George Washington, Consul Willshire Butterfield, William Irvine

Correspondence

Official Letters Between Washington and Brig. Gen. William Irvine

George Washington, Consul Willshire Butterfield, William Irvine

Correspondence
Official Letters Between Washington and Brig. Gen. William Irvine

ISBN/EAN: 9783744687645

Printed in Europe, USA, Canada, Australia, Japan

Cover: Foto ©ninafisch / pixelio.de

More available books at **www.hansebooks.com**

WASHINGTON-IRVINE CORRESPONDENCE

THE OFFICIAL LETTERS

WHICH

PASSED BETWEEN WASHINGTON AND BRIG.-GEN. WILLIAM IRVINE AND BETWEEN IRVINE AND OTHERS CONCERNING MILITARY AFFAIRS IN THE WEST FROM 1781 TO 1783

ARRANGED AND ANNOTATED

WITH AN INTRODUCTION CONTAINING AN OUTLINE OF EVENTS OCCURRING PREVIOUSLY IN THE TRANS-ALLEGHANY COUNTRY

ILLUSTRATED

By C. W. BUTTERFIELD

Author of "Crawford's Campaign against Sandusky," "History of the Discovery of the Northwest by John Nicolet" and other works

MADISON, WIS.
DAVID ATWOOD
1882

DAVID ATWOOD,
PRINTER AND STEREOTYPER,
MADISON, WIS.

PREFACE.

The correspondence between General Washington as commander-in-chief of the American army and Brigadier General William Irvine, while the latter was in command of the Western Department, headquarters at Fort Pitt, Pittsburgh,—a period extending from early in November, 1781, to October 1, 1783,—is given to the public as a contribution to Revolutionary history, having, it is thought, an interest and value as illustrating the most important events which transpired in the west during the last years of the struggle of the colonies for independence. The letters in the text which follow this correspondence are all either to or from Gen. Irvine: they generally relate to military matters in the trans-Alleghany country and are mostly written by officers—civil or military.

The selection of Gen. Irvine, at a critical period, to take charge of military affairs in the west, was a wise one. How his perseverance brought the repairs of Fort Pitt so nearly to completion as twice to cause the abandonment by the enemy of expeditions against it; how, until the close of the war, his firmness and urbanity preserved order at Pittsburgh; and how his prudence and sagacity gave confidence to the distracted border, and something of efficiency to its militia;—will hereafter fully appear. His letters are characterized by clearness in descriptions, faithfulness in statements and carefulness in details.

In the introduction as well as in the numerous illustrative notes added to the letters which follow it, facts have been given with but little reliance upon tradition. Contemporaneous publications and manuscripts have been diligently sought for and carefully compared, and the substance of the principal events found in them noted; or such extracts made from them as, it is believed, would tend to elucidate the various points needing illustration. If, therefore, statements are made running counter to some in current histories of the west, it is not that the latter have been overlooked, but because, after due consideration and the closest scrutiny, they have been found erroneous.

It would seem to be an editor's privilege (if, indeed, it is not his duty) to correct verbal and grammatical mistakes or inaccuracies, in bringing forth the letters of a person after his death, written without any design of publication; but, in doing this, great caution should be observed that the writer's meaning and purpose are not changed or affected. This rule has been applied in the following pages. In a few places, words have been omitted which, if expressed, might give pain to living persons. In each, the fact of an omission is indicated.

Several letters written by Irvine to his wife while he was in charge of Fort Pitt and its dependencies, have been omitted for reason of their referring largely to family affairs; those only being printed which are considered of importance in illustrating matters appertaining to the General's command in the Western Department; in explaining his mode of living while there; or, in describing the condition of the country and its society. Some have also been omitted which were written to Irvine by militia officers stationed upon the frontiers, asking for supplies of ammunition and provisions; giving information as to the marching of their commands to different posts, etc. These, it is thought, would convey little if any information of interest to the reader. A few others have been excluded because of their being repetitions in the main, or because of their having no relation to events transpiring in the west.

I must express my high appreciation of the kindness of Lord Derby in transmitting through the American Legation in London, copies of letters and documents in Her Majesty's State Paper office. They are, in general, extravagant in their estimate of the number of men killed of the Americans under Col. Wm. Crawford, and erroneous as to the intent of the borderers; but some of them proved to be of value as illustrative of Gen. Irvine's correspondence and as corroborating (and, in some instances, correcting) American accounts of incidents occurring in the Sandusky country during the year 1782. I am indebted to Dr. Wm. A. Irvine, grandson of Gen. Irvine, for much the larger part of the letters appearing in this volume and for many favors in connection with their preparation for publication. I take pleasure in acknowledging, also, in a special manner, my obligations to Mr. Isaac Craig and Mr. Geo. Plumer Smith, for a like generous assistance and for valuable suggestions while the work was going through the press. My thanks, for kindly aid, are likewise due to Lyman C. Draper, LL.D., Dr. Wm. H. Egle, C. C. Baldwin, Esq., and Boyd Crumrine, Esq.

MADISON, WISCONSIN, 1882.   C. W. B.

CONTENTS.

INTRODUCTION.

	Pages.
CHAP. I.— The West to the Commencement of the Revolution,	1–5
II.— War Inaugurated upon the Western Border of Pennsylvania and Virginia. 1776–1777,	6–12
III.— Hostilities Increase upon the Ohio. 1777–1778,	13–20
IV.— An Expedition Undertaken against Detroit — Its Failure. 1778–1779,	21–34
V.— Progress of the Western Border War. 1779–1781,	35–64
VI.— Biographical Sketch of William Irvine,	65–70

WASHINGTON-IRVINE LETTERS.

Washington to Irvine, Nov. 1, 1781,	71
Irvine to Washington, Dec. 2, 1781,	72
Washington to Irvine, Dec. 18, 1781,	83
Washington to Irvine, Dec. 21, 1781,	84
Irvine to Washington, Feb. 7, 1782,	89
Washington to Irvine, March 8, 1782,	94
Irvine to Washington, March 17, 1782,	96
Washington to Irvine, March 22, 1782,	98
Irvine to Washington, April 20, 1782,	99
Irvine to Washington, May 2, 1782,	109
Irvine to Washington, May 7, 1782,	112
Irvine to Washington, May 21, 1782,	113
Washington to Irvine, May 22, 1782,	120
Irvine to Washington, June 16, 1782,	121
Irvine to Washington, July 1, 1782,	122
Washington to Irvine, July 10, 1782,	125
Irvine to Washington, July 11, 1782,	126
Washington to Irvine, Aug. 6, 1782,	129
Irvine to Washington, Oct. 29, 1782,	133
Washington to Irvine, Dec. 11, 1782,	141
Irvine to Washington, March 6, 1783,	142
Irvine to Washington, March 28, 1783,	144
Irvine to Washington, April 16, 1783,	148
Washington to Irvine, April 16, 1783,	149
Irvine to Washington, May 8, 1783,	150
Washington to Irvine, Sept. 16, 1783,	151

APPENDIXES.

	Pages.
A.—Irvine to the President of Congress,	153–156
B.—Correspondence with the Continental Board of War; also with the Secretary at War and his Assistant,	157–199
C.—Correspondence with the Superintendent of Finance,	200–213
D.—John Pierce, Paymaster-general, to Irvine,	214–216
E.—Correspondence with the Deputy and Assistant Quartermaster-general,	217–224
F.—Correspondence with John Moylan, Clothier-general, and Jacob S. Howell, his Deputy,	225–228
G.—Correspondence with the Governors of Pennsylvania,	229–265
H.—Correspondence with Benj. Harrison, Governor of Virginia,	266–271
I.—William Davies, Virginia Secretary at War, to Irvine,	272–276
J.—Correspondence with the Lieutenant of Washington County, Pennsylvania,	277–320
K.—Correspondence with the Lieutenant of Westmoreland County, Pennsylvania,	321–339
L.—Irvine to his Wife,	340–348
M.—Miscellaneous Correspondence,	349–423
INDEX,	425–430

THE WASHINGTON AND IRVINE PORTRAITS.

The portrait of Washington in this work is from a Stuart picture; that of Irvine, from an oil painting by B. Otis, after one by Robert Edge Pine, an eminent English artist, who came to America in 1784. The original was taken in New York, when Irvine was a member of Congress — aged forty-eight.

WASHINGTON-IRVINE CORRESPONDENCE.

INTRODUCTION.

CHAPTER I.

THE WEST TO THE COMMENCEMENT OF THE REVOLUTION.

The vast extent of country lying between the Alleghany mountains on the east, the Mississippi on the west, and bordered by the great lakes on the north, was first explored by Frenchmen, and to a very limited extent occupied by them. They had here their forts, trading-posts, and missions, — few in number it is true, yet sufficiently numerous to exert a powerful influence over the Indians, whom they usually endeavored to conciliate and attach to their interest. France, therefore, by right of discovery as well as by occupation, claimed, as against the civilized world, this region as her own. But Frenchmen soon had rival claimants to the trans-Alleghany country. England, through her colonies, coveted the goodly land. In the very nature of things, a contest for supremacy could not long be postponed. By proclamations and perishing inscriptions, as well as by the erection of military posts, France sought to establish firmly the Alleghanies as the eastern boundary of her possessions, while English enterprise not only carried a nominal occupation into the Ohio valley but pushed the fur-trader far beyond it. England demanded explanations for French encroachments. France answered with menaces and increased exertions to gain a permanent foot-hold in the Ohio region. Hostilities commenced and continued until, in 1755, war was fully inaugurated. France at first was victorious. Braddock's defeat was a humiliating blow to Great Britain and her American colonies. However, in the end, Wolfe and Amherst conquered Canada, and French domination in North America was almost wholly overthrown.

Although possession of a large portion of the country northwest of the Ohio was yielded to England by France in 1760, yet no title to this extensive region had been acquired of its Indian occupants, who sullenly acquiesced in the change. They had been the close and trusted allies of the French, but the triumph of English arms caused them to make peace with the conquerors — a peace prompted more by fear than friendship. Indifference and neglect of the British government, outrages of fur-traders, brutality of English soldiery, intrusion of provincial settlers upon lands of border tribes, fabrications and wiles of French trading-companies — all conspired to arouse their war-spirit. Their leader was Pontiac, a war-chief of the Ottawas. Every English post west of Niagara and the Alleghanies fell a prey to savage fury, Ligonier, Fort Pitt (Pittsburgh), and Detroit, only excepted. The western frontiers were, as in the previous war, overrun with merciless foes. But England and her colonies soon conquered the Indians, dictating preliminary treaties of peace to them in 1764, which were completed not long afterward. For the next ten years, there was as much quiet along the Ohio as could have been expected from the presence of savages upon one side of the river and the rapid approach of white settlers to the other.

At the close of Pontiac's war, there were not to be found any settlements in the upper Ohio country. Up and down the Monongahela and its branches every white settler had been expelled. From the headsprings of the Alleghany to its union with its sister stream, there were no habitations other than of savages. At the junction of these rivers, where the city of Pittsburgh now sits enveloped in the smoke of its thousand industries, there was very little to indicate the presence of civilization save Fort Pitt. Outside that post, there was not an inhabited hut of even a trader. Down the Ohio on the left was an uninhabited region; so, also, on the right — up the Beaver, the Muskingum, the Scioto, and down the parent stream to its mouth. Settlements upon the waters of the Monongahela by adventurous Virginians, begun before the commencement of the contest between England and France for the Ohio country, had but an ephemeral existence. Houses and cornfields of English traders, which then dotted the margin of the Ohio and its tributaries in a few places, were destroyed by the French in this war for supremacy; and though others afterward appeared, nearly all vanished before the devastating hand of the foe in 1763. Pittsburgh, dating its origin from English occupation of the head of the Ohio in 1758, attained, by the spring of 1761, to the dignity of a population numbering three hundred and thirty-two, occupying one hundred and four houses. Doubtless both had considerably increased by May, 1763, when most of its log cabins were leveled to the ground, and the occupants of all driven into the fort for protection against the wild warriors of Pontiac's confederation.

Notwithstanding the king of England's proclamation of 1763, prohibiting colonial governors from granting warrants for lands to the westward of the sources of the rivers running into the Atlantic, and forbidding all persons purchasing such lands or settling on them without special license from the crown, emigration two years thereafter broke through the barriers of the Alleghanies, rolling into the valley of the Ohio from that time forward with a resistless tide; so that the purpose of royalty in limiting settlements to the east side of the mountains — whether to set bounds to the aspirations of the colonies or a temporary expedient to quiet the minds of the Indians — was signally frustrated. In 1765, Pittsburgh again started — this time upon a permanent but not rapid career to prosperity and greatness. Emigrants to the Ohio valley were, generally, either such as came to secure fertile and cheap lands, or they were traders with the Indians. The former class was looked upon by the various tribes claiming the country, as trespassers; and it was the policy of the home government as well as Pennsylvania so to treat them. Those who came to cultivate the soil were largely from Virginia, but the traders were mostly Pennsylvanians.

Two principal highways were followed in coming over the mountains: the northern route was known as Forbes', or the Pennsylvania road; the southern, as Braddock's, or the Virginia road. Parties from Maryland or Virginia in emigrating to the Ohio country, traveled the last mentioned route. Settlements soon extended. In 1768, the Indian title to a considerable portion of western Pennsylvania, east and south of the Alleghany and Ohio rivers, was purchased, leaving, however, it and much more in dispute as between the Penns and Virginia, while large tracts were claimed by individuals under grants from some of the Indian tribes. These grants needed confirmation by the crown to be valid.

Pittsburgh grew slowly. About twenty houses, and these occupied by traders, were all that the place could boast of in 1770. The number increased, however, in the next two years to thirty. Probably not less than fifty constituted the town at the commencement of 1774. From Fort Pitt, far up the Monongahela and along many of its branches, were settlements. Upon eastern tributaries of the Ohio, and down that stream for more than one hundred miles were to be seen cabins of frontiermen; but not a single settler had yet ventured across that river. Small cultivated fields broke in upon the monotony of the wilderness for a short distance up the east side of the Alleghany from Pittsburgh, while toward the mountains, Forbes' road was, in general, the northern limit of civilized habitations.

Augusta county, Virginia, at the beginning of 1774, comprehended not only the whole of the northwestern portion of the present state of West Virginia, but also a large part of what is now southwestern Pennsylvania including Pittsburgh; that is, such was then the claim of Virginia. On the other hand, Westmoreland county had been formed the year previous by Pennsylvania, to include all of that state, as at present constituted, west of the Laurel Hill. This conflict of jurisdiction caused serious trouble. The southern line of Pennsylvania had not been extended farther to the westward than a short distance beyond the Monongahela, and it was not till ten years subsequent to this date that it was finally completed.

The county-seat of Westmoreland county was Hannastown, about thirty-five miles from Pittsburgh on Forbes' road, where (and at Ligonier still further eastward) Pennsylvania interests were paramount. In many of the other settlements, the citizens were largely in sympathy with Virginia. However, across the Alleghany and Ohio, in the Indian country, the influence of the fur-traders was the leading one with the various tribes. These dealers dreaded above all things an Indian war. Most of them lived in the northern settlements, especially at or near Pittsburgh — the principal depot west of the mountains for Indian supplies.

In 1774, the Virginia county of Fincastle included, south and southwest of Augusta county, the lower portions of the valley of the Great Kanawha and extended westward so as to comprehend the whole of the present state of Kentucky, but no where crossed the Ohio. All was, however, uninhabited. It was only that part of the county lying to the eastward of this that was settled. The presence of Virginia and Pennsylvania land-claimants and surveyors, along the Ohio in 1773, and in the spring of the next year, precipitated hostilities with the Shawanese and Mingoes, whose observance of the peace of 1764 had been far from cordial, especially toward the citizens of Virginia. Lord Dunmore's war ensued. Wakatomica, an Indian town located upon the Muskingum, was destroyed by the Virginians, with out-lying villages. The battle of Point Pleasant, at the mouth of the Great Kanawha river, on the tenth of October, 1774, when victory over the savages was purchased at a price well-nigh commensurate with defeat, compelled the Indians to sue for peace, negotiations for which, near their villages on the banks of the Scioto, were rendered famous by the eloquent speech of Logan, the Mingo chief.

The day of the revolution now began to dawn. Quickly, after the battle of Lexington, were the fires of patriotism lighted west of the mountains. The hearts of many of the backwoodsmen were soon aglow with enthusiasm for the cause of liberty. 'On the sixteenth of May, 1775, conventions were held at Pittsburgh and Hannastown for citizens to give expression to their views and sentiments regarding the acts of the mother country, and to take initiatory steps toward providing for the common defense. The boundary troubles for the time were forgotten. In the fall, a number of frontiermen enlisted for Virginia service. The commencement of 1776 found the trans-Alleghany settlements not greatly behind the seaboard in their determination to repel, by force of arms, aggressions of parliament and the king.

CHAPTER II.

WAR INAUGURATED UPON THE WESTERN BORDER OF PENNSYLVANIA AND VIRGINIA. 1776—1777.

At the commencement of the struggle of the colonies for independence, the scattered settlements to the westward of the Alleghanies had little to fear from invading armies of Great Britain. Their dread was of a more merciless foe. Nor were their apprehensions groundless; for the Indians of the northwest, influenced by British gold and the machinations of English traders and emissaries, early gave evidence of hostile intentions. Explanations by the United States, made in 1775 and 1776, to some of the tribes at treaties held with them at Pittsburgh, that the questions in dispute did not necessarily affect their interests, were to little purpose. Gradually they arrayed themselves against the Americans, the more remote nations being the first to attach themselves to the British. Painted and plumed warriors soon carried destruction and death to the dismayed frontiers, — the direct result of a most ferocious policy, adopted by England in opposition to the advice of some of the best and ablest statesmen, — "letting loose," in the language of Chatham, "the horrible hell-hounds of savage war" upon the exposed settlements.

The deadly strife thus begun, was made up on the side of the Indians largely of predatory incursions of scalping parties, the tomahawk and scalping-knife sparing neither age nor sex, while the torch laid waste the homes of the unfortunate bordermen. It is difficult fully to appreciate the appalling dangers which beset the frontiers; for, to the natural ferocity of the savages, there was added the powerful support of Great Britain, lavish in her resources, whose western agents, especially at the commencement of the war, were noted for their zeal in obeying the behests of their government.

The principal point of British power and influence in the

northwest was Detroit, where Lieutenant-Governor Henry Hamilton, who paid a bounty for scalps, but withheld it for prisoners,[1] was in command. Being captured by Virginians early in 1779, he was succeeded before the close of that year by Major A. S. De Peyster, who, although carrying out the policy of his government, did so in the spirit of an enlightened humanity.[2] Indian depredations upon the western frontier of Virginia[3] and Pennsylvania, and in the infant settlements of Kentucky,[4] drew, to a great extent, their inspiration from that post. It was there the Wyandots, from its immediate vicinity and from the Sandusky — a river flowing north into Sandusky bay — were enlisted in the interests of Great Britain. It was there these Indians, and the Shawanese from the Miami and Scioto rivers — northern tributaries of the Ohio — received aid to pillage and destroy. And it was there that these and other tribes were made close allies of the English, and then turned loose upon the exposed settlements of the west. These they assailed with an

[1] "Governor Hamilton gave standing rewards for scalps, but offered none for prisoners, which induced the Indians, after making their captives carry their baggage into the neighborhood of the fort [Detroit], there to put them to death."—Va. Council, 16 June, 1779. "When we arrived there [on the bank of the Detroit river], we found Governor Hamilton, and several other British officers, who were standing and sitting around. Immediately.... the Indians produced a large quantity of scalps; the cannon fired; the Indians raised a shout; and the soldiers waved their hats, with huzzas and tremendous shrieks, which lasted some time. This ceremony being ended, the Indians brought forward a parcel of American prisoners, as a trophy of their victories; among whom were eighteen women and children, poor creatures, dreadfully mangled and emaciated, with their clothes tattered and torn to pieces in such a manner as not to hide their nakedness; their legs bare and streaming with blood, the effects of being torn with thorns, briers, and brush..... If I had had an opportunity, I should certainly have killed the Governor, who seemed to take great delight in the exhibition." — Leeth's Narrative, pp. 10, 11. This is an exceedingly rare production; so rare, indeed, that the pamphlet entire, which is now before me, has only been obtained by gathering three distinct parts of it, from as many states.

[2] "De Peyster got above three hundred prisoners out of the hands of the Indians." (See "Miscellanies" of that officer, p. 246, note).

[3] By "the western frontier of Virginia" is meant — and the words are used with that signification in the following pages — no farther to the westward than the Ohio, nor to the southwestward than the mouth of the Great Kanawha, although the claims of Virginia, at that date, included the whole of Kentucky, and, before the close of the revolution, the Illinois country also; but, by her deed of cession to the United States of 1784, and by the admission of Kentucky into the Union in 1792, and that of West Virginia in 1863, she was reduced to her present limits.

[4] The few settlements in Kentucky experienced, during the revolution, all the horrors of savage warfare; but a consideration of the events transpiring there during that period, closely connected as some of them were with incidents upon the western borders of Pennsylvania and Virginia, is beyond the scope proposed for this work.

indiscriminate thirst for blood that could seldom be restrained, even under the humane authority of De Peyster.

The important post, however, of Fort Pitt was in possession of the Americans; and it continued the center of government authority and interest west of the Alleghanies during the revolutionary contest. The peculiar nature of the war in the trans-Alleghany country made it incumbent on the officers of the patriot army in charge of affairs there to direct, so long as the struggle continued, their military operations almost wholly with a view to the security of the exposed settlements. To this end, expeditions several times marched into the enemy's country, generally organizing at Fort Pitt, or receiving material aid from that post. These enterprises were not always successful. Some, indeed, were highly disastrous. Nor were the British and their Indian allies usually more fortunate in their principal endeavors against the frontiers. It was the continual inroads of small numbers of savages, though the latter were frequently pursued, and a just retribution was occasionally visited upon them, that brought to the homes of the backwoodsmen innumerable woes.

On the eleventh day of September, 1775, Captain John Neville[1] took possession, under orders of Virginia, of the dilapidated fort at Pittsburgh,[2] at the head of one hundred of the militia of that commonwealth, and held it, "covering and protecting" the border until early in 1777, when his force was relieved by another company.[3] At the time orders were issued to garrison Fort Pitt, a small force was directed to occupy Fort Fincastle, at the mouth of Wheeling creek,[4] and one was also ordered stationed at Point Pleasant, at the mouth of the Great Kanawha river.[5] Fort Pitt, near which, previous to its commencement by the English in 1758, was Fort Duquesne of the French,

---
[1] Neville was born in Virginia, in 1731; died near Pittsburgh, 29th July, 1803.

[2] Penn. Arch., IV, 650. Henning's Va. Stat., vol. 9, p. 13. Craig's Hist. of Pittsburgh, p. 122.

[3] It was resolved by the Virginia Council, Feb. 7, 1777, that "Col. Dorsey Pentecost, lieutenant of Yohogania county, Virginia [then the Virginia county which included Pittsburgh, as claimed by that state], raise one hundred militia to garrison Fort Pitt; and that Capt. Robert Campbell, 1st Lieut. Thad. Kelley, 2d Lieut. Wm. Anderson, and Ensign John Ward, with their [that] Yohogania company, are to command there."

[4] Now the site of the city of Wheeling, West Virginia.

[5] Within the present county of Mason, West Virginia.

was abandoned and partly demolished by the British in 1772, but was again occupied in 1774, in a partisan way, by Virginia militia, to enforce in the vicinity the laws of that province, and its name changed to Fort Dunmore. This occupation, however, was brought to an end in July, 1775, and the name fully restored when Lord Dunmore became odious to Virginia patriots.

The Indian policy of Neville, while in command at Fort Pitt, was one of strict neutrality, powerless, however, to a great extent with all the western tribes, except the Delawares. These Indians were principally located upon the Muskingum.[1] Their most important village was Coshocton.[2] In holding this nation in check, he was powerfully aided by George Morgan, congressional agent of Indian affairs of "the middle department"[3] in the west, also by commissioners of the United States, who made treaties with them, and by Moravian missionaries, who had brought Indian converts from the Susquehanna and Beaver rivers, in Pennsylvania, to the Tuscarawas valley, where they were living in towns some distance above Coshocton, on the Tuscarawas river.

Although Hamilton, at Detroit, had, as early as September, 1776, exerted himself to organize small parties of savages against the "'scattered settlers on the Ohio' and its branches," yet the war upon the western border was not fully inaugurated for nearly a year after. But the frontiers of Virginia, meanwhile, were sorely afflicted with savage incursions, mostly by a lawless gang of the Mohawk Pluggy, located upon the Olentangy, or Whetstone, the principal eastern tributary of the Scioto, some distance above its confluence with that stream.[4] This band was without tribal organization and.

---

[1] This river was known as the Muskingum as far up as the mouth of Sandy creek, its main eastern affluent, for several years after that date. It is now called the Tuscarawas as far down as the mouth of the Walhonding, or White Woman, its chief western tributary, and is so distinguished in the following pages.

[2] Synonyms: Cooshacking, Coochocking, Goshochking, Goschachguenk, etc. It was the site of the present town of Coshocton, county-seat of Coshocton county, Ohio.

[3] Such was the designation of one of three Indian departments previously created by congress. It included the country west of the Alleghanies. This region, as one of the military divisions of the United States, was known as the "western department" during the revolution.

[4] The site of Pluggy's town was identical with that of the present town of Delaware, Delaware county, Ohio. For determining its location, I have relied mainly upon an

marauded upon the border settlements independent of surrounding nations. So galling did these visitations become that the distressed commonwealth, upon the recommendation of congress, determined, in the spring of 1777, to send an expedition against Pluggy's town; but the project, after considerable preparation, was laid aside lest it should cause the Delawares and Shawanese to take up the hatchet.

On Sunday, the first day of June, 1777, Brigadier General Edward Hand of the continental army, "famed for his splendid horsemanship," arrived at Fort Pitt unaccompanied by troops,[1] except an escort of militia light horse,[2] which had met him west of the mountains, and assumed the chief command at Pittsburgh.[3] Not long after his arrival, Hand resolved upon an expedition against the savages,—seemingly a timely movement, for up to the last of July there had been sent out from Detroit to devastate the western settlements, fifteen parties of Indians, consisting of two hundred and eighty-nine braves, with thirty white officers and rangers. The extreme frontier line needing protection on the north reached from the Alleghany mountains to Kittanning[4] on the Alleghany river forty-five miles above Pittsburgh, thence on the west, down that stream and the Ohio to the mouth of the Great Kanawha. The only posts of importance below Fort Pitt, at this date, were Fort Henry[5] at Wheeling, and Fort Randolph at Point Pleasant:[6] the former was built at the commencement of Lord Dunmore's war in 1774; the latter was erected by Virginia, in 1775. Rude stockades and block houses were multiplied in the intervening distances and in the most exposed settlements. They were defended by

---

authentic copy of James Wood's MS. journal of a visit to the western tribes, in 1775. I have before me an original letter of 1779, written by Killbuck, a Delaware chief, to Col. Daniel Brodhead, also throwing light upon the subject. Geo. Morgan (Hildreth's Pion. Hist., p. 110) simply locates the place upon the upper waters of the Scioto. All other printed authorities which have fallen under my notice, are equally vague.

[1] Francis Dunlavy's declaration for a pension — 1832: MS. copy. The original is one of the completest on file in the pension office relating to revolutionary service.

[2] Hand to his wife, from Pittsburgh, 4 June, 1777, MS.

[3] Hand's garrison was of a mixed nature — regulars, independents, and militia. — Dunlavy's declaration for a pension, MS.

[4] Where is now located the town of that name, county-seat of Armstrong county, Pennsylvania.

[5] Formerly Fort Fincastle.

[6] The site of the present town of Point Pleasant, Mason county, West Virginia

small detachments from a Virginia regiment,[1] also by at least one independent company,[2] and by squads of militia on short tours of duty. Scouts likewise patrolled the country where danger seemed most imminent. But the wily savage frequently eluded their vigilance and fell with remorseless cruelty upon the homes of the bordermen. The suffering from this irregular warfare — legitimate from the stand-point of the Indian, but wanton and murderous in its instigators — was terrible.

It was the belief of General Hand that nothing but penetrating the country of the savages and destroying the settlements of the "perfidious miscreants" could "prevent the depopulation of the frontiers."[3] The Wyandots, and particularly the Mingoes — Pluggy's-town Indians — were the most troublesome. A demand by the Fort Pitt commander of two thousand men from the western counties of Pennsylvania and Virginia, to attack these enemies, was not responded to with alacrity, although eight hundred men were embodied including regulars at Forts Pitt and Randolph.[4] "I have many difficulties," wrote Hand to a friend, "to encounter; yet I hope to drink your health in pure element at Sandusky before Christmas."[5] Late in the autumn, having been deceived as to the strength and spirit of the people, he abandoned the expedition. "I fully expected," he wrote, "to be able to give the Wyandots a specimen of what their perfidy so justly deserves; but, to my great mortification, I am obliged to relinquish the design."[6] There was a lack both of men and supplies. One reason for the failure was a want of concert between General Hand and the lieutenants and militia officers of the border counties of

---

[1] The Thirteenth Virginia, usually called, at that time, the West Augusta regiment.
[2] Capt. Sam. Moorhead's independent company of Pennsylvania troops.
[3] Hand to Sup. Ex. Council of Pa., 24 July, 1777, in Penn. Arch., V, 443.
[4] Hand to Washington, 9 Nov. 1777, MS.
[5] Hand to Wm. Russell, 14 Oct., 1777, MS. The General, in using the term "at Sandusky," meant, at the Wyandot Indian town of Upper Sandusky, then located upon the upper waters of the Sandusky river, in what is now Wyandot county, Ohio.
[6] Hand to the governor of Va., 9 Nov., 1777, MS. Extensive preparations had been made for this, the first expedition projected in the west against Sandusky. It was apparently the intention of Hand to have attacked the Pluggy's town Indians as well as the Wyandots.

Virginia and Pennsylvania.[1] Another element militating against unity of action was the existence of the boundary controversy between the two states. Although at the beginning of trouble with the mother country this had been suffered to slumber, and although delegates in congress had early in the war urged the people of the disputed territory to mutual forbearance, it again stirred up partisan hatred, stifling in a greater or less degree many patriotic resolutions of the borderers, to the detriment of the western country generally. The most, therefore, that Hand could accomplish was, a partial protection of the settlements by acting on the defensive only. "If I can assist the inhabitants to stand their ground," he wrote, " I shall deem myself doing a great deal."[2]

---

[1] A distinction is properly drawn between the lieutenants of the various counties of these two states and the officers of the militia therein. The former were appointed by the respective commonwealths and had control of, and general supervision over, military affairs of the county wherein each resided. They received the title of colonel. Under their orders were the officers of the various battalions of militia in the different counties.

[2] Hand to his wife, 2 Nov., 1777, MS. It had been General Hand's intention to assemble his forces at Fort Randolph, marching thence across the Ohio into the enemy's country (Withers' Border Warfare, pp. 151, 152); and several companies of Virginia militia reached that post for the intended expedition. Hand afterward dropped down the river to the fort, but "without an army, and without provisions for those who had been awaiting his coming. It was then determined to abandon the expedition."—Ib. p. 155.

CHAPTER III.

HOSTILITIES INCREASE UPON THE OHIO. 1777-1778.

About the time General Hand commenced his labors to organize an expedition against the savages, the Mingoes upon the Scioto, and the Wyandots upon the Sandusky, with a few Shawanese and Delawares, began the laying of a scheme to capture Fort Henry. On the first day of September,[1] that post was beset by about two hundred Indians,[2] the first attempt of the savages against this frontier, in force, after the commencement of the war in the west. The assailants, having successfully ambushed a portion of the garrison, withdrew across the Ohio with a trifling loss.[3] Fifteen of the Americans were killed, and five wounded.[4] On the twenty-sixth of the same month, forty-six men started from Fort Henry on a reconoitering expedition down the Ohio. The next day, on their return, when about eight miles below Wheeling, on the Virginia side of the river, they were attacked by forty Wyandots.[5] Twenty-one were killed, several wounded,[6] and one captured.[7] The whole region west of the mountains, because of these disasters and the enforced evacuation of the small post at Kittanning,[8] was now

---

[1] David Shepherd to Hand, from Fort Henry, 3 Sept., 1777, MS. John Gibson to same, 4 Sept., 1777, MS. Hand to Russell, 14 Oct., 1777, MS.
[2] "Between two and three hundred:" Shepherd to Hand, 15 Sept., 1777, MS. "Two hundred and ten warriors:" White Eyes to Geo. Morgan, 23 Sept., 1777, MS.
[3] "One killed and nine wounded:" David Zeisberger to Hand, 22 Sept., 1777, MS.
[4] Shepherd to Hand, 15 Sept., 1777, MS.
[5] Zeisberger to Hand, 22 Sept., 1777, MS.
[6] Shepherd to Hand, 27 Sept., 1777, MS. John Van Matre to Ed. Cook, 28 Sept., 1777, MS. Daniel McFarland to Hand, 30 Sept., 1777, MS. James Chew to same, 3 Oct., 1777, MS. Hand to his wife, 9 Oct., 1777, MS.
[7] His name was Jacob Pugh. Compare Hildreth's Pion. Hist., 128; also Doddass' Hist. Ind. Wars W. Va., 279. This ill-starred expedition is known in western border annals as "Foreman's Defeat."
[8] "Being convinced that, in your present situation, you are not able to defend yourself, much less to render the continent any service, you will withdraw from Kittanning, bringing everything away, portable, leaving the houses and barracks standing:" Hand to Capt. Samuel Moorhead, 14 Sept., 1777, MS. The place was occupied by troops for the first time in the spring of that year. There were then only a few cabins at that point. Fort Armstrong was afterward built there.

thoroughly alarmed. Many feared the Alleghanies would again become the western frontier line of the settlements. "We have no prospects," wrote a citizen of the western department, "but desolation and destruction." "There are very few days," he continued, "that there is not a murder committed on some part of our frontiers."[1]

The Shawanese Indians, whose villages were upon the Scioto and Miami, and whose principal chief was Cornstalk,[2] did not readily join the Wyandots and Mingoes in their hostility to the Americans.[3] Farther removed from British intrigue at Detroit, and influenced by the neutral Delawares, it was not until the autumn of 1777, that a majority of the nation resolved to unite with their neighbors against the border. But Cornstalk and his clan remained friendly. Anxious to promote peace, two of his warriors came to Captain Matthew Arbuckle, then in command at Fort Randolph, making inquiries and professing friendship. These were detained by the commandant, who feared they were spies.[4] Afterward, Cornstalk himself came. He, too, was deprived of his liberty. "I am well satisfied," wrote Arbuckle, "the Shawanese are all our enemies."[5] On the tenth of November, the four Indians — for Cornstalk's son was then with them — were killed in cold blood by the uncontrollable militia at the post, in revenge for the death of one of their number, slain that day in the woods by a hostile savage.[6] "From this event," wrote General Hand, "we have little reason to expect a reconciliation with the Shawanese."[7] They proved, finally, the most unrelenting of foes.

In January, 1778, Lieutenant-Colonel George Rogers Clark, who had planned a secret expedition against the Illinois country,

---

[1] Archibald Lochry to Sup. Ex. Council of Pa., 4 Nov., 1777, in Penn. Arch., V, 741.
[2] Cornstalk commanded the Indians at the battle of Point Pleasant, 10 Oct., 1774, and was foremost in the treaty with Lord Dunmore soon after, on the banks of the Scioto.
[3] "Two tribes of the Shawanese declare for us; two are against us:" Hand to Jasper Yeates, 12 July, 1777, MS. "The neutral portion are wavering:" Arbuckle to Wm. Flemming, 26 July, 1777, original letter.
[4] Arbuckle to Hand, 6 Oct., 1777, MS.
[5] Same to same, 7 Nov., 1777, MS.
[6] Affidavit of Jno. Anderson and others, 10 Nov., 1777, MS. Hand to Geo. Morgan, 24 Dec., 1777, MS.; also to the continental board of war of same date, MS. The militia were of those intended for Hand's expedition against Sandusky.
[7] Hand to the continental board of war, 21 Dec., 1777, MS., just cited.

then in possession of England, arrived in the western department to enlist soldiers for the enterprise. By the end of the month, he had all his recruiting parties properly disposed, and at Redstone-old-fort,[1] he prepared boats, light artillery and ammunition. Many of the backwoodsmen opposed the undertaking; and he only succeeded in collecting, with some aid east of the mountains, about one hundred and fifty men, when, on the twelfth of May, he "set sail for the falls" of the Ohio, "leaving the country," he wrote, "in great confusion — much distressed by the Indians." "General Hand," he added, "pleased with my intentions, furnished me with every necessary I wanted."[2] He was re-enforced on his way down the river by a small number of troops at Fort Randolph. His men were mostly Virginians, and all were in the Virginia service. The result of the campaign was, the reduction of the British posts between the Ohio and Mississippi rivers — Kaskaskia, St. Phillips, Cahokia, Prairie du Rocher, and Vincennes; — a conquest, as it proved, of great importance to the United States, reflecting also much credit upon Virginia. The commander of the expedition won for himself the title of "The Heroic."

In February, 1778, General Hand, having previously received intelligence that a quantity of stores was lodged by the British at an Indian town on the Cuyahoga river,[3] formed a project for capturing them.[4] Gathering a party of about five hundred men at Fort Pitt, mostly from Westmoreland county,[5] he proceeded on the expedition. But heavy rains falling, and the snows of winter melting, he was obliged to relinquish his design, after having arrived at a point a considerable distance above the mouth of Beaver, on the Mahoning river.[6] Just at this place, Indian tracks were discovered, conjectured to be of warriors on a marauding expedition into the settlements. These were fol-

---

[1] Now Brownsville, Fayette county, Pennsylvania.
[2] Clark to Geo. Mason, 19 Nov., 1779, in Clark's Campaign in the Illinois (Cincinnati: Robert Clarke & Co., 1869), p. 25.
[3] This stream flows into Lake Erie at the city of Cleveland, Ohio.
[4] Hand to Wm. Crawford, 28 Dec., 1777, and 5 Feb., 1778, in The Washington-Crawford Letters (Cincinnati: Robert Clarke & Co., 1877), pp. 66, 67.
[5] That is to say, from the territory acknowledged to be Westmoreland county by Virginia, at that date. Gen. Hand, in his correspondence, recognized residents of the territory claimed by Virginia, as Virginians.
[6] The point reached was in the present Mahoning county, Ohio.

lowed to a camp, "supposed to contain between fifty and sixty Indians," which was immediately attacked; "but, to my great mortification," wrote the commander, "only one man, with some women and children, was found." The Indian and one of the squaws were killed. "Another woman was taken," adds the chagrined and thoroughly disgusted general, "and with difficulty saved; the remainder escaped."[1] The prisoner reported that ten Monsey Indians — Delawares — were making salt about ten miles further up the Mahoning.[2] A detachment was sent to secure them. This enterprise proved even more inglorious than the first. The enemy "turned out to be four women and a boy," wrote Hand, "of whom one woman only was saved." "In performing these great exploits," are the felicitious words of the commander, "I had but one man — a captain — wounded, and one drowned."[3] This, the first expedition in force to march into the Indian country from Pittsburgh after the war began, was long remembered in the west as "the squaw campaign."

At the very time, in 1777, when the hostility of the Wyandots could no longer be a matter of doubt upon the border, news was brought across the Ohio by friendly Indians, of the suspicious conduct of some of the resident Americans in the vicinity of Fort Pitt; especially of Alexander McKee, who had formerly been deputy Indian agent at Pittsburgh, and had, as early as in April, 1776, been put upon his parol by a committee of whigs at Pittsburgh, not to give any "aid or comfort" to the British.[4] "He must be an enemy to the United States," wrote Arbuckle, from Point Pleasant, "for the grenadier squaw[5] and her friends, who are now at this garrison, say that he has engaged his Indian friends to carry off his effects to their towns; which being accomplished, he would then make his escape to Detroit."[6] Well had it been for the western country if

---

[1] Hand to Yeates, 7 March, 1778, MS.
[2] This was in what is now Trumbull county, Ohio.
[3] Hand to Yeates, 7 March, 1778, MS., just cited. The substance of this communication is reiterated by Gen. Hand in a letter to Maj.-Gen. Gates, same date. Hand's successor at Fort Pitt apologized for this raid upon the Delawares, to Capt. Pipe, principal war-chief of that tribe.
[4] Amer. Arch., 4th Series, Vol. V, pp. 818-820, 1092. The Olden Time, Vol. II, p. 104.
[5] The grenadier squaw was a sister of Cornstalk, the Shawanese chief.
[6] Arbuckle to Hand, 26 July, 1777, MS.

this arch-traitor had been at once secured. As it was, he was suffered to remain at large, upon his promise previously made, not to correspond with, or give any intelligence to, the enemies of the United States, or to leave the neighborhood of Fort Pitt without permission.

During the summer of 1777, many persons were arrested on suspicion of tory proclivities in western Pennsylvania and northwestern Virginia. Among them were some prominent men at Pittsburgh, including George Morgan. Even General Hand was suspected, so distrustful had western patriots become. Morgan was triumphantly acquitted. McKee, after being confined to his own house, was paroled anew. Hand, afterward, ordered him to report at York, Pennsylvania, to the continental board of war; but, feigning sickness, he remained at Pittsburgh.[1]

By the first of March, 1778, the excitement against the tories, in the west, had to a great degree subsided. On the twenty-eighth of that month all this was changed; for, on that day, not only McKee, but Matthew Elliott, who had lately arrived from Quebec, claiming to be a prisoner returned on parol, but, in reality, having a captain's commission from the British in his pocket, and Simon Girty, an Indian interpreter,—fled from the vicinity of Fort Pitt to the enemy.[2] These three renegades[3] afterward proved themselves active servants of the British government, bringing untold misery to the frontiers, not only while the revolution continued, but throughout the Indian war which followed that struggle. Their influence was immediately exerted to awaken the war-spirit of the savages. Going directly to the Delawares, they came very near changing the neutrality of that nation to open hostility against the United States;— frustrated, however, by the prompt action of General Hand, and of Morgan, who was still Indian agent at Fort Pitt,

---

[1] During the excitement in 1777, west of the mountains, caused by the general distrust, one man, supposed to have been a leader of the tories, lost his life under suspicious circumstances. Many depredations were also committed upon the property of suspected persons.

[2] Hand to Maj.-Gen Gates, 30 March, 1778, MS. Same to Yeates, same date, MS. Same to Col. Wm. Crawford, same date, MS. See, also, Penn. Arch., VI, 445; Heckewelder's Narr., p. 170. Four others fled to the enemy, at the same time,— Robert Surplus, one Higgins, and two negroes belonging to McKee.

[3] "Of that horrid brood called refugees, whom the devil has long since marked as his own."— Hugh H. Brackenridge, Pittsburgh, 1782.

and by the timely exertions of the Moravian missionaries upon the Tuscarawas. After leaving the Delawares, these traitors proceeded westward, inflaming the Shawanese and other tribes to a white heat of rapacity against the border settlements. Thence they made their way to Detroit.

The flight of these men to the enemy was soon followed at Fort Pitt by other disturbances. The minds of some of the soldiers of the garrison were poisoned by the wiles of disaffected persons in the vicinity. Several of them,[1] including a few citizens, on the night of the twentieth of April, stole a boat and fled down the Ohio. Luckily they were overtaken at the mouth of the Muskingum by a party sent after them and the ringleaders killed or captured.[2] Six of the soldiers and two citizens escaped.[3] "I hope to see some of the captured hanged in a few days," was the emphatic language of General Hand.[4] Two were shot, one hanged, and two whipped, the latter receiving one hundred lashes each.[5]

On the sixteenth of May, a number of Wyandots, under the lead of the Half King,[6] their principal chief, together with some Mingoes,[7] crossed the Ohio river and assailed Fort Randolph. The savages endeavored to draw the garrison into an ambuscade, but Captain William McKee, who was then in command, having received intelligence of their coming, was too wary for them. Only one of his men was killed and one wounded. The enemy had three wounded. After killing or driving off all the stock belonging to the fort, the Indians, who, during the day, kept up a scattering fire, but at too great

---

[1] "A sergeant and twenty odd men": John Proctor to Thomas Wharton, 26 Apr., 1778, in Penn. Arch., VI, 445.
[2] Hand to Maj.-Gen Gates, 28 Apr., 1778, MS.
[3] Hand to his wife, 28 Apr., 1778, MS.
[4] Hand to Maj.-Gen. Gates, 14 May, 1778, MS. Same to his wife, 15 May, 1778, MS.
[5] In addition to the authorities already cited, I have consulted, in connection with the tory troubles in the west, during 1777 and 1778, Zach. Morgan to Hand, 29 Aug., 1777, MS.; Thomas Brown to same, from "Redstone Fort," same date, MS.; Hand to Yeates, 16 Sept., 1777, MS.; same to his wife, 9 Oct., 1777, MS.; same to continental board of war, 9 Nov., 1777, MS.; same to same, 21 Dec., 1777, MS.; same to Alex. McKee, 7 Feb., 1778, MS.; same to Sampson Mathews, 27 June, 1778, MS.; Report of Cong. Com., at Fort Pitt, relative to Geo. Morgan, 27 March, 1778, MS.; Journals of Cong. for 1777, 1778.
[6] So called by the English. By the Wyandots, he was known as Sastaregi (Appendix to Hist. West. Penn., p. 144), or as Sarstarrateze (MS. statement of William Walker); by the Delawares, as Pomoacan (Heckewelder's Narr., p. 285. note).
[7] Their combined force numbered one hundred: Zeisberger to Morgan, 9 June, 1778, MS.

Introduction. 19

a distance either to do or receive much damage, at nightfall retired, soon making their way up the Great Kanawha to attack the Greenbrier settlement.[1] Timely notice sent by express from Fort Randolph fortunately averted, to a great extent, the impending destruction. The enemy, however, assailed one of the country forts — the most exposed one — on the twenty-ninth, but were gallantly repulsed. It was guarded, when first attacked, with only twenty-five men. The savages commenced the assault at sunrise and continued their firing until three o'clock in the afternoon, when a relief of sixty-six men forced their way into the inclosure through the enemy's lines, without loss.[2] The siege continued until night, when the savages disappeared, after having seventeen of their number killed. Of the Virginians, four only were slain.[3]

The activity displayed by the British Indians all along the western border, during the fall of 1777, induced Pennsylvania and Virginia to bestir themselves to protect their distant settlements. Congress, urgently appealed to by these suffering states, determined to make common cause with them against the enemy. Commissioners[4] acting under authority of the United States were sent to Fort Pitt to inquire into the disaffection of the frontier people, and to provide for carrying the war into the enemy's country.[5] They reported that the

---

[1] Capt. Wm. McKee to Hand, 21 June, 1778, MS.
[2] This force was under command of Col. Samuel Lewis and Capt. Arbuckle.
[3] Arbuckle to Hand, 2 June, 1778, MS. The fort attacked was Andrew Donnelly's. Compare Withers' Border Warfare, pp. 178, 179. The relief party marched from a fort where is now located Lewisburg, Greenbrier county, West Virginia. The letter of Arbuckle, just cited, corrects a few of the statements of Withers.
[4] Sampson Mathews, Geo. Clymer, and Sam'l McDowell.
[5] Journals of Cong., 20 Nov., 1777. On that day, congress —

"*Resolved*, That three commissioners be appointed to repair, without delay, to Fort Pitt; that they be instructed to investigate the rise, progress, and extent of the disaffection in that quarter, and take measures for suppressing the same and bringing the deluded people to a sense of their duty; that the said commissioners be invested with full powers to suspend, for misconduct, any officers in the service of the United States employed in that quarter, and appoint others in their room, and to confine, in safe custody, all such officers against whom they shall have satisfactory proof of being offenders against the rights and liberties of America.

"[*Resolved*], That the said commissioners be directed to cultivate the friendship of the Shawanese and Delawares, and prevent our people from committing any outrages against them; that they be empowered to engage as many of the Delaware and Shawanese warriors in the service of the United States as they judge convenient; that they be empowered and directed, for effectually checking the progress of the enemy, to concert with

western Indians were stimulated in their hostility by the British commandant[1] at Detroit. They drew up and presented to General Hand an elaborate plan[2] for the protection, by the militia alone, of the frontiers, until recommendations made by them to congress could be approved and carried into execution. On the second of May, 1778, congress resolved to raise two regiments in Virginia and Pennsylvania, to serve for one year unless sooner discharged, for protection of the western frontier, and for operation thereon; — twelve companies in the former and four in the latter state. It was likewise determined that, as General Hand had requested to be recalled from Pittsburgh, a proper person should be sent to relieve him. Washington was called upon to make the nomination. After much consideration upon the subject, he named Brigadier General Lachlan McIntosh, an officer of worth and merit, a Georgian by birth. "I part with this gentleman," wrote the commander-in-chief, "with much reluctance." "I know," are his words from his camp at Valley Forge, "his services here are, and will be, materially wanted." Washington had a high estimation of his fitness for the position assigned him: "His firm disposition and equal justice, his assiduity and good understanding, added to his being a stranger to all parties in that quarter, pointed him out as a proper person; and I trust extensive advantages will be derived from his command, which I could wish was more agreeable. He will wait on congress for their instructions."[3] On the twenty-sixth, McIntosh was notified of his appointment.

Brigadier General Hand a plan of carrying the war into the enemy's country, and cause the same to be executed with all convenient dispatch."...

[1] Lieut.-Gov. Henry Hamilton.

[2] A copy of this plan, or "Agreement," as it is called, is before me. It has no date.

[3] Washington to congress, 12 May, 1778, in Sparks' Washington, V, 361.

CHAPTER IV.

AN EXPEDITION UNDERTAKEN AGAINST DETROIT—ITS FAILURE. 1778-1779.

It was suggested to congress by the commissioners sent to Fort Pitt, that a defensive war upon the western border would not only prove an inadequate security against inroads of the savages, but would, in a short time, be more expensive than a vigorous attempt to force them to sue for peace. Thereupon that body determined that an expedition should be immediately undertaken to reduce, if practicable, the fort at Detroit, and compel the hostile Indians inhabiting the country contiguous to the route between Pittsburgh and that post, to cease their aggressions. Three thousand men — the number proposed by the commissioners[1] — were to be engaged in the service. Virginia was requested to call forth as many militia, not exceeding twenty-five hundred, as should be judged necessary to complete the number appropriated for the undertaking. The continental board of war was directed to coöperate with Brigadier General McIntosh, who was soon to have command of affairs in the west, in measures necessary for the enterprise, and give him such instructions as might appear best adapted to promote the expedition. Over nine hundred thousand dollars were voted to defray expenses, and a person was appointed to procure provisions, packhorses, and other necessaries for the army. To give effect to the action of congress, a plan was immediately set on foot for raising the necessary force and for the purchase of supplies for the expedition. Fifteen hundred men were to march by way of the Kanawha to Fort Randolph, and a like number, assembling at Pittsburgh, was to drop down the Ohio to the same post, whence all were to move into the enemy's country.

---
[1] Hand to Archibald Lochry and Providence Mounts, May 4, 1778, MS.

Before congress determined to begin active measures against Detroit and the hostile savages, Washington, upon receipt of information concerning Indian ravages upon the western frontier, had ordered the eighth Pennsylvania regiment, a choice body of men, who had been raised to the westward — one hundred of them having been constantly in Morgan's rifle corps — to prepare to march to Pittsburgh, a detachment having already been sent to that department. At the head of these troops was Colonel Daniel Brodhead. Previous to this, the men of the thirteenth Virginia[1] remaining at Valley Forge, had been placed under marching orders for the same destination, as they, too, were enlisted in the west. The others, numbering upwards of one hundred, were already "at or near Fort Pitt." The command of this regiment was given, temporarily, to Colonel John Gibson.

The advance of the regulars toward Pittsburgh commenced on the eleventh of June,[2] but was interrupted by Indian ravages in the valley of Wyoming. On the twelfth of July, McIntosh, then at Carlisle, Pennsylvania, on his way over the mountains, having been informed of the depredations of the savages to the northward, sent the eighth Pennsylvania up the Susquehanna, to stop the progress of the enemy, and encourage the militia to stand in their own defense; he, soon afterward, pursued his journey to Pittsburgh, where he arrived early in August.[3] General Hand, who had seen considerable service previous to his taking charge of the western department, gladly relinquished the command, — returning at once over the mountains to more active duties and wider fields of usefulness.[4] The turning aside of Colonel Brodhead's regiment retarded, of course, its progress toward Fort Pitt. After reaching a point as far up the Susquehanna as Muncy, where

---

[1] Afterward numbered the ninth, then the seventh, and, finally, the first Virginia regiment.

[2] "Col. Brodhead will march to-morrow with his regiment:" Washington to McIntosh, June 10, 1778, MS.

[3] "General McIntosh has at length arrived. . . . Day after to-morrow, I hope to set forward to Lancaster:" Hand to his wife, from Pittsburgh, 6 Aug., 1778, MS.

[4] Hand was born 31 Dec., 1744, in King's county, Ireland; succeeded Gen. Stark in command at Albany, in October, 1778; was made adjutant-general, in 1780; was a member of congress in 1784–5; died 3 Sept., 1802, near Lancaster, Pennsylvania.

he did good service, Brodhead returned with his force to Carlisle. He resumed his march toward Pittsburgh not long afterward, where he arrived about the tenth of September.[1]

As early as July, it became apparent that success, in an expedition against Detroit, could not reasonably be expected, unless the force destined for that service could march from Pittsburgh by the first of September, as had been suggested by the Fort Pitt commissioners; that the necessary supplies could not, by any means, be procured within the time limited; and that an extraordinary rise in the price of some articles since the campaign was first determined on would cause the expense of the undertaking, even if practicable, to exceed the estimate in an enormous degree.[2] Congress therefore resolved, that the expedition, for the present, should be deferred. McIntosh was directed to assemble at Pittsburgh fifteen hundred continental troops and militia, and proceed, without delay, to destroy such towns of the hostile tribes as he, in his discretion, should think would most effectually tend to chastise and terrify the savages and check their ravages on the western frontiers. The Fort Pitt commander was, however, more ambitious. He declared "that nothing less than Detroit was his object." Congress asked Virginia to supply him with as many militia as he should call for, " to make up the complement of men destined for an incursion into the towns of the hostile Indians;" but McIntosh kept his eye on Detroit, notwithstanding.[3] He was willing to "defer" the expedition against that post; that was all. The scheme of marching a force by way of the Kanawha to Fort Randolph, to be joined by an army at that post moving down the Ohio, was abandoned.

Upon the arrival of McIntosh in the western department, there were but two fixed stations, beside Fort Pitt, west of the Alleghanies, occupied by continental troops. These two

---

[1] Brodhead's MS. orderly book shows him (Brodhead) to have been at Ligonier on the sixth of September, and at Fort Pitt on the twelfth, when it speaks of his "late arrival."

[2] The estimate, by the commissioners at Pittsburgh, for the expedition, was $609,538.

[3] "The regular troops and new levies were equal to such an undertaking [an excursion into the Indian country], but General McIntosh's views were much more extensive . . . he was determined to take Detroit." — Brodhead to Maj.-Gen. Greene, 26 May, 1779, in Penn. Arch., XII, 118.

were Fort Randolph and Fort Hand.[1] There were, however, thirty or forty other smaller stations, or forts, at different times garrisoned by militia; some between Wheeling and Pittsburgh; others upon the waters of the Monongahela and the Kiskiminetas; and not a few in the interior parts of the settlements;—" which were frequently altered, kept, or evacuated, according to the humors, fears, or interest, of the people of most influence." General Hand had been obliged to yield to this, as his chief dependence was upon militia. These forts, in view of the fact that they were very expensive and would be of little service now that the war was to be carried into the enemy's country, McIntosh resolved to break up as soon as he could, without giving too much offense to the people, whose assistance he so much required.

That the frontiers might not be wholly deprived of means for defense while the army marched into the Indian country, the lieutenants of Monongalia and Ohio counties, Virginia,[2] were authorized to raise a ranging company jointly, to scout continually along the Ohio river "from Beaver creek downwards," where the savages usually crossed to annoy the settlements. Archibald Lochry, lieutenant of Westmoreland county, Pennsylvania, was empowered to organize two such companies, to scour the frontiers on the north, as a protection from scalping parties of the northern Indians. Independent companies had been raised for the sole purpose of maintaining Fort Pitt, Fort Hand, and Fort Randolph, as these posts were expected soon to be evacuated by their garrisons.

McIntosh had not been long in the west when he discovered that a number of store-houses for provisions, which had been built at public expense, were at great distances apart, difficult

---

[1] Fort Hand, erected in the spring of 1778, and named in honor of Brig.-Gen. Hand, was located in Westmoreland county, about fourteen miles north of Hannastown. "About a mile south of the ford of the Kiskiminetas; and the ford was about six miles above the mouth of the stream:" MS. Statement of Samuel Murphy, 1846.

[2] Three counties—Yohogania, Monongalia, and Ohio—were formed by Virginia in 1776, out of the district of West Augusta, the latter having previously been set off from Augusta county. Yohogania included — so Virginia claimed — a considerable portion of what is now southwestern Pennsylvania. To the south of this, down the Ohio river, was Ohio county. Eastward of Ohio county, lying upon the waters of the Monongahela and its branches, was the county of Monongalia. The lieutenant of Monongalia county was Col. John Evans; of Ohio county, Col. David Shepherd.

Introduction. 25

of access, and scattered throughout the border counties. At each of these, a number of men was required. These buildings were given up, as the provisions in them intended for the expedition proved to be spoiled. In place of them, one general store-house was built by a fatigue party, "in the fork of the Monongahela river," where all loads from over the mountains could be discharged, without crossing any considerable branch of any river.

The commissioners at Fort Pitt proposed to congress that a treaty be held on the twenty-third of July, at Pittsburgh, with the Delawares, Shawanese, and other Indians. Congress approved the suggestion, and resolved that three persons should be appointed to negotiate with the savages. Virginia was requested to send two and Pennsylvania one commissioner for that purpose. Messengers carrying presents had already been dispatched to the Delawares and Shawanese, with invitations to attend the conference.[1] Two Virginians,[2] representing the United States, repaired to Fort Pitt, but Pennsylvania neglected to send a representative.[3] This caused some disappointment. From the wilderness across the Ohio, no Indians came but Delawares, as a large majority of the Shawanese were now openly hostile to the United States. The former tribe was represented by their three principal chiefs.[4] It was September before the parties met for consultation; and a treaty was not finally signed until the seventeenth of that month.[5] By its terms, not only were the Delawares made close allies of the United States and "the hatchet put into their hands,"—thus changing, and wisely too, the neutral policy previously acted upon,—but consent was obtained for marching an army across their territory.[6] They stipulated to join the troops of the general government with such a number of their best and most

---

[1] The messenger sent to the Shawanese was James Girty; but, like his brother Simon, he was induced to desert the cause of his country. He remained with the Indians.
[2] Andrew and Thomas Lewis.
[3] George Morgan solicited the appointment, but none was made.
[4] White Eyes, Captain Pipe, and John Killbuck, Jun.
[5] This treaty has been several times published.
[6] The territory of the Delawares, as claimed by them at that date, was bounded on the east by French creek, the Alleghany, and the Ohio,—as far down the last mentioned stream as Hockhocking, at least; on the west, by the Hockhocking and the Sandusky. They even advanced claims to the whole of the Shawanese country.

expert warriors as they could spare, consistent with their own safety. A requisition for two captains and sixty braves was afterward made upon the nation by the American commander.

McIntosh now opened a road to the Beaver. There, just below its mouth, upon the right bank of the Ohio,[1] he built, by fatigue of the whole line, a post with barracks and stores, where loads could be carried, either by land or water; and where, should there be a failure of sufficient troops and supplies to carry forward the expedition during the autumn, a footing, at least, would be secured, considerably advanced toward the enemy's country. This would enable the commander to be better prepared for another attempt in the spring, and show the foe, at the same time, that he was in earnest in his progressive movements.[2] The post was called Fort McIntosh, in honor of its projector. It was built under the immediate supervision of a competent engineer.[3] It was furnished with bastions and protected by artillery. It was a "good, strong fort," — the first military post of the United States erected upon the Indian side of the Ohio.[4]

As early as the eighth of October, the headquarters of the army were removed from Fort Pitt to the new fort,[5] where a considerable force — the largest collected west of the Alleghanies during the revolution — was assembled, consisting, beside the continental troops, of militia, mostly from the western counties of Virginia.[6] But the want of necessary supplies prevented any immediate forward movement. On the third day of November, cattle from over the mountains arrived,

---

[1] At the site of what is now the borough of Beaver, in Beaver county, Pennsylvania.

[2] Such were the reasons given by McIntosh himself, to Washington, for the erection of the post.

[3] Le Chev'r de Cambray.

[4] Fort McIntosh was "a regular stockaded work, with four bastions, and defended by six pieces of artillery." It was built of hewn logs; its figure was an irregular square, the face to the river being longer than the side to the land. It was about equal to a square of fifty yards; was well built, and strong against musketry, although the opposite side of the river commanded it entirely, and artillery placed there could have reduced it.

[5] Orderly book of McIntosh, 1778, MS.

[6] McIntosh's entire force was about thirteen hundred. The militia numbered "at least one thousand." — Brodhead to Maj.-Gen. Greene, 26 May, 1779, previously cited. They were mostly from what was then Berkeley, Frederick, Rockingham, Augusta, Botetourt, Yohogania, Monongalia, and Ohio counties, Virginia. MS. Memoranda of Francis Dunlavy. McIntosh's orderly book, 1778, MS. Jour. Va. Ex. Council, July, 1778, MS.

but they were extremely poor, and could not be slaughtered for want of salt.[1]

Alarming intelligence now reached McIntosh from the wilderness west. He was reproached for his tardiness by friendly Indians, who threatened that all their nations would unite in the Tuscarawas valley to give him battle, and oppose his progress to Detroit. Orders were, therefore, immediately issued for twelve hundred men to get ready to march. On the fifth of November, the movement of the army westward commenced, including the whole force, except one company, which was left under command of Lieutenant-Colonel Richard Campbell, of the thirteenth Virginia regiment, to bring on the "long-looked for supplies."[2] For fourteen days, the march continued before the Tuscarawas was reached,[3] a distance of only about seventy miles from Fort McIntosh. This slow progress was caused by the "horses and cattle tiring every four or five miles." It was upon this river, where the army had now encamped, that the commander anticipated meeting the enemy; but only a few Delawares from Coshocton, and some Moravian Indians[4] were found, and they were friendly. The gathering of the savages to impede his march, he was told, had been abandoned.[5]

At this juncture, McIntosh was informed that the necessary supplies for the winter had not reached Fort McIntosh, and that very little could be expected. He was thus disappointed in all his "flattering prospects and schemes" against Detroit. There was now no other alternative but to return as he came, without effecting any valuable purpose, thereby confirming

[1] Salt sold in Pittsburgh, at that date, at twenty dollars a bushel.
[2] McIntosh to Washington, 27 Apr , 1779, in Sparks' Corr. Amer. Rev., vol. II, p. 284. Jacob White's pension statement, 1833, MS. copy. Dunlavy's pension statement, MS. copy, previously cited. McIntosh's orderly book, 1778, MS.
[3] That is to say, there were fourteen marching days. The army did not make its camp upon the Tuscarawas until November 21st; McIntosh's orderly book, 1778, MS. McIntosh, in his letter to Washington, of 27 Apr., 1779, just cited, says: "We were fourteen days upon our march." The route was the same as the one followed by Colonel Henry Bouquet, on his march against western Indians in 1764. For a description of the course taken by that officer, consult Bouquet's Expedition against the Ohio Indians, Philadelphia printed, London reprinted, 1766, pp. 11–13; or, Robert Clarke & Co.'s reprint, Cincinnati, 1868, pp. 46–51.
[4] The Moravian Indians (themselves mostly Delawares) were of those gathered in the valley of the Tuscarawas, by Moravian missionaries.
[5] That the enemy seriously contemplated meeting McIntosh in the valley of the Tuscarawas, there is no evidence.

the savages in the opinion already formed of the weakness of the Americans, and combining them all more completely with the British,—or, to build a strong stockade fort upon the Tuscarawas, and leave as many men as provisions would justify, to secure it until the next season, to serve as a bridle upon the Indians in their own country.[1] The commander, with the unanimous approbation of his principal officers, chose the latter alternative; and a post was commenced where there had been one formerly,[2] on the west bank of the river, below the mouth of Sandy creek,[3]— the whole army being employed upon it while provisions lasted; not, however, without some trouble, as the militia whose homes were west of the mountains, were in a mutinous condition. The fortification was a regularly laid out work, inclosing less than an acre of ground, and was named Fort Laurens, in honor of the president of congress. It was the first military post of the government erected upon any portion of the territory now constituting the state of Ohio. Leaving a garrison of one hundred and fifty men, with scanty supplies, under command of Colonel John Gibson, to finish and protect the work, McIntosh, with the rest of his army, returned, very short of provisions,[4] to Fort McIntosh, where the militia under his command were discharged "precipitately."[5]

Washington soon after, in ignorance of McIntosh's movements beyond the mountains, declared that the latter ought to decide finally, if he had not already done so, whether he could,

---

[1] Such were the reasons given by McIntosh to Washington, sometime afterward, for building Fort Laurens. "I am the more particular in giving my reasons," said he, "for building Fort Laurens, as ——, ——, and their dependents, for want of other matter, have cried it down, as a designed slaughter-pen, impossible to maintain; and endeavored to prejudice the whole country against it, although the former laid the plan that was afterwards adopted for taking and keeping Detroit."—McIntosh to Washington, 27 April, 1779, previously cited.

[2] Compare Bouquet's Expedition, London reprint, p. 13, or Cincinnati reprint, pp. 51, 52, as to the erection of a fort upon the right bank of the Tuscarawas, in 1764, by Col. Bouquet. The fortification commenced by McIntosh was close by the site of Bouquet's.

[3] A short distance south of the present village of Bolivar, Tuscarawas county, Ohio.

[4] "On our march in, we were obliged to eat beef-hides, which had been left to dry; they were first roasted:" Statement of Stephen Burkham, 1845, MS. "Thirty-six dry hides were cut up and roasted in one night:" Ellis' Recollections, 1845, MS.

[5] McIntosh to Washington, 11 Jan., 1779, MS. Mem. of Francis Dunlavy, MS. The army left Fort Laurens on the morning of the 9th Dec., arriving at Fort McIntosh the 13th.

with the force, provisions, stores, prospect of supplies, and means of transportation, which he then had, advance to Detroit; and whether the advantages or disadvantages of a winter expedition preponderated. The return of the Fort Pitt commander to the Ohio river was an emphatic decision, already given, in opposition to a winter campaign against that post.

McIntosh now made such disposition of his continental troops and independent companies for the winter as, in his judgment, would protect the border, and facilitate future operations. The eighth Pennsylvania regiment was assigned to Fort Pitt. The men left in Fort Laurens were a part of the thirteenth Virginia. The residue, with the independent companies, were divided between Fort McIntosh, Fort Henry, Fort Randolph, and Fort Hand; with a few at inferior stations. There was not one of the militia retained under pay at either of these posts.

After the main army left Fort Laurens, the work upon that post was continued. "I have already finished setting up the pickets," wrote the officer in charge, toward the latter part of December, "and, in a few days, I think I can bid defiance to the enemy." "The distressed situation of the men," he continued, "prevents the work from going on as briskly as it otherwise would." In the meantime, he had opened negotiations with the friendly Delawares at Coshocton for the purchase of some cattle. "With these," he added, "I am in hopes we shall have beef enough, and that we shall have a sufficient quantity of flour until a farther supply can be sent us."[1]

The disappearance into the Indian country from Fort Pitt and vicinity, in the early part of the year 1778, of McKee and other tories, added greatly to the terror in the border settlements naturally inspired by the knowledge of the hostile attitude of the western savages. "What may be the fate of this county," is the language of a resident of Westmoreland, in the latter part of April, "God only knows; but, at present, it wears a most dismal aspect." On the twenty-eighth, a settlement "at and about Wallace's fort," in that county, was at-

---

[1] Col. John Gibson to McIntosh, from Fort Laurens, 21 Dec., 1778, MS.

tacked, and twenty men who were out reconnoitering the woods, had nine killed and their captain wounded. Four of the enemy were killed. By the middle of May, the northern road leading over the mountains from Pittsburgh had become the frontier line in that direction. A captain, who, with nine men, chiefly continental soldiers, was bringing grain from the neighborhood to Fort Hand, was, on the seventh of July, surprised by a party of savages. The officer[1] and seven of his command were killed. There were, also, frequent incursions of scalping parties across the Ohio, at different points below Wheeling, notwithstanding the progress of the American army westward of that river. These were continued until late in the autumn. From Fort Henry to Fort Randolph, there were few, if any, obstacles presented to this advance of the foe into the settlements lying on the east and west forks of the Monongahela and their branches. Suddenly would the savages make their appearance, frequently where least expected; then followed the bloody work of the tomahawk and scalping-knife; and, as suddenly as they came, would the murderers disappear.

While McIntosh was at Fort Laurens, he ordered one hundred and fifty militia from Westmoreland county, to march as secretly as possible to "the forks of the Alleghany river," and endeavor to destroy some Indians settled on French creek, who were the perpetrators of much of the mischief done in the northern settlements. The men reached a point within "ten miles of the savages, when they returned," declared McIntosh, "without seeing the face of a single Indian."[2] "We proceeded on to French creek," is the subsequent language of the officer having chief command of the expedition, "where we found the Indian town evacuated." "I then went on further than my orders called for," he adds, "in quest of Indians; but our provisions being nearly exhausted, we were obliged to return."[3]

---

[1] Capt. Miller, of the eighth Pennsylvania regiment.
[2] McIntosh to Washington, 11 Jan., 1779, MS., previously cited.
[3] This was the first expedition in force to the northward from the vicinity of Fort Pitt, during the war. It was commanded by Col. James Smith. For this officer's account of the march, see his Narr. (Lexington, Ky., 1799), p. 75, or Robert Clarke & Co.'s reprint (Cincinnati, 1870), p. 135-137. Mention of the "French creek expedition," as it was called, is to be found in Col. Rec. of Pa., XIV, 662.

Introduction.

More than half the month of January, 1779, wore away without anything of importance occurring to the westward of Pittsburgh, when Samuel Sample, an assistant quartermaster, sent by Colonel Gibson from Fort Laurens to Coshocton, for corn and other articles, had one man killed,[1] and another desperately wounded,[2] by treacherous Delawares.[3] Toward the close of the month, Captain John Clark, of the eighth Pennsylvania regiment, who had commanded an escort of provisions to Gibson, was, on his return, with a sergeant and fourteen men, when only about three miles distant from the fort, attacked by seventeen Indians, chiefly Mingoes, led by Simon Girty, the renegade from Pittsburgh, who, immediately after his arrival at Detroit, was employed in the Indian department as interpreter, and sent back to the savages. The Americans suffered a loss of two killed, four wounded, and one taken prisoner. The remainder, including the captain, fought their way back to the fort. Letters written by the commander of the post, and containing valuable information, were captured by Girty.[4] McIntosh, upon receipt of this intelligence, endeavored to send supplies to the garrison by way of the Ohio and Muskingum rivers, but the attempt proved abortive.[5] By the middle of February, provisions began to grow scarce. The commander sent word to McIntosh at Fort Pitt, informing him of the state of affairs, concluding with these brave words: "You may depend on my defending the fort to the last extremity."

On the twenty-third, a wagoner was sent out of Fort Laurens for the horses belonging to the post, to draw wood. With him went a guard of eighteen men. The party were fired upon by lurking savages and all killed and scalped in sight of the fort,

---

[1] John Nash, of the thirteenth Virginia regiment; killed Jan. 22d.
[2] Peter Parchment, of the same regiment as Nash; wounded on the 27th of the same month; he finally recovered.
[3] Gibson to McIntosh, from Fort Laurens, 13 Feb., 1779, MS.
[4] Capt. John Killbuck to Gibson, 3) Jan., 1779, original letter. Heckewelder to same, 8 Feb., 1779, original letter. McIntosh to Lochry, 29 Jan., 1779, in Penn. Arch., VII, 173.
[5] "I am now happily relieved by the arrival of Maj. Taylor here, who returned with one hundred men and two hundred kegs of flour. He was six days going up the Muskingum river about twenty miles, the waters were so high and stream so rapid; and as he had about one hundred and thirty miles more to go, he judged it impossible to relieve Col. Gibson in time, and therefore returned, having lost two of his men sent to flank him upon the shore, who were killed and scalped by some warriors coming down the Muskingum river!" McIntosh to Washington, from Fort Pitt, 12 March, 1779, MS.

except two, who were made prisoners.[1] The post was immediately thereafter invested by the Indians — mostly Wyandots and Mingoes — in force.[2] They continued the siege until the garrison was reduced to the verge of starvation; a quarter of a pound of sour flour and an equal weight of spoiled meat constituting a daily ration. The assailants, however, were finally compelled to return home, as their supplies had also become exhausted.

Before the enemy left, a soldier managed to steal through their lines, reaching McIntosh on the third of March, with a message from Colonel Gibson informing him of his critical situation.[3] The Fort Pitt commander immediately made exertions to set on foot an expedition for his relief. In the event of not meeting the foe upon the Tuscarawas, McIntosh planned, in his own mind, to march before his return, against Sandusky and destroy the Wyandot towns; "and if we could not get any supplies there," are his words, "proceed farther."[4] On the nineteenth of March, with about two hundred militia quickly raised from the counties west of the mountains, and over three hundred continental troops from Fort McIntosh and Fort Pitt, he left the former post upon his second march to the Tuscarawas;[5] arriving there in four days,[6] to find the siege of Fort Laurens abandoned and the savages gone. A salute, fired by the garrison upon the arrival of the relief in sight of the post, frightened the packhorses, causing them to break loose, scattering the supplies in the woods and resulting

---

[1] McIntosh to Washington, 12 March, 1779, MS., just cited. Brodhead to same, 21 March, 1779, MS.

[2] "The attacking party consisted of one hundred and eighty:" Hildreth's Pion. Hist., p. 138. "Near three hundred:" Heckewelder to McIntosh, 12 March, 1779, MS. Hildreth is the better authority in this matter. He cites Geo. Morgan, who got his information from the Delaware chiefs. The cunning foe, it seems, by stratagem, made their number so appear, that eight hundred and forty-seven were counted from one of the bastions of the fort.

[3] "A messenger came to me the third of March, instant, who slipped out of Fort Laurens on the night of Sunday, the twenty-eighth of February, by whom Col. Gibson would not venture to write:" McIntosh to Washington, 12 Mar., 1779, previously cited.

[4] McIntosh to Washington, 3 Apr., 1779, MS.

[5] McIntosh to Washington, 19 March, 1779, MS. Orderly book of McIntosh, 1779, MS. Col. Brodhead was left in command of Fort McIntosh.

[6] McIntosh to Washington, 3 Apr., 1779, MS., previously cited. McIntosh's orderly book, MS.

in the loss of a number of the horses and of some of the provisions.

The men in the fort were found in a most deplorable condition. For nearly a week, they had subsisted on raw hides and such roots as they could find in the vicinity after the Indians had gone. McIntosh called a council of war and laid before the officers assembled his plan for marching against the Wyandots and striking a blow at their towns on the Sandusky. But the project was unanimously opposed; as the ground, so early in the season, was very wet, and there was a scanty supply of forage for their horses and less than two weeks' provisions for the whole army. So the matter was dropped.[1] Leaving one hundred and six men, rank and file, of the eighth Pennsylvania regiment, under command of Major Frederick Vernon, to garrison the post, and a supply of food for less than two months, he returned with the residue of his force to Fort McIntosh, reaching there after a march of six days.

In April, 1779, McIntosh, dispirited and with health impaired, retired from the command of the western department,—his request, previously made to congress for that purpose, having been granted.[2] He soon repaired to Washington's headquarters.[3] This was the abandonment by the general government, for the time, of offensive measures in the west. Something had been gained by the forward movement from Fort Pitt, although at the expense of a number of lives and much treasure. The attention of the savages had, to some extent, been diverted from the border, and the anxiety at Detroit considerably increased. In the management of affairs in the western department not immediately connected with aggressive

---

[1] McIntosh to Washington, 8 Apr. (just cited) and 3 May, 1779, MS. letters.

[2] "Whereas Brigadier [General] McIntosh, commanding a detachment of the army at Fort Pitt, hath requested leave to retire from that command,

"*Resolved*, That the commander-in-chief be directed to appoint a proper officer to succeed to the said command; and that Brigadier-General McIntosh, on being relieved, repair to the main army, or to such post as shall be assigned to him by the commander-in-chief."—Journals of Cong., 20 Feb., 1779.

[3] He was in Philadelphia as early as the twenty-fourth of April: Penn. Arch., VII, 342. His letter written to Washington on the twenty-seventh was dated in "Camp," which Sparks (Corr. Amer. Rev., II, 284) erroneously supposed meant Pittsburgh. Beside, the context clearly indicates that he was writing east of the mountains: "When I first went there [west of the mountains], I found," etc.

movements beyond the Ohio, McIntosh had exercised good judgment. He had carefully avoided interfering with the troublesome boundary question, although often applied to by both sides; as it was wholly out of his power to remedy the evil. He had preserved cordial relations with the several county lieutenants and had been active and vigilant in protecting the exposed settlements. The erection of Forts McIntosh and Laurens as a precautionary measure was approved by the commander-in-chief. "The establishing of posts of communication," he wrote, "which McIntosh has done for the security of his convoys and the army, is a proceeding grounded on military practice and experience." Congress having directed the appointment of a successor to the retiring officer, Washington, on the fifth of March, made choice of Colonel Daniel Brodhead, of the eighth Pennsylvania regiment, who was then first in rank, in the western department, under General McIntosh.[1]

[1] McIntosh was born near Inverness, Scotland, 17 March, 1725. His father's family, himself included, came with General Oglethorpe to Georgia, in 1736. He became colonel of the first Georgia regiment in the early part of the revolution; was soon made a brigadier-general; killed Button Gwinnett, a signer of the declaration of independence, in a duel, in 1777; was captured at Charleston, South Carolina, May 1ª, 1780; became a member of congress, in 1784; an Indian commissioner, in 1785; died in Savannah, Georgia, 20 Feb., 1806.

CHAPTER V.

PROGRESS OF THE WESTERN BORDER WAR. 1779–1781.

While in charge of Fort McIntosh, Brodhead was notified of his appointment to the command of the western department, in a complimentary letter from the commander-in-chief. Said Washington: "From my opinion of your abilities, your former acquaintance with the back country, and the knowledge you must have acquired upon this last tour of duty, I have appointed you to the command."[1] It was a selection gratifying to Pennsylvania, as the colonel was a citizen of that state. The whole force turned over to him by McIntosh, including continental and independent troops, consisted of seven hundred and twenty-two men, stationed at Fort Laurens and Fort McIntosh, Fort Henry and Fort Randolph, Fort Hand and Fort Pitt. At the last mentioned post, Brodhead soon established his headquarters.[2] A few other stations were garrisoned with small detachments.

The wanton ravages and murders by Indians of the Six Nations, the year previous, in the exposed settlements of Pennsylvania and New York, particularly at Wyoming and Cherry Valley, determined Washington to send a formidable expedition against them. Four thousand men were to penetrate their country from the waters of the Susquehanna; while five hundred from Pittsburgh, by way of the Alleghany, were to coöperate as circumstances might permit. Brodhead received, from the commander-in-chief, explicit orders concerning the movement from Fort Pitt. These directions were given careful thought. "The strictest attention," was his assurance to Washington, "shall ever be paid to all the in-

---
[1] Washington to Brodhead, 5 Mar., 1779, MS. Compare Patterson's Hist. Backwoods, p. 234.
[2] Orders from Pittsburgh were issued by him as early as April 13th: MS. Instructions— Brodhead to Lieut. Lawrence Harrison, of the 13th [9th] Va. Reg't. This regiment had been recently numbered the 9th, a fact then unknown at Pittsburgh.

structions your excellency may, from time to time, be pleased to give me." "I shall be happy," said he, previously, "if we can move by the first of June." But the idea of coöperation from Pittsburgh with the other forces marching against the New York Indians, was soon abandoned. The uncertainty of timing it well, and a want of sufficient information of the country through which Brodhead would have to pass, together with the difficulty of providing supplies in time, and the removal of troops, which would uncover the region around Fort Pitt, thereby giving confidence to the western savages, already too much inclined to hostility, were the principal inducements prompting the commander-in-chief to lay aside all thoughts of aid from the western department. But the expedition against the hostile portion of the Indians of the Six Nations was not abandoned.

In his instructions to Brodhead, mention was made, by Washington, of the boundary troubles in the west. "There is one point," are his words, "upon which I will take the liberty of dropping you a caution, though perhaps it may have already struck you, which is, the policy and propriety of not interesting yourself in the dispute subsisting between the states of Pennsylvania and Virginia, on account of their boundaries." The advice of Washington was not lost upon Brodhead. He turned his thoughts to the protection and wants of the whole trans-Alleghany region, irrespective of boundary lines. "His excellency, the commander-in-chief," he wrote, on the fifteenth of April, "has now honored me with the command of the western department, and my whole attention shall not be wanting to strike terror in our enemy and secure the settlements in this fertile country."

The condition of Fort Laurens early engaged the attention of Brodhead. Major Vernon, at that post, experienced, from the commencement of his charge, many hardships. Scarcely had the command been turned over to him when small parties of savages began to make their appearance in the vicinity. He soon had two men killed, out of a party of forty who were outside the fort gathering fire-wood.[1] The throwing of supplies

[1] Vernon to McIntosh, from Fort Laurens, 26 March, 1779, MS. Same to Brodhead,

into the post was attended with much difficulty and expense, and its evacuation seemed desirable. But "it is to be preserved," wrote Washington, "if, under a full consideration of circumstances, it is judged a post of importance, and can be maintained without running too great a risk." The commander-in-chief was apprehensive its abandonment would give great encouragement to the savages about Detroit,— which was his reason for holding it; not on account of any opinion of its usefulness as a protection to the border. Brodhead found "that the state of provisions there" was by no means what he had supposed it to be.[1] The language of Vernon, in a letter from the fort, dated the twenty-ninth of April was expressive and startling: "Should you not send us provisions in a very short time, necessity will oblige us to begin on some cow-hides the Indians left."

"I am just now fitting out one hundred and fifty men," wrote Brodhead, on the fourth of May, "to escort a small quantity of supplies to Fort Laurens." "Indeed," was his earnest declaration, in addition, "I cannot send a larger party; as the Indians are at present very troublesome on the northern frontiers of Westmoreland, and a large party would consume all the salt provisions on the march; as for fresh ones, I have none."[2] But the greatest part of the garrison, by the middle of the month, had to be sent in, or they would have perished by starvation, as no relief had arrived. Major Vernon held the post ten days longer with only twenty-five men, living on herbs, salt, and cow-hides, when supplies from Fort Pitt, escorted by a party of regulars, who marched by a new route,[3] reached the fort.

same date, MS. The attack was made in the morning of the day on which these letters were written. Ensign John Clark was one of the killed.

[1] Brodhead to Lochry, 23 Apr., 1779, MS.
[2] Brodhead to Washington, MS. letter.
[3] The relief was commanded by Capt. Robert Beall, of the 13th [9th] Va. Reg't. They dropped down the Ohio to an old, deserted Mingo town, at the mouth of Cross creek, just below the present Steubenville, Ohio; marching thence to Fort Laurens.—Brodhead to Beall; MS. Instructions. Same to Maj. Vernon, at Fort Laurens, 14 May, 1779, MS. Same to Lieut. John Hardin, of the 8th Pa. Reg't, same date, MS. The detachment was detained for a time, at Fort McIntosh, "while the garrison at Fort Laurens were starving:" Brodhead to Capt. John Clark, June 6th, 1779, MS. This new route to Fort Laurens was not again used,—"the old Tuscarawas path" being taken in subsequent marches to and from that post.

At this time, the garrison were so much reduced for want of provisions that they were scarcely able to stand on their feet. " I dare say," are the words of Brodhead to the Fort Laurens commander, on the thirtieth, " you took good care not to suffer your starved men to eat too much at a time, after the supplies arrived, and that the whisky added to their relief." Past the middle of June, the post was relieved by seventy-five men, well supplied with provisions, under command of Lieutenant-Colonel Campbell.[1] Vernon returned to Fort Pitt, but his detachment was left at Fort McIntosh.[2] After being once more seriously threatened by the Indians in force, Fort Laurens, early in August, was evacuated; orders to that effect having been previously sent by Colonel Brodhead,[3] that the garrison stationed there might be added to troops already collected at Pittsburgh for a contemplated expedition against the northern Indians. Before the soldiers left, two of their number were killed by lurking savages within sight of the post. As the fort might again be occupied, Colonel Campbell was enjoined not to destroy it. It was never after garrisoned. It remained intact during the war, but was subsequently demolished.

Turning our eyes from the wilderness beyond the Ohio, to the northern settlements of Westmoreland, we see that, as early as the twenty-sixth of February, 1779, Indian depredations began therein. On that day, about twenty miles east of Pittsburgh, on the main road leading over the mountains, eighteen persons — men, women, and children — were either killed or taken prisoners.[4] It is not surprising, therefore, that the first care of Brodhead, after assuming command in the west, was, to protect the northern frontier. His first order[5] directed a de-

[1] Brodhead to Campbell, MS. Instructions, 14 June, 1779. Same to Vernon, same date, MS. Instructions. Same to Campbell, 16 June, 1779, MS. letter.
[2] Brodhead's orderly book, 1779, MS. Zeisberger to Campbell, at Fort Laurens (no date), MS.
[3] The first order to leave was issued by Brodhead on the 16th July: Brodhead to Campbell, MS. Instructions. This informed the commander that the post was to be evacuated as soon as horses could be sent to bring in the stores; subsequent orders were more pressing and imperative.
[4] McIntosh to Washington, 12 Mar., 1779, MS., before cited.
[5] Brodhead to Lieut. Lawrence Harrison, 13th [9th] Va. Reg't, 13 Apr,, 1779, MS., previously cited.

tachment from Fort Pitt to occupy the vacant Fort Crawford, located a few miles up the Alleghany.[1] The soldiers were instructed to scout on the waters of that river, as well as on Puckety creek, and upon the Kiskiminetas as far as Fort Hand, thereby to protect, as much as possible, from the death-dealing savages of the north, the exposed settlements to the eastward of Pittsburgh. General Washington, with "a full sense of the importance, necessity, and duty, of taking the most vigorous and speedy measures for the support and protection of the frontiers," decided to order to the westward Colonel Moses Rawlings' corps of three companies from Fort Frederick, Maryland, to assist in protecting the exposed settlements, and, at the same time, to promote the coöperation of troops from Fort Pitt with the army to be sent against Indians of the Six Nations, by erecting posts at Kittanning and Venango. Although the plan for the movement of a force from Pittsburgh was soon laid aside and the building of the two forts abandoned, the march of the Maryland corps was not countermanded.

Pursuant to a resolution of congress, Pennsylvania determined to raise five companies of rangers for service to the westward. Militia, also, were ordered "to march with all possible expedition" from the eastward, "for the immediate protection of the counties of Bedford and Westmoreland."

"The Indians seem to have taken quarters in Westmoreland," Brodhead wrote, on the fourteenth of April, "but they lost one of their scalps yesterday."[2] On the twenty-sixth, Fort Hand was attacked by a considerable force of the enemy.[3] It was defended by Captain Samuel Moorhead, commanding his independent company, then numbering only seventeen men inside the fortification. The post was assailed about one o'clock in the afternoon, and a continual firing kept up until

---

[1] Fort Crawford stood a little way above the mouth of Puckety creek, on the Fort Pitt side of the Alleghany. Compare Penn. Arch., second series, Vol. IV, p. 701. It was in what is now Burrell township, Westmoreland county, near the line of the Alleghany Valley railroad.

[2] MS. Instructions: Brodhead to Lieut. Gabriel Peterson, of the 8th Pa. Reg't.

[3] "Supposed to be not less than one hundred;" M orhead to Brodhead, 27 Apr., 1779, MS. "Capt. Moorhead thinks there were about one hundred:" Brodhead to Lochry, 30 Apr., 1779, MS.

nearly mid-day of the twenty-seventh, when the foe retired. The garrison had none killed. Three were wounded — one soon died. There were a few women in the fort, who busily employed themselves during the attack in running bullets for their brave defenders. A company of forty men marched from Pittsburgh to intercept the enemy,[1] but the attempt proved a failure. On the same day of the appearance of the savages around Fort Hand, the Indians attacked the settlement at Ligonier, killing one man and taking two prisoners.

"The savages," wrote a resident of Westmoreland, on the first day of May, "are continually making depredations among us; not less than forty people have been killed, wounded, or captured, this spring." The arrival of Rawlings' corps before the close of the month gave some confidence to the inhabitants, who had already fallen upon a mode of self-protection, by raising two companies of rangers, under the authority previously given Colonel Lochry by General McIntosh. A re-enforcement of militia from Cumberland county, also, reached Westmoreland, giving additional security to the frontier. The company raised for the purpose of defending Fort Randolph, but employed elsewhere, was, in the fall of 1778, ordered by McIntosh to garrison that post. When Brodhead assumed command of the western department, he found this force reduced to twenty-nine men. So small a number at so great a distance from inhabitants, could answer no salutary purpose. The post was, therefore, ordered evacuated,[2] the men reaching Pittsburgh with the stores, in safety, about the first of June. As soon as the fort was abandoned, it was burned by the Indians. Fort Henry now marked the southern line of defense in the western department.

A threatened attack by rangers and savages from Canada, induced Brodhead to keep a watchful eye in the direction of Venango and the Indian towns far up the Alleghany. Scouts were frequently sent "to reconnoiter the Seneca country." A party from Fort Pitt, of twenty white men and a young Del-

---

[1] Brodhead to Lieut. B. Neilly, 8th Pa. Reg't, 30 Apr., 1779, MS.
[2] MS. Instructions: Brodhead to "Capt. [Sam.] Dawson, of the 8th Pa. Reg't, or the commanding officer [Capt. O'Harra] at Kanawha," 14 Apr., 1779. Same to Capt. Dawson, 23d of same month, MS.

aware chief, "all well painted," and commanded by Captain Samuel Brady, of the eighth Pennsylvania, while upon a mission of that nature, "fell in with seven Indians," not many miles above Kittanning. These savages had penetrated across the northern border, upon a marauding expedition. They had killed a soldier between Fort Crawford and Fort Hand, and a woman and four children in one of the settlements; they had also taken two children prisoners.[1] The Indians were attacked by Brady and his band, their captain killed, their plunder re-taken, and the two prisoners rescued. It was the opinion of Brodhead that a garrison, respectable in size, stationed at Kittanning, would afford better protection against these attacks by the northern savages, than many little forts scattered through the settlements. One hundred and twenty continentals, rank and file, under command of Lieutenant-Colonel Stephen Bayard, of the eighth Pennsylvania, were, therefore, ordered from Fort Pitt, on the sixteenth of June, to erect a stockade, similar to Fort Crawford, at that place.[2] The post was soon completed, and, in honor of one of the revolutionary generals,[3] was named Fort Armstrong.

Although the line of defense on the north reached from Fort Ligonier to Fort Armstrong, including Fort Hand, Fort Crawford, and a number of smaller stockades, yet it required the watchful care and continued effort of Brodhead to protect the settlements of Westmoreland. "The Indians sometimes take a scalp from us," he wrote on the sixth of August, "but my light parties, which I dress and paint like savages, have retaliated in several instances." This petty defensive warfare was now to be followed by offensive operations of considerable magnitude on part of the Fort Pitt commander. "I have told his excellency, the commander-in-chief," are his words, "that I can more effectually protect the settlements with one thousand men acting offensively, than with three times that number on a defensive plan." The con-

[1] Brother and sister, children of a Mr. Henry.
[2] Brodhead to Bayard: MS. Instructions.
[3] Maj.-Gen. John Armstrong, then of Carlisle, Pennsylvania. During the old French war, he led an expedition against what was then the Indian town of Kittanning, (the site of the present town of that name), which proved successful.

stant inroads of the northern Indians induced him to continue his appeals to Washington, for the privilege of leading a force from Fort Pitt into their country. "With great pleasure," he wrote, on the twenty-fifth of June, "I can now inform your excellency, that I have upwards of four hundred head of beef cattle, and near a thousand kegs of flour, with which, had I your permission, I conceive I could make a successful expedition against the Senecas." He also informed the chief executive of Pennsylvania that he had a considerable quantity of provisions; and he declared with confidence, that he "could make a succeesful campaign up the Alleghany;" "but," said he, "I am not at liberty to do it." However, the consent of the commander-in-chief was finally obtained, and immediate preparations began; for the terms of service of more than two hundred of his best men would expire before the middle of August, and it was just between harvest and seeding time when a number of volunteers from the country might reasonably be expected; beside, should the expedition be delayed, Indian corn would be ripe, and could be carried off by the enemy; this, the commander hoped to prevent. Brodhead was willing and anxious to coöperate with Major-General John Sullivan, who was now in command of the expedition against Indians of the Six Nations, but he feared it would be impracticable.

The friendly Delawares were solicited to join the army at Fort Pitt with as many of their braves as could be spared. The small posts of the department, garrisoned by continental or provincial troops, were ordered evacuated, that their commands might be rendered available for the enterprise. As many soldiers as could well be spared from the large ones were directed to march to Pittsburgh for the same purpose. The provincial companies in Westmoreland were called in. Exertions were made to induce volunteering. Militia from the neighborhood were ordered to Fort Pitt. By the eleventh of August, six hundred and five, rank and file, with a number of Delawares, were collected. The force began its march that day under the lead of Brodhead, with Colonel Gibson second in command. The army, having one month's supplies, advanced up the Alleghany, — the provisions, except live cattle, being transported by water, under an escort of one hundred men, — to the mouth of the Mahoning, above Kittanning.

The stores were now loaded on packhorses, and the troops continued their march up the river. An advance party of fifteen light infantry and eight Delawares, under command of Lieutenant John Hardin, of the eighth Pennsylvania regiment, fell in with thirty or forty warriors, coming down the Alleghany, in seven canoes. A sharp contest ensued. The enemy were defeated, the savages losing five of their number killed and several wounded. All their canoes, with their contents, were captured. Three men of the Americans were slightly wounded; also, one of the Delawares.

Brodhead proceeded up the river as far as the Indian village of Buckaloons,[1] its inhabitants fleeing upon his approach. The army threw up a breastwork of trees not far away,[2] and a garrison of forty men was left to guard provisions. The remainder of the force marched up the river to the mouth of the Conewango, near which was the deserted village of that name.[3] The troops then moved up the latter stream to within about four miles of the present state boundary line, where several towns were found, just vacated. "On my return," wrote Brodhead, "I preferred the Venango road." A village, twenty miles up French creek from its mouth, was visited. Every Indian town seen by the army during the expedition was burned. Many acres of corn were laid waste, and a valuable booty secured.[4] The army reached Pittsburgh the fourteenth of Sep-

---

[1] On the flats south of the Brokenstraw, Warren county, Pennsylvania. Called Kachnlodagon, in 1749; O. H. Marshall, in Mag. of Amer. Hist., Vol. II, p. 130.

[2] "On a bluff, on the Alleghany river, half a mile above the Brokenstraw."— Dr. Wm. A. Irvine to the writer.

[3] Now Warren, Warren county, Penn. This was a Seneca village as early, at least, as 1749; O. H. Marshall. It was called Kanaňagon (Conewango.)

[4] The Olden Time, II, 309; Penn. Arch., XII, 155, 165; N. Y. Gaz., 1 Nov., 1779; N. H. Gaz., 2 Nov., same year; Turner's Hist. Holland Purchase (N. Y.), p. 661; Sparks' Washington, VI, 384; Young's Hist. Chautauqua County, N. Y., pp. 50, 51; Dunlavy's pension statement, 1832, already cited. A letter from Brig.-Gen. Wm. Irvine to Washington, 2 May, 1782 (Irvine to Washington of that date, post), throws light upon the expedition. I have also before me, MS. statements of Blacksnake, Capt. Decker and Charles O'Bail, 1850, giving the Seneca traditions of the campaign. These locate the place where Lieut. Hardin had his skirmish with the Indians, "at or near an island, three or four miles below Brokenstraw." As to the expedition generally, see also, Mag. Amer. Hist., Vol. III, pp. 649-673.

tember, without the loss of a man.[1] Brodhead, although unable to join his force with the army of General Sullivan, received the thanks of Washington and congress, for his successful enterprise.[2]

Notwithstanding the failure of McIntosh, in his endeavors beyond the Ohio, the commander-in-chief continued to keep an eye to the westward. "Try to ascertain," he early wrote Brodhead, "the most favorable season for an enterprise against Detroit." It is not surprising, therefore, that the Fort Pitt commander returned from his expedition to the northward filled with enthusiasm for an immediate undertaking to capture that post;— he was in hopes, also, of punishing the Shawanese on his way. Before the end of September, he wrote: "I have applied, sometime past, for leave to make an expedition against Detroit, but fear it will again be put off until the season is too far advanced." By the first of October, he became despondent: "It is uncertain whether I shall have leave to make another expedition. I can only say that if I do not, it will not be owing to the want of a most anxious inclination on my part." But the orders of Washington previously given were, to act on the defensive only, until further instructions.

In June, 1778, David Rogers, who, on the fourteenth of January preceding, had been selected by Virginia to proceed to New Orleans to purchase supplies for the use of the troops of that state, raised a party of about thirty men in the region of what is now Brownsville, Fayette county, Pennsylvania, and, in keel-boats, floated down the Ohio and Mississippi. He did not reach New Orleans until after considerable trouble and delay. When he arrived, he found he would have to return to St. Louis, to obtain the goods, for which he was given

---

[1] "Upon the return march, a young man named John Ward was badly injured by his horse falling on a rock, in a creek. This accident occurred in what is now Butler county, Pennsylvania, where there is a township and post office, called 'Slippery Rock.'"— Dunlavy.

[2] "*Resolved*, That the thanks of congress be given to his excellency, General Washington, for directing, and to Colonel Brodhead and the brave officers and soldiers under his command, for executing, the important expedition against the Mingo and Monsey Indians and that part of the Senecas on the Alleghany river, by which the depredations of those savages, assisted by their merciless instigators, subjects of the king of Great Britain, upon the defenseless inhabitants of the western frontiers, have been restrained and prevented."— Journals of Cong., 27 Oct., 1779.

an order. From the latter place, in the autumn of 1779, he made his way up the Ohio to the falls, where he was re-enforced. Early in October, with about seventy men, he continued up the river to a point above the mouth of the Licking, but below that of the Little Miami, when he discovered Indians. Rodgers made a disposition of his force upon the Kentucky side of the Ohio to surprise the enemy, but was himself attacked and the larger portion of his men killed or taken prisoners. Forty bales of dry goods, a quantity of rum and fusees, together with "a chest of hard specie," fell into the enemy's hands. Rogers was killed.[1]

As the fall of this year wore away, the anxiety on the part of Brodhead for a campaign against Detroit was not lessened. "Winter expeditions," he reasoned, "are generally attended with great loss of horses and cattle, except where large magazines of forage are laid in and can be transported; but the British garrison and shipping will be a full compensation for every loss of that kind." "It will," he confidently added, "likewise secure the future tranquility of this frontier." But Washington could furnish neither men nor supplies necessary for such an important enterprise; still, he desired Brodhead not to discontinue his inquiries and preparations as far as convenient; "for," said he, "it is an object of too great importance to be lost sight of."

The attention of the savages to the westward during the first half of 1779, was not wholly given to the garrison in Fort Laurens. The settlements upon the waters of the Monongahela and the Ohio were, during that period, frequently harassed by war parties; and, after the evacuation of that post, up to the setting in of winter, the Mingoes, Wyandots, and Shawanese continued their murderous forays to the southward and southwestward of Pittsburgh. The two tribes last mentioned, it is true, throughout most of the year, made loud protestations of friendship, and manifested, apparently, a strong desire for peace; but Brodhead, although at times inclined to

---

[1] Heckewelder to Brodhead, 23 Oct., 1779, MS. Brodhead to Washington, 22 Nov., 1779, in Penn. Arch., XII, p. 189. Royal London Gaz., 15 July, 1780. Burnet's Notes, pp. 292, 293. Collins' Hist. Ky., vol. II, pp. 115, 116, 117.

give ear to their speeches, was nevertheless so mistrustful of
them — especially of the Shawanese — as to importune Washington several times for permission to march against them.

The terms of enlistment of the two ranging companies authorized by General McIntosh and raised in Westmoreland county — one of which was commanded by Captain Matthew Jack, the other by Captain Nehemiah Stokely — expired during the summer; but their places were filled by two others, one under command of Captain Joseph Irwin, the other of Captain Thomas Campbell. These companies were enlisted in the same county, under the resolution of congress for raising five in all, for service in the west. Brodhead was authorized to call upon these companies only in the event of their services being needed upon an expedition against the enemy; otherwise, they were to take orders from the lieutenant of Westmoreland county. Until this was fully understood, some trouble was caused, yet no serious results ensued.

From the time of the return of Brodhead from his expedition against the Seneca Indians to the end of the year, a good degree of quietude existed along the northern frontier. Rawlings' corps, now very much reduced in number, was still in the western department. These troops and those of the eighth Pennsylvania and ninth Virginia regiments were placed for the winter in such positions as, in the opinion of the commander, would best protect the western country. Fort Armstrong and Fort Crawford were evacuated. The principal points garrisoned were Wheeling, Holiday's Cove (in what is now Hancock county, West Virginia) and Fort McIntosh, down the Ohio; Fort Pitt, at Pittsburgh; and Fort Hand, Fort Wallace and Hannastown, on the northern frontier: the two last mentioned were occupied by the ranging companies of Captains Irwin and Campbell, whose terms of service expired during the ensuing winter. Meanwhile, Captain Moorhead's independent company, which, for nearly three years, had been doing duty on the frontiers of Westmoreland county, was removed to Fort Pitt, and made a part of the eighth Pennsylvania regiment.

The spring of 1780 opened gloomily upon the western frontier. As early as the middle of March the Indians began their depredations. At a sugar camp on Raccoon creek, a stream flowing into the Ohio, on the left, thirty-three miles by the course of the river below Pittsburgh, five men were killed and three girls and three boys taken prisoners. About this time, two boats, in descending the Ohio, were attacked a few miles below Captina creek, which empties into the Ohio on the right, twenty-one miles below Wheeling, and one of them captured. In the boats were some families on their way to Kentucky. Several men and a small child were killed. Twenty-one persons — men, women and children — were made captives. Among them was Catharine Malott, a girl in her teens, who subsequently became the wife of Simon Girty, the refugee from Pittsburgh.[1]

The visitations of the savages were earlier than was expected, considering the severity of the season. Brodhead called together the county lieutenants of the western department to consult upon the alarming state of affairs. It was determined to strike, if possible, the Shawanese, whose ravages were particularly severe. Active measures were taken to protect the border. Forts Armstrong and Crawford, which had been evacuated late in the previous year, were again garrisoned. The counties in the west were called upon for over eight hundred militia, to go upon an expedition against the Shawanese, but they came in slowly. Indian marauds into the settlements, and lack of provisions, together with the boundary controversy, caused the abandonment, finally, of the enterprise. Brodhead had been informed that a re-enforcement of continentals with supplies would be sent him, but none came.

By the last of April, the Indians had become exceedingly troublesome; — over forty men, women and children had fallen victims to their ferocity in the country south and southwest of Fort Pitt. These depredations were quickly followed by others to the northward. It really began to look as though the county of Westmoreland would again become a wilderness.

---

[1] Penn. Arch., VIII, p. 153 — XII, p. 218. MS. Shane Papers. West. Christ. Adv., vol. II, pp. 1, 5, 9, 14. MS. Statement of Mrs. Sarah Munger, last surviving child of Simon Girty, 1864.

A large part of the population north of the Youghiogheny — the principal eastern tributary of the Monongahela — was forced to fly to the several forts of that locality for safety. The utmost exertions of local companies and of the half-clad, half-starved regulars — now only the cullings of the last year's men, many having been sent over the mountains on account of the pressure of the war upon the sea-board — were put forth to protect the homes of the borderers, but with little effect. The war if possible, the commander fully realized, must be carried to the homes of the savages; and, above all, as it was now seen, to the homes of the Wyandots, who were more powerful for mischief to the border than either of the other tribes acting against it. In June, Captain Isaac Craig with a detachment from the fourth Pennsylvania regiment of artillery reached Fort Pitt. On the tenth of July, Brodhead informed the lieutenants of the counties of the western department of his intention to attack the Indian towns upon the Sandusky by the time corn should come to perfection. "The enterprise," said he, "must be secret and the execution rapid."

The resolution of the commander to assail the Wyandots was a timely one; for, scarcely had a week gone by, before a considerable number of them—over thirty warriors — struck the settlements to the southwest of Fort Pitt, having crossed the Ohio five miles below Fort McIntosh. Early information enabled Brodhead to send a detachment down the river to intercept the savages. The movement proved entirely successful; nearly the whole war party was killed; not, however, until some unsuspecting harvesters had been surprised and shot.[1]

"How happy should I be," is the language of Brodhead in August, "if it were in my power to attack the Wyandots and Mingoes at this time." Difficulties, however, had already interposed. The Maryland corps in August deserted their posts on the frontier of Westmoreland, and, in a body, marched to the other side of the mountains. The time for starting was postponed until the twelfth of October. Meanwhile, the colonel was informed that no help need be expected from the commander-in-chief.

---

[1] Heckewelder to Brodhead, 14 Aug., 1780, MS.

"It is much to be regretted," are the words of Washington, "that the state of our regular troops will not admit of a detachment sufficient to reduce the posts of the enemy to the westward, or even to undertake anything offensive against the hostile tribes of Indians." "If a sufficient quantity of provisions can be obtained," wrote Brodhead to the commander-in-chief on the fifth of September, "I will yet visit the Wyandots by the first of November." But insurmountable obstacles were encountered. On the seventeenth of October, all his hopes had vanished. "In full confidence that a sufficient supply of provisions," he wrote, "would, sooner or later, be furnished for the troops in this district, as well as for such number of militia as policy or the exigencies of affairs might render necessary to call into action, I, with a view to cut off the Wyandots and other Indian towns that were very troublesome to our settlements, called for a draft from the militia, at three different times, and was as often disappointed in obtaining provisions."

Brodhead's mortification at this failure was great. Under the comparative quietude of defensive measures only, he grew impatient. His temperament was ardent; his bravery undoubted. No one more fully realized the importance of acting on the offensive, in Indian warfare; and especially at this juncture in the affairs of the western border was such a policy desirable. "I cannot but lament the repeated disappointments we have met with," are his despairing words, "for want of resources to enable us to retaliate on the hell-hounds of the forest. But I must console myself with a consciousness that the blame lies not at my door." "The want of provisions," wrote Washington, "is a clog to our operations in every quarter." "The smallness of your force," he continued, "will not admit of an expedition of any consequence had you magazines. You must therefore of necessity, confine yourself to partizan strokes, which I wish to be encouraged." [1] Under all these discouragements, the gallant colonel maintained his equanimity: "I am sensible it would be greatly to my advantage to retire, but I love the

---

[1] Washington to Brodhead, 13 Oct., 1780, MS.

cause in which we are engaged and wish to entertain the pleasing reflection that I did not quit the field until I had seen the freedom of my country fully established."

The punishment received by the Wyandots in July below Fort Pitt did not check the marauds of the savages into other settlements; especially were their visits frequent into the exposed parts of northwestern Virginia. About the middle of August, ten men were killed at one time, in Monongalia county. A month subsequent, seven were massacred or taken prisoners upon the waters of Tenmile creek. * "The state of our frontiers," were the disconsolate words of a citizen of Monongalia in October, " is really deplorable; even while some of us are engaged in burying our neighbors, others are falling a sacrifice to the hellish inventions of the savages."

An event afterward took place which tended to increase the efficiency of the militia upon the frontiers to the south and southwest of Pittsburgh. This was the passage of an act by the general assembly of Pennsylvania, March 28, 1781, erecting into a new county called Washington, all the territory between the Monongahela and Ohio and extending south and west to the boundary line between that state and Virginia. A county lieutenant — James Marshel — was appointed for the county thus created. His efficiency in organizing new battalions was at once recognized.

From the time that Brodhead had taken command at Fort Pitt, he had made the most strenuous endeavors to preserve friendly relations with the Delawares, who, ever since the war began, had been objects of suspicion to the borderers. It was not known, of course, at what moment they might take up the hatchet, in which event their proximity to the settlements would give them great advantages for mischief. Besides, it was well understood that some of them were actually hostile while the nation at large was, professedly, the ally of the United States. The inability of the government to carry out treaty stipulations, and the influences and threats of the British and their Indian allies, induced them finally, though unwillingly, to rise against the border, only a small band remaining in the interest of the United States. Thus the Indian war, early in 1781, became general,— not a single tribe in the country beyond the Ohio remaining friendly.

The commander of the western department was early informed of the defection of the Delawares. "The people at Coshocton," wrote John Heckewelder, a missionary, from one of the Moravian villages,[1] upon the Tuscarawas, to Brodhead, on the twenty-sixth of February, "have been very busy in trying to deceive you this long time." "I indeed believe," he continued, "that the greater part of them will be upon you in a few days." "They have arranged themselves in three parties," he added, "and, if I am right, one party is gone already; but I hope they will receive what they deserve." And thus wrote, also, a friendly Delaware Indian from the Moravian towns: "Everybody here knows that the Coshocton men are getting ready to go and fight you." Now, the leader of these hostile Delawares was the war-chief Winganund. Brodhead, acting upon a suggestion of the patriotic missionary,[2] determined, thereupon, to carry the war to the homes of the Coshocton Indians.[3]

It was well that Brodhead made this resolve, for, at that very time, the Delawares were earnestly soliciting the British commandant at Detroit to send traders among them, declaring that they would no longer listen "to the Virginians," who, they said, had deceived them. The artful but humane De-Peyster encouraged them, but added: "I am pleased when I see what you call *live meat*, because I can speak to it and get information; *scalps* serve to show that you have seen the enemy, but they are of no use to me; I cannot speak to them."[4]

On the seventh of April, the commander left Fort Pitt with over one hundred and fifty regulars, on an expedition against

---

[1] There were three of the Moravian Indian villages — New Schœnbrunn, Gnadenhuetten and Salem. They were all located in the valley of the Tuscarawas, some distance above Coshocton, and within the present limits of Tuscarawas county, Ohio.

[2] "If it shall be concluded on that a body of men should march to Coshocton to punish these wicked people," etc.— Heckewelder to Brodhead, in Penn. Arch., VIII, p. 771.

[3] Brodhead to Col. David Shepherd, 5 March, 1781, original letter. Compare Penn. Arch., IX, pp. 39, 52, 57, 97; The Olden Time, II, pp. 389-392.

[4] De Peyster's "Miscellanies," p. 253. By *live meat*, he meant "prisoners, styled so by the Indians."

the Delawares, dropping down to Wheeling where David
Shepherd, lieutenant of Ohio county, Virginia, had collected
one hundred and thirty-four of the militia of his county, including officers.[1] With them were a few friendly Indians —
Captains Montour and Wilson and three other warriors[2] —
who evinced a keen desire for the scalps of the hostile Delawares. On the tenth, the united force made its way across the
Ohio, taking the nearest route to Coshocton. Shepherd's division consisted of four companies. The savages were completely surprised. Their town was laid waste; also a village
of theirs just below.[3] Fifteen of their warriors were killed
and over twenty prisoners taken. Large quantities of peltry[4]
and other stores were destroyed, and about forty head of cattle
killed. The Americans then proceeded up the valley to Newcomer's town, where there were about thirty friendly Delaware
Indians, who were occupying the place. From them, as well
as from the Moravian missionaries and their converts, whose
towns were not far away, the troops experienced great kindness, obtaining a sufficient supply of meat and corn to subsist
themselves and their horses to the Ohio. The plunder brought
in by the troops sold for a large sum.[5] The expedition proved
a decided success; for the hostile Delawares now entirely forsook the valley of the Tuscarawas and Muskingum, never
again occupying either as a permanent abode — drawing back
to the Scioto, the Mad river and the Sandusky, receiving mean-

---

[1] *Roster of Col. Shepherd's Division:* David Shepherd, colonel; Samuel McColloch, major; Isaac Meeks, adjutant; William McIntyre, quarter master; James Lemon, sergeant major; Jonathan Zane, spy; Captain Joseph Ogle, two lieutenants, one ensign, two sergeants, and sixty-four privates; Captain Benjamin Royce, one lieutenant, two sergeants, and twenty-seven privates; Captain Jacob Lefler, one sergeant, and nine privates; Captain William Crawford, one sergeant, and thirteen privates. Time of service, from April 10th to April 28th (1781), inclusive.

[2] Brodhead to Huntington, August 23, 1781.

[3] Known at this time as "Indaochale;" but, when previously occupied by Moravian Indians, it was called "Lichtenau." It was in what is now Tuscarawas township, Coshocton county, Ohio, two and a half miles below Coshocton.

[4] Not "poltry," as printed in Penn. Arch., IX, p. 161.

[5] Brodhead to Shepherd, 16 March and 3 April, 1781, original letters. Shepherd's pay roll of the Coshocton campaign, original MS. Brodhead to the commanding officer of Monongahela militia, 5 Apr., 1781, in Brodhead's MS. letter book for that year. Brodhead to Sup. Ex. Council, 22 May, 1781, in Penn. Arch., IX, p. 161. Same to Congress, 23 May, 1781, in Penn. Packet of June 5th, 1781, which was Brodhead's official report of his "Coshocton Campaign."

while, every encouragement from the British commander at Detroit, who now addressed them as his "children."[1] The friendly Delawares, at Newcomer's town, put themselves under the protection of Brodhead and marched with him to Fort Pitt for safety. It was well they did, for, in a few days, eighty hostile Delawares, headed by a chief of the same tribe, came to the Tuscarawas valley in pursuit of them.

Although the failure of McIntosh in his designs upon Detroit had discouraged further attempts in that direction, yet Washington ever kept in view an undertaking against that post, to be carried into execution with a continental force. He well knew that so long as it continued in possession of the enemy it would be a constant source of trouble to the whole western frontier; but the want of men and supplies as Brodhead at Fort Pitt fully realized, had thus far rendered it impossible to move successfully in the enterprise. Finally, however, the governor of Virginia informed the commander-in-chief that he thought he should be able, with the aid of some artillery and stores already at Pittsburgh, to accomplish this most desirable object. George Rogers Clark was to command the expedition. Washington, who favored the enterprise and determined to give it all the aid in his power, believed it could not be committed to better hands. Of Clark, he wrote: "I have not the pleasure of knowing the gentleman; but, independently of the proofs he has given of his activity and address, the unbounded confidence which I am told the western people repose in him, is a matter of vast importance; as I imagine a considerable part of his force will consist of volunteers and militia, who are not to be governed by military laws, but must be held by the ties of confidence and affection to their leader." Brodhead was enjoined to give countenance and assistance to the enterprise. He was assured that, while offensive operations were going forward against Detroit and the Indians in alliance with the British in that quarter, the posts in the western department would, with small garrisons in them, and by the exercise of proper vigi-

[1] De Peyster to the Delawares, June 7, 1782, in "Miscellanies" of that officer, pp. 233, 234.

lance, be perfectly secure. This assurance, however, did not satisfy the ambition of Brodhead. His restless spirit could hardly brook confinement within the walls of Fort Pitt while others were, probably, soon to gather laurels which he had fondly imagined were to encircle his own brow. But, being a true friend of his country, he would obey orders though he could not conceal his chagrin: "I have hitherto been encouraged to flatter myself that I should sooner or later be enabled to reduce Detroit. But it seems the United States cannot furnish either troops or resources for the purpose, but the state of Virginia can." And again: "I have just received instructions from the commander-in-chief to detach my field pieces, howitzers and train, also a part of my small force, under Colonel Clark, who, I am told, is to drive all before him by his supposed unbounded influence in the western country."

On the seventh of May, 1781, Brodhead left Fort Pitt for Philadelphia on public business,[1] giving the command of that post and the western department, during his absence, to Colonel John Gibson, whom he thus addressed: "Having obtained leave from his excellency, the commander-in-chief, to proceed to Philadelphia and represent the affairs of this department, I intend to set out immediately. You will remain in command until it is determined that you are otherwise ordered by proper authority. Should this happen before my return, the command will then devolve on Lieutenant-Colonel [Stephen] Bayard."[2]

The arrival of Clark in the trans-Alleghany country awakened much enthusiasm in many of the settlements of both states in aid of his expedition. But, in some, owing principally to the unsettled state of affairs caused by the boundary controversy, a determined opposition was manifested. Brodhead, also, had availed himself of a certain discretion given him by the commander-in-chief to withhold some supplies. However, definite orders having been received by Gibson from Washington, after Brodhead's departure, all the articles de-

---

[1] Brodhead to Baron Steuben, September 6, 1781, MS.
[2] Brodhead to Gibson, May 6, 1781, MS. For a biographical sketch of Bayard, see Appendix M,—Bayard to Irvine, April 5, 1783, note.

Introduction. 55

manded were turned over to Clark which it was thought could be spared consistent with the safety of the garrison at Fort Pitt. Finally, with volunteers and militia obtained from the country,[1] and a regiment of Virginia state troops — Colonel Joseph Crockett's — together with the detachment of artillery at Fort Pitt commanded by Captain Isaac Craig,[2] in all about four hundred men,[3] having three field pieces, ordnance and other stores,— Clark, near the close of July,[4] moved down the Ohio from Pittsburgh for the falls (Louisville), stopping at Wheeling on the way. "He left this place with a great many boats large and small," says a writer at Pittsburgh, about a month after, "a very large quantity of flour, some salt, a good deal of whisky and very little beef, and that little he chiefly lost before he got to Wheeling where he continued some days. . . . At and about Wheeling, he was joined by numbers from that country, to what amount I cannot tell, and deserted by near a hundred of the militia who left this place with him."[5]

A Pennsylvania force composed of volunteers and a company of state troops (rangers) raised for the defense of Westmoreland county, all under command of Archibald Lochry, lieutenant of that county, on its way down the river to join Clark, was, on account of information derived from an intercepted note of the latter by the enemy, attacked by Indians under command of Captain Joseph Brant (Thayendanegea) and George Girty (who, after his brothers Simon and James had joined the enemies of his country, had deserted and was now in the employment of Great Britain) on the twenty-fourth of August, about eleven miles below the mouth of the Great Miami, in what is now the the state of Indiana. Every

---

[1] Clark to Shepherd, original letters of 2d, 8th and 18th of July, 1781, MS.
[2] Craig to Clark from Fort Pitt, July 2?, 1781, original letter. Gibson to Washington, August 23, 1781, MS. Captain (afterward Major) Craig's command at Fort Pitt was a detachment from the fourth Pennsylvania regiment of artillery, and a detachment of artillery artificers. Captain Craig left Carlisle for Fort Pitt May 23, 1780, and reached that post June 25, following. (Ante, p. 48.)
[3] Gibson to Washington, just cited.
[4] MS. Mem. of Capt. Craig, of July 29, 1781. Compare Penn. Mag. of Hist. and Biog., Vol. IV. p. 248.
[5] Ephraim Douglass to Gen. James Irvine, 29 Aug. 1781, in Penn. Mag. of Hist. and Biog., just cited.

man present of the Americans — numbering in all over one hundred — was killed or captured.[1] Colonel Lochry was among the slain. Because of this unfortunate event and the passing of an act by Virginia authorizing its governor to stop the expedition, causing the non-arrival of other expected re-enforcements, Clark, who was at the falls, was compelled to abandon the enterprise.[2] Captain Craig, with his command, made his way back to Fort Pitt, where he arrived, after many hardships, on the twenty-sixth of November.

Brodhead returned to Pittsburgh on the eleventh of August. He was then involved in a controversy with some of his officers who had preferred charges against him. Immediately upon his arrival and while preparations were making for his trial, a question of rank arose between him and Colonel Gibson. It proved a bitter quarrel — a contest for the command of the department. He wrote Washington on the nineteenth, that, by the clamor of some disaffected persons and others, he found himself in the most disagreeable situation he ever experienced. On the twenty-ninth matters had not improved. "Things here," he again wrote the commander-in-chief, "are in the utmost confusion; some officers confessing me to be the commanding officer, and others, Colonel Gibson; nor is it likely they will change until your excellency's pleasure is expressed." It was claimed by Colonel Gibson and his adherents that, as they interpreted the instructions of the commander-in-chief, they could not with propriety be commanded by Brodhead until he had cleared himself of the charges exhibited against him which were then pending.[3]

---

[1] Statement of Robert Orr, MS. Brig. Gen Wm. Irvine to Congress from Fort Pitt, December 3, 1781, Appendix A. Penn. Packet, March 12, 1782 (No. f57). Devereux Smith to Gen. Irvine, September 13, 1782, Appendix M. Consult also, in this connection, Vermont Hist. Soc. Coll., II, pp. 342, 344; McBride's Pion. Biog., I, pp. 278-287; Penn. Arch., IX, pp. 333, 458, 468, 574; Col. Rec. Pa., XIII, pp. 155, 167, 324; Sparks' Corr. Amer. Rev., III, p. 456.

[2] Clark to the Gov. of Va., from "Fort Nelson" (Louisville), October 6, 1781, MS. For further information concerning Clark's intended attack on Detroit, see The Olden Time, Vol. II, pp. 344, 345.

[3] "John Gibson, Col. commanding at Fort Pitt; Fred'k Vernon, Major 8th Pa. Reg't; Uriah Springer, Capt.,7th Va. Reg't;" and eleven other officers; — to Brodhead, Aug. 19, 1781, MS. The charges were principally, that he had speculated with the public funds. (Penn. Arch., IX, pp. 97, 306.)

"Dissensions run high in every department of our transmontane country," wrote a close observer of affairs from Pittsburgh. "Those between Virginia and Pennsylvania are not yet entirely healed, and a variety of new ones have been created; the citizen is opposed to the soldier and a variety of parties formed from opinion, prejudice, or prospects of interest among themselves abstracted from their quarrels with the army about which they are also divided — and have had the fortune or address to create divisions among the military people themselves, two of whom, the highest in rank, are at this time contending for the command and each supported by his friends and adherents."[1].

Just before the departure of Clark from Fort Pitt and before the return of Brodhead from the east, the former suggested to Gibson that, with the troops who were to be left behind on account of being illy supplied with clothing, and with as many volunteers or militia as could be called out readily for that purpose, he ought to make an excursion against the Wyandots upon the Sandusky; Clark would, at the same time, begin his march from the mouth of the Miami river against the Shawanese, on his way to Detroit, which was intended to be about the fourth of September. The matter was laid before Brodhead immediately upon his arrival at Pittsburgh, who approved of the enterprise, and, claiming the right of command, issued circular letters to the county lieutenants to aid the undertaking. Early in September, at Fort McIntosh, was the time and place fixed upon for rendezvous. It was determined that the country people going upon the expedition should be considered volunteers and might elect their own officers; that each man should provide himself with a horse and thirty days' provisions; and that the whole should bring as many spare horses as would mount one hundred and fifty regulars — the number Gibson proposed to take with him upon the occasion, from Fort Pitt.[2] Preparations were immediately made for the enterprise. A number of volunteers

---

[1] Ephraim Douglass to Gen. James Irvine from Pittsburgh, August 23, 1781, in Penn. Mag. of Hist. and Biog., IV, p. 247.

[2] Gibson to Washington, 25 Aug., 1781, MS.

was enrolled — leading citizens of the country taking an active part in aiding the project, and offering their services for the campaign. "An expedition," wrote Brodhead, on the twenty-third of August, "against the Sanduskies, is in contemplation." As he considered himself, at that time, in command of the western department, he expressed his desire to promote the undertaking. To Washington he wrote: "The troops will rendezvous at Fort McIntosh, on the 4th and 5th of next month; the country appears desirous to promote it [the expedition]; and I intend to command it, if they, the militia and volunteers, do not suffer themselves to be induced into a belief, that I have no right to command."

At the moment when every thing seemed auspicious for the success of the enterprise alarming intelligence reached Fort Pitt from the banks of the Tuscarawas. David Zeisberger, one of the Moravian missionaries there, had dispatched a messenger to the commander at Pittsburgh with a written message to the effect that a large number of Indians — about two hundred and fifty in all — was approaching the settlements with the intention, probably, of going to Wheeling, but they might attack some of the other posts. "They will try," said he, "to decoy the garrison out where they will lie in ambush." "The party is headed," continued the missionary "by Matthew Elliott and a few English and French. The Indians are Wyandots, Delawares, Monseys, and a small number of Shawanese." "You will be careful," he added, "not to mention that you had this intelligence from our towns; for it would prove dangerous for us if the Indians should get knowledge of it; which might happen by a prisoner, if they should take one."[1]

"Last evening I was honored with your obliging letter," was the response of Brodhead to the missionary, "for which be pleased to accept my best thanks. We shall be upon our guard and give the wicked a warm reception."[2] The commanding officer at Fort Henry (Wheeling) was soon informed by Brodhead of the coming of the enemy. "You will imme-

---

[1] David Zeisberger to Brodhead, Aug. 18, 1781, MS. Just what Zeisberger feared would happen did take place, as will hereafter be shown.
[2] Brodhead's MS. letter book, August 25, 1781.

diately put your garrison in the best posture of defence," he wrote, "and lay in as great quantity of water as circumstances will admit, and receive them coolly. They intend to decoy your garrison, but you are to guard against stratagem, and defend the post to the last extremity." "You must not fail," he added, "to give the alarm to the inhabitants within your reach, and make it as general as possible, in order that every man may be prepared at this crisis." Brodhead also sent letters to the county lieutenants and one to the commandant of Fort McIntosh, with information of the threatened attack.

As might be expected, the excitement was intense all along the border. Fort Henry was immediately placed in a proper condition for defense. The borderers everywhere put themselves in readiness to meet the foe. "The country has taken the alarm," wrote Brodhead, "and several hundred men are now in arms upon the frontier." It was not long before the Indians made their appearance, as was expected, in the vicinity of Wheeling, being but a part, however, of those who were at the Moravian Indian towns. Of three boys outside of Fort Henry, at the time, one was killed, and one — David Glenn — was made prisoner. The other effected his escape inside the fortification, slightly wounded. In a moment, the garrison was ready to receive the savages. The latter, seeing the borderers fully prepared for them, soon disappeared, doing but little mischief, except killing all the cattle they could find.[1] Their depredations up Wheeling and Buffalo creeks, however, were, before they re-crossed the Ohio, much more serious. They killed and captured several persons.[2]

The intelligence sent by Zeisberger, the Moravian missionary, to Brodhead was not well kept.[3] The captured boy, Glenn, informed the savages "that the garrison at Wheeling and the country in general were alarmed and on their guard; that they had been notified of the intention of the Indians by

---

[1] De Hass' Hist. Ind. Wars W. Va., p. 258. Heckewelder's Narr, pp. 262, 263. Dr. Joseph Doddridge's MSS. Gibson to Washington, September 30, 1781, MS. Statement of Mrs. Lydia Cruger, 1845, MS.

[2] Statement of Henry Jolly, 1838, MS. Dr. Jos. Doddridge's Narr. of the second and third attacks upon Fort Henry, MS. Statement of Mrs. Lydia Cruger, 1845, MS.

[3] Zeisberger, it seems, sent two expresses.

letters sent to Pittsburgh by the Moravian ministers. This exasperated the warriors so much that they took the missionaries prisoners, tied them, and destroyed everything they had, and ordered the whole of the Moravian Indians to get up and move off with their families, or they would cut them all off, which they were obliged to consent to."[1] The day after the arrest of the ministers, another party of savages returned from the border settlements to Gnadenhuetten, bringing with them as prisoner a white man who had been captured some distance from Wheeling. He corroborated the story of the boy-prisoner as to the missionaries having sent word to Fort Pitt of the intentions of the Indians.

The missionary establishments upon the Tuscarawas were thus broken up, news of which was brought to Gibson at Pittsburgh by a Moravian Indian woman who made her escape from the warriors and came into that place on the seventh of September. The information soon spread through all the settlements of the border counties. The missionaries and their converts were taken to the Sandusky river by the savage allies of Great Britain, under the lead of that "infamous rascal, Matt. Elliot,"[2] where, at a point a little over two miles south of the present Upper Sandusky, county-seat of Wyandot county, Ohio, but on the opposite (east side) of the river, they prepared to spend the winter. Upon their arrival in the Wyandot country, they were left in great destitution. The ministers were compelled to visit Detroit to be examined by De Peyster, the commandant, touching their correspondence with the Americans. They were afterward permitted to return to the Sandusky, as the evidence in possession of the Detroit commander was not sufficient for their detention. They had, however, on many occasions favored the Fort Pitt commanders with important information, to the prejudice of the English and British Indians; and this, too, of their own free will.[3] Their fidelity to the Americans was, so long as

---

[1] Gibson to Washington, from Fort Pitt, September 30, 1781, MS.
[2] Brig. Gen. Wm. Irvine, from Fort Pitt, to his wife, December 29, 1781, Appendix L.
[3] Gibson to Jefferson, from Fort Pitt, May 33, 1781, MS. Compare also, Penn. Arch., VII, pp. 516, 524, 511 — VIII, pp. 152, 153, 170.

Introduction.　　　　　　　　61

they remained upon the Tuscarawas, always to be relied upon.

Not long after and while the Wyandots were upon the Walhonding on their way back, with the missionaries and the Moravian Indians, to Sandusky, seven of their number, of whom three were sons of the Half King,[1] left the main body and again marched for the border, raiding into a small settlement on Harman's creek, in Washington county, taking one prisoner — a man about sixty years of age. The savages immediately started on their return, but were soon pursued by a number of settlers, to the Ohio river, where they were overtaken and all killed except one; and he, their leader, Scotash by name, escaped wounded. The white prisoner was released. Andrew Poe, one of the pursuers, his gun missing fire, boldly sprang upon and grappled two of the Indians — sons of the Half King. During a most violent struggle, which was continued first on shore and then in the river, Andrew killed one of the Indians but was himself badly wounded. Adam Poe, a brother, coming to his relief, shot the other savage. Meanwhile, Andrew then in the water, by mistake received a second wound from one of his own men. The settlers lost one killed.[2]

The conflict of authority at Fort Pitt, together with the Indian invasion, caused a postponement of the expedition against Sandusky. Finally, the contest between the commanders continuing, the enterprise was wholly abandoned.[3] Washington put an end to the dispute, by ordering Brodhead to

---

[1] "As early as the spring of 1779, the three sons of the Half King went, in company, to war against the border."— Heckewelder to Brodhead, April 9, 1779, MS. It was, therefore, not a new thing for all three to be together upon a marauding expedition.

[2] Recollections of the Captivity of Thomas Edgington, as related by his son, Geo. Edgington, 1845, MS. Pension statement of Adam Poe, 1833, MS. copy. Statement of Wm. Walker, MS. Consult, in this connection, Heckewelder's Narr., pp. 279, 281, 303; Smith's Hist. Jeff. College, p. 391, note; De Hass' Hist. Ind. Wars W. Va., p. 336. McKnight's Western Border, p. 413. Schweinitz' Life and Times of David Zeisberger, p. 517. But neither of the savages killed was named Big Foot (there was never a Wyandot chief so called); nor was either of the sons of the Half King of unusual size. It is with regret that I am compelled thus to spoil, somewhat, the romance of the famous fight of "Andrew Poe and Big Foot," which story has long been the delight of youthful readers.

[3] Gibson to Shepherd, September 12, 1781, original letter. Brig. Gen. Wm. Irvine, from Fort Pitt, to Washington, December 2, 1781, post. Sparks' Corr. Amer. Rev., III, p. 432. The Olden Time, II, p. 531.

resign his command during the dependence of his trial, to Colonel Gibson, the latter to "assume the like command at the post of Fort Pitt and its dependencies, as had been committed to Colonel Brodhead."[1] On the seventeenth of September, 1781, the latter quietly turned over his charge as directed by the commander-in-chief, and was relieved from the command in the west.[2]

---

[1] Washington to Brodhead, September 6, 1781, MS. Same to Gibson, same date, MS. Washington's letter to Gibson was as follows:

"HEAD OF ELK [now Elkton, Maryland], *Sept.* 6th, 1781.

"*Sir:*— Colonel Brodhead having been directed, in my letter to him of this date, to resign his command at Fort Pitt, during the dependence of his trial, on sundry accusations brought against him whilst in command [the principal of which was for speculating with public funds], you will immediately upon the receipt of this assume the like command at the post of Fort Pitt and its dependencies, as has been committed to Colonel Brodhead.

"Mr. [Alexander] Fowler, who appears to have been a principal in the accusation brought against Colonel Brodhead, insisting that he has a right in this instance to act as judge advocate, from his having been in that capacity for some time past, you will, from the manifest impropriety in this case, direct that Mr. Fowler do not appear nor act as deputy advocate, in taking the depositions necessary on this trial, nor in any other way in the present case as judge advocate; and you will appoint some person whom you shall think proper, to act in such manner as directed in any former letters on this occasion. In this way I hope to have this disagreeable dispute speedily issued.

"I am, etc.,
"G. WASHINGTON.

"To Col. John Gibson,
"Fort Pitt."

Washington's letter to Brodhead was in these words:

"HEAD OF ELK, *Sept.* 6th, 1781.

"*Sir:*— I have received your letter of 23d Augt., with its enclosures. Had you adverted to the plain construction of mine of the 5th of May, you would not have been in doubt as to the propriety of your holding the command at Fort Pitt, while your trial was preparing and hearing. As you seem to have misconstrued my meaning in that letter, I have now to request, in positive terms, that you do immediately, on receipt of this, resign your command to Col. Gibson, who will immediately thereupon assume the same command as has been committed to you.

"In the meantime, I request that this unhappy dispute may be brought to as speedy an issue as possible.

"I am, dear sir, your most humble servant,
"GEO. WASHINGTON.

"Col. Brodhead."

[2] Gibson to Washington, September 30, 1781, MS. Daniel Brodhead was born at Marbletown, Ulster county, New York, in 1736. His great grandfather, Daniel Brodhead, was a royalist and captain of grenadiers in the reign of Charles II. He came with the expedition under Colonel Nichols in 1664, that captured the Netherlands (now New York) from the Dutch, and settled in Marbletown in 1665. His son Richard, and *his* son Daniel, the father of the subject of this sketch, also resided in Marbletown. Daniel Brodhead, Sr., in 1738, removed to a place called Dansville, on Brodhead's creek, near Stroudsburgh, Monroe county, Pennsylvania, when Daniel Brodhead, Jr., was an infant. The latter and his brothers became famous for their courage in conflicts with the In-

Introduction.

The western department was, at this time, in much confusion. When the savages were at the Moravian Indian villages upon the Tuscarawas, it came to the ears of the missionaries that the enemy expected to be joined by a party from Canada, consisting of British Americans and Indians, to the number of a thousand, who were reported to be on their way. "Guy Johnson," wrote Zeisberger to Brodhead, "is coming down by Presque Isle [now Erie, Pennsylvania] with a thousand men to make a diversion and stop General [George Rogers] Clark's proceeding down the river [Ohio]; because they had intelligence that he [Clark] would come to Detroit with an army."[1] There was some foundation for this report. It was proposed by the authorities in Canada (though afterwards given up) to make a diversion from that country to co-operate, by way of Fort Pitt, with an expedition from the southern army of the British, up the rivers Potomac and Susquehanna.[2]

At this juncture, Fort Pitt was little better than a heap of ruins. The regular force stationed there was wholly incompetent to the exigencies of the service. The controversy

---

dians on the border, their father's house having been attacked by the savages December 11th, 1755. Daniel became a resident of Reading in 1771, where he was deputy surveyor. In July, 1775, he was appointed a delegate from Berks county to the provincial convention at Philadelphia. At the breaking out of the revolution, Daniel was elected a lieutenant-colonel (commissioned October 25, 1776), and subsequently became colonel of the eighth Pennsylvania regiment; his promotion was March 12, 1777, to rank from September 29, 1776. He participated in the battle of Long Island, and in other battles in which Washington's army was engaged. He marched to Fort Pitt, as has already been stated, in the summer of 1778, his regiment forming a part of Brigadier-General Lachlan McIntosh's command in the western department. Here, as we have seen, he served until the next spring, when he succeeded to the command in the west, headquarters at Fort Pitt. He retained this position until September 17, 1781, as above mentioned, making a very efficient and active commander, twice leading expeditions into the Indian country, in both of which he was successful; but was superseded in his command at Pittsburgh by Colonel John Gibson, as indicated in Washington's letter to that officer, just given. Brodhead was, at that date, colonel of the 1st Pennsylvania regiment, to which position he was assigned January 17, 1781. After the war, he was surveyor general of Pennsylvania. He was appointed to that office November 3, 1789, and held the place eleven years, he having previously served in the general assembly. He died at Milford, Pike county, in that state, November 15, 1809. He was twice married. By his first wife he had two children; by his second, none. In 1872, at Milford, an appropriate monument was erected to his memory.

[1] Zeisberger to Brodhead, August 18, 1781, MS., previously cited. Compare also, Penn. Mag. of Hist. and Biog., IV, p. 248.

[2] Haldimand to Sir Henry Clinton, September 29, 1781, in Vermont Hist. Soc. Coll., II, p. 312.

about the command of the post had greatly increased the disorder. The garrison was in want of pay, of clothing, of even subsistence itself, and, as a consequence, was in a mutinous condition. The militia of the department was without proper organization; and when called into service, destitute, to a great extent, of military knowledge and discipline.

The civil government of the country was even in a worse state than the military, on account of the excitement regarding the boundary between Pennsylvania and Virginia. Both states, before the war, had asserted their claims to, and exercised an organized jurisdiction over, the disputed territory. As between the two commonwealths, the quarrel was brought to an end, virtually, in 1779; but bitter feeling still existed among the people — the line was not yet run. As a consequence of having long contemned the authority of a neighboring state, many had come into open disrespect of their own. Hence, there was a restlessness prevailing in the country, and a desire, on the part of some, to emigrate into the wilderness beyond the Ohio to form a new state.

Such was the disorder — the confusion — which beset the western department at the moment of the threatened invasion. Washington fully appreciated the difficulties. Something must be done and done quickly. Above all things, a commander was needed at Fort Pitt, possessed not only of courage and firmness, but of prudence and judgment. The commander-in-chief, with great care and concern, looked about him for such a person. His choice for the position, after due deliberation, fell upon a resident of Carlisle, Pennsylvania, an officer at the head of the second brigade of that state — Brigadier General William Irvine.

CHAPTER VI.

BIOGRAPHICAL SKETCH OF WILLIAM IRVINE.

William Irvine was born in county Fermanagh, Ireland, November 3, 1741. His ancestry originally emigrated from Scotland. His elementary education commenced at a grammar school in Enniskillen, and was completed at the college of Dublin. He then entered the army as a cornet, but owing to a quarrel with his colonel resigned his commission. He afterward became a student of medicine and surgery, receiving, at the close of his studies, an appointment as surgeon of a British ship of war. This was during the old French war. While in the line of duty, he became acquainted with the condition of society in this country; and, a few months after the declaration of peace, he came to America, settling in the interior of Pennsylvania, where he afterward married Anne Callender, daughter of Robert Callender. The result of the marriage was a family of ten children — five sons and five daughters. At Carlisle, his place of residence, he soon gained the general confidence of the people, both as citizen and in the practice of his profession.

Irvine early took part in the controversy which resulted in national independence. A meeting was held in Philadelphia, followed by similar assemblages in different counties. A provincial convention assembled in that city July 15, 1774, which promptly recommended the selection and sitting of a general congress and passed resolutions of the most patriotic character. Of this convention, Irvine was a diligent and influential member.

On the 6th of January, 1776, he was appointed (his commission being dated the 9th) to raise and command a regiment — the sixth of the Pennsylvania line. At its head, he marched to the mouth of the river Richelieu in Canada. On the 7th, of June, his regiment and three companies of Colonel Anthony Wayne's embarked in batteaux, under command of Gen. Thompson, and proceeded to Nicolet, where they were joined by Col. Arthur St. Clair, who had almost seven hundred men under his command. An attempt was then made against the vanguard of the British army, stationed at Three Rivers, about forty miles below, in hopes to surprise it, but resulting in the loss to the Americans of about twenty-five men killed and two hundred made prisoners. Of the latter were the general in command and Colonel Irvine, who were carried to Quebec. Irvine was not exchanged until April 21, 1778, although released on parol August 3d, after his capture.

Irvine was promoted to the command of the second Pennsylvania brigade, being commissioned brigadier-general May 12, 1779. From the date of his exchange as a prisoner of war, his career was an honorable one both as patriot and soldier. He took an active part in the service. He was in the battle of Monmouth, where he won special honors. But history has been strangely silent concerning them. He was actively engaged in the northern campaigns until the revolt of the Pennsylvania line at the beginning of 1781. After this, he was employed in recruiting, until, in September of that year, he was ordered by congress, upon the recommendation of Washington, to the command of the western department, headquarters at Fort Pitt, Pittsburgh.

Irvine assumed command in the west early in November, 1781. His first efforts were directed to the re-formation of the continental forces stationed at Pittsburgh.

Not very long after his arrival, he received instructions to employ his garrison in repairing the fort. He immediately began the task, so as to meet, if possible, any emergency which might arise in case of an attack by the enemy. New pickets were prepared; and, to encourage the soldiers, Irvine labored with his own hands. This had a happy effect. Every officer followed his example. The greatest activity prevailed. In a short time the fort was put in a tolerable condition for a successful defense. But the work did not stop here. It was continued for many months. In January, 1782, Irvine left his post for a short visit to his home in Carlisle, and to confer with congress and the commander-in-chief concerning affairs in the western department; having, however, previous to his departure, put the frontiers in as good state of defense as was practicable. Colonel John Gibson was in command during his absence.

On the 8th of March, Washington sent instructions to Irvine at Carlisle to proceed with all convenient despatch to Fort Pitt, and when he should have arrived there to take such measures for the security of the post and for the defense of the western frontier, as the continental force there stationed, combined with the militia of the neighboring country, would admit. He reached that post on the 25th, finding, upon his arrival, the country people in a frenzy of excitement because of Indian raids. James Marshel, the lieutenant of Washington county, Pennsylvania, had ordered out some militia to march across the Ohio river to the valley of the Tuscarawas, there to attack some hostile savages believed to be occupying what for a short time previous had been the deserted villages of the Moravian Indians. The force was commanded by David Williamson. Upon his arrival, he found a considerable number of men, women and children of "Moravians," and, it is said, some warriors. In the end, all were killed except two boys, who made their escape.

The garrisons at Forts Pitt and McIntosh were, upon the commander's return, in a mutinous condition. Great firmness had to be exercised by Irvine. The result was, before the end of May, besides the frequent application of "one hundred lashes well laid on," two of the soldiers suffered the death penalty. Meanwhile, owing to the increased boldness of the savages in penetrating into the exposed settlements, the country people became clamorous to be led against the Wyandot towns upon the Sandusky river, in what is now northwestern Ohio, whence came the greater portion of the warriors depredating upon the western border of Pennsylvania and of so much of Virginia as lay upon the upper Ohio river. Irvine finally gave his consent to an expedition against these Indians, and exerted himself to the best of his ability to forward the enterprise; issuing instructions to the one to be elected to command for his guidance. The campaign proved unsuccessful, the borderers suffering a loss of about fifty men. Colonel William Crawford, who led them into the wilderness, was captured by savages and burned at the stake.

Notwithstanding the departure of the volunteers against Sandusky, Irvine did not relax his watchful care over the inhabitants upon the border. A large portion of his time, after the return of the expedition until fall, was taken up in preparing for another enterprise against the same Indian settlements. This expedition he was to command in person. However, upon the assurance of the commander-in-chief of the British forces in America that the savages had all been required to desist from further hostilities, it was, by order of General Washington, laid aside. The ensuing winter brought with it, occurrences of but little moment in the western department. Irvine again visited his home in the spring, arriving there in March, 1783. He left Lieutenant Colonel Stephen Bayard in command at Fort Pitt.

Not long subsequent to his reaching Carlisle, he wrote Washington congratulating him upon the glorious news of peace which had just arrived in America. "With great sincerity," was the reply of the commander-in-chief, "I return you my congratulations." At the request of Washington, Irvine again returned to Pittsburgh, arriving out in May; here he remained until his final departure on the 1st day of October, 1783, when he turned over his command to a small continental force, his garrison having previously been furloughed, except a small detachment.

Irvine returned to his home in Carlisle, with health much impaired by exposure in the service. Pennsylvania acknowledged her gratitude for his labors by the donation of a valuable tract of land on Lake Erie, below Erie, Pennsylvania, known, afterward, as "Irvine's Reserve."

The general was a member of the council of censors of his state in 1783 and 1784. On the 26th of March, 1785, he was appointed to examine and select the donation lands promised the troops of Pennsylvania. He reported the result of his mission in November following. He advised the acquisition by purchase from the United States of the "triangle," which gave to his state a frontage (and one of the best harbors) on Lake Erie. He was afterward elected a member of congress from the Cumberland district (1786-8) under the confederation. He took an early interest in internal improvements, not only of his own state but of the country at large. In 1790, he was elected, a member of the constitutional convention of Pennsylvania, which framed the constitution adopted September 2nd, of that year. In 1791, he was a commissioner to establish the boundary line between the counties of Huntingdon and Mifflin, his state, which had been in dispute. He settled the difficulty to the satisfaction of both parties. Irvine was a member of the board of commissioners appointed to arrange the national account between the several states and the general government, which began with the war for independence. The labors of the commission were concluded on the 29th of June, 1793, to the satisfaction of all concerned.

Irvine was again honored, by the voters of the Cumberland district, with a seat in congress — this time, elected to the third congress (1793-1795), under the constitution of the United States. In 1794, he was appointed a commissioner with Andrew Elliott, to lay out the towns of Erie, Waterford, Warren and Franklin, Pennsylvania; he was also appointed one of the commissioners in an endeavor to settle the difficulties of the so-called "Whisky Insurrection" in western Pennsylvania. Negotiations, however, failed and troops were ordered to march against the insurgents. Irvine as senior major general commanded the Pennsylvanians under Governor Mifflin. A successful march of the forces from eastern Pennsylvania, and of those from New Jersey, Maryland and Virginia, resulted in quelling the disturbance.

General Irvine was one of the thirteen presidential electors of Pennsylvania chosen in 1797, when John Adams was elected president. In 1798, he was appointed commander-in-chief of the Pennsylvania proportion of the quota of eight thousand militia ordered out by congress to serve during the expected French war. Upon the election of Jefferson to the presidency,

Irvine was appointed intendant of military stores — an important office, as it included the charge of arsenals, ordnance, supplies of the army, and supervision of Indian affairs. He was afterward made president of the Pennsylvania society of the Cincinnati, he having been elected treasurer at its first organization on the 4th of October, 1783. He died in Philadelphia (to which place he had removed from Carlisle) of an inflammatory disorder, on the 29th of July, 1804. He was a zealous patriot, a judicious statesman, an able military commander. In a word, he was a careful, intelligent, and conscientious executor of all public trusts confided to his management, and was noted as a man of incorruptible integrity.

THE WASHINGTON-IRVINE LETTERS.

I. — WASHINGTON TO BRIG.-GEN. WILLIAM IRVINE.

HEADQUARTERS NEAR YORK, *November* 1, 1781.

Sir: — During the time of my being occupied in the siege of York,[1] I received a letter from Colonel Gibson,[2] commanding, at that time, at Fort Pitt,[3] inclosing sundry proceedings of courts martial held at that post, among which are two capital cases, on which sentences of death are decreed by the court.

Being informed by congress that you have been ordered to

---

[1] Yorktown was completely invested by the American and French forces on the thirtieth of September, 1781. On the nineteenth of October following, Lord Cornwallis surrendered. General Washington remained at his "Headquarters near York" until the fifth of November, when he proceeded by way of Mount Vernon to Philadelphia. It was five days before his departure that the above letter to Irvine was written, as its date indicates.

[2] Col. John Gibson, of the seventh Virginia regiment, who has already been frequently mentioned. For a biographical sketch of Gibson, see note to his letter to Irvine of Jan. 28, 1782, Appendix M.

[3] A fort — Duquesne — was built at this point — Pittsburgh — by the French at the commencement of the old French war, but was burned by them in 1758, immediately before the occupation of the place by the British under General Forbes. It was a strong fortification of earth and wood stockaded. In December, 1758, the British erected a small stockade, with bastions, within two hundred yards of the ruins of the French post. The next year, however, was commenced a more formidable fortification. It was near the site of Fort Duquesne, and was named Fort Pitt. It remained in possession of a British force until the latter part of the year 1772, when it was abandoned and considerably, though not wholly, destroyed. During the year 1773 a citizen of Pittsburgh — Edward Ward — had possession of what was left. It was, in 1774, re-occupied and somewhat repaired by Captain John Conolly, under orders from Lord Dunmore, as a Virginia post, and its name changed to Fort Dunmore, though the Pennsylvanians still adhered to "Fort Pitt," which name was fully restored when Dunmore became odious to Virginia. It was vacated by Conolly just at the commencement of the revolution. Its first occupation after that struggle began was by Virginia troops under Captain John Neville, in 1775, as previously related, who were superceded early in 1777 by others raised in the immediate neighborhood of Pittsburgh. (See Introduction, p. 8, note 3.) Following these, as already mentioned, was a continental garrison, first under Brigadier General Edward Hand, afterward under Brigadier

the command of that post,[1] I have to inform you that the sentence of Meyndert Fisher, one of the above, is not approved; and that upon application from his friends and some particular information respecting him, I have to request that he be liberated from his confinement.

The case of John Hinds I know nothing of more than is contained in his trial. You will, therefore, please to order him to execution, or pardon him, as you shall think particular circumstances and the necessity of example may require.[2]

II.— IRVINE TO WASHINGTON.

FORT PITT, *December* 2,[3] 1781.

Sir:— At the time congress directed me to repair to this place,[4] I took for granted your excellency would have information thereof, through different channels; and knowing how

---

General Lachlan McIntosh, whose successor was Colonel Daniel Brodhead, followed by Colonel John Gibson, in command in October, 1781, as indicated in the above letter.

[1] The orders of congress were expressed in the following resolutions, passed by that body September 24, 1781:

"Resolved, That Brigadier General Irvine be and hereby is ordered to repair forthwith to Fort Pitt, and take upon him the command of that garrison until further orders.

"That Brigadier General Irvine be and hereby is authorized and directed to arrange the troops which compose the garrison of Fort Pitt and its dependencies in such manner as to retain no more officers than are absolutely necessary for the number of non-commissioned officers and privates at those parts.

"That Brigadier General Irvine be and hereby is authorized and directed to arrange the staff departments within his command so as to retain no more officers or persons in those departments than the service absolutely demands.

"That he be and hereby is further empowered to call in from time to time such aids of militia as may be necessary for the defense of the post under his command and the protection of the country. And, for this purpose, the executives of the states of Virginia and Pennsylvania are requested to direct the proper officers of the militia in their respective states to obey such orders as they shall from time to time receive from Brigadier General Irvine for the purpose aforesaid."

[2] Irvine, of course, liberated Fisher. What action was taken in Hind's case, a note to the next letter shows.

[3] The day of the month is omitted in this letter as copied in Irvine's letter-book, but is inserted, as above, in the original sent Washington.

[4] The instructions given by congress to Irvine, who was then in Philadel-

very particularly you were at that moment engaged,¹ I did not think proper to give unnecessary trouble. This, I flatter myself, will excuse me to your excellency for not writing sooner. Previous to my arrival,² Colonel Gibson had received

phia, were dated September 24, 1781. He did not leave the city immediately for Pittsburgh, for the reason that a "small supply of cash" expected from congress had not been received. The time of his starting for Carlisle and the west was, probably, on the 9th of October, as the following letter written by the president of congress to the president of the supreme executive council of Pennsylvania, indicates (a similar one being sent the governor of Virginia):

PHILADELPHIA, October 8th, 1781.

"<i>Sir:</i>— As Brigadier-General Irvine proposes to set out to-morrow in order to take command at Fort Pitt, and may very probably have occasion for the aid of the militia in the vicinity of that post, I thought it proper to procure a copy of his instructions and to transmit them to you. They are accordingly herewith enclosed; and I rest assured every suitable measure will be adopted for affording him effectual support by the militia in case of necessity. I have the honor to be, with the highest respect, sir, your excellency's most obedient servant, THO. McKEAN, President.
"His Excellency Joseph Reed, Esquire."

¹ Washington and Rochambeau reached LaFayette's headquarters near Williamsburg, on the 14th of September. Here they remained until the 30th, when they completely invested Yorktown. Irvine's appointment to the western department was made by congress (24 Sept.) during the active operations of Washington, immediately preceding the commencement of the siege. This work was what Irvine refers to as engaging the particular attention of the commander-in-chief.

² The exact day of the arrival of General Irvine at Fort Pitt and his assuming command of the post, is not known. The following is the first entry in his orderly book:

"FORT PITT, Nov. 6th, 1781.

"Parole, <i>General.</i>   Countersign, <i>Joy.</i>

"General Irvine has the pleasure to congratulate the troops on the great and glorious news. Lord Cornwallis, with the troops under his command, surrendered prisoners of war on the 19th of October last, to the allied army of America and France, under the immediate command of his Excellency General Washington. The prisoners amount to upwards of five thousand regular troops, near two thousand tories, and as many negroes, besides a number of merchants and other followers.

"Thirteen pieces of artillery will be fired this day at 1 o'clock, in the fort, at which time the troops will be under arms, with their colors displayed. The commissary will issue a gill of liquor extraordinary to the non-commissioned officers and privates on this joyful occasion.

"Accurate regimental returns [are] to be made to-morrow morning at

your letter directing him to take the command, which was acquiesced in by Colonel Brodhead; and things went on in the usual channel, except that the dispute[1] occasioned Colonel Gibson's intended expedition against Sandusky being laid aside,[2] and perhaps it also prevented many other necessary arrangements. The examination of evidences on the charges against Colonel Brodhead, is still taking, and I am informed will continue some weeks.[3]

Agreeable to my orders from congress, to retain no more officers here than sufficient for the men, I have made the following arrangments: re-formed the remains of the late eighth Pennsylvania regiment into two companies, and call them a detachment from the Pennsylvania line, to be commanded by Lieutenant-Colonel Bayard.[4] Baron Steuben had some time ago directed Colonel Gibson to re-form his regiment[5] also into two companies, retaining with him the staff of the regiment; and to send all the supernumerary officers down into Virginia.

---

9 o'clock, of the officers and dates of their commissions, together with rolls of non-commissioned officers, drums, fifes, and privates,—accounting for every man, where he is, how employed, and time so employed."

[1] The dispute here spoken of was the one already mentioned as subsisting, previous to Brodhead's yielding the direction of affairs at Fort Pitt to Gibson, between these two officers as to the right of command.

[2] "The intended expedition against Sandusky" was an enterprise against the Wyandots and other hostile Indians located upon the upper waters of the Sandusky river in what is now the northwestern part of the state of Ohio, which had been planned, as heretofore stated, at Fort Pitt, and which "the dispute" caused to be "laid aside."

[3] Charges, it will be remembered, had been preferred against Brodhead, among other things for speculating with public money, to substantiate which, witnesses were then being examined. He was afterward honorably acquitted.

[4] The eighth Pennsylvania regiment, under command of Daniel Brodhead as colonel, marched, as previously explained, to Fort Pitt in the summer of 1778 to take part in an expedition under Brigadier-General Lachlan McIntosh against Detroit. The enterprise, it has already been seen, proved abortive, but the regiment remained in the western department; when, upon the arrival of Irvine, "its remains" were re-formed into a "detachment from the Pennsylvania line," to be commanded by Lieutenant Colonel Stephen Bayard, as above indicated; the whole consisted of only two companies, the first commanded by Capt. Clark and Lieuts. Peterson and Reed; the second by Capt. Brady and Lieuts. Ward and Morrison.

[5] The seventh Virginia regiment, afterward the first. This regiment, pre-

The re-formation was so made; but the officers were so distressed for want of clothing and other necessaries, that they were not able to proceed. However they are now making exertions, and I hope will soon set out. I have ordered the supernumerary officers of the Pennsylvania line to repair forthwith to their proper regiments in the line.[1] The whole of the troops, here, are thrown into four companies. I have been trying to economize; but every thing is in so wretched a state, that there is very little in my power. I never saw troops cut so truly a deplorable, and at the same time despicable, a figure. Indeed, when I arrived, no man would believe from their appearance that they were soldiers; nay, it would be difficult to determine whether they were *white men*. Though they do not yet come up to my wishes, yet they are some better.

As it does not rest with me to decide on the propriety or impropriety of any person's conduct, I shall only make a few general observations. The consumption of public stores has, in my opinion, been enormous, particularly military stores; and I fear the reason given for it will not be justifiable, namely: that the militia would all fly if they had not powder and lead given them, not only when in service, but also to keep in their houses. It is true the county lieutenants,[2] and others who are

---

viously the ninth, was originally the thirteenth Virginia. It was raised west of the mountains largely through the exertions of Col. William Crawford, and was known on the border as the "West Augusta regiment;" so called from the district of West Augusta, Virginia.

[1] The supernumerary officers included Colonel Brodhead, Major Frederick Vernon and others. The two named, under the arrangement then in force, belonged to the first Pennsylvania regiment. Stephen Bayard was lieutenant colonel of the same regiment (afterward, January 1, 1783, of the third); but he remained at Fort Pitt, as already explained, in command of the "detachment from the Pennsylvania line."

[2] According to the militia laws of Pennsylvania and Virginia, each company was commanded by a captain, two lieutenants and an ensign; each batallion by a colonel, lieutenant colonel and major; and the whole in a county by a county lieutenant. Besides this the latter officer had a general supervision of military affairs within his county, with the rank of colonel. The western department, at the date of Irvine's arrival at Fort Pitt, included the counties of Westmoreland and Washington in Pennsylvania, Monongalia and Ohio in Virginia; in each of which there was a county lieutenant; in the two former counties, there were, also, sub-lieutenants.

called responsible men, have promised to be accountable; but I am certain not an ounce can ever be again collected. I find by the returns, that near two thousand pounds of powder, and four thousand pounds of lead, have been issued to the militia since the dispute commenced between Colonels Brodhead and Gibson, chiefly by orders of the former, besides arms, accoutrements, etc., and not a man called into actual service. The magazine is nearly exhausted. There is not now as much remaining as has been issued since the first of last September.

I presume your excellency has been informed by the governor of the state of Virginia,[1] or General Clark,[2] of the failure of his [Clark's] expedition.[3] But lest that should not be the case, I will relate all the particulars that have come to my knowledge. Captain Craig,[4] with the detachment of artillery under him, returned here the 26th instant.[5] He got up with much difficulty and great fatigue to the men, being forty days on the way, occasioned by the lowness of the water. He was obliged to throw away his gun-carriages, but brought his pieces and best stores safe. He left General Clark at the rapids [Louisville, Ky.]; and says the general was not able to prosecute his intended plan of operation for want of men, being able to collect in the whole only about seven hundred and fifty. The buffalo meat was all rotten; and, he adds, the general is ap-

---

[1] "Richmond (Virginia), Dec. 29. The honorable Thomas Nelson, Jr., Esq., our late governor, having resigned on account of ill state of his health, the honorable Benjamin Harrison, Esq., speaker of the house of delegates, is elected in his room."—Penn. Packet, Jan. 10, 1782 (No. 831).

[2] For a biographical sketch of Geo. Rogers Clark, see Appendix M,—Clark to Irvine, August 10, 1782, note.

[3] See Introduction, pp. 53–56.

[4] Captain (afterward Major) Isaac Craig was, as we have before seen, in command, at Fort Pitt, of a detachment from the fourth Pennsylvania regiment of artillery, and of a detachment of artillery artificers, and was sent down the Ohio with Clark. His was one of the most efficient — one of the best disciplined bodies, of soldiers in the west. For a biographical sketch of Craig, see Appendix M,— Craig to Irvine, April 1, 1783, note.

[5] "The 26th instant;" that is, the 26th of November, 1781. Irvine evidently commenced writing his letter the last of that month although it was not finished until the 2d December.

prehensive of a visit from Detroit,[1] and is not without fears the settlement will be obliged to break up, unless re-enforcements soon arrive from Virginia. The Indians have been so numerous in that country that all the inhabitants have been obliged to keep close in forts, and the general could not venture out to fight them.

A Colonel Lochry, lieutenant of Westmoreland county, in Pennsylvania, with about one hundred men in all, composed of volunteers and a company raised by Pennsylvania for the defense of said county, followed General Clark, who, it is said, ordered Lochry to join him at the mouth of Miami, up which river it had previously been agreed on to proceed. But General Clark having changed his plan, left a small party at the Miami, with directions to Lochry to proceed on to the falls after him, with the main body. Sundry accounts agree that this party, and all Lochry's, to a man, were waylaid by the Indians and regulars (for it is asserted they had artillery) and all killed or taken. No man, however, escaped either to join General Clark or return home. When Captain Craig left the general, he could not be persuaded but that Lochry with his party had returned home.[2] These misfortunes threw the people of this country into the greatest consternation and almost despair, particularly Westmoreland county, Lochry's party being all the best men of their frontier. At present, they talk of flying early in the spring, to the eastern side of the mountain, and are daily flocking to me to enquire what support they may expect.

I think there is but too much reason to fear that General Clark's and Colonel Gibson's expeditions falling through will

---

[1] At this date, as ever since the commencement of the revolution, Detroit was the center of British power and influence in the northwest. Lieutenant-Governor Henry Hamilton commanded the post until early in 1779. His successor was Major Arent Schuyler De Peyster. Depredations upon the exposed borders of Pennsylvania and Virginia (including Kentucky) by the savages, drew, to a great extent, their inspiration and were given direction from this point. (See Introduction, p. 7.) Indian expeditions were sometimes under the command of British officers accompanied by regulars and rangers. It was a visit of this nature that Clark, in the fall of 1781, at Louisville, Kentucky, stood in apprehension of.

[2] See Introduction, pp. 55, 56; also Appendix G,— Irvine to Moore, December 3, 1781.

greatly encourage the savages to fall on the country with double fury, and perhaps the British from Detroit to visit this post, which, instead of being in a tolerable state of defense, is in fact nothing but a heap of ruins. I need not inform your excellency that it is, at best, a bad situation for defense. I have been viewing all the ground in this vicinity, and find none equal for a post to the mouth of Chartiers creek,[1] about four miles down the river. This was pointed out to me by Captain [Thomas] Hutchins [geographer], before I left Philadelphia, who says there is no place equal to it any where within forty miles of Fort Pitt.

I think it best calculated, on many accounts. First, the ground is such that works may be constructed to contain any number of men you please, from fifty to one thousand. It is by nature almost inaccessible on three sides, and on the fourth no commanding ground within three thousand yards. Secondly, as it would effectually cover the settlement on Chartiers creek, the necessity for keeping a post at Fort McIntosh[2] will of course cease. In case of making that the main post,[3] Fort Pitt should be demolished, all except the north bastion, on which a strong block-house should be built. A small party in it would as effectually keep up a communication with the settlement on Monongahela as the whole garrison now does; for the necessary detachments to Fort McIntosh, Wheeling,

---

[1] Chartiers creek rises in Washington county, Pennsylvania, flows a north-northeast course, and empties into the Ohio on the south side, four miles below Pittsburgh.

[2] See Introduction, p. 26.

[3] "Whether the point recommended was McKee's rocks, or the hill immediately west of the mouth of the creek [Chartiers], is not very clear; although the assertion that there was no commanding ground within three thousand yards, would incline us to select the latter as the point. It is not a little singular that the general's correspondent [Washington] had, twenty-seven years before, examined the point at the junction of the rivers [Pittsburgh] as well as McKee's rocks, and expressed his opinion in favor of the former."—Craig's *Olden Time*, Vol. II, pp. 532, 533.

Before Washington's first visit to this country, Christopher Gist, who had been appointed surveyor for the Ohio company and was familiar with both localities, was directed to lay off a town and fort near the mouth of Chartiers creek. This was in 1752. The site thus selected was not improved.

etc., so divide the troops that no one place can ever be held without a large body of troops. Indeed, I do not like Fort McIntosh being kept a post in the present situation of things.

If the enemy at Detroit should take it into their heads to make us a visit, that would be an excellent place for them to take by surprise; whence they could send out Indians and other partisans to lay the whole country waste before we could dislodge them. We have (I think idly) too much of our stores there. I have been making efforts to bring up the greater part; but though it is almost incredible, yet it is true that, of all the public boats built here, not a single one was to be found when I came here, except one barge and one flat. I expect two boats up, loaded, this day. It is, I believe, universally agreed that the only way to keep Indians from harassing the country is to visit them. But we find, by experience, that burning their empty towns has not the desired effect. They can soon build others. They must be followed up and beaten, or the British, whom they draw support from, totally driven out of their country.

I believe if Detroit was demolished, it would be a good step towards giving some, at least temporary, ease to this country. It would cost them at least a whole summer to rebuild and establish themselves; for, though we should succeed in reducing Detroit, I do not think there is the smallest probability of our being able to hold it. It is too remote from supplies. I have been endeavoring to form some estimates, from such information as I can collect, and I really think that the reduction of Detroit would not cost much more, nor take many more men, than it will take to cover and protect the country by acting on the defensive. If I am well informed, it will take seven or eight hundred regular troops and about a thousand militia; which number could pretty easily be obtained for that purpose, as it appears to be a favorite scheme over all this country. The principal difficulty would be to get provisions and stores transported. As to taking a heavy train of artillery, I fear it would not only be impracticable, but an incumbrance; two field pieces, some howitz, and perhaps a mortar [would suffice]. I do not think, especially under present circumstances, that it would be possible to carry on an expedition in such a manner as to promise success by a regular siege. I would therefore propose to make every appearance of setting down before the place, as if to reduce it by regular approaches. As soon as I found the enemy fully impressed with this idea, attempt it at once by assault.

I mean to write to congress for leave to go down the country in January, to return in March, if they make it a point that I should continue here.[1] I can scarcely think they will wish me to remain with four companies of men. The power of calling out the militia of this country is more ideal than real, especially till the lines between Virginia and Pennsylvania are determined, and actually run. Neither civil nor military law will take place until then.[2] Whether I am to be

---

[1] See Irvine to the president of congress, 3 Dec., 1781, Appendix A.

[2] For several years, the country around the head-waters of the Ohio had been a subject of dispute between Pennsylvania and Virginia, the boundary line between the two provinces not having been run. Mason and Dixon's line had been extended from the northwest corner of Maryland to a point some distance west of the Monongahela, by the Penns and Lord Baltimore, in 1767; but with this line Virginia had nothing to do. This province, as early as 1752, began to assert a claim to what was afterwards recognized as southwest Pennsylvania; however, the quarrel did not assume a very threatening aspect until the legislature of the latter province embraced, in 1773, all the disputed territory in the new county of Westmoreland. Lord Dunmore as governor of Virginia then attempted to enforce jurisdiction over the country about Pittsburgh, it being claimed as part of Augusta county, Virginia. "Fort Pitt was seized by a band of armed partisans, headed by Captain John Conolly, and its name changed to Fort Dunmore. New counties were formed from which delegates were sent to the Virginia legislature. Justices and other civil officers were commissioned by the authorities of Virginia. Court houses were erected and Virginia courts regularly held within the limits of the present counties of Alleghany and Washington, in Pennsylvania. The people were divided in their allegiance; arrests, counter-arrests, and other violent acts frequently occurred during this seven years' contest. The breaking out of the revolutionary war in 1775, and a recommendation by congress on the subject, abated the civil strife." The controversy ended, virtually, in 1779 and the following year, as between the two states, Virginia yielding her claims to the disputed territory. During the fall of 1782, a temporary line was run as far as the Ohio river, beginning where Mason and Dixon's ended. But this was subsequent to the date of Irvine's letter. The people, therefore, were still "divided in their allegiance;" hence it was that neither civil nor military laws could well be enforced in the disputed territory. However, as

continued here or not, I am pretty certain it might be of use for me to go down, in order the better to concert measures proper to be taken either with your excellency or congress; for, as matters now stand, it is clear to me this country must be given up. The militia, however, promise pretty fair, and I have had no ground for differing with them yet. There are no provisions laid in, nor is there even sufficient from day to day. The contract made by Mr. [Robert] Morris [superintendent of finance], for supplying this post, has not been fulfilled on the part of the contractor[1] in any tolerable degree; nor would the contract answer here, even if complied with. However, as I must write particularly to the board of war on this subject,[2] and have exceeded the moderate bounds of a letter, I fear I have already tired, and taken up too much of your excellency's time.

P. S.— I have been told of three persons who were prisoners with the enemy, and have lately made their escape. I have sent in search of them but could not find them out. The lieutenant of Washington county [James Marshel] has promised to bring one of them to me as soon as possible. If they have any material accounts, I shall inform your excellency

---

will be hereafter seen, Irvine found but little difficulty in calling out the militia when needed. One requisition upon the lieutenant of Washington county had already been promptly responded to.

[1] The contractor was Michael Huffnagle, a resident of Hannastown, Westmoreland county, Pennsylvania. David Duncan, also a resident of Westmoreland, attended to the contractor's business at Fort Pitt.

[2] Irvine's letter to the board of war was written the next day. (Appendix B.) The secretary at war — Major General Benjamin Lincoln — was the successor of this board; but he had, at the above date, been so short a time in office that the fact was unknown to Irvine. Why there was a necessity for writing to the board, the following order will show: —

"[Continental] WAR OFFICE, *September* 29, 1781.

"*Agreed*, That General Irvine be authorized and directed to regulate the issues of provision by the contractors at Fort Pitt and its dependencies in such manner as will best suit the circumstances of those posts, consistent with the contract, and give temporary direction on the subject, reporting to this board any regulations he may make and the orders given in consequence, which are to be subject to the revision and alteration, if necessary, of the board. By order of the board. JOS. CARLETON, *Sec*."

the earliest possible. They have come from different places, and I am told all agree that great preparations are making to attack this country, at several places, at the same time. Speaking of prisoners, leads me to beg your excellency's opinion or instructions respecting an exchange in this quarter, or a negotiation carried on with the commander at Detroit.[1] I find numbers of poor people are taken in this district; some were taken at the commencement of the war, and are yet languishing in prison, in Canada, for they send all down to Quebec or Montreal. I cannot learn that any attempt has ever been made, on either side, to exchange them. John Hinds and Myndert Fisher have both been confined here a whole year, and are under sentence of a court-martial. I request your excellency's orders respecting them. I am informed the proceedings of the court were sent to headquarters a considerable time since.[2]

[1] The British commandant at Detroit at this time was Arent Schuyler De Peyster, major of the eighth regiment of foot, afterward lieutenant colonel of the same regiment. (See Appendix M,—De Peyster to Irvine, July 10th, 1783, note.)

[2] From this, it will be seen that Irvine had not received Washington's letter of the first of November, though it must have come to hand shortly after, as the order for the release of Fisher from confinement was dated the seventh of January and the one for the release of Hinds the day after, as shown by the following from Irvine's MS. orderly book:

"FORT PITT, *January* 7, 1782.

"At a general court martial held the 25th of July last, of which Lieutenant Colonel [Stephen] Bayard was president, John Hinds, a fifer, in the 7th Virginia regiment was tried for desertion, and assisting a disaffected Indian to make his escape to the enemy. The court are of opinion he is guilty, and sentence him to suffer death. His excellency General Washington confirms the sentence.

"At the same court, Myndert Fisher was tried for holding a traitorous correspondence with the enemies of the United States. The court are of opinion he is guilty, and sentence him to be hanged. The commander-in-chief disapproves the sentence, and orders him to be liberated from confinement. He is, therefore, to be released immediately.

"FORT PITT, *January* 8, 178?.

"His excellency General Washington having been pleased to leave to General Irvine to execute or pardon John Hinds, as he should judge proper, General Irvine, through motives of humanity and compassion for his youth, as well as warm solicitation of some of his officers in his favor, is induced to pardon him. He is to be released from confinement."

III.—WASHINGTON TO IRVINE.

PHILADELPHIA, *December* 18, 1781.

Dear Sir: — I have received your favor of the 2d instant. I am not at all surprised to hear that you found matters in disorder to the westward; it is generally the case when a dispute arises respecting command, as the parties make it a point to thwart each other as much as possible. Perhaps what is past cannot be amended, as Colonel Brodhead may say that the delivery of ammunition to the county lieutenants was necessary.[1] But you will judge of the propriety of the measure in future.

I am sorry to hear of the failure of General Clark's expedition, of which I was always doubtful, as it was to be carried on with militia. But of this I am convinced, that the possession or destruction of Detroit is the only means of giving peace and security to the western frontier; and that when it is undertaken, it should be by such a force as should not risk a disappointment. When we shall have it in our power to to accomplish so desirable an end, I do not know. It will depend upon the exertion of the states in filling up their regular batallions.

I cannot undertake to determine upon the propriety of removing our principal post from Fort Pitt to Chartiers creek. It is a matter in which I suppose a variety of interests is concerned, and which must therefore be decided upon by congress. Should you obtain leave to come down this winter, you will have an opportunity of laying the matter fully before them.[2]

I wish you had been particular upon the manner in which the contractors of Fort Pitt, etc., have been deficient, and had

---

[1] This was in answer to Irvine's remarks concerning the waste of ammunition by the militia of the western counties.

[2] The letter of Irvine to the president of congress of the 3d of December, 1781 (Appendix A), was referred to the secretary of war, who reported that for a variety of reasons it was inexpedient, at that time, to remove the post from Pittsburgh to Chartiers creek, whatever might be done in the future. (See Washington to Irvine — next letter.)

given your reasons for thinking that the contract upon its present establishment will not answer. I would immediately have laid them before Mr. Morris. If your representations should not have been made before this reaches you, no time should be lost in doing it.[1]

I have directed our commissary of prisoners, who is now at Elizabethtown, negotiating a general exchange, to endeavor to include the prisoners in Canada. I cannot see what end would be answered by your opening a treaty with the commandant of Detroit upon that subject, as we seldom or never have a prisoner in our hands upon the quarter where you are.

In my letter of the 1st of November, I acquainted you with my determination upon the cases of Hinds and Fisher.

IV.—WASHINGTON TO IRVINE.

PHILADELPHIA, *December* 21, 1781.

Dear Sir:— The secretary at war, to whom your letter of the 3d instant to congress was referred, reported that, for a variety of reasons, which it is not at present necessary to repeat, it was judged inexpedient to remove the principal post from Fort Pitt to Chartiers creek, at this moment, whatever might be done in future, and that you should be instructed "immediately to employ the garrison in repairing the old fort and the block-house which commands it, and that, when you had made the necsssary arrangements, you should be permitted to repair to congress, that the benefit of your advice might be had in digesting measures for the security of the frontiers."[2] The report having been submitted

---

[1] This matter was laid before the board of war by General Irvine in his letter to that body of December 3, 1781; also in a further communication upon the same subject, on the 14th of that month. (See Appendix B.)

[2] Soon after receiving this notification, Irvine began making preparations for his contemplated trip over the mountains. On the 10th of January, 1782, he sent a requisition to James Marshel, the lieutenant of Washington county, for one subaltern, one sergeant and fifteen privates, of the militia, to relieve the garrison at Fort Henry (Wheeling) by the 1st of February. (See Appendix J,— Irvine to Marshel, of that date.) He, also, sent circular letters to

to me by congress, with direction to give order upon it, as I should think proper, I have concurred in opinion with the secretary at war, and must therefore desire you to follow the measures recommended by him.

the sub-lieutenants of Westmoreland and one to Marshel, with information that he was to go down to Philadelphia on public business connected with his department; that he was not certain what length of time he might be detained there; and that, during his absence, Colonel John Gibson would have command at Fort Pitt. As he was apprehensive there might be a necessity for calling out the militia before his return — especially as his garrison must continue to be employed in repairing the fort — they should, on the requisition of Gibson, who would be the best judge when such necessity might arise, order out such numbers as he should call for, not exceeding fifty, for one tour of duty; the tour not to exceed one month's time. "I hope," said Irvine, "to return by the first of March, before which time I presume there will not be much danger of any damage being done; at the same time, I think it most prudent to take every proper precaution." (See Irvine to Cook, first letter in Appendix K.)

The following is from Irvine's MS. orderly book:

"FORT PITT, *Jan'y* 15, 1782.

"As the general will be absent some time, he requests Colonel Gibson to use every possible exertion to put this post in a good state of defense as possible; for this purpose, he will employ the garrison whenever the weather will admit.

"The general observes that more men are returned on furlough than what are entitled by resolution of congress; and is informed that this indulgence is generally abused by overstaying the time allowed, equally injurious to service and to other men who are as well entitled to the same indulgence. He therefore directs that officers commanding corps will take effectual measures to call in all whose furloughs are expired; and that in future no man is to be furloughed without the knowledge and consent of the commandant." Irvine left the next morning.

The following orders were issued by Irvine, from Dec. 5, 1781, to January 14, 1782, inclusive:

"FORT PITT, *December* 5, 1781.

"When there is flour sufficient in store, the bread must be baked at least one day before it is issued to the troops. The general directs the quartermasters to pay strict attention to the quality of the provisions, and when they think it unwholesome or unfit for use, they will make immediate report thereof, in order that inspection may be made. Major [Samuel] Finley will send a copy of this order to the contractor."

"PITTSBURGH, *December* 7, 1781.

"Neither non-commissioned officers nor privates shall retain or use in public service, arms or accoutrements which are private property. All, therefore,

Whether we shall or shall not be in condition to prosecute an enterprise against Detroit in any short time, I do not know.

who are possessed of such are at liberty to dispose of them as they think proper. All rifles (public property) and accoutrements belonging thereto, and all the ammunition in the hands of the troops, are to be instantly collected by the quartermasters, which, together with what they may have on hand unissued, are to be delivered into the military store; and [the quartermasters are to] make out new returns to complete each man to three rounds which must be made up.

"All returns for arms, accoutrements or ammunition [are] to be examined and signed by [the] officer commanding [each] corps, when [they are to be] delivered to the inspector for signing also, who will hand them to the commanding officer.

"The general expects that officers of every rank will exert themselves to prevent unnecessary destruction or embezzlement of arms, ammunition, clothing and public property of every kind. He is sorry to observe that so little progress has been made in the mode proposed in altering and enlarging the soldiers' clothes and for repairing the barracks so as to make the quarters comfortable. It is in vain for men to allege, in excuse, that they have not money to purchase thread, needles, etc., or to pay taylors, when it is evident that their credit is large with vendors of whiskey.

"No arms [are] to be loaded till further orders, excepting when the officer of the day shall judge it expedient in the night, which is to be noted in the daily reports."

"Fort Pitt, *December* 12, 1781.

"The several corps will provide coal and wood for themselves in such manner as the commandants may think best; the coal pit to be occupied by turns, day and day about, at first, till all have some days' supply; afterwards, each three days to be determined by lot who shall have the first day for the present in this business. The artillery and the Pennsylvania detachment will work together and Capt. Livergood's company with Col. Gibson's regiment. Each will supply the blacksmith's, armorer's, and the general's family, in rotation, with such quantities as Mr. [Samuel] Sample shall direct, who will also assign boats and teams in due proportion as the case will admit.

"The general requests the officers to make such arrangements as [that] the men will be kept as short time as possible on fatigue in each tour and never to exceed two days. Boatmen, carters, and colliers, who have skill in the business, may render it necessary to keep them constantly in the employ. These men will be entered in the quartermaster's books, to be allowed the same additional pay as soldiers taken from the line of the army to drive wagons; as this is the mode adopted in all armies. The general flatters himself there will be no more cause of complaint for want of these articles [of fuel]. If the troops should hereafter suffer, he hopes they will attribute it to the real cause (indolence), which he will not charge them with without good evidence."

But, as a consideration of that point may be brought on when you come down, it may be well for you to prepare yourself with the necessary information respecting the strength of the

[An order for December 15, 1781, is given hereafter. See Appendix M,—Capt. John Finley to Irvine, February 2, 1782, note.]

"FORT PITT, *December* 18, 1781.

"General Irvine thinks proper to republish this extract from general orders, dated at West Point, July 24, 1779, that no person may plead ignorance in future:

"'Any soldier who presumes to fire his musket without leave from the commanding officer of his regiment (who is not to give it but in cases of necessity, and then will acquaint the general of it) is to receive fifteen lashes on the spot and to pay one-sixth of a dollar for the cartridge to the quarter-master of the regiment, who will lay out the money arising this way for the use of the sick. A similar punishment shall be inflicted on any soldier who will, through neglect, waste or lose any of his ammunition. The guard nearest the spot where the gun is fired is to send a file of men for the offender.'"

"FORT PITT, *December* 24, 1781.

"All officers who shall obtain leave of absence will acquaint the brigade major thereof."

"FORT PITT, *December* 25, 1781.

"A detachment of troops in this garrison, consisting of one sub[altern], one sergeant, one corporal, one drum and eighteen privates, will parade to-morrow at twelve o'clock, with their arms, accoutrements and packs for a command of two weeks.

"Detail.

"The general orders the rolls of each company to be called by the orderly sergeant in the barrack rooms after tattoo beating, at which time an officer of each corps will be present and see the rolls called, reporting the absentees to the commanding officer of each corps, that the delinquents may be punished for a breach of former general orders."

"FORT PITT, *January* 1, 1782.

"G. O. [General Orders.]

"Patrick Leonard, John Cain and Martin Shuster are to be released from their confinement. The general hopes this lenity will excite them to better conduct in future."

"HEADQUARTERS, FORT PITT, *January* 2, 1782.

"G. O.

"There will be a general inspection of the troops at this post the 4th instant. All fatigue parties will be present at the examination. The troops will appear clean, their arms and accoutrements in good order.

"The officers will make returns of the strength of the companies they command, accounting for all absentees, together with the alterations, specifying the quantity of clothing delivered their companies since last inspection, and

post, that of the garrison, and the means that ought to be employed to give the expedition a tolerable certainty of success.

of the arms, ammunition and accoutrements of each company, distinguishing such as are in the hands of the men absent on command, etc., from those present, and of camp equipage delivered each company, the quantity on hand and the deficiency since the preceding examination.

"The regimental quartermasters will make out returns of the articles they have drawn since the last inspection, both from the assistant quartermaster and deputy field commissary of military stores, the issues they have made to each company, the stores on hand and the deficiencies that have happened.

"The regimental clothiers will make out returns of all the articles of clothing by them received and delivered and on hand.

"The assistant quartermaster [will make] out a return of the articles of his department issued to the several regiments and others and returned by them to him.

"The deputy field commissary of military stores will make out a similar return."

"FORT PITT, *January* 12, 1782.
"General Orders.

"A detachment will parade to-morrow morning at troop-beating prepared for a command of two weeks.

"Detail for the Pennsylvania detachment:

"Sub[altern].	Serg't.	Drum.	R[ank] and File.
1	0	1	9

"At a garrison court martial, of which Captain [Isaac] Craig was president.— Matthias Ward and David Fitzgibbons, corporals in Captain [Samuel] Brady's company, were tried for attempting to murder Indian Moses, a Delaware. The court are of opinion that the evidence against them does not amount to positive proof, and therefore acquit them of the charge. The general agrees with the court in opinion that no positive proof has been made against them, but thinks the circumstances are strong and pointed, and he cannot help lamenting that any person who bears the name of a soldier should be so destitute of humanity or the manly virtues necessary to stamp the profession as to do or say anything even to create a suspicion of so base an act. Matthias Ward and David Fitzgibbons are to be released from their confinement after this order shall have been read at the head of the troops of the garrison, they being present.

"At the same court, John Cupps, soldier in Captain [John] Clark's company, was tried for leaving his guard. The prisoner pleads guilty to the charge. The court finds him guilty of a breach of the 4th article, 12th section of the articles of war, and sentence him to receive one hundred lashes on his bare back by the drummer of the garrison. The general being determined not to let crimes of so heinous a nature escape punishment, approves the sentence, and orders it to be put in execution at retreat-beating this afternoon.

V.—IRVINE TO WASHINGTON.

PHILADELPHIA, *February* 7, 1782.

Sir: — The present strength of the garrison at Fort Pitt is two hundred and thirty. At least thirty of these are unfit for field duty, and several even garrison duty. From this number detachments are made to garrison Forts McIntosh and Wheeling, the first distant thirty miles, the latter eighty. Fort Pitt is in a bad state for defense; Fort McIntosh pretty easily repaired. If Fort Pitt were in the best state, the work is too extensive for less than a garrison of at least four hundred and fifty men to make a tolerable defense. Fort McIntosh would take one hundred and fifty to defend it properly, and be able to send patrolling parties towards Wheeling.

Wheeling should have twenty-five or thirty men, and an equal number at some intermediate post. From Fort Pitt to

---

"At the same court William Straphan, soldier in Captain Brady's company, was tried for insolence to Lieutenant Crawford, to which charge he pleads guilty. The court sentence him to fifty lashes. The general approves the sentence; but at the particular request of Lieutenant Crawford, is pleased to remit the punishment of William Straphan, who is to ask Lieutenant Crawford's pardon at the head of the corps to which he belongs, after which he is to be released.

"At the same court Samuel McCord and John Britain, soldiers in the 7th Virginia regiment, were tried for being concerned in killing a cow, the property of John Ferry. The court acquit them of the charge. Samuel McCord and John Britain are to be released from their confinement. John Lockhart, [confined] on suspicion of killing a cow, is to be immediately released."

"FORT PITT, *January* 12, 1782.
"After Orders.

"The punishment ordered to be inflicted on John Cupps is to be postponed till to-morrow at troop-beating, and also reading the sentence to Ward and Fitzgibbons. The other prisoners are to be released immediately."

"FORT PITT, *January* 14, 1782.
"General Orders.

"As soon as the principal evidence [witness], David Tate, arrives, a court martial will assemble for the trial of Mr. John Johnson, forage master. Colonel Gibson will preside."

the Laurel Hill,[1] northwards, it would take two hundred men in actual service from the first of April to the last of October to guard that quarter from the incursions of the savages. By this arrangement, it would take nine hundred and fifty men to act on the defensive the whole of the summer season. The number of militia in Washington county is said to be two thousand; in Westmoreland, one thousand. The inhabitants are dispirited, and talk much of making their escape early in the spring to the east side of the mountain, unless they see a prospect of support.

The Indians have all left us, except ten men,[2] and, by the best accounts [the hostile tribes beyond the Ohio], are preparing to make a stroke in the spring, either against General Clark, at the rapids [Louisville, Ky.], or Fort Pitt, which, my informant could not with certainty say, but was positive one or the other was intended. I am apprehensive, from the steps taken by the commandant at Detroit, that something serious is intended. First, thirteen nations of Indians have been treated with in the beginning of November; at the conclusion, they were directed to keep themselves compact, and ready to assemble on short notice. Secondly, the Moravians are carried into

---

[1] The Laurel Hill is a mountainous range in the southwestern part of Pennsylvania, to the eastward of Pittsburgh, and having a northerly and southerly trend. At the Youghiogheny river, going north, it becomes Chestnut Ridge, and the range east of it receives the name of Laurel Hill.

[2] These Indians were friendly Delawares. The Delaware tribe, located upon the Tuscarawas and Muskingum rivers, in the present state of Ohio, had, for a considerable time after the commencement of the revolution, remained neutral. Finally, the nation became an ally of the Americans. British influence, however, and the inability of the United States to carry out treaty stipulations, subsequently alienated, as already related, a large portion from American interests, resulting in their taking up the hatchet against the border in the spring of 1781. To punish the Delawares, Colonel Daniel Brodhead, commanding at Fort Pitt, marched, in April of that year, against Coshocton, their principal village, the site of the present town of that name, the county seat of Coshocton county, Ohio. His expedition, as previously shown (Introduction, p. 51), was successful. The hostile Delawares were driven from the valleys of the Tuscarawas and Muskingum, except a few who still adhered to the Americans. These returned with Brodhead to Fort Pitt; and the "ten men" mentioned by Irvine were a portion of this party.

captivity, and strictly watched, and threatened with severe punishment if they should attempt to give us information of their movements.[1] Thirdly, part of five nations are assembled at Sandusky. The Shawanese and Ottawas have settled nearer Detroit than formerly. There is no magazine of provision laid in at any of our posts to hold out a siege; ammunition exhausted; no craft to transport materials for repairing the fort or to keep up a communication with Fort McIntosh or Wheeling or to supply these posts with provision or stores in case of exigence.[2]

[1] Before the commencement of the revolution, some Moravian Indians, as they were called, moved from the Susquehanna under the guidance of two Moravian missionaries, to the banks of the Tuscarawas river, in what is now the eastern part of the state of Ohio. These Indians soon received an accession to their numbers by the arrival from Beaver river, Pennsylvania, of more "converts." Two villages were built upon the eastern bank of the stream upon territory set apart for them by the Delaware Indians. Up to the beginning of hostilities between the colonies and the mother country, the Tuscarawas mission was, most of the time, in a prosperous condition, under the lead of David Zeisberger, with several assistants. During the revolutionary contest, down to the summer of 1781, the missionaries held a position, outwardly, of strict neutrality between the contending parties, though, in reality, they were secret and most valuable correspondents of the American commanders at Fort Pitt. A confession of this fact, made by two prisoners to the British and their Indian allies, caused the breaking up of the mission in September, 1781, by a force of western Indians, assisted by a few whites, and the transporting of all the Moravian Indians and missionaries westward to the Sandusky river, in the northwestern part of what is now the state of Ohio. (See Introduction, p. 60.) Here, as Irvine says, they were strictly watched. At the time of the breaking up of the mission, there were three villages, all within what is now Tuscarawas county, Ohio. The most northern was New Schœnbrunn, on the west bank of the Tuscarawas; the middle one was known as Gnadenhuetten, situated on the east bank of the river; while the lower one, on the west side of the stream, was called Salem.

[2] Irvine had previously "briefed" this portion of his letter as follows: "Washington county is said to have two thousand fighting men. They could furnish one-third — equal to seven hundred; the remaining three hundred from Westmoreland, and out of that number two hundred volunteer horse.

"Westmoreland robbed of its best men by Lochry's defeat; the generality of the people on the out-frontiers preparing to quit their habitations.

"The fort at Pitt in no repair, and at best not tenable.

"The garrison weak — too weak to defend Fort Pitt, much less Fort McIntosh.

To carry on an expedition against Detroit would take two thousand men, to give a tolerable certainty of success; the time would be three months, and the best season to march from Fort Pitt, the 1st of August. Then the waters are low; morasses and soft, rich meadows dried up; by land totally preferable to any part by water, the enemy having entire command of the lake with armed vessels; the navigation of rivers uncertain; besides, the number of boats, and waste of time, would make it more expensive than land carriage.[1] Pack-horses to carry provision would be better and more certain than wagons; but, as a road must be cut for artillery, the ammunition and military stores would be transported with greater facility and more safety in wagons. One thousand horses would carry flour for two thousand men for three months. Beef must be driven on foot. Twenty-five wagons would carry military stores sufficient for the train, which should consist of two twelve-pounders, two sixes, one three-pounder, one eight-inch howitzer and one royal.

At least one-half should be regular troops. If it is necessary to keep half the number of troops to act on the defensive that it will to act offensively, and three months are sufficient to complete the expedition, then the only difference in the expense will be transportation of provision and stores; as acting on the defensive, seven months will be the least, and the same quantity of provision will be consumed and ammunition wasted. If we act offensively it will draw the whole attention of

---

"If you quit Pitt and possess McIntosh, all communication with the inhabitants may easily be cut off. If you relinquish McIntosh altogether, the enemy will make a place of arms of it, and Pitt will not be tenable with any numbers.

"The soldiery undisciplined.

"Not a sufficiency of provisions laid in, nor to be laid in, for a siege.

"No water craft to keep up a communication between Pitt and McIntosh, and to supply the latter in an exigency with stores and provisions.

"Ammunition exhausted."

[1] The reader is referred to the opinion of Col. Alexander Lowrey, as given in a letter written to Irvine by George Gibson, February 5, 1782, (Appendix M,) as to the impracticability of marching in the spring for Detroit, from Fort Pitt.

the enemy to their own defense, by which our settlements will have peace; and such of the militia as do not go on the expedition will have time to raise crops. On the contrary, continual alarms will keep them from these necessary duties. The garrison at Detroit is three hundred regular troops, the militia (Canadians), from seven hundred to one thousand; the number of Indians that could assemble in ten days' notice, to a certain point, about one thousand.[1]

Query. Should we be able to take Detroit, shall we hold it? If not, what advantage will the bare reduction of the place be of, if immediately evacuated?

Answer. The reduction of Detroit in the fall of the year will prevent an intercourse with the western Indians for a whole year, as it would be late in the succeeding summer before the British could reëstablish themselves, during which time we might either open a trade with such savages as would ask for peace; or, by frequently penetrating into, and establishing posts in their country, oblige them to retire to such a distance as would put it out of their power to harass the back inhabitants. It would be attended with great expense and vast risk to support a garrison at Detroit, as long as the British possess the lower part of Canada, and have the command of Lake Erie.

The present garrison is too weak to repair the fort [that is, Fort Pitt], and perform other necessary duties; no cash to pay artificers; the troops in bad temper for want of pay;[2]

---

[1] A memorandum of Irvine is as follows:

"THE ENEMY'S FORCE IN DETROIT.

Regular troops	300
Refugees at *Roche de Bout* [on the Maumee]	70
Militia at the largest computation	1,000
	1,370

Thirteen nations of Indians mustered in April, 1780, 1,150 warriors."

[2] That General Irvine was not unmindful of the suffering of the garrison he had left at Fort Pitt, and that he continued to make every exertion to relieve their wants, is evident from the following extract from the proceedings of the supreme executive council of Pennsylvania:

"In Council. Philadelphia, Friday, March 1, 1782.

' . . . General Irvine attended in council and represented that there was too much reason to fear a revolt of the troops stationed at Fort Pitt

under very bad discipline; too long in one station, as they have formed such connections as make them tenacious of the rights of citizens, while they at the same time retain all the vices common to a soldiery. What is contained in the foregoing report is all that occurs to my memory at present necessary to trouble your excellency with.

VI.— WASHINGTON TO IRVINE.

PHILADELPHIA, *March* 8, 1782.[1]

INSTRUCTIONS.

Sir:— You will proceed with all convenient despatch to Fort Pitt, the object of your command, and you will take such measures for the security of that post and for the defense of the western frontier, as your continental force, combined with the militia of the neighboring country, will admit. Under present appearances and circumstances, I can promise no further addition to your regular force than a proportion of recruits[2] for the Virginia and Pennsylvania regiments, which are already upon the western station; consequently offensive operations, except upon a small scale, cannot just now be brought into contemplation. You may, however, still continue to

---

from the want of pay, that application had been made to the superintendent of finance [Robert Morris] for the purpose of obtaining money for paying the said troops, and that he had returned for answer, 'he could not think of making a partial pay of the troops.'

• "The council considering the great importance of preserving a force on the frontiers for the protection of the inhabitants, were of opinion that measures should be immediately taken for satisfying the said troops; and thereupon "*Ordered*, That Mr. Vice President [James Potter]. Mr. [Christopher] Hays, Mr. [Dorsey] Pentecost and Doctor [Joseph] Gardner be a committee for conferring with a committee of the general assembly on the situation of the frontier defense, if the honorable house shall think proper to appoint such a committee."

[1] For the sake of convenience and uniformity, the date of this letter (or, rather, of these instructions) is transferred from the conclusion to the commencement. In the original, the ending is in these words: "Given at Headquarters, at Philadelphia, the 8th of March, 1782."

[2] For information concerning these recruits,— their number, where stationed, and the proportion to be sent to Fort Pitt, see next letter.

keep yourself informed of the situation of Detroit, and the strength of the enemy at that place.

With respect to the subject of the letters which you have lately received from Colonel Gibson,[1] I can only repeat what I have said to you personally. You must endeavor to convince both officers and men that measures are actually taking to put them upon such a footing with regard to their provisions, clothing, and pay, that it is to be hoped they will ere long have no reason to complain. They will have already found the difference between their past and present mode of obtaining provisions and clothes; and they cannot therefore doubt that the only remaining difficulty, which is on account of pay, will be removed as soon as the financier [Robert Morris] can reap the advantages of the taxes for the current year, which are but just laid, and cannot therefore come yet into use. The officers and men must, upon a moment's reflection, be convinced of the wisdom of applying the public money in hand to procuring victuals and clothes. They cannot be dispensed with even for a day; and when both are assured that certificates of pay, due to the 1st of the present year, will be given with interest, and that pay thenceforward will be more regular and as frequent as the public treasury will admit, they ought to be satisfied.

Should the troops comprising the western garrison be discontented with their situation, and think that they are partially dealt by, you may make them an offer of being relieved and of taking their chance of the emoluments, which they may suppose accrue to those serving with either the northern or southern armies. There may be policy in this offer, because, if I am not mistaken, most of the men who have connections in the upper country, would rather remain there at some disadvantage than be brought away from their families.

You will make such arrangements as shall comport with

---

[1] Colonel John Gibson, it will be remembered, was left in command at Fort Pitt, upon Irvine's departure over the mountains. The letters from Gibson to Irvine have not been found. Their contents, however, may be judged of by consulting Capt. John Finley's letter to Irvine, February 2, 1782 — Appendix M.

the above instructions and the strictest principles of economy, with General Knox[1] and the quartermaster-general respecting military and other stores necessary for the posts under your orders; and you will, I am persuaded, use every means in your power to prevent any waste or embezzlement of them.[2]

VII.—IRVINE TO WASHINGTON.

CARLISLE [Pa.], *March* 17, 1782.

Sir:—The inclosed is the best return[3] that could at present be obtained of the recruits and old soldiers of the Pennsylvania line, actually assembled at this post; exclusive of these, I am informed there are about seventy at Lancaster, who are chiefly for the regiments of cavalry and artillery; but as accurate returns are gone to Colonel [Richard] Humpton,[4] I hope they will reach him before your excellency leaves Philadelphia. Colonel Richard Butler[5] also wrote on this subject previous to my arrival here.

From present appearances, I do not expect that the number will exceed three hundred by the 10th of April, including cavalry, artillery and infantry, after which time I am of opinion

---

[1] Brigadier General Henry Knox. He was in command of the artillery of the main army, at date of the above instructions, and had, in the fall previous, contributed greatly to the successful result at Yorktown.

[2] These instructions were sent to Irvine at Carlisle, Pennsylvania, his home, where he was then tarrying with his family.

[3] Irvine's "return" has not been found.

[4] Richard Humpton was born in Yorkshire, England, about the year 1733. As a captain in the British army, he distinguished himself in the attack on St. Malo. While stationed in the West Indies, he resigned his commission, came to Pennsylvania, and fixed his residence on one of the upper branches of the Susquehanna. He was appointed lieutenant colonel in the Flying Camp, July 16, 1776, from which he was transferred to the colonelcy of the eleventh. At the battle of Brandywine, he had a horse shot under him. He commanded the sixth Pennsylvania in 1781 and 1782, holding that position at the date of the above letter. In 1783, he was at the head of the second regiment, and was the same year breveted a brigadier general. After peace, he settled on a farm, holding, until his death, which occurred the 21st of December, 1804, the office of adjutant general of militia.

[5] For a biographical sketch of Butler, see Appendix M,—Butler to Irvine, March 23, 1782, note.

few will be obtained by the ordinary mode of recruiting; and I think it would be best to call in all the parties, except one officer from each corps. As the cavalry, it seems, have been indulged with leave to enlist for their own corps, particular instructions from your excellency respecting their equipment, and whether they are to march under Colonel Butler, may be necessary. I find that there is a sufficient number of officers, now in the state, belonging to the southern detachment[1] (who came home sick or on furlough) to marshal the recruits to that army, and will direct them all to assemble here, and put themselves under Colonel Butler, until he receives your excellency's orders. Colonel Butler, among other matters, will require your orders for the number to send to Fort Pitt, which, agreeable to the mode proposed by your excellency's instructions to me, should be one-sixth part. Should there be commands for any more field officers of the line,[2] agreeable to the usual mode of doing duty, the colonels now unemployed will stand in rotation — Colonel William Butler,[3] Humpton, Brodhead; but General Hand[4] will doubtless be able to regulate

---

[1] The following extract from a letter to Brigadier General Anthony Wayne, written by Washington on the 8th of April, 1781, will give the reader an idea of what is meant by Irvine, in speaking of the "southern detachment: "The critical situation of our southern affairs and the re-enforcements sent by the enemy to that quarter, urge the necessity of moving as large a proportion of the Pennsylvania line as possible without a moment's loss of time." Wayne, it will be remembered, was one of the brigadiers of that line.

[2] The principal officers, at the above date, in the Pennsylvania line, were, of the infantry regiments, as follow: Arthur St. Clair, major general; Anthony Wayne and William Irvine, brigadier generals; Daniel Brodhead, colonel of the first regiment; Walter Stewart, colonel of the second; Thomas Craig, colonel third regiment; William Butler, lieutenant-colonel commandant fourth regiment; Richard Butler, colonel fifth regiment; Richard Humpton, colonel of the sixth regiment.

[3] William Butler, at that date lieutenant-colonel of the 4th Pennsylvania regiment, was a younger brother of Richard Butler. He was at the head of his regiment during all its active service, its colonel being a prisoner on parole. In October, 1778, he made an excursion into the Indian settlements of Unadilla and Anaquago, which were destroyed. He retired from the lieutenant colonelcy of the 4th Pennsylvania regiment, January, 1783. (For particulars of his military services, see Penn. Arch., second series, vol. X, pp. 484-488.)

[4] See Introduction, p. 22, note 4.

this business. I shall proceed to-morrow to Fort Pitt,[1] consequently cannot take cognizance of any matters in the interior part of the state. I have, however, in the meantime, written to the secretary at war, to prevent delay, giving my opinion that arms and accoutrements should be forwarded here for the recruits, in order that they may be completely ready to move in any direction when they shall receive your excellency's command.

Should anything turn up to put it in your excellency's power to march a detachment to the westward, Col. Richard Butler is well acquainted in that country, and would be an useful officer. However, this is only meant by way of information.

VIII.— WASHINGTON TO IRVINE.

PHILADELPHIA, *March* 22, 1782.

Dear Sir: — You will be pleased to make yourself acquainted as accurately, but with as much secrecy as possible, with the nearest and best route from Fort Pitt to Niagara, whether up the Alleghany river and thence through the woods, or by the river Le Bœuf,[2] and along the side of the lake [Erie]. You will in both cases mention the different distances of land and water transportation. The Indians and traders who have been used to traverse the country above mentioned, must be well acquainted with it. In order to deceive those of whom you inquire, appear to be very solicitous to gain information respecting the distances, etc., to Detroit — the other matter you may converse upon as if curiosity was your only inducement.[3]

[1] Irvine, as will be seen in his next letter to Washington, arrived at Fort Pitt on the 25th of March. It is probable, therefore, that he left Carlisle on the 18th, as he intended when he wrote the above.

[2] By "the river Le Bœuf" is meant French creek, Pennsylvania. At an early day, it was frequently called the river Aux Bœufs, or Beef river. Fort Le Bœuf stood on the north bank of the inlet to Le Bœuf lake, just east of the present Susquehanna and Waterford turnpike, in what is now Erie county, that state.

[3] It is probable that juvenile readers will not see in this paragraph such an

I shall leave town this day to go to the army upon the North river. Your letters to me may be put under care to the secretary at war.

IX.—IRVINE TO WASHINGTON.

FORT PITT, *April* 20, 1782.

Sir: — I arrived here the 25th of March. At that time things were in greater confusion than can well be conceived. The country people were, to all appearance, in a fit of frenzy. About three hundred had just returned from the Moravian towns, where they found about ninety men, women and children [Moravian Indians, usually so stated], all of whom they put to death,[1] it is said, after cool deliberation and considering the matter for three days. The whole were collected into their church and tied when singing hymns.[2] On [after]

---

outgrowth of the story of the cherry tree and little hatchet, as to excite in them raptures of delight; but, to more mature minds, "the end justified the means."

[1] As the killing of these Indians occurred at Gnadenhuetten, the middle village, upon what is now known as the Tuscarawas river, in Tuscarawas county, Ohio, before that time occupied by the Moravian Indians and their teachers, it is usually known as "the Gnadenhuetten affair."

[2] Concerning the expedition to the "Moravian towns"— known in history as " Williamson's expedition," from Col. David Williamson, the one who commanded it — and the investigation which followed, only a brief account in this connection can be given.

Early in 1782, war parties committed sundry depredations upon the border. The first was the killing of John Fink, a young man, near Buchanan fort. The particulars are as follow: "On the 8th of February, 1782, while Henry Fink and his son John were engaged in sledding rails on their farm in the Buchanan settlement, several guns were simultaneously discharged at them, and before John had time to reply to his father's inquiry whether he was hurt, another gun was fired and he fell lifeless. Having unlinked the chain which fastened the horse to the sled, the old man galloped briskly away. He reached his home in safety, and immediately moved his family to the fort."—*Wither's Border Warfare,* pp. 232, 233.

The next maraud was the taking from their homes of Mrs. Robert Wallace and her three children on Raccoon creek, of which the following is an account: " By a gentleman who lately arrived here [Philadelphia] from the westward, we have the following information: that, about the 8th ult., a woman [Mrs. Robert Wallace] and four [three] children were taken prisoners by the Indians,

their return, a party came and attacked a few Delaware Indians, who have yet remained with us, on a small island close by this garrison, killed two who had captains' commissions in

---

25 miles west of Fort Pitt. Happily a heavy snow falling the same night prevented much more mischief, as there were upwards of forty Indian tracks found in the snow next morning. [See, post, p. 318 and note thereto.] This naturally threw the people in the neighborhood into the greatest consternation and will be a means of causing much distress, unless timely relieved. General Irwin [Irvine] is now on his way to Pittsburgh; he will do every thing possible for the assistance of the distressed inhabitants. If the general has money to pay the militia, etc., there is no doubt he will find men enough to keep the Indians at a distance, and to enable the farmers to put in their crops in due season."— *Pennsylvania Packet*, March 30, 1782 (No. 865).

Both of these accounts are referred to in the following: "I am told this day that the Indians have made sundry depredations on the frontiers of this country, during the last open spell of weather, on Raccoon creek and up the Monongahela, I think at a place called Buchanan. I fear this is the beginning of more than usual calamity."— *Thomas Scott to Pres't Moore, from Washington county, February 20, 1782.* (See, also, post, p. 239, note 4, third clause, where these depredations are referred to.) The next raid of the Indian warriors resulted in the capturing of John Carpenter, on Buffalo creek, particulars of which are hereafter given (see, p. 101; p. 239, note 4; p. 241, notes 3 and 4).

These marauds, coming so early in the year, took the borderers by surprise, causing, as we have seen, "the greatest consternation," as no visitations were expected before about the first of April. (Post, p. 341.) The belief was prevalent that "enemy Indians" (that is, warriors — hostile savages) were upon the Tuscarawas (then called the Muskingum), occupying the previously deserted Moravian Indian towns. Thereupon, the lieutenant of Washington county ordered out a number of the militia against them. They assembled upon the bank of the Ohio, intending to cross over to the Mingo bottom on the west side of the river — a point some forty miles by land and seventy-five by water below Pittsburgh. The weather was very cold and stormy and the river high. This discouraged some and they turned back; others, however, succeeded in getting safely to the Indian side of the Ohio. The militia marched under command of Col. David Williamson, of the third battalion of his county. Upon reaching the Tuscarawas, a considerable number of *Moravian* Indians were found — men, women and children; all of whom were taken prisoners except two, who were killed as the town — Gnadenhuetten — was reached. Subsequently, the whole were put to death, two boys only escaping. It is said that, with the killed, were, also, some "enemy Indians." Such, in a word, was the origin, progress and result of Williamson's expedition. The first reference to it published, was the following: "Philadelphia, April 6. A very important advantage has lately been gained over our savage enemies on the frontiers of this state, by a party of

our service, and several others; the remainder effected their escape into the fort, except two who ran to the woods, and have not since been heard of. There was an officer's guard

---

the back county militia. We hope to give particulars in our next."—*Pennsylvania Packet*, April 9, 1782 (No. 868).

But how was it that these "Moravians" had returned to the Tuscarawas after the breaking up of the missionary establishments there, as already explained (ante, p. 60)? The answer is this: Impelled by a scarcity of provisions, about 150 men, women and children, having received permission from the Wyandots upon the Sandusky, started for their old homes where there was plenty of corn still standing left ungathered of the last year's growth. Reaching the valley they pursued their labors until captured, as just mentioned, by the Washington county militia under Col. Williamson.

Some time after the return of the militia, an inquiry into the "Gnadenhuetten affair" was ordered by Pennsylvania and Virginia, at the request of congress;—the steps taken and what the results were, are hereafter mentioned. All accounts *strictly contemporaneous* that have been found, whether printed or in manuscript, in anywise relating to this expedition, are given in these pages. But, as a discussion of the events which transpired after the militia reached the valley of the Tuscarawas does not come within the scope proposed for this work, none will be entered upon. The following is the first account published of the expedition:

"In a late paper we gave an account that a woman and three children had been carried off by the savages from their habitation near Fort Pitt; and in our paper of the 9th [6th] inst. we mentioned an advantage being gained over those Indians. By a gentleman who arrived here on Saturday last from Washington county we have the following particulars: That on the 17th of Feb. last the wife and three children of one Robert Wallace, an inhabitant on Raccoon creek (during his absence from home), were carried off by a party of Indians. Mr. Wallace, on his return home in the evening, finding his wife and children gone, his house broke up, the furniture destroyed, his cattle shot and laying dead about in the yard, immediately alarmed the neighbors, and a party was raised that night, who set out early the next morning; but unfortunately a snow fell, which prevented their following, and they were obliged to return. About this time, a certain John Carpenter was taken prisoner from the waters of Buffalo creek in said county, and another party had fired at a man, whom they missed, and he escaped from them. These different parties of Indians, striking the settlements so early in the season, greatly alarmed the people, and but too plainly evinced their determination to harass the frontiers, and nothing could save them but a quick and spirited exertion. They therefore came to a determination to extirpate the aggressors and, if possible, to recover the people that had been carried off; and having received intelligence from a person who was taken prisoner last fall (but had made his escape and come home a few days before), that the Indian towns on the Muskingum had not moved as they had been told, a number of men properly provided, collected and rendezvoused on the Ohio, opposite the Mingo Bot-

on the island at the same time, but he either did not do his duty or his men connived at the thing; which, I am not yet able to ascertain. This last outrage was committed the day before I arrived; nothing of this nature has been attempted since.[1]

tom, with a design to surprise the above towns. The weather was very cold and stormy, the river high and no boats or canoes to transport them across. These difficulties discouraged some, but 160 determined to persevere, and they swam the river, in doing of which some of their horses perished with the severity of the cold. When they got over, officers were chosen, and they proceeded to the towns on the Muskingum, where the Indians had collected a large quantity of provisions to supply their war parties. They arrived at the town in the night, undiscovered, attacked the Indians in their cabins, and so completely surprised them that they killed and scalped upwards of ninety (but few making their escape), about forty of which were warriors, the rest old men, women and children. About eighty horses fell into their hands, which they loaded with the plunder, the greatest part furs and skins, and returned to the Ohio, without the loss of one man, and at the place where they chose their officers they held a vendue. And in order to prevent the inhabitants from bidding against the adventurers, they divided the spoil equally between officers and men, first reimbursing those who had lost their horses in swimming the river. [In the foregoing, "fall" should doubtless be "February."]

"The person above mentioned to have escaped from the enemy says, that he was taken by six Indians, two of which called themselves Moravians, and spoke good Dutch, and were the most severe and ill-natured to him. He was taken to the above towns, and from thence four of the above Indians set out with him for St. Duskie. The second day of their march, in the morning, he was sent out for the horses when he left them; and, being a good woodsman, came off clear and got to Fort Pitt. [This was Carpenter: see p. 243, note.]

"While at Muskingum the two Moravian Indians learnt him an Indian song, which they frequently made him sing, by way of insult, and afterward interpreted to him in obscene language; and he left them at Muskingum where they staid, in order to go out with the next party against our settlements.

"Our informant further says, that last Thursday two weeks, upwards of 300 men, properly equipped on horseback, set out for St. Duskie. It is hoped they will succeed in their expedition, and hereby secure themselves from the future encroaches of the savages."—*Pennsylvania Packet*, April 16, 1782 (No. 872).

[1] The borderers who committed "this last outrage" were not the same organized party that took part in the "Gnadenhuetten affair," as the language of Irvine might be construed to mean. The killing was done on Smoky, or Killbuck's Island, since gone. The following will be found of interest as relating to the transactions:

"And before this time a party had come from the Chartiers, a settlement south of the Monongahela, in the neighborhood of this town [Pittsburgh], and

A number of wrong-headed men had conceived an opinion that Colonel Gibson was a friend to Indians, and that he must be killed also. These transactions, added to the then mutinous disposition of the regular troops, had nearly brought on the loss of this whole country. I am confident, if this post was evacuated, the bounds of Canada would be extended to the Laurel Hill in a few weeks. I have the pleasure, however, to inform your excellency that things now wear a more favorable aspect. The troops are again reduced to obedience,[1] and I

---

had attacked some friendly Indians on the island in the Ohio (Killbuck's Island), under the protection of the garrison, and had killed several, and amongst them some that had been of essential service to the whites, in expeditions against Indian towns, and on scouting parties in case of attacks upon the settlements. One to whom the whites had given the name of Wilson (Captain Wilson) was much regretted by the garrison."—Loudon's *Indian Wars*, Vol. 1, pp. 54, 55.

The faithful services of the unfortunate Delaware captain just mentioned, had long been appreciated at Fort Pitt, as shown by the following certificate:

"FORT PITT, *November* 18, 1781.

"I certify that in consequence of the faithful service of Captain Wilson (an Indian), as well as to encourage him to be active in future expeditions and detachments, I did, last spring, make him a present of a small black horse, belonging to the United States.

"DANIEL BRODHEAD, Col. 1st P. Reg."

[1] The following communication from the non-commissioned officers and soldiers of the seventh Virginia regiment to General Irvine, written probably soon after his return to Fort Pitt, clearly sets forth their grievances:

"To the Honorable Brigadier General William Irvine, Esq., commanding western department:

"We, the non-commissioned officers and soldiers of the 7th Virginia regiment, having heard the speech your honor made to the troops at this post, do present you with these few lines, as follow:

"We have been at this post almost four years, and have been without pay two years and three months of the time; this undoubtedly your honor must be acquainted with. Your honor likewise saw when you first arrived here in what a deplorable condition we were, for want of clothing, almost naked, several days wanting provisions, in cold, open barracks with little fuel or fire— these extremities made us to utter things much to the prejudice of the character of soldiers; but that thing of murder, mutiny or desertion we abhor and disdain — it never was our real intentions, and we should look upon every one that has had that bad opinion of us to be our enemies. We have always been ready to exert ourselves in the service of our country, but more particularly, on these frontiers, entrusted to our charge. We are too sensible of the troubles and inconveniences (although there is but a handful of regular troops

have had a meeting or convention of the county lieutenants and several field officers, with whom I have made arrangements for defending their frontiers, and who promise to exert themselves in drawing out the militia, agreeably to law, on my requisitions.[1] The few remaining Indians, chiefly women and

---

here) if this post should be evacuated. Though we have been upbraided by the country inhabitants for our fidelity — they calling us fools, cowards and a set of mean fellows for staying without our pay and just dues — yet we think more of our honor than to listen to any advice than what is given to us by our officers.

"It is reported amongst the soldiery that the officers of our regiment and the Indians have received pay; if it is so, we are sorry that the Indians should be paid in preference to us. But this is news we cannot well credit. We are well assured your honor is too much of a soldier's friend.

"We thought it very hard when the depreciation money was paid to the Pennsylvania line and none to the Virginia; and if the Indians have received pay, we think this harder.

"We are very sorry the country is not better able to pay the troops employed in its service; but we must needs know and consider within our breasts, that when the war commenced the country was young and unprepared, and must of consequence be much in debt; but we hope it will overcome all in a short time, to our great joy and satisfaction, and we have no further reason to complain. We have nothing further to add, but remain your honor's most obedient and faithful soldiers of the 7th Virginia regiment."

[1] Notes taken by Irvine at this convention were as follow:

"Arrangement of troops in the western district.

"Forts Pitt and McIntosh garrisoned by regular troops. Westmoreland county to keep in actual service sixty-five men. These are formed into two companies, under the direction of a field officer. They are to be constantly ranging along the frontier (and do not occupy any stationary post) from the Alleghany river to the Laurel Hill.

"Washington county to keep in actual service 160 militia, to range along the Ohio, from Montour's Bottom to Wheeling, thence some distance along the southern line — under two field officers.

"I have not yet been able to draw any from the counties of Virginia, even for their own defense. The lieutenants say, in excuse, that they have not received any instructions for this purpose from government; that they are not able, etc. I have written the governor on this subject."

The foregoing notes were afterward extended, thus:

"Lieutenants and sub-lieutenants and field officers of the several counties west of Laurel Hill assembled at Fort Pitt, Friday, April 5, 1782, at the request of General Irvine, to concert measures for the defense of the frontiers. [There were] present for Westmoreland [county] Colonel [Edward] Cook, lieutenant; Colonel [Charles] Campbell, sub-lieutenant. For Washington [county], Colonel [George] Vallandigham, sub-lieutenant; Colonel [David]

children, are exceedingly troublesome to us, as they dare not stir out of the fort; not one of the warriors will even venture on a reconnoitering party. I think they would be better in some more interior part of the country, where they could be both cheaper fed and clothed. Besides, it is not only incon-

Williamson, Colonel [Thomas] Crooks, Maj. [James] Carmichael, James Edgar, Esq. For Ohio county, Colonel [David] Shepherd, lieutenant; Major [Samuel] McColloch.

"The aforenamed persons unanimously agreed that the best mode of defending the frontier will be to keep flying bodies of men constantly on the frontier, marching to and from the different places; three companies for Washington and two for Westmoreland. Forts Pitt and McIntosh to be garrisoned by regular troops. Westmoreland county is to keep in actual service sixty-five men; these are to be formed into two companies, under the direction of a field officer. They are to be constantly ranging along the frontier, and not occupy any stationary post, from the Alleghany river to the Laurel Hill. Washington county is to keep in actual service 160 militia, to range along the Ohio, from Montour's Bottom to Wheeling; thence some distance along the southern line, under two field officers. I have not been able to draw any from the counties of Virginia, even for their own defense. The lieutenants say, in excuse, that they have not received any instructions for this purpose from government; that they are not able, etc. I have written the governor [of Virginia] on this subject."

Two weeks after the before-mentioned meeting at Fort Pitt, Irvine issued the following:

"Instructions for Major Scott.

"*Sir:*— Four companies of militia are called out for the purpose of defending the frontier of Washington county. You are to take command of two companies, who are to be kept constantly in motion from Montour's Bottom to Decker's or Mingo Bottom [a station on the east side of the Ohio]. As the whole of this frontier is entrusted to your charge, I have no doubt you will make such arrangements and dispose of these two companies so as best to answer the purpose.

"It will therefore be incumbent on you to visit the companies frequently and see that the men are alert and attentive to duty; but above all, you will dispose of them in such a manner as that very short intervals will take place between the different parties marching and counter-marching. You will direct the officers commanding companies or parties, should they discover signs of an enemy, to alarm not only the other companies and parties, but they are to inform the neighboring settlements, and to be extremely cautious at the same time to guard against false alarms or reports. You will also direct them to send me notice of any material occurrence by express (one of their men), the lower company to that next this way, the officer commanding there to send one of his men — the first to return to his company.

"You will make weekly returns to me of the number of men and officers

venient but improper to have them among the troops, who are, without them, crowded in dirty, bad barracks. I beg your excellency's instructions how to dispose of them. Their chief, Killbuck,[1] has a son and brother at Princeton college, whom he is anxious to see.

Captain [Uriah] Springer,[2] of the Virginia line, marched,

actually on duty under you; and you will direct each captain or officer commanding a company, in the last week of the month, to make out a muster-roll of his company, pointing out the day of the month each man joined, and also if any left him, and what day, noting the cause. This muster-roll must be sworn to by the officer and certified either by Colonel [James] Marshel [lieutenant of Washington county], one of the sub-lieutenants, a justice of the peace, or by you. When so completed it must be transmitted to me. You will likewise compare with the officers their returns of men, the muster-rolls and provision returns, and with them correct any mistakes.

"It is impossible to give instructions so minute but what circumstances may intervene either to make an alteration necessary or something done which is not at first, nor can be, foreseen. A great deal must therefore depend on your own judgment and prudence. Among other matters, however, you will take particular care that no unnecessary waste of public property of any kind is committed.

"Given under my hand at Fort Pitt, April 18, 1782.

"WM. IRVINE, B. Gen'l.

"To MAJOR SCOTT, Washington Militia."

[1] John Killbuck, Jr., an hereditary chief of the Delawares, son of John Killbuck and grandson of King Newcomer, was born in 1737, near the Lehigh Water-Gap, in Northampton county, Pennsylvania. Early in the revolution he was at the head of the council of his nation, upon the Tuscarawas and Muskingum, in what is now the eastern part of Ohio. He remained true to the United States after a large part of the Delawares went over to the British Indians, putting himself and a small number of followers under the protection of the commander at Fort Pitt, where he was at the date of the above letter. Some years afterward he joined the Moravian Indians, being named, at baptism, William Henry. Subsequent to the victory of Wayne over the allied nations, he was urged by his tribe, which had become reconciled to him, to resume his office of chief, but this he declined. He died in 1811, in Goshen, Tuscarawas county, Ohio.

[2] "Died, at his residence near Connellsville, Fayette county, Pennsylvania, on Thursday, 21st ult., Major Uriah Springer in the 73d year of his age. His father's family was amongst the first settlers west of the Alleghany mountains before the revolutionary war. Uriah, at the age of nineteen, was commissioned by Lord Dunmore, then governor of Virginia, an ensign in a company of rangers organized for the protection of this frontier, and was the first officer that commanded the stockade at this place [Brownsville] in 1774,

some time since, with three Indians and as many white men, towards Sandusky, for the purpose of gaining intelligence; but the Indians proved too timid for him to venture to go all the way. He of course returned, without being able to accomplish anything. I thought it too great a risk, but it was by his request, and that of the Indians, who were very solicitous.¹ It was proved on one of the party, named [John] Eels,

commonly called Redstone Old Fort. He was subsequently commissioned in the Virginia line and served as captain in the army of the revolution until the end of the war. After the peace of 1783, he continued in the small military establishment of the country and served in several campaigns against the Indians. After the treaty of Greenville, by Gen. Wayne, he retired to his family. During the late war [1812-15], although advanced in years, he was appointed brigade inspector and served a winter campaign on the northwestern frontier. He has left an aged widow [Sarah], daughter of the late Colonel [William] Crawford [and formerly a widow of William Harrison], who [both] fell a sacrifice to Indian barbarity at [not far from] Upper Sandusky."—*Brownsville* [Pa.] *Observer*, 1826, cited in Hazard's Register, Vol. I, p. 416.

¹ General Irvine's instructions to Captain Springer were as follow:

"FORT PITT, *April* 12, 1782.

"*Sir:*— The nature of the service you go on is such that confining you by particular instructions might defeat the purpose intended.

"In general, however, I wish you to consider your command (on account of the smallness of your number) more in the light of an reconnoitering party than calculated for offensive operations against the enemy. You will, therefore, proceed with great caution; your route first, for thirty or forty miles, inclining up the Alleghany river. Should you not discover any traces of an enemy on that route, you will proceed toward Sandusky, where you will use every prudent means in your power to gain intellegence of the strength and intentions of the enemy; whether any white men are among them; and whether they are regular British troops or refugees, or as they call themselves — "rangers;" who now commands at Detroit; what the strength of the garrison is; or whether they have received, this spring, re-enforcements of men, provisions, etc. The best mode, I think, of obtaining this end would, if practicable, be by capturing one or more white men.

"If you should discover such symptoms of bodies of the enemy being on their march, so large as to endanger any of our posts, or the settlements on the frontier of this country, you will either return or send me notice by one of your party whom you can confide in, as in your judgment the case may merit. Should you meet a smaller party than your own, I make no doubt you will give a good account of them, provided you can effect it without risk of frustrating your principal object. Given under my hand at Fort Pitt, this 12th day of April, 1782.   "WM. IRVINE, B. Gen'l.

"Captain URIAH SPRINGER."

that he intended betraying Captain Springer, and all the party, into the hands of the enemy. I directed a board of officers to inquire into his conduct, who were of opinion he should suffer death. I ordered him executed; he was shot on the 12th instant, seemingly much to the satisfaction of the other Indians.[1]

Civil authority is by no means properly established in this country, which I doubt not proceeds in some degree from inattention in the executives of Virginia and Pennsylvania. Not

---

[1] John Eels, the Indian, was executed for "an intention of making his escape to, and joining the enemy, and also trying to prevail on others to do the same," as will appear from the following record of General Irvine's orders inquiring into the guilt or innocence of the accused:

"FORT PITT, *April* 11, 1782.

"A board of officers will assemble immediately at Colonel Gibson's quarters to inquire into and report their opinion to the general whether John Eels, an Indian, is guilty of an intention of making his escape to and joining the enemy and of his trying to prevail on others to do the same; and also to give their opinion in case he did go, whether it was or not evidently his intention to discover to the enemy the design of the party under Captain Springer, of which he was to have been one. Colonel Gibson [is to be] president; Lieutenant-Colonels Wuibert and [Stephen] Bayard, Major [Isaac] Craig and Captain [John] Clark, members. If the board is of opinion John Eels is guilty, they will please to mention in their report what punishment should be inflicted."

"FORT PITT, *April* 12, 1782.

"At a board of officers of which Colonel Gibson is president,— to inquire and report their opinion whether John Eels, an Indian, is guilty of an intention of making his escape to and joining the enemy, and trying to prevail on others to do the same, and also to report their opinion whether it was not evidently his intention to discover to the enemy the design of the party under Captain Springer, of which he was to have been one; the board reports to General Irvine as their opinion that John Eels, an Indian, is guilty of an intention of making his escape to and joining the enemy, and also trying to prevail on others to do the same. The board further reports it is their opinion that if he had gone off, Captain Springer and the party under his command must have been discovered and the design of the party. The board is of opinion that John Eels ought to suffer death as a traitor. The general confirms the opinion of the board, and directs that John Eels, an Indian, shall be shot to death this day at one o'clock at the foot of the gallows on the bank of the Alleghany river. The major of brigade will see this order executed. A party consisting of one subaltern, one sergeant, one corporal, one drum, one fife, and twenty rank and file, properly armed and accoutred will attend at the execution,— to parade at half past twelve."

running the boundary line is, I think, a proof of this, which is at present an excuse for neglects of duty of all kinds, for at least twenty miles on each side of the line. More evils will arise from this neglect, than people are aware of. Emigrations and new states are much talked of. Advertisements are set up, announcing a day to assemble at Wheeling, for all who wish to become members of a new state on the Muskingum. A certain Mr. J———[1] is at the head of this party; he is ambitious, restless, and some say disaffected. Most people, however, agree he is open to corruption; he has been in England since the commencement of the present war. Should these people actually emigrate, they must be either entirely cut off, or immediately take protection from the British, which I fear is the real design of some of the party, though I think a great majority have no other views than to acquire lands. As I apprehended taking cognizance of these matters would come best from the civil authority, I have written to the governors of Virginia[2] and Pennsylvania[3] on the subject, which I should not have done, till I had first acquainted your excellency thereof, but for this consideration, namely, that the 20th of May is the day appointed for the emigrants to rendezvous; consequently, a representation from you would be too late, in case the states should think proper to take measures to prevent them.[4] I am much embarrassed by the scanty and irregular supply of provision. I intend to write to Mr. Morris on this head.

X.—Irvine to Washington.

Fort Pitt, *May* 2, 1782.

Sir:—I did not receive your excellency's letter of the 22d of March until two days ago. I shall observe your directions respecting the roads, etc., leading to Niagara. As yet, I have

---

[1] This blank is filled, in the original, with the surname of the leader of the new state scheme. I have thought best to omit it.

[2] See Irvine to Governor Benjamin Harrison, April 20, 1782, Appendix H.

[3] See Irvine to Wm. Moore, May 9, 1782, Appendix G.

[4] Gen. Irvine had previously mentioned the subject of emigration to the Indian country and of a new state, to the governor of Pennsylvania, in a letter dated December 3, 1781 (see first letter of Appendix G); and, in reply, that official suggested a plan to divert the attention of the people from the scheme.

not been able to fall in with any person who has even a tolerable knowledge of them. There has been very little communication with that quarter since last war; and few of the people who were then employed are now living. Several of the officers who went with Colonel Brodhead, in 1779, up the Alleghany, say they marched about one hundred and seventy miles to a creek called Connewango.[1] They were informed that it took its rise about thirty miles from that place in a small lake; that, at this lake, the waters divided; other small streams run out of it towards Niagara, and that thence the country was pretty level and neither rivers nor morasses of any consequence in the way. As far as Colonel Brodhead went, it was almost impassable either by water or land. The greater part of the way along the river was one continued defile. They went in September: at that season, it was with difficulty they got up some small canoes, and this on the main branch of the Alleghany. They took pack-horses along. Some say they were at one time not more than thirty miles from General Sullivan's line of march, or rather I believe the extreme point he marched to.[2]

I have it in report from officers and others, that French creek from Venango[3] to Le Bœuf[4] is so full of timber that

[1] This creek rises on the line between Chautauqua and Cattaraugus counties, New York, flowing along their boundaries, then curving across the southeast part of the first mentioned county, receiving, meanwhile, Cassadaga creek and the outlet of Chautauqua lake; pursuing thence a south course, to the Alleghany river, which it enters at Warren, in Warren county, Pennsylvania. An army moving from Pittsburgh up the Alleghany to the mouth of the Connewango, thence up that creek and through Chautauqua lake to its head, would have had a portage of only eight miles to Lake Erie.

[2] See Introduction, pp. 42–44, where particulars of Brodhead's expedition are recited. Major-General John Sullivan in August, 1779, commanded an expedition against the Indians of the Six Nations from Tioga Point on the Susquehanna. He laid waste their settlements, especially upon the Genessee river, which was the farthest point to the westward reached by him. On his way out, he inflicted a severe defeat upon the Indians under Brant and the Tories under Sir John Johnson, at what is now Newtown, New York.

[3] Venango was the site of a French fort which was destroyed in August, 1759. It was afterward occupied as a British post, the garrison being murdered by the savages in 1763. It was at or near the present town of Franklin, Pennsylvania.

[4] The French burned Fort Le Bœuf at the same time Venango was destroyed.

it would take great labor to clear it, and that, in the summer season, it is a very small stream. From Le Bœuf to Presq' Isle,[1] the old bridged road is entirely rotten and under water. These gentlemen assert that it would be easier to make a new road than to repair the old one. By these accounts, it appears almost impracticable to march any but light troops, without artillery or heavy stores or baggage. I will, however, continue to get the best accounts in my power and transmit them to your excellency.

In my letter of the 20th of April, I mentioned that the troops were reduced to obedience. Since that time, desertions have been numerous, and though nothing like general mutiny has taken place, yet several individuals have behaved in the most daring and atrocious manner, two of whom are now under sentence and shall be executed to-morrow, which I hope will check these proceedings.[2]

I have sent several officers mounted after the deserters, who

---

This post, like Fort Venango, was afterward occupied by the British, but the garrison was cut off in Pontiac's war, except one officer and seven men.

[1] There was a fort at Presq' Isle erected by the French, but destroyed by them when Fort Le Bœuf and Fort Venango were burned. It was a British post subsequently; but its garrison was cut off in the war of 1763, by the savages. It occupied the site of the present city of Erie, Pennsylvania.

[2] The following is from the MS. orderly book of General Irvine:

"*April* 30, 1782.

"After Orders.

"At a general court martial, of which Colonel Gibson is president — John Phillips and Thomas Steed, soldiers in the seventh Virginia regiment, were tried for mutiny and disobedience of orders in opposing by violence and making an actual attack upon their officer [Lieutenant Samuel Bryson of the second Pennsylvania regiment] when in the execution of his office [as commandant of Fort McIntosh], by which a post of consequence belonging to the United States was in danger of falling into the hands of the enemy. The court having duly considered the evidence and the defense of the prisoners are of opinion that they are guilty of a breach of the third and fifth articles of the second section of the articles of war, and do sentence the prisoners Thomas Steed and John Phillips to suffer death.

"It is always with pain that General Irvine orders any punishment inflicted on a soldier; but, in crimes of so heinous a nature, which, in their tendency, endanger not only the safety and lives of some thousands of the good people of this part of the country, but ultimately might be attended with ruinous consequences to the cause and interests of the United States — on these principles, the general would think himself criminal were he to suffer men so

take different routes; and I sent by them circular letters to the county lieutenants and militia officers, by which means I hope to have some of them taken.[1]

XI.— IRVINE TO WASHINGTON.

FORT PITT, *May* 7, 1782.

Sir:— Since my last letter to your excellency, [Lieutenant] Colonel Wuibert,[2] the engineer, has been continually teasing me

---

evidently guilty of the highest crimes which a soldier can possibly be guilty of, to escape. The general approves and confirms the sentence."

The following petition was sent to Irvine by the condemned soldiers:

"*To the Honorable Brigadier General William Irvine, Esq., commanding the Western Department:*

"*Honorable Sir:*— Your poor, unhappy, dying petitioners humbly beg of your honor's goodness to spare our lives for the space of some time longer that we may make our peace with the Almighty God, we being in a bad situation to resign our mortality and change it to immortality. We hope and beg of your honor to grant us this request in this our last dying moments, and we hope the Almighty God will ever bless and requite your goodness hereafter.

"From your honor's sincere, penitent and humble petitioners,

"JOHN PHILLIPS,
"THOMAS STEED.

"FORT PITT GUARD HOUSE, *April* 30, 1782."

The following additional orders were issued by Irvine:

"FORT PITT, *May* 2, 1782.

"John Phillips and Thomas Steed, soldiers in the seventh Virginia regiment under sentence of death, are to be executed to-morrow forenoon between the hours of eleven and twelve o'clock."

"FORT PITT, *May* 3, 1782.

"Morning Orders.

"One subaltern, one sergeant, one corporal, one drum and all the fifers in the garrison, twenty rank and file, properly armed and accoutred will attend the execution. Captain Brady as officer of the day will see it performed. The party will parade at eleven o'clock.

"Notwithstanding the general is determined to keep up subordination and strict discipline, he nevertheless has feelings of humanity. Though constrained by duty to make examples in full expectation that the example shown this day will evince this, and in compassion for his youth, in hopes he may be reclaimed and yet make a good soldier and citizen, the general is pleased to pardon John Phillips." Steed was executed. (See Appendix M,— Bryson to Irvine, April 29, 1782.)

[1] See Marshel to Irvine, May 1, 1782, Appendix J.

[2] A lieutenant-colonel in the continental corps of engineers.

for leave to go to Philadelphia, which I informed him I could by no means grant without your permission. If your excellency has nothing more in view for him in this quarter than barely to superintend repairing the works at this post, his attendance may, without injury to the service, be dispensed with, especially as Major [Isaac] Craig of artillery is on the spot, whose knowledge of the executive part I have more dependence on than Colonel Wuibert's. This accompanies his letter on the subject.[1]

XII.— IRVINE TO WASHINGTON.

FORT PITT, *May* 21, 1782.

Sir:— A number of the principal people of this country made application to me, about two weeks since, for my consent to their collecting a body of volunteers to go against Sandusky,[2] which I agreed to on these express conditions: that they did not mean to extend their settlements,[3] nor had anything in view but to harass the enemy, with an intention to protect the frontier, and that any conquests they might make should be in behalf and for the United States; that they would be governed by military laws as militia; that they must collect such numbers as might probably be successful; and, lastly, that they would equip themselves and victual at their own expense. They are accordingly assembling this day at the Mingo Bottom,[4] all on horseback, with thirty days' pro-

---

[1] The desired permission was granted. See Appendix M,— Wuibert to Irvine, no date.

[2] By "Sandusky," General Irvine meant a Wyandot Indian town and settlement upon the Sandusky river in what is now Wyandot county, Ohio. It was then a rendezvous for British Indians of the northwest, preparatory to their striking the western borders of Pennsylvania and Virginia. Near by were located Shawanese, Mingoes, Monseys, Delawares and Ottawas. It was in easy communication with Detroit, headquarters of British troops for the whole country west of Niagara.

[3] Irvine here refers to the scheme of some of the borderers of making new settlements upon the western or Indian side of the Ohio river, especially upon the Muskingum — the "new state scheme."

[4] The Mingo Bottom here spoken of by General Irvine was on the east side of the Ohio, a little above but across the river from what is now Steubenville,

visions. They have asked of me only a few flints and a small supply of powder.

As they will elect their officers, I have taken some pains to get Colonel [William] Crawford[1] appointed to com-

---

Ohio. There was also a Mingo bottom below, on the west side of the Ohio (ante, p. 100, note), at which place the volunteers, after crossing the river, were to choose their officers and march thence directly for Sandusky.

[1] William Crawford was born in Westmoreland county, Virginia; his family, however, early moved to Frederick county, beyond the Blue Ridge. Here he married Hannah Vance. He was about ten years older than Washington, but was taught by the latter the art of surveying. Up until the commencement of the old French war, Crawford's principal duties were such as usually appertain to a farmer's life. In 1755, he forsook the compass and the plow for

"The pomp and circumstance of glorious war,"

receiving from the governor of Virginia a commission as ensign. He was first employed in garrison duty, or as a scout upon the frontiers. In 1758, he marched with the Virginia troops under Washington to Fort Duquesne, which post was reached and occupied in November. Crawford remained in the service, being promoted first to a lieutenantcy — afterwards commissioned as captain. At the close of hostilities, he returned to his home and resumed his labors of farmer and surveyor. In Pontiac's war, which followed the seven years' war, he took an active part, doing efficient service in protecting the frontiers from savage incursions.

While in the Virginia army, Crawford became familiar with the country watered by the Monongahela and its branches. He had, indeed, become enamored of the trans-Alleghany region, and resolved, at some future day to make it his home. The time had now arrived to put his resolution into practical effect. Early, therefore, in the summer of 1765, he reached the Youghiogheny river, where, at a place then known as "Stewart's Crossings," in what is now Fayette county, Pennsylvania, he chose his future residence; moving his family, consisting of his wife and three children, over the mountains in the spring of 1766. With Crawford, at this place, the next year, Washington opened a correspondence, which continued until near the time of the above letter. (See *The Washington-Crawford Letters*. Cincinnati: Robert Clarke & Co.)

Among the first employments of Crawford after his removal, besides farming, were surveying and trading with the Indians. During the year 1770, he was appointed one of the justices of the peace for his county, Cumberland, then the most westerly county of Pennsylvania. In the autumn of that year, he received a visit, at his humble cabin upon the Youghiogheny, from Washington, who was then on a tour down the Ohio. Crawford accompanied his friend to the Great Kanawha, the party returning to "Stewart's Crossings" late in November, whence Washington leisurely made his way back to Mt. Vernon.

mand, and hope he will be. He left me yesterday on his way down to the place of rendezvous. He does not wish to go with a smaller number than four hundred; whether this

In March, 1771, Bedford county having been formed from that part of Cumberland including the home of Crawford, he was appointed by Governor Penn one of the justices of the peace for the new county; and in 1773, the erection of Westmoreland from Bedford taking in his residence, he was commissioned one of the "justices of the court of general quarter sessions of the peace, and of the county court of common pleas" for that county. As he was first named on the list of justices, he became by courtesy and usage the president judge of Westmoreland — the first to hold that office in the county. He was, the same year, appointed surveyor for the Ohio company, by the college of William and Mary.

In 1773, Lord Dunmore, the governor of Virginia, paid a visit to Crawford at his house upon the Youghiogheny, the occasion being turned to profitable account by both parties; by the Earl, in getting reliable information of desirable lands; by Crawford, in obtaining promises for patents for such as he had sought out and surveyed. The next year — 1774 — occurred "Lord Dunmore's war," a conflict between the Virginians on the one side, and the Shawanese and Mingoes, principally, on the other. In this contest, Crawford was a prominent actor; — first as captain of a company on a scouting expedition, building, subsequently, along with Major Angus McDonald, a fort at the present site of Wheeling; afterwards as major in command of troops belonging to the division of the army which descended the Ohio to the mouth of Hocking river, in what is now the state of Ohio. The only fighting done in the Indian country after the bloody battle of Point Pleasant on the tenth of October, was by a detachment under Crawford, in what is now Franklin county, Ohio, where he surprised and destroyed two Mingo villages, securing some prisoners as well as considerable amount of plunder, and rescuing two white captives.

The interest taken by Crawford in this war operated greatly to prejudice his Pennsylvania friends against him; for, among them, the conflict had been an exceedingly unpopular one. Crawford, who, at first had sided with Pennsylvania in the boundary controversy subsisting between it and Virginia, now took part with the latter; so he was ousted from all offices held by him under authority of the former province. In December, 1774, he had been commissioned by Dunmore a justice of the peace and a justice of oyer and terminer for the county of Augusta, the court to be held at Fort Dunmore (Pittsburgh). He did not qualify, however, for these offices until after he had been superseded in those held by him under Pennsylvania authority. Augusta county, as claimed by Virginia, included Crawford's home upon the Youghiogheny; afterwards the district of West Augusta was formed out of that county. Crawford's place of residence then fell in that district. Finally, when Yohogania county was established, his cabin came within its boundaries and so remained until Virginia relinquished her claim to southwestern Pennsylvania.

number will assemble I cannot say. He pressed me
for some officers. I have sent with him Lieutenant

> Crawford not only took office under Virginia, but he became an active
> partisan in extending the jurisdiction of his native province over the disputed
> territory. Some of his acts were doubtless oppressive, though he soon atoned
> for them in his patriotic course upon the breaking out of the revolution.
> The partisan feeling in his breast immediately gave place to the noble one of
> patriotism. He struck hands with Pennsylvanians in the cause of liberty.
> In 1776, Crawford entered the revolutionary service as lieutenant-colonel of
> the fifth Virginia regiment — William Peachy, colonel. He remained with
> his regiment until called to the command of the seventh in place of William
> Dangerfield, resigned. Afterwards, being assigned to the duty of raising a
> new regiment — the thirteenth Virginia — he resigned his command of the
> seventh. His time thus far had been spent east of the mountains; but now,
> late in the year, he returned to his home; as the thirteenth — "West Augusta
> regiment" — was to be raised west of the Alleghanies. In August, 1777,
> with about two hundred of his new levies, Crawford joined the main army
> under Washington, who was then near Philadelphia. He rendered efficient
> service in the preliminary movements which resulted in the battle of Brandy-
> wine, and in that contest not only took an active and prominent part, but
> came near being captured. He was also, it seems, in the battle of German-
> town. Just before this, General Joseph Reed wrote Washington that he had
> "Colonel Crawford" with him, "a very good officer."
> Late in 1777, Crawford returned to his home, having been sent to the west
> by Washington to take a command under Brigadier-General Edward Hand.
> The commander-in-chief, in writing to the board of war on the twenty-third
> of the following May, spoke of Crawford as "a brave and active officer."
> His being ordered to the western department, lost him the command of the
> thirteenth Virginia and his place in the continental line, which Washington,
> although he regretted the circumstance, could not get restored to him. Under
> Brigadier-General Lachlan McIntosh, who succeeded Hand in August, 1778,
> at Pittsburgh, Crawford took command of the militia of the western counties
> of Virginia and had in charge the building of Fort McIntosh at what is now
> Beaver, in Beaver county, Pennsylvania. He marched with that officer into
> the Indian country in November, in command of a brigade, and was present
> at the building in December of Fort Laurens, upon the west bank of the
> Tuscarawas river, in what is now Tuscarawas county, Ohio. He returned
> soon after to his home, and, in the spring, again marched under McIntosh
> into the wilderness to the relief of that post. Crawford had now but few
> prospects before him in a military way, nevertheless he lost no opportunity,
> when called upon, in serving his country; for he still held his commission as
> colonel, and continued to hold it until his death.
> Notwithstanding the time spent by him in the army, Crawford found leis-
> ure to fill several positions of honor and trust to which he had been called by
> his fellow citizens at home. In November, 1776, he was appointed deputy-
> surveyor of Yohogania county, and sat at intervals in 1777 and the following

Rose,[1] my aid-de-camp, a very vigilant, active, brave young gentleman, well acquainted with service; and a surgeon.[2]

year as one of its judges. In 1778, he was one of the commissioners for adjusting and settling the boundary line between Yohogania and Ohio counties, Virginia; and, in 1779, was commissioned as surveyor of his county, continuing in that office to the time of his death, which occurred before the return of the expedition spoken of by Irvine as assembling at Mingo Bottom. (See last note to letter XIV, following.)

[1] John Rose, familiarly known at Fort Pitt as "Major Rose." His real name was Gustavus H. de Rosenthal, or, more correctly, Henri Gustave Rosenthal. He was a Russian nobleman. Becoming involved in a duel, he killed his antagonist and fled his country. He arrived in America in the early days of the revolution; made his appearance in the cantonments of the patriot army, and gave his name as simply John Rose, studiously concealing his rank and birth. He was a fine looking young man; spoke the French language, and having taken a brief course of surgery, in Baltimore, was appointed subsequently surgeon of the seventh Pennsylvania regiment, having previously done duty as a surgeon's mate in one of the army hospitals. At length, owing to a feeling of jealousy on the part of some of the American officers against foreigners, he resigned his position in his regiment and volunteered as surgeon in the navy of the United States, only to be taken prisoner by the British and carried to New York. After being exchanged, he returned to Pennsylvania; was made ensign in a company of the fourth regiment of that state, and lieutenant on the first of April, 1781. On the eighth of July following, General Irvine appointed him his aid. Upon Irvine taking command at Pittsburgh, he brought with him Lieutenant Rose; and, as above stated, when the expedition against Sandusky was planned, he was permitted by the general to accompany it. He still kept his secret, but Irvine had had strong suspicions ever since first making his acquaintance, of his exalted character and station. He remained in the west until the return of the general from Fort Pitt, occasionally, as duty required, visiting Carlisle and Philadelphia. The troops under Irvine were paid off, for the last time, by him. In the fall of 1783, he was secretary to the council of censors of Pennsylvania, and in the spring of 1784 sailed for Europe, to return to his home, having received complete immunity from his sovereign. Before leaving he revealed his real history to Irvine. Pennsylvania rewarded him in land for his valuable services. Afterward, he held an office of honor under the emperor of Russia. He was born in 1753 and died in Rival June 26, 1829.

[2] Dr. John Knight. He was born in Scotland in the year 1751. He subsequently, in England, gained some knowledge of medicine. He came to America in 1773. Migrating to the west, he enlisted in 1776, as a private in the thirteenth Virginia regiment,—afterward the ninth, but at date of the above letter, the seventh, of which John Gibson was colonel. Soon after enlisting, he was made sergeant, and was in the battles of Brandywine, Germantown, and other engagements. On the ninth of August, 1778, he was appointed surgeon's mate of his regiment, which office he held at the time he

These two are all I could venture to spare. Several were solicitous for my going, but I did not think myself at liberty, consistent with the spirit of your excellency's instructions; nor are we in such a situation that I could take a single continental soldier along, particularly as the volunteers are all mounted. If their number exceeds three hundred, I am of opinion they may succeed, as their march will be so rapid they will probably in a great degree effect a surprise.

I cannot find a man in this country who has a tolerable knowledge of the road to Niagara. There are numbers who are acquainted to the heads of Alleghany; thence, I think, the people of the state of New York are better acquainted than any this way.

P. S.— The volunteers have sent requesting my instructions [1]

---

was spared by Irvine to go upon the Sandusky expedition. He continued his duties as surgeon's mate until the close of the war. On the fourteenth of October, 1784, he married Polly Stephenson, daughter of Richard Stephenson, half brother of Colonel William Crawford. He subsequently moved to Shelby county, Kentucky, where he died on the twelfth of March, 1838, the father of ten children.

[1] The "instructions" afterward sent by Irvine were as follow:

"FORT PITT, *May* 14, 1782.

"To the officer who will be appointed to command a detachment of volunteer militia, on an expedition against the Indian town at or near Sandusky.

"SIR — When an officer is detached, though he may have general instructions, yet much must depend on his own prudence. On such an expedition as the present, where a variety of unexpected events may take place, I think it would be vain to attempt being particular. In general, however, it is incumbent on me to give such ideas as I think may be of use.

"The object of your command is to destroy with fire and sword (if practicable) the Indian town and settlements at Sandusky, by which we hope to give ease and safety to the inhabitants of this country; but if impracticable, then you will doubtless perform such other services in your power as will, in their consequences, have a tendency to answer this great end.

"Previous to taking up your line of march, it will be highly expedient that all matters respecting rank or command should be well determined and clearly understood, as far at least as first, second and third. This precaution, in case of accident or misfortune, may be of great importance. Indeed, I think whatever rank or grade may be fixed on to have commands, their relative rank should be determined. And as it is indispensably necessary that subordination and discipline should be kept up, the whole ought to understand that, notwithstanding they are volunteers, yet by this tour they are to get credit for it in their tours of militia duty; and that for this and other

(which I will send) for the officer who may be appointed to command. The troops behave remarkably well since a few examples have been made.[1]

good reasons, they must, while out on this duty, consider themselves, to all intents, subject to the militia law and regulations for the government of the militia when in actual service.

"Your best chance for success will be, if possible, to effect a *surprise;* and though this will be difficult, yet, by forced and rapid marches, it may, in a great degree, be accomplished. I am clearly of opinion that you should regulate your last day's march so as to reach the town about dawn of day or a little before, and that the march of this day should be as long as can well be performed.

"I need scarcely mention to so virtuous and disinterested a set of men as you will have the honor to command, that, though the main object at present is for the purposes above set forth, viz., the protection of this country, yet you are to consider yourselves as acting in behalf and for the interest of the United States. That, of course, it will be incumbent on you especially who will have the command, and on every individual, to act, in every instance, in such a manner as will reflect honor on, and add reputation to, the American arms — always having in view the law of arms, of nations, or independent states.

"Should any prisoners, British, or in the service or pay of Britain or their allies, fall into your hands — if it should prove inconvenient for you to bring them off. you will, nevertheless, take special care to liberate them on parole, in such a manner as to insure liberty for an equal number of our people in their hands. There are individuals, however, who, I think should be brought off at all events, should the fortune of war throw them into your hands. I mean such as have deserted to the enemy since the declaration of independence.

"On your return, whatever your success may be, you will please to make report to me. I very sincerely wish you success; and am, dear sir, your obedient servant, W. IRVINE."

The following extract from a letter written by Irvine to John Lyon more than seventeen years after these instructions were sent, is confirmatory of them:

"Colonel Crawford was on the continental establishment of the Virginia line. The troops under his command, at the time he fell, were volunteer militia, part Virginians and part Pennsylvanians, and a few continental officers whom I sent to assist him. All the troops both regulars and militia in that quarter, were at that time under my orders. In looking over my instructions to the officer who should be appointed to command that expedition — the volunteers were allowed to chose one, and they elected Colonel Crawford — I find he was enjoined to regulate rank of officers before he took up his line of march, and to impress on their minds that the whole must from the moment they marched be in all respects subject to the rules and articles of war for the regular troops."

[1] Of the "few examples" referred to by Irvine, one was that of Thomas Steed of the seventh Virginia regiment, executed, it will be remembered, on

XIII.— WASHINGTON TO IRVINE.

HEAD QUARTERS, NEWBURGH, *May* 22, 1782.

Sir: — I have been favored with your two letters of the 20th of April and 2nd of May and am much obliged by your vigilance and attention.

An extract respecting the removing and supporting of the Indians, I have transmitted to the secretary at war, and desired him to take measures for the relief and comfort of those distressed wretches.[1]

---

the 3d of May. He and the Indian, John Eells, were the only ones who had, up to the date of the above letter, suffered capitally (although a number had received "one hundred lashes well laid on ") since Irvine's advent in the western department. Another, however, soon followed; — James Gordon being executed on the 26th day of May, for repeated desertion and re-enlisting. He was tried by court martial on the 24th of the month for the offenses just named, and found guilty of the first and third articles of the sixth section of the articles of war and sentenced to death. The order approving the sentence read as follows:

"Gordon, from his own confession, appears to have made a trade of enlisting and deserting. So great an offender has no right to expect pardon. Such daring perjury and such willful and premeditated determination, so often repeated (to desert and re-enlist), are proofs of the most hardened and abandoned villainy. The general confirms the sentence."

The warrant for his execution was in these words:

"*Sir:* — James Gordon having repeatedly transgressed the laws of God and his country, and though he has long escaped justice, he has at length been caught, tried and sentenced to die, by a general court martial; which sentence has been approved. You will, therefore, cause him to be taken from the place of his present confinement, to the usual place of execution, this day, immediately after troop beating, where he is to be shot to death; for so doing, this shall be your warrant.

"Given under my hand at Fort Pitt, May 26th, 1782.

"WM. IRVINE, B. Gen'l.

"To Capt. BENJ. BIGGS, officer of the day."

The final order for his execution was as follows:

"Morning orders, May 26, 1782. James Gordon, under sentence, is to be shot this morning at troop beating. A detachment properly armed and accoutred will attend the execution. All the troops will be marched by corps to the place without arms. Captain Biggs, as officer of the day, will see this order executed. The new guard will remain with their corps until after the execution."

[1] For directions of the secretary at war concerning these Indians, see Appendix B,—Lincoln to Irvine, May 30, 1782.

Any further particulars you can obtain of the route to Niagara and its practicability, you will please to forward to me as early as possible; the more minute and circumstantial, the better.

XIV.—IRVINE TO WASHINGTON.

FORT PITT, *June* 16, 1782.

Sir: — In my letter of the 21st of May, I mentioned to your excellency that a body of volunteer militia was assembling at the Mingo Bottom to go against Sandusky. The inclosed letters, one from Colonel Williamson,[1] second in command, and the other from Lieutenant Rose,[2] my aid-de-camp, contain all the particulars of this transaction which have yet come to my knowledge. I am of opinion had they reached the place in seven days, instead of ten, which might have been done, especially as they were chiefly mounted, they would have succeeded. They should also have pushed the advantage evidently gained at the commencement of the action. They failed in another point which they had my advice and indeed positive orders for, namely, to make the last day's march as long as possible and attack the place in the night. But they halted in the evening within nine miles and fired their rifles at seven in the morning before they marched. These people now seem convinced that they cannot perform as much by themselves as they sometime since thought they could. Perhaps it is right that they should put more dependence on regular troops. I am sorry I have not more to afford them assistance.[3]

---

[1] See Williamson to Irvine, June 13, 1782, Appendix M.

[2] Rose to Irvine, June 13, 1782, Appendix M.

[3] This letter differs somewhat from the copy retained by Irvine, which reads as follows:

"FORT PITT, *June* 16, 1782.

"*Sir:* — In my letter of the 21st of May, I mentioned to your excellency that a body of volunteer militia were assembling at the Mingo Bottom to go against Sandusky. The inclosed letters, one from Colonel Williamson, second in command, and the other from Lieutenant Rose, my aid-de-camp, contain all the particulars of this transaction which have yet come to my knowledge. I am of opinion the cause of their failure was owing to the slowness of the

XV.— IRVINE TO WASHINGTON.

FORT PITT, *July* 1, 1782.

Sir: — Your excellency's letter of the 22d May did not come to hand till yesterday. The 17th of June I sent one active, intelligent white man with an Indian to explore the country towards Niagara. I shall take the earliest oppor-

march, and not pushing the advantage they had evidently gained at their first commencing the action. They were ten days on the march, when it might have been performed in seven, particularly as they were chiefly mounted; my advice was to attack the *town in the night*, but instead thereof they halted within ten miles in the evening and did not take up their line of march till seven in the morning. These people now seem convinced that they cannot perform as much by themselves as they sometime since thought they could; perhaps it is right that they should put more dependence on regular troops. I am sorry I have not more to afford them assistance." [Immediately following the word "knowledge," in this copy, are the following words, which have a line drawn over them: "Dr. Knight, mentioned in Mr. Rose's letter, is one of the regimental surgeons of this garrison, whom I spared to Colonel Crawford and is also missing."]

Of the volunteers who went upon the expedition against Sandusky, about two-thirds were from Washington county; the residue, except a few from Ohio county, Virginia, were from Westmoreland. The final rendezvous was at the Mingo bottom on the west side of the Ohio river, where, on the twenty-fourth day of May, four hundred and eighty, finally, congregated. They distributed themselves into eighteen companies. The general officers elected were: For colonel-commandant, Colonel Wm. Crawford; for four field majors (to rank in the order named), David Williamson, Thomas Gaddis, John McClelland, and James Brenton; for brigade major, Daniel Leet. Dr. John Knight went as surgeon; John Rose, as aid. The guides were Thomas Nicholson, John Slover and Jonathan Zane.

The volunteers began their march the next day for Sandusky. All were mounted. On the fourth of June, the enemy were encountered a short distance north of what is now Upper Sandusky, Ohio. They numbered something over three hundred, consisting of about two hundred savages —Wyandots, Delawares, Mingoes, and "Lake Indians"— and a company of rangers from Detroit, under command of Captain William Caldwell. A battle ensued, with the advantage on the side of the Americans. The loss of the enemy was five kil'ed — four Indians and a ranger — and eleven wounded, including Capt. Caldwell; the American loss was five killed and nineteen wounded. The next day (June 5th) the enemy were re-enforced by not less than one hundred and forty Shawanese and by a small detachment of rangers. Crawford called a council of war and it was decided to retreat.

The return march began soon after dark of the same day, but was attended

tunity after their return of communicating their observations to your excellency, if they appear useful. The inclosed copy of a letter to General Lincoln [1] will inform your excellency of the wishes of the inhabitants of this country, and also of my mode of treating their applications.[2] I hope that, as well as

---

with considerable confusion. The main portion of the retreating army was joined the next morning by some straggling parties, so that the whole numbered about three hundred; and the retreat was continued. Quite a number were missing; among them were Col. Crawford, Dr. Knight, Major McClelland and John Slover. In the afternoon (June 6th), the volunteers were overtaken by a force of the enemy, in what is now Crawford county, Ohio, and a warm engagement ensued; but the pursurers were driven off, with a loss to the Americans of three killed and eight wounded. The expedition finally reached the Mingo bottom on their return; and re-crossed the Ohio on the thirteenth of June, having with them a number of their wounded. The next day the army disbanded. The entire loss was about fifty men. Of those taken by the enemy, only two escaped — Dr. Knight and John Slover. A number of the captured were tomahawked; but Colonel Crawford, his son-in-law (Wm. Harrison), and a few others (all of whom had been made prisoners), were tortured at the stake. The first named perished miserably, amidst the most terrible suffering, on the eleventh of June, in what is now Wyandot county, Ohio. (For an extended narrative of this campaign, see "An Historical Account of the Expedition against Sandusky, under Col. William Crawford, in 1782; With Biographical Sketches, Personal Reminiscences, and Descriptions of Interesting Localities; Including, also, Details of the Disastrous Retreat, the Barbarities of the Savages, and the Awful Death of Crawford by Torture.")

[1] See Irvine to Lincoln, 1 July, 1782, Appendix B.

[2] The following account describes the incipient steps taken for another expedition against Sandusky: —

"Whereas our friends and countrymen [under Col. Wm. Crawford] hath unfortunately miscarried on a late expedition against the Indians [at Sandusky], which was intended for the good of our country in general,— we conceive we should be lost to our entire and common interest as well as the memory of our fellow citizens if we did not use our utmost exertion to retaliate and convince our enemies that that brave handful of men has not fallen unregarded.

"To carry this expedition with apparent success, we propose acting under General Irvine upon it; and as the continental troops under his command cannot be supplied with the necessary quantity of provisions through the usual channels, we do hereby pledge our faith and honor to furnish the provision and the necessary horses for its transportation — annexed to our names respectively, for such regular officers and soldiers as General Irvine may command on said expedition, exclusive of the necessary quantity for our own subsistence; and do acknowledge to be bound by the same ties to render any

this way of communication, will meet your excellency's approbation. I would not presume to go on any account without your excellency's express orders, or at least permission, did I not conceive that before the day appointed for rendezvousing, I will receive information if any movements are intended this way, this campaign, as, by that time, it will be full late enough to undertake anything more than on a small partisan way. By the best accounts I can obtain, we may lay out our accounts to have to fight the Shawanese, Delawares, Wyandots, Mingoes and Monseys; in all, about five hundred. They are all settled in a line from lower Sandusky near Lake Erie, to the heads of the Miami, not more than seventy miles from the two extremes. Upper Sandusky lies near the center. If all these could be beat at once, it would certainly nearly, if not entirely, put an end to the Indian war in this quarter. Should this be the case, it would be much best that some continental troops should be convened for a variety of reasons, which I need not trouble your excellency with an explanation of at present; which are inducements for me to think of going with so few regulars. In a few weeks, I hope to have the fort in a tolerable state of defense against small arms, so that there will be less risk in being absent a few weeks with some of the best of the troops than heretofore.[1]

---

personal service, or furnish a man to do the same without fee or reward except government at their own convenient time think proper to reimburse us.

"Given under our hands at Stewart's Crossings [now New Haven, Fayette county, Pennsylvania], this 22d day of June, 1782.

"[Under the head of personal service there is then put down forty-one men; under rations of flour, thirty-one hundred and eighty; under rations of meat, fifteen hundred and five; horses, ten.] This subscription is made from two companies only. There is reason to believe there will be more subscribed from them.

"ROBERT BEALL,
"THOMAS MOORE,
"Captains of Militia."

[See Appendix K,— Irvine to Cook, June 26, 1782.]

[1] De Peyster, commanding at Detroit, early received intelligence of the contemplated movement of General Irvine and informed General Haldimand, his superior, of the fact. The latter, in a letter to Sir Guy Carleton, on the 28th of July, said:—

"A letter from Major De Peyster says that General Irvine is to take the

XVI.—WASHINGTON TO IRVINE.

HEADQUARTERS, NEWBURGH, *July* 10, 1782.

Sir:—I have been favored with your letter of the 16th of June, apprising me of the disaster that befell the militia at Sandusky. I am persuaded you did everything in your power to insure them success. I cannot but regret the misfortune, and more especially for the loss of Colonel Crawford, for whom I had a very great regard.[1]

---

route of Tuscarawas; a party of militia, the Shawanese country; and Colonel Clark, the Wabash, with artillery. That this expedition, though given out as intended against the Indian villages, he is informed is, in reality, a concerted plan against Detroit, which Mr. Irvine brought with him from congress. In consequence of this intelligence, I have re-enforced the upper country with about two hundred men."

[1] Washington and Crawford were intimate friends. The latter was captured by the Delaware Indians, upon the Sandusky expedition, and suffered, as already explained, a horrible death by torture. When Irvine wrote his letter to Washington, of the 16th of June, to which the above was an answer, he had not learned the terrible details; all that he knew was that Crawford was missing; and this he learned from the two letters which he inclosed. By referring to his letter of the 16th of June (ante, p. 121), it will be seen, that he does not mention the subject himself.

The following certificate written by Irvine while major general of Pennsylvania militia is not only confirmatory of the fact of his having aided and abetted the expedition against Sandusky, but of the good conduct of Major Rose and Colonel Crawford; also, of the "particular esteem and high regard" in which the last mentioned was held by Washington:

"I certify that Colonel William Crawford, of the Virginia line of continental troops, was elected by a body of volunteers, partly of Virginia and partly of Pennsylvania, in the year 1782, during the time I commanded at Fort Pitt and country around, to the supreme command of said volunteers who meant to march into the Indian country, to attack several of their towns (of this election I was informed by the county lieutenants, both of Virginia and Pennsylvania, west of the Alleghany mountains, not only by verbal communication of some of them, but by written report of all of them), in which they requested my approbation and aid. I accordingly furnished the party with some ammunition and sent written instructions to the commandant (ante, p. 118, note 1); and I also sent two continental officers to assist Col. Crawford: Major Rose, my own aid-de-camp, and Doctor Knight, surgeon of one of the regiments under my command. (Ante, p. 117.) After the defeat, the second in command [Col. David Williamson] then informed me that it was owing, in a great degree, to the bravery and good conduct of Major

XVII.— IRVINE TO WASHINGTON.

FORT PITT, *July* 11, 1782.

Sir: — Dr. Knight, a surgeon I sent with Colonel Crawford, returned the 4th instant to this place.[1] He brings an account of the melancholy fate of poor Crawford. The day after the main body retreated, the colonel, doctor, and nine others, were overtaken, about thirty miles from the field of action, by a body of Indians, to whom they surrendered. They were taken back to Sandusky, where they all, except the doctor, were put to death. The unfortunate colonel, in particular, was burned and tortured in every manner they could invent.

The doctor, after being a spectator of this distressing scene was sent, under guard of one Indian, to the Shawanese town, where he was told he would share the same fate the next day; but fortunately found an opportunity of demolishing the fellow, and making his escape.[2] The doctor adds, that a certain Simon Girty, who was formerly in our service, and deserted with McKee, and is now said to have a commission in the British service, was present at torturing Colonel Craw-

---

Rose that the retreat was so well effected. I mention these circumstances in order to refute a report that the colonel undertook this expedition without my consent, and in other respects disobeyed my orders.

"I also certify that no officer of the party ever reported to me any misconduct of the colonel's, and that I never reported any to my superiors against him; so far from it, that I find in my correspondence with the commander-in-chief (General Washington) that he lamented the misfortune of Col. Crawford's death extremely, as he was an officer for whom he had a particular esteem and high regard.   WILLIAM IRVINE, Major General."

[1] "I saw Knight on his being brought into the garrison at Pittsburgh; he was weak and scarcely able to articulate. When he began to be able to speak a little, his Scottish dialect was much broader than it had been when I knew him before. This I remarked as usual with persons in a fever, or sick; they return to the vernacular tongue of their early years. It was three weeks before he was able to give anything like a continued account of his sufferings.— H. H. Brackenridge, in Loudon's *Indian Wars*, Vol. I, pp. VIII, IX.

[2] Owing to the peculiar wording of this sentence, it might be inferred that Knight escaped *after* his arrival at the Shawanese villages; but such was not the fact. He was told at the place where Crawford was burned that he would suffer the same fate; and he made his escape on his way to the towns where he was to be tortured.

ford,[1] and that he, the doctor, was informed by an Indian, that a British captain commands at Sandusky; that he believes he was present, also, but is not certain; but says he saw a person there who was dressed and who appeared like a British officer.[2] He also says the colonel begged of Girty to shoot him [Crawford], but he paid no regard to the request.

A certain [John] Slover has also come in yesterday, who was under sentence at the Shawanese town. He says a Mr. William Harrison, son-in-law to Colonel Crawford, was quartered and burned. Both he and the doctor say they were assured, by sundry Indians they formerly knew, that not a single soul should in future escape torture; and gave, as a reason for this conduct, the Moravian affair. A number of people inform me, that Colonel Crawford ought to be considered as a continental officer, and are of opinion retaliation should take place. These, however, are such facts as I have been able to get. Dr. Knight is a man of undoubted veracity.[3]

---

[1] Simon Girty was born on an island in the Susquehanna river in the then province of Pennsylvania, and when a boy was captured by the savages, and adopted by the Seneca tribe of Indians. He afterward returned to the settlements, locating at Pittsburgh. He fled to the enemy across the Ohio, along with Alexander McKee and others, in the spring of 1778. (See Introduction, p. 17.) Arriving at Detroit, he was engaged in the Indian department and sent back into the Ohio wilderness with his headquarters among the Wyandots, upon the Sandusky river. He immediately entered upon a career of savage ferocity against the border settlements of Pennsylvania, Virginia and Kentucky. He was in the battle of the 4th of June, 1782, between the volunteers under Crawford and the enemy, taking part with the latter, and was present, as above stated, at the torturing of the unfortunate colonel. He had no commission in the British service. He and Crawford were well acquainted.

[2] The person dressed like a British officer and referred to as having been seen by Knight at the torture, was Captain Matthew Elliott, a renegade royalist, who, as previously mentioned, escaped to the enemy along with Alex. McKee and Simon Girty, from the vicinity of Pittsburgh, in 1778. Knight had not made his acquaintance at the latter place. Elliott, however, did not have command at Sandusky; it was Captain William Caldwell. The latter was not present at the burning of Colonel Crawford. Elliott belonged to the British Indian department. (See Appendix M,— Rose to Irvine, June 13, 1782, note.)

[3] John Slover was, as already noticed, one of the guides to the expedition against Sandusky. He was captured by the savages, but succeeded in making his escape. His narrative was soon published, along with that of Dr.

This account has struck the people of this country with a strange mixture of fear and resentment. Their solicitations for making another excursion are increasing daily, and they are actually beginning to prepare for it.

Knight's. Both are to be found in a pamphlet entitled, "Narrative of a late Expedition against the Indians; with an Account of the Barbarous Execution of Col. Crawford; and the Wonderful Escape of Dr. Knight and John Slover, from Captivity, in 1782. Philadelphia: Printed by Francis Bailey, in Market street. M,DCC,LXXIII." An X, in the date, is accidentally omitted. Copies of the original edition of this work are exceedingly rare. Subsequent but imperfect editions have been published from time to time. A small one was printed in Nashville, in 1843, and there is a Cincinnati reprint of this, in 1867. The narratives have also been printed, with more or less variations from the original, in several border histories.

In the original pamphlet is the following address by the publisher — Francis Bailey, printer of the *Freeman's Journal*, in Philadelphia:

"To the Public: The two following narratives [Knight's and Slover's] were transmitted for publication, in September last [1782]; but shortly afterward the letters from Sir Guy Carlton, to his excellency, General Washington, informing that the savages had received orders to desist from their incursions, gave reason to hope that there would be an end to their barbarities. For this reason, it was not thought necessary to hold up to view what they had heretofore done. But as they still continue their murders on our frontier, these narratives may be serviceable to induce our government to take some effectual steps to chastise and suppress them; as from hence, they will see that the nature of an Indian is fierce and cruel, and that an extirparation of them would be useful to the world, and honorable to those who can effect it."

Immediately following the address is this letter:

"Mr. BAILEY: Enclosed are two narratives, one of Dr. Knight, who acted as surgeon in the expedition under Col. Crawford, the other of John Slover. That of Dr. Knight was written by himself at my request; that of Slover was taken by myself from his mouth as he related it. This man, from his childhood, lived amongst the Indians; though perfectly sensible and intelligent, yet he can not write. The character of Dr. Knight is well known to be that of a good man, of strict veracity, of a calm and deliberate mind, and using no exaggeration in his account of any matter. As a testimony in favor of the veracity of Slover, I thought proper to procure a certificate from the clergyman to whose church he belongs, and which I give below.

"These narratives you will please publish in your useful paper or in any other way you may judge proper. I conceive the publication of them may answer a good end, in showing America what have been the sufferings of some of her citizens by the hands of the Indian allies of Britain. To these narratives, I have subjoined some observations which you may publish or omit, as it may be convenient.
"H. H. BRACKENRIDGE.

"PITTSBURGH, *Aug*. 3, 1782.

XVIII.— WASHINGTON TO IRVINE.

HEAD QUARTERS, *August* 6, 1782.

Sir: — I have to acknowledge the receipt of your two letters of the 1st and 11th of July; the former containing the plan of a proposed expedition, on which you mention you are

---

"(Certificate of the Clergyman.)

" ' I do hereby certify that John Slover has been for many years a regular member of the church under my care, and is worthy of the highest credit.

" ' WILLIAM RENO.'

"(An Episcopalian.)"

Brackenridge, to whom the world is indebted for the narratives of Knight and Slover, was an eminent lawyer and author of Pittsburgh, from 1781 until his death in 1816. The last fifteen years of his life, he was one of the judges of the supreme court of Pennsylvania. He was noted for his talents, learning, and eccentricity. He was the author of "Modern Chivalry," "Incidents of the Whisky Insurrection," and other works. The "observations" he speaks of, in his letter to Mr. Bailey, were printed by the latter, with the narratives of Knight and Slover. They are, as the writer quaintly calls them, "observations with regard to the animals, vulgarly styled Indians." They contain, however, nothing in relation to the expedition against Sandusky.

The narrative of Knight, up to the commencement of the retreat of the army, contains little that is not suppliable from other sources; after that event, however, his account of what he saw and suffered, is exceedingly valuable and complete. He throws no light, of course, upon the retreat of the army; neither does Slover. The narrative of the latter is not as well connected as that of the former; yet, of the general truthfulness of his story, there can be no question. Both narratives, it will be noticed, were written immediately after the return of these men from captivity. There was no printing done in Pittsburgh until the establishment and issuing of the *Pittsburgh Gazette*, in July, 1786; hence, the publication of the pamphlet in Philadelphia.

All the statements have been examined that could be found, made by Knight and Slover after their return, not contained in their printed narratives. Most of these are either in manuscript or in the Philadelphia newspapers of 1782, furnished by western correspondents. From these sources a few additional facts can be obtained, all corroborative, however, of their original statements. Subsequent relations of deserters and of the savages themsleves fully substantiate their authenticity and correctness. "After a treaty or temporary peace had taken place, I saw traders who had been with the Indians at Sandusky and had the same account from the Indians themselves which Knight gave of his escape."— Brackenridge, in Loudon's *Indian Wars*, Vol. I, pp. VIII, IX.

solicited to take the command, and covering a copy of your letter to the secretary at war [1] on that proposition. I have not given you my ideas on this expedition, as the plan, if adopted, must have began its execution before my letter would have reached you. If attempted, I can only give you my good wishes for its success.[2]

---

[1] See Irvine to Lincoln, July 1, 1782, Appendix B.

[2] Irvine, in anticipation of being absent from Fort Pitt upon this expedition, wrote out the following instructions:

I.—IRVINE TO LIEUTENANT COLONEL WUIBERT.

"FORT PITT, *September* 13, 1782.

"*Sir:*—During the time of the excursion I am about to make with part of the troops comprising this garrison and some militia, you will please carefully to examine what further repairs may be indispensably necessary to make on this post; in doing of which, you will calculate with as much accuracy as possible, the quality and quantity of materials and number of artificers and laborers required to complete the work. When this is done, you will please to reconnoiter the ground in the vicinity of the post and determine (in your judgment) the places an enemy will be most likely to approach by. But, in a particular manner, I wish you also to reconnoiter an eminence on the northwest side of the Alleghany, immediately opposite the fort, and fix on the most advantageous spot for erecting either an inclosed redoubt or block house. Of all which, I beg you will have plans made, and estimates also of labor, at my return. As to having any actual work performed, I do not expect it; the troops will be so few, they cannot perform any and do the necessary military duty. Major Craig will command all the troops; and I make no doubt from the good understanding I know you to be on with this gentleman, but your time will pass agreeably.

"I am, sir, your obedient, humble servant,

"WM. IRVINE.

II.—IRVINE TO MAJOR ISAAC CRAIG.

"FORT PITT, *September*, 1782.

"*Sir:*—In my absence (on the intended excursion) the command of this post will devolve on you. Your knowledge of every circumstance relative to the defence of it, and the resources you have to depend on, together with the entire confidence I repose in your prudence, render it unnecessary to trouble you with prolix instructions.

"The advanced season and the precautions I have recently taken (by sending parties up the Alleghany) nearly convince me that you will have little to fear from that quarter; notwithstanding, you must not depend on probabilities, but guard against possibilities. To the westward, we shall doubtless draw all the enemy's attention.

"You are already informed how I intend the militia from Virginia and Pennsylvania are to be employed, unless this post should appear in danger; in

I lament the failure of the former expedition, and am particularly affected with the disastrous fate of Colonel Crawford.[1] No other than the extremest tortures that could be

that case, you will doubtless draw in as many of them as you may judge necessary. If matters remain quiet as late as the 15th of October, the militia from the lower country may be discharged; as their services after that time, I think, will be an unnecessary fatigue on them, and expense to the public.

"In case, however, of an actual investiture of the post, or that circumstances threaten, you will apply to the lieutenants of Westmoreland and Washington counties, whom I will direct before my departure to order men to your relief on your requisition. I am persuaded you have not, under these several circumstances, much to fear, except a surprise; and if the enemy have information of our movements, an enterprising partisan may possibly think it a favorable opportunity, as he may suppose you will be off your guard, depending too much on the effects of our expedition.

"You are well acquainted with the state of the magazine and all the stores, as well as the difficulty and expense attending supplying the post; and you are also too well acquainted with the state of the public finances to make it necessary for me to say much on the score of economy; you know it ought to be extreme. As to the ordinary police or standing orders at the post, you will doubtless adhere to them, except in cases where circumstances may render it indispensably necessary to vary or deviate from.

"*Private.*— I am afraid there are such men in this country who are not too good (in order to favor a scheme of a new *state*) to devise plans to get possession of this post and particularly the stores. You will, therefore, scrupulously guard against their devices — some of which may probably be false alarms to induce you to call in militia, *or rather volunteers*, whom you may have difficulty to get out.

"I am, dear sir, with much regard, your obedient, humble servant,

"WM. IRVINE."

[1] In a letter addressed by Washington to President William Moore, of Pennsylvania, dated July 27, 1782, is this reference to Crawford: "It is with the greatest sorrow and concern that I have learned the melancholy tidings of Col. Crawford's death. He was known to me as an officer of much care and prudence, brave, experienced and active. The manner of his death as given in letters of Gen. Irvine, Col. Gibson, and others, was shocking to me; and I have this day communicated to the honorable, the congress, copies of such papers as I have regarding it."

Col. Crawford, before starting upon the Sandusky expedition, made his will, as follows:

"In the name of God, amen. I, William Crawford, of the county of Westmoreland, and state of Pennsylvania, being in perfect health of body and sound memory, do make, ordain and constitute this my last will and testament, in manner and form following, that is to say: I give and bequeath unto my much beloved wife, Hannah Crawford, all that tract of land whereon

inflicted by savages, I think, could have been expected by those who were unhappy enough to fall into their hands; especially under the present exasperation of their minds, for the treatment given their Moravian friends. For this reason, no persons, I think, should, at this time, submit themselves to fall alive into the hands of the Indians.

I now live, situate, lying and being on the river Youghiogheny, in the county and state aforesaid, during her natural life. I do also give and bequeath unto my said wife one negro man named Dick, and one mulatto man Daniel; also all my household furniture and stock of every kind and nature whatsoever, for and during her natural life, and after the decease of my said wife, the above mentioned negroes, Dick and Daniel, to descend to my loving son, John Crawford, and after his decease, to the heirs of his body lawfully begotten.

"I give and bequeath unto my loving son, John Crawford, and his heirs lawfully begotten, five hundred acres of land to be laid off out of lands located down the river Ohio by me, to be laid off by my executors, reserving to my son the choice of said lands, and also the tract of land whereon I now live at Stewart's Crossings, at the decease of my said wife, Hannah, and at the decease of said son, John Crawford, to descend to his son, William Crawford, and his heirs forever; but if he die without heirs, then and in that case to descend to his next oldest brother. And I do give and bequeath unto Moses Crawford, son of the above said John Crawford, and to his heirs forever, four hundred acres of land, to be laid off out of my lands located down the river Ohio as before mentioned.

"I do give and bequeath unto Richard Crawford, son of the above said John Crawford, and to his heirs forever, four hundred acres of land, out of, and to be laid off as above mentioned. I do give and bequeath unto Anne McCormick, daughter of William and Effe McCormick, four hundred acres of land, to be laid off as above mentioned. Also I do give and bequeath unto Anne Connell, all that tract of land whereon she now lives, lying and being on the north side of Youghiogheny river, about two miles from said river and on Braddock's old road, together with all the stock of every kind whatsoever, and all the household furniture and farming utensils now in her possession, for and during her natural life; and after the said Anne Connell's decease, my will is and I do hereby ordain that the said land, goods and chattels of every kind whatsoever be sold by my executors and the money arising therefrom be equally divided amongst her four children, to-wit: William, James, Nancy and Polly; but nevertheless, in case the said Anne Connell should think it more proper that the two boys, or either of them, the said William or James, should keep the said land, etc., that then and in that case the said lands, goods and chattels of every kind be appraised, and one equal fourth of the said appraisements be paid to the other children as they may arrive at the age by law affixed, or the survivor of them.

" Also, I do give and bequeath unto William Connell, son of the said Anne

XIX.—IRVINE TO WASHINGTON.

FORT PITT, *October* 29, 1782.

Sir:— I would have marched the 20th of September into the Indian country with about eight hundred militia and a small detachment from this post, had I not received letters on the eighteenth [inst.] from the secretary at war[1] and council of Pennsylvania:[2] — the first informing me that General Hazen's regiment[3] was ordered up, and the latter promising men and money to carry the business with effect. As the militia

---

Connell, and his heirs forever, five hundred acres of land located by me down the Ohio river, there being a warrant for that quantity in his name from the land office, Virginia. I also give and bequeath unto James Connell, son of the said Anne Connell, and his heirs forever, five hundred acres of land down the river Ohio, there being a warrant for that quantity in his name, which was also located by me as above mentioned, as soon as they arrive at full age. Also, I do give and bequeath unto Nancy and Polly, daughters of said Anne Connell, six hundred acres of land located by me down the river Ohio, to be equally divided between them by my executors.

"And my will is that after my accounts are adjusted and settled and all my just debts and legacies and bequeaths paid, that all and singular my estate, real and personal, of every kind whatsoever (except a mulatto boy named Martin, which I give to my son John Crawford, and a mulatto girl named Betty, which is to continue with my wife Hannah), be equally divided between my three beloved children, viz.: John Crawford, Effe McCormick and Sarah Harrison, and their heirs forever. And I do will, constitute, and appoint my much beloved wife, Hannah Crawford, my loving brother, John Stephenson, and William Harrison, executrix and executors of this my last will and testament, ratifying and confirming this to be my last will and testament.

"In witness whereof, I have hereunto set my hand and affix my seal this sixteenth day of May, in the year of our Lord one thousand seven hundred and eighty-two.

"W. CRAWFORD. [SEAL.]

"Signed, sealed, published, pronounced and declared by the said William Crawford as his last will and testament in presence of us: Thomas Gist, John Euler, Mary Wright, Nancy McKee."

[1] Lincoln to Irvine, September 7, 1782, Appendix B.

[2] The letter here spoken of as from the "council of Pennsylvania," was written by Gov. Moore, of that state, September 4, 1782. See Appendix G.

[3] The continental regiment of Brigadier-General Moses Hazen, which had previously been guarding prisoners in Pennsylvania. For a history of this regiment, see Hist. Mag., Feb., 1872, p. 92; also, Penn. Arch., second series, vol. XI, p. 99.

had orders to march previous to this, I countermanded them
and began to prepare for acting on a larger scale,— directing
the militia to assemble again at the time proposed to me for
moving from this place, namely: the 8th of October. From
that date till the 23d, I was in a state of the greatest suspense
and uncertainty, as the troops did not arrive nor was there any
reason assigned why they did not.

The letters, it seems, for directing the expedition to be laid
aside [1] were trusted to some persons traveling on their private
business; and I should not have got them to this day, had I
not sent officers on the different roads to gain intelligence of
the march and hasten Hazen's regiment.[2] One of these picked
up the letters. So much having been said and so many attempts made, I confess I should have been pleased to put the
matter to trial; as I believe we should have been able to chastise the savages severely; no number of Indians whatever, in
my opinion, can fight a thousand men under proper discipline
or regulation. However, I presume it must be best laid aside,
doubtless for good reasons. Indeed, I never could see any
great advantages gained by excursions of this kind; at least,
they have not been lasting: nothing short of destroying the
British posts from which they receive the means to carry on

---

[1] See Lincoln to Irvine, September 27, 1782, Appendix B, for one of these.
[2] With one of the officers he sent the following:

"FORT PITT, *September* 30, 1782.

"*Sir:*— I am instructed by the secretary at war that part of General Hazen's regiment is ordered to this post. The time being now nearly elapsed within which he intended they should arrive, I begin to be anxious to know how far you are advanced; and as it is also necessary I should know what provision, if any, horses and stores of every kind you have under your convoy, I have sent Captain [Samuel] Brady to meet you and make these and other inquiries, to whom you are to communicate all matters respecting your corps or convoy necessary for the commanding officer here to know.

"He has my orders to return immediately on meeting you. As much, very much, will depend on your speed, I make no doubt you will make forced marches. He will also inform you of the necessity hereof, and can give you the best information of the route you should come, being well acquainted with the country. I am, sir, your obedient, humble servant,

"WM. IRVINE, B. Gen'l.

"To the officer commanding a detachment of General Hazen's regiment, on the march to Fort Pitt."

war, or establishing posts in their country, will effectually answer the end. I am very anxious about General Clark. If my last messenger to him arrived safe, he will have reason to think I am now in the Indian country; and it was not possible for me to inform him of my countermand in time. I have, however, used every precaution and stratagem. in my power to draw the attention of the Delawares and Wyandots this way, to prevent their aiding the Shawanese, whom he determined to attack at the same time I did the others. I have some hope he will have the former alone to deal with, if he should proceed.[1] I fear the Indians will not be restrained by the British. They have killed so late as the 6th inst. in this neighborhood, but this may have been done by some small party, who were out before orders reached them.[2]

---

[1] The Delawares and Wyandots were, at this date, principally upon the Sandusky river directly on the line between Fort Pitt and Detroit, and their territory would have been the objective point of Irvine had he proceeded with the expedition as had been contemplated. South of these, principally upon the upper waters of the Great Miami, and at no very great distance, were seated the Shawanese. The plan was well laid between the two American commanders to strike all three of these tribes at the same time: Irvine, from the east, would engage the Wyandots and Delawares; Clark, from the south (Kentucky), would attack the Shawanese. The last part of the programme was carried out.

[2] "As to the savages, I have the best of assurance that from a certain period not very long after my arrival here, no parties of Indians were sent out, and that messengers were dispatched to recall those who had gone forth before that time." — Sir Guy Carleton to Washington, from New York, September 12, 1782.

"DETROIT, 29 *Sept.*, 1782.

". . . . I have a very difficult card to play at this post and its dependencies. . . . It is evident that the back settlers will continue to make war upon the Shawanese, Delawares and Wyandots, even after a truce shall be agreed to between Great Britain and her revolted colonies; in which case, whilst we continue to support the Indians with troops (which they are calling loud for) or only with arms, ammunition and necessaries, we shall incur the odium of encouraging incursions into the back settlements; for it is evident that when the Indians are on foot, occasioned by the constant alarms they receive from the enemy's entering their country, they will occasionally enter the settlements and bring off prisoners and scalps; so that whilst in alliance with a people we are bound to support, a defensive war will, in spite of human prudence, almost always terminate in an offensive one."— Col. A. S. De Peyster to Gen. Haldimand.

If a peace with the British should not take place, I am almost certain there will be no rest here while they possess Canada; and I think they will attempt gaining possession as far as the Ohio, agreeable to their Quebec bill,[1] if we cannot wrest the lower part of Canada from them. It is probable they will send troops up the lake[2] next spring in order to do this. If they do, they will meet little obstruction as far as the Alleghany,[3] unless measures are adopted to counteract

[Extract from the Penn. Packet, 1 Oct., 1782 (No. 944).]

"PHILADELPHIA, *October* 1, 1782.
"A gentleman is arrived in town who left Fort Pitt on Wednesday, the 18th ult. He informs, that altho' the Indians have been much more quiet lately than some time before, yet an attack from them was expected at Fort Weeling [Wheeling], on the Ohio, some distance southeast of Fort Pitt."

[1] The object of the Quebec bill, which passed the parliament of Great Britain during the crisis immediately preceding active hostilities of the revolution, was to prevent Canada — that is, the province of Quebec — from joining with the other colonies. The bill not only regulated the affairs of that province, but extended its boundaries to the Ohio and Mississippi rivers, over the region which included, besides Canada, the area of the present states of Ohio, Indiana, Michigan, Illinois and Wisconsin, in utter disregard of the charters and rights of Massachusetts, Connecticut, New York and Virginia.

[2] Irvine's meaning is, "up Lake Erie."

[3] Irvine here has reference to the Alleghany river, which stream unites with the Monongahela at Pittsburgh to form the Ohio.

"It is much to be desired that a uniform orthography of this name should be adopted. In New York, it is commonly written *Allegany;* in Pennsylvania, *Allegheny;* and in Virginia and the Southern States, *Alleghany.* As nearly all the works on general geography, even those published in New York and Pennsylvania, spell the name ALLEGHANY, the citizens of those states might, it is believed, without any unmanly concession, or without the slightest abandonment of what is due to the dignity of sovereign states, conform in this respect to the usage of the majority. The impropriety, not to say absurdity, of this discrepancy in the spelling, will be seen by referring to a representation of New York and Pennsylvania on the same map. We shall there find one and the same river named *Allegheny* near its source; while further down, for the distance of some 40 or 50 miles, it is *Allegany,* and then again *Alleghany* for the rest of its course. If we have occasion to speak of the mountains, we must, according to this method, call them *Allegany* in a description of New York, *Allegheny* in an article on Pennsylvania, and *Alleghany* in treating of Virginia or any of the Southern or Western States."— Lippincott's *Gazetteer of the World,* art. ALLEGHANY.

The spelling here recommended would yield the *a* to New York; the *h* to Pennsylvania: a fair compromise, surely. It is adopted in these pages.

them. The most effectual way (in my opinion) in this quarter would be for us to establish a post on the lake early in the spring, build two stout row galleys, each for one hundred men, and to mount two twelve-pounders with other smaller guns. These, from the accounts I have, would be quite equal to destroy all their fleet. This business must undoubtedly be managed with secrecy and dispatch and arrangements made for holding the post; otherwise, it could not answer any other purpose than a temporary loss of their vessels; as they could soon rebuild them if we did not hold the command. Almost all the necessary irons and anchors for boat building are here ready made; but there is no heavier artillery than six-pounders, which are too small even for this post.

The old causeway, as it is called, to Presq' Isle is so much out of repair it would take immense labor and waste much time to make it passable;[1] besides, the navigation of the Alleghany river and French creek is at best uncertain; in summer, none at all. Cuyahoga river, or creek, by all accounts, would be a proper place for such a post.[2] From the mouth of Beaver creek[3] and Fort McIntosh to the navigable part of this river is only about seventy miles, through a tolerable champaign country. However, I intend to have it explored soon by an intelligent officer, who for fear of discovery or cause for anybody taking umbrage, shall go equipped and under the idea of a hunting excursion.[4]

---

[1] As early as 1759, the road from Venango to Le Bœuf was described as being "trod and good;" thence to Presq' Isle, about half a day's journey, as "very low and swampy and bridged almost all the way."

[2] The Cuyahoga river rises in the central parts of Geauga county, Ohio, whence it runs into Portage and Summit counties, gradually turning northwestwardly into and across Cuyahoga county, entering Lake Erie at Cleveland. It has a total length of about sixty miles. The point referred to by Irvine was undoubtedly at or near the mouth of the river.

[3] The Mahoning river and Shenango, uniting in what is now Lawrence county, Pennsylvania, form the Beaver river, usually called, at an early day, the "Big Beaver." Slippery Rock and Conoquenessing creek flow into it near to the dividing line between Beaver and Lawrence counties. The river then flows southward through nearly the middle of Beaver county, and empties into the Ohio at Rochester, close to the borough of Beaver.

[4] Major Isaac Craig of the artillery was the "intelligent officer" Irvine had

I shall not, at present, trouble your excellency with any further detail of this matter, as it is probable your general arrangements may render such an undertaking unnecessary, or that circumstances will not allow; however this may be, I presume the suggestion that such a plan might be effected will not be disagreeable to you. The expense would be considerable, but not more than must be spent in acting on the defensive and making partial fruitless excursions. It cannot,

in view, as will appear by the following order; but the general gave up "the idea of a hunting excursion:"

"FORT PITT, *Nov.* 11, 1782.

"*Sir:*—I have received intelligence through various channels that the British have established a post at Lower Sandusky [now Fremont, Ohio], and also information that it is suspected they intend erecting one at either Cuyahoga creek or Grand river [now Fairport, Ohio]. But as these accounts are not from persons of military knowledge, nor to be fully relied upon in any particular, and I am anxious to have the facts well established, you will therefore proceed with Lieutenant Rose, my aid-de-camp, and six active men, in order to reconnoiter these two places, particularly Cuyahoga. As your party is so small, you will use every precaution to avoid being discovered, which service I expect you will be able to perform, as they will probably be relaxed in discipline at this advanced season of the year. When you have reconnoitered these posts (if any), you may try to take a prisoner, provided it can be done without much risk of losing any of your party; which must be guarded against at all events, as it is not your business to come to action; my reasons for allowing you so small a party being to avoid discovery.

"I know your zeal will excite you to go lengths, perhaps even beyond your judgment, in order to effect the purposes of your excursion. But, notwithstanding my earnest desire to obtain accurate accounts of the matters mentioned herein, you will please to keep in view that I am extremely solicitous that every man may be brought back safe, and that one man falling into the hands of the enemy may not only ruin your whole present business, but also prevent future discovery.

"As it may be necessary for you to detach or separate from Mr. Rose, it will be proper for you to give him a certified copy of this order.

"I am, sir, your obedient, humble servant,

"WM. IRVINE, B. Gen'l.

"Major CRAIG."

"The major, with his party, started on their expedition on the 13th of November, taking with them one horse with a supply of provisions; they crossed Big Beaver river at its mouth, and Little Beaver some distance above its mouth; thence they proceeded in a direction south of west, as if bound to the Indian town at the forks of the Muskingum, pursuing that course until night, and then turned directly north, and traveled all night in that direction. This was done to mislead and elude the pursuit of Indians who may have followed

however, be performed at all unless a magazine of salt provision is laid up here this winter, which is very practicable; there are great quantities of pork in the country.

This fort [Fort Pitt] has been much repaired in the course of the summer. A new row of picketing is planted on every part of the parapet where the brick revetment did not extend, and a row of palisading nearly finished in the ditch; so far, also, with sundry other small improvements; but, above all, a complete magazine, the whole arched with stone. I think I

them. When they arrived, as they supposed, within a day's march of the mouth of the Cuyahoga, they left one man with the extra provisions. It was the intention, upon rejoining this man, to have taken a fresh supply of provisions, and then proceed to examine the mouth of Grand river, one of the points which the enemy was reported to have in view. General Irvine, in his instructions, had treated it as a point of less importance than the Cuyahoga, but yet worthy of attention. The weather proved very unfavorable after the separation, the major, with his party, was detained beyond the appointed time, and the soldier with the horse, had disappeared; so that when they reached the designated place, weary and half famished, they found no relief, and had before them a journey of more than one hundred miles, through a hostile wilderness. The examination of Grand river had, of course, to be abandoned, and the party was compelled to hasten back to Fort Pitt.

"The travel back was laborious and painful, the weather being tempestuous and variable. The party pursued the most direct course homeward. Before they reached the Connequenessing, near about, as Major Craig thought, where Old Harmony now stands, the weather became extremely cold, and they found that stream frozen over, but the ice not sufficiently firm to bear the weight of a man. The following expedient was then resorted to as the best the circumstances allowed: A large fire was kindled on the northern bank of the Connequenessing, and when it was burning freely, the party stripped off their clothes; one man took a heavy bludgeon in his hands to break the way, while each of the others followed with portions of their clothes and arms in one hand and a firebrand in the other. Upon reaching the southern bank of the stream, these brands were placed together and a brisk fire soon raised, by which the party dressed themselves, and then resumed their toilsome march. Upon reaching the Cranberry plains, they were delighted to find encamped there a hunting party consisting of Captain Uriah Springer and other officers, and some soldiers, from the fort. There, of course, they were welcomed and kindly treated, and, partaking of the refreshments in their cases so necessary and desirable, they resumed their journey and arrived at the fort on the evening of the 2d of December."—*Sketch of the Life and Services of Isaac Craig, by Neville B. Craig*, pp. 41-44. Consult, in this connection, the W. R. and N. O. Hist. Soc. tract, No. 22.

may venture to assert, it is a very elegant piece of workmanship as well as most useful one. It has been executed under the direction of Major Craig.[1]

I have used the most rigid economy in every instance. The whole expense is but a trifle. Though the troops labored hard, yet, from the smallness of their number and unavoidable interruptions, some necessary repairs remain yet unfinished. Some parts of the ramparts and parapets are much broken down. A new main gate and draw bridge are wanted and some small outworks are necessary to be erected, which cannot be effected this winter, as it is now high time to lay in fuel and make some small repairs on the soldiers' barracks to make them habitable.

If I am to be continued in service and command here, I shall be much obliged to your excellency for leave to visit my family at Carlisle in the dead of winter, when I suppose there can be no risk in my being absent from the post. Besides, I shall then be directly on the line of communication to this place, and will not stay longer than you may judge proper. I should not trouble your excellency with this request, was not the necessity for paying some attention to my private affairs very urgent; notwithstanding, if it is, in any measure, incompatible with your views, or inconsistent with my duty, I will cheerfully submit to your excellency's pleasure in the matter.

---

[1] About this time, a detachment composed of three hundred British and five hundred Indians was formed in Canada, and after reaching the south side of Lake Erie, embarked on Chautauqua lake with twelve pieces of artillery, with the intention of attacking Fort Pitt; but the expedition was abandoned before proceeding further, in consequence of the reported repairs and strength of the post. General Irvine, in August, picked up at Fort Pitt a number of canoes which had drifted down the river; and he received repeated accounts in June and July, from a Canadian who had deserted to him, as well as from friendly Indians, of this armament, but he was ignorant at the time where it had assembled. Notwithstanding the enterprise was given up by the enemy, as just mentioned, another project was immediately entered into and carried out with effect, by a portion of the detachment marching against Hannastown, a settlement to the eastward of Pittsburgh. (See Appendix B,— Irvine to Lincoln, July 16, 1782; also, Appendix G,— Irvine to Moore, same date.)

XX.— WASHINGTON TO IRVINE.

HEAD QUARTERS, NEWBURGH, *December* 11, 1782.

Sir:— Your letter of the 29th of October came to hand a few days since.

Viewing the matter on every side, I think it best the expedition was laid aside. Your reasoning on the subject is very just — such excursions serve only to draw the resentment of the savages; and I much fear, that to the conduct of our people may be attributed many of the excesses which have been committed on our frontiers.

I am obliged to you for the plan you suggest. I wish always you would propose to me any enterprises you may think of advantage, and my endeavors shall not be wanting to promote them when our circumstances will admit.

The expedition to Lake Erie is far above any means we have in our power. We cannot advance a single farthing, and to undertake it with any prospect of success or advantage, we should have such a command of money as to induce a number of ship carpenters to accompany a sufficient detachment; otherwise it would be impossible for us to build vessels there without the enemy's knowledge; and then they could, and doubtless would, build vessels with heavier metal as fast as we.

As to laying in a magazine of salted provisions, that should be done whether an expedition is undertaken on a large scale or not, and the contractors should take measures for that purpose.

I shall be glad to hear from you when you have explored the country you mention.

From every appearance I do not imagine our parties will be distressed during the winter; and, as your command will be continued, if your private affairs require your presence, I shall have no objection to your visiting your family for a reasonable time whenever the situation of your post will admit it. Of that you can best judge.[1]

---

[1] Irvine left Fort Pitt to visit his family in Carlisle the last of February, turning the command of that post and its dependencies over to Lieutenant-

XXI.—IRVINE TO WASHINGTON.

CARLISLE, *March* 6, 1783.

Sir:— I was honored with your excellency's letter of the 7th December. Neither the situation of things at Fort Pitt, nor my state of health would admit of my coming down the country much sooner. I got here two days ago, only. There have been no murders committed by the savages this win-

---

Colonel Stephen Bayard, then of the third Pennsylvania regiment. He reached home March 4th. (See next letter.) Before his departure, he issued the following instructions to Bayard:

"FORT PITT, *February*, 1783.

"*Sir:*— In my absence from this post the command will devolve on you. As you are so well acquainted with the duty and police of the garrison, and my mode of conducting matters generally, it will be unnecessary for me to descend to many or minute particulars. You are also well acquainted with the state of the stores and all public property, and how necessary economy is in every instance; particularly as it is not only difficult to have stores brought here, but the transportation of them is immense.

"Let not the report of peace or anything short of an order from proper authority for evacuating this post or disbanding the troops be the smallest inducement for you to suffer any deviation from discipline and exact performance of all military duties.

"Should the savages commit murder on the frontier and application is made to you, or you hear of it with certainty, you will give such assistance to protect the inhabitants as in your power, consistently with the safety of the post. The assistance ought to be mutual, as the defense of the country and post depends much on each other. You will, therefore, cultivate a friendly intertercourse with the militia officers (if their services should become necessary). I make no doubt you will make the best arrangements and render every service in your power comporting with these instructions.

"Should any matters come to my knowledge of consequence to the command or troops of this garrison, you shall have the earliest notice possible. The post at McIntosh will also claim your attention. I have given the present commandant particular instructions, which will do for standing orders during my absence, unless circumstances change very materially. I am, with great regard, dear sir, your obedient, humble servant,

"WM. IRVINE, B. Gen'l."

"P. S.—Should a necessity arise for demanding a few volunteer militia, to perform a scout, it will be far most advantageous they should be joined to a few regulars and all supplied with a certain number of days' provision from this place.

"W. I.

"Lt. Col. Bayard."

ter, except one Mr. Madison, who was killed at Kanawha [1] (when with a party surveying), the 15th of January.

I have heard nothing lately from any of the Indian nations, but have got accounts through a private channel that Sir John Johnson [2] was at Detroit in October last and told the Indians they must remain quiet till spring; that there was a prospect of peace; but if it did not take place, he would find ample employment for them. Great preparations are making and magazines laying up at their several posts on Lake Erie; and every measure seems to threaten some capital stroke from them to the westward this spring or summer.

If we are not in a situation to perform enterprises on a large scale, we ought at least to try something in the partisan way. I have in view to surprise a small post called Fort Schlosser,[3] at a carrying place at the lower end of Lake Erie;

---

[1] By Kanawha is here meant the Great Kanawha. This stream is formed by the Gauley and New river, and enters the Ohio at Point Pleasant, West Virginia, a distance of two hundred and sixty-seven miles by the course of the latter stream, below Pittsburgh. In early times, the name was generally written Kenhawa.

[2] Sir John Johnson was the son of Sir William Johnson, who, for a long time previous to the revolution was colonial agent and sole superintendent of the affairs of the Six Nations and other northern tribes. Sir John was born in 1742, and upon the death of his father in 1774, succeeded to his title and estates as well as to the post of major general of militia. Early in 1776, the whigs attempted to secure his person, but with about seven hundred followers he fled from the interior of New York to Canada. He was soon commissioned a colonel, raised two battalions, called the Royal Greens; and became one of the most active and one of the bitterest foes that the whigs encountered during the revolution. He invested Fort Stanwix in August, 1777, and at Oriskany defeated General Mercer. In 1780, he was himself defeated by General Van Rensselaer at Fox's Mills. Soon after the close of the war, Sir John went to England, but returned in 1785, and resided in Canada. He was superintendent of Indian affairs until his death, which occurred at Montreal on the 4th day of January, 1830. He was, for a number of years, a member of the legislative council of Canada. The British government, to compensate him for his losses, made him several grants of land. His son, Sir Adam Gordon Johnson, born in 1781, succeeded to his father's title.

[3] Fort Schlosser was situated nearly two miles above the cataract of Niagara on the east side of the river. Near this point was the French post Fort du Portage, which was burned in 1759. The fort was rebuilt by the British in 1760, and named Fort Schlosser. It was, along with Fort Niagara, briefly

accomplishing this, though small in itself, might be attended with happy effects, not less perhaps than saving Fort Pitt or the post at the falls of the Ohio;[1] particularly if the stroke can be made when they have a quantity of provision at the place. It will at any time harass and embarrass them, and might cause such delay as to frustrate their plan. I know it will be a hazardous undertaking, chiefly occasioned by Indians who live in the vicinity. The garrison live in the most perfect state of security — only one officer and twenty-five men. I think early in the month of May will be not only the most likely time to succeed, but answer greater ends; as, at that season they generally begin to transport over the lake [Erie] their provisions and stores, and seldom have any other guard employed than barely enough to work their vessels.

Since my arrival at this place, the reports and appearance of peace are so flattering I begin to persuade myself there will be little occasion for my returning to Fort Pitt; however, in order to avoid disappointment or delay, I have sent my aid-de-camp [Lieutenant John Rose] to the secretary at war, in order to transact several matters relative to the post, which cannot be so well done by letter; and, in the mean time, will prepare for returning to my command the 1st of April, unless otherwise directed by your excellency or the secretary at war.

XXII.— IRVINE TO WASHINGTON.

CARLISLE, *March* 28, 1783.

Sir:— The general face of affairs is so much changed since I wrote to your excellency the 6th instant, that I think it most advisable for me to remain here, and not return to Fort Pitt

---

invested by the savages in 1763, but was not captured. During the revolution, as before that time, the portage around the falls terminated at this point; its commencement being about eight miles below, at what is now Lewiston, Niagara county, New York.

[1] In 1780, a fort was built "at the falls of the Ohio," at what was then (or soon after) Louisville, Kentucky, and called Fort Nelson, in honor of Thomas Nelson, at that date governor of the state of V.rginia, which state included the whole of Kentucky. In 1782, a larger and more commodious fort was constructed on the same site. It contained about an acre of ground.

till I receive your orders, especially as everything is quiet in that quarter and the post in good order. Both Virginia and Pennsylvania troops, of whom the garrison are composed (being enlisted for the war expressly), will not think themselves obliged to do one hour's duty after the peace is announced. And should they be disbanded before measures are taken for securing the stores, great waste and perhaps total destruction will take place. I may call a militia guard, but that will be small security, I assure you. . . .

As there is no paymaster at the post, Mr. Morris and the paymaster general have prevailed on Lieutenant Rose, my aid-de-camp, to make one month's payment to the troops, in order to save the expense of an appointment for that purpose; I will therefore let him proceed immediately.[1] Perhaps the

---

[1] The meaning of Irvine is that Rose would immediately proceed to Fort Pitt. The general's order was as follows:

"CARLISLE, *April* 1, 1783.

"You will immediately proceed to Fort Pitt and pay the troops of that garrison, agreeably to the directions of the paymaster general. You will keep an account of the expenses of your journey and charge the same to the United States. WM. IRVINE, B. Gen'l.

"To Lieutenant JOHN ROSE."

Rose's account of the expenses of his journey, as rendered, was as follows: "The United States,

"To John Rose, Lieutenant 3d Penn. Reg't, *Dr.*
"To my expenses on a journey from Carlisle to Fort Pitt, being six
 days, at $2.00 per day, - - - - - - - $12.00."
[Instead of the dollar mark ($), the *word* is given.]

The following is the correspondence between Rose and the paymaster general while the former was acting-paymaster at Fort Pitt:

"PHILADELPHIA, *March* 21, 1783.

"*Sir:*— As you have been so kind as to undertake to pay the troops for me at Fort Pitt, I do hereby authorize you to draw bills on me for the monthly subsistence of the officers there, agreeably to the rates of the establishment signed by the secretary at war now given to you. You will be cautious not to pay any persons but those on the *present* arrangement. You will take duplicate receipts from each officer and transmit me one set with your accounts as often as safe conveyances occur.

"If you can find a sale for your bills on me, you will be pleased to pay to the privates of the infantry half a dollar a week, and to the non-commissioned officers and the privates of the other corps in the same proportion, until you have paid to them one month's pay, which is to be for January, 1783, and

order for paying the men only half a dollar a week may be dispensed with, and that they may receive the whole at once, but he will proceed in the mode directed till your excellency's pleasure is signified.

I understand the paymaster general is gone to settle with the main army, and I presume some person will also be sent for this purpose to the southern army. The troops at Fort Pitt are considered as of the latter, but in this business I conceive them unconnected, and that it would be expedient to have some person appointed for this purpose, and this can not take duplicate vouchers, as in the case of the officers' subsistence. Mr. Tannehill, the gentleman who has lately transacted my business at Fort Pitt, being discharged and having the sum of forty-seven dollars and thirty-ninetieths in his hands of the public monies, you will please to receive the same from him and apply it to the public use.

"As he has not sent down his last vouchers, I will thank you to pay an attention to their being forwarded. I am, sir, with respect, your most obedient servant, JOHN PIERCE, P. G.

"Captain JOHN ROSE."

"FORT PITT, *May* 5, 1783.

"*Sir:*— Inclosed I transmit to you the accounts and vouchers of one month's pay and four months' subsistence paid the officers at this post, continued on the present arrangement. Lieutenant Samuel Bryson's pay of the second Pennsylvania regiment remains in my hands, he having obtained leave of absence before my arrival here.

"Empowered by your instructions, I have given Mr. William Wilson, or his order, a draft on you of a hundred and sixty dollars. I expect the discharge of it will meet with no delay when presented, as the receipts for the disbursements of the money accompany this letter.

"The soldiers here have refused receiving their pay for one month at the weekly rates proposed; but should they be paid, are the muster-rolls to be the guide to the paymaster, or is he to confine himself to the regulated establishment of the army, namely: some companies muster a double number of drums and fifes, etc.? Again, men who were mustered in January, but since discharged the service, are these, upon application made by them, to receive this pay? And again, prisoners of war and others, not mustered in January, but now actually on the spot doing duty, are they to be included?

"With much economy I shall be able to rake up subsistence for May; after that, the garrison will depend upon your goodness and care to forward it in cash. You will please to favor me with a few lines signifying the receipt of my accounts and vouchers delivered you by Mr. Blackwood. I am, etc.

"JOHN ROSE.

"JOHN PIERCE, Esq., Paymaster General."

be done after they are separated from the officers now with them. They have confidence in my promise to them last year (by your excellency's order) that they might depend on being treated, in every respect, equal to any other troops of the army. And I think I may venture, without creating a suspicion of vanity, to assure your excellency that this confidence is heightened by the unremitting pains I have taken to have them provided for, and at the same time exact discipline kept up, but for this I have been compensated by the good order established and the cheerfulness and alacrity with which they

"FORT PITT, *June* 8, 1783.

"*Sir:*— My accounts and vouchers for the payment of the subsistence for May accompany this letter. I now retain cash for bills sold General Irvine to the amount of nineteen hundred eighty-four dollars, the exact sum requisite to pay the soldiery at this post one month's pay. Though they refused to take it at the weekly rates proposed, as I mentioned to you in a former letter, yet I make no doubt they will request and expect it in one payment as soon as the time is elapsed it would require to pay it in the first mode prescribed. General Irvine, therefore, wishes I should reserve this sum until I could receive your instructions on this head.

"But as this sum includes all the public money remaining in his hands, and as I have no prospect of any farther sale of any bills upon you, I shall be necessitated to apply a part of the sum mentioned to the subsistence of the officers. Should you determine to pay the troops of this post their month's pay agreeable to this requisition in one payment, you will please to transmit me by the bearer of this letter as much money as will be necessary to pay the officers their subsistence for the time they are likely to be continued here. By Mr. John Irwin, you will find a very safe conveyance. He promises to wait on you for an answer to this and my letter of the 5th of last month favored by Mr. Blackwood. I am, etc., JOHN ROSE.

"JOHN PIERCE, Esq., Paymaster General."

"PAY OFFICE, PHILADELPHIA, *July* 21, 1783.

"*Sir:*— Yours of the 5th of May last with the accounts inclosed I have received, and your bill for one hundred and sixty dollars is duly honored. In answer to that letter, I will say, we are obliged to take muster rolls for our sole guide, which are sufficient vouchers for payment of moneys. You must take care that your payments be as small as possible, for which reason it is much the best to omit the discharged men, if in your power; and if a larger number of drums and fifes are mustered than what are allowed in the establishment, the muster master ought to be called on to answer for such allowance; but we have no power to alter it. If, in February rolls, men are mustered for January, the January pay will be drawn with the February, and so on from time to time.

perform all kinds of duty. In the meantime I will direct Lieutenant-Colonel Bayard, the present commanding officer, to keep the troops together in all events, till he receives positive orders to the contrary.

If your excellency should think proper to direct my return to Fort Pitt, I shall be greatly obliged by your limiting the time of my stay,— some attention to my health being necessary, as it is much impaired. And I farther beg whatever orders or instructions you judge necessary may be, as soon as convenient, forwarded to me at this place.

Sir:— The most glorious news of a general peace, honorable for America, arrived here two days ago. On this happy occasion, I pray your excellency may be pleased to accept my sincere congratulations. That you may long live to enjoy the well-earned fruits of your labors is the ardent wish of, sir, etc.

XXIII.— IRVINE TO WASHINGTON.

CARLISLE, *April* 16, 1783.

Sir:— I have received a letter this day from Lieutenant-Colonel Bayard,[1] at Fort Pitt, informing me that the savages

---

"I have also received yours of the 8th of last month. I have not the least doubt but you may pay the soldiers their month's pay for January all at once; but as for the subsistence money due the officers for this year, we have not the way of paying them, but by notes granted by Mr. Hilligas payable monthly. I could send them some of them if I thought it would answer the purpose. The officers of the main army receive them and the contractors receive them commonly for provisions supplied the officers. I am, sir, your most obedient servant, PHILIP AUDEBERT, Assistant Paymaster General.

"P. S.— The paymaster general is at headquarters. Mr. Morris' notes, payable in six months from the 10th day of June, are ready for three months' pay of the army, and you may have them whenever you please.

"L't JOHN ROSE."

The promptness of Rose's settlement with the paymaster general is indicated by the date of the following receipt:

"PAY OFFICE, PHILADELPHIA, *November* 5, 1783.

"Received of L't John Rose fifty-four dollars and 3-90, being the full balance of his account settled in this office while acting as paymaster at Fort Pitt. PHILIP AUDEBERT, A. P. M."

[1] Bayard to Irvine, April 5, 1783, Appendix M.

have killed and taken a number of families, nearly at the
same time, in different quarters of the country, both on the
frontiers of Virginia and Pennsylvania; seventeen persons are
said to be killed and scalped in one small settlement on Wheeling creek.[1] This stroke has been very unexpected; numbers
of people were returning to their places in confidence that
these wretches would not dare to continue the war unsup-
ported.

I presume this conduct will give force to a temper already
pretty prevalent among the back settlers, never to make peace
with Indians; and, indeed, I am almost persuaded it will be
next to impossible to insure peace with them till the whole of
the western tribes are driven over the Mississippi and the lakes,
entirely beyond the American lines, — which will not now be
very difficult, but would take two summers at least, and be attended with great expense; yet I am certain not so great as
holding treaties, and have much better effect, as all the sums
heretofore expended in treating and presents have been worse
than thrown away. I have not yet been honored with your
excellency's acknowledgment of the receipt of my letters of
the 6th and 28th March.

XXIV.— WASHINGTON TO IRVINE.

HEAD QUARTERS, *April* 16, 1783.

Sir:— In reply to your favor of the 28th of March, I have
to observe that it is probable that a dissolution of the army is
not far distant, but as it is uncertain when the proclamation
of peace and cessation of hostilities will be ordered by congress;[2] and as it is of much importance, for the reasons mentioned by yourself, among others, that you should be present

---

[1] Wheeling creek enters the Ohio on the left, at the distance of ninety-three miles, by the river's course, below Pittsburgh. Its mouth is the site of the present city of Wheeling, West Virginia.

[2] The preliminary articles of peace were signed at Paris, November 30, 1782; the general — or as it was then generally styled, the definitive — treaty, at the same place, January 20, 1783. It was ratified by congress, April 11th, following, and publicly proclaimed the 19th of the same month, three days after the date of the above letter.

at your post, previous to and at the taking place of that event; I have to desire that you will proceed immediately to Fort Pitt, where your influence and prudence may be much needed.

Particular instructions respecting the security and disposition of the stores, after disbanding the troops now at the garrison, it is not in my power to give you at this time. These you will probably soon receive from the secretary at war, and will depend upon the arrangements which shall be adopted for a peace establishment, which are now under consideration.[1] On this decision, also, will probably depend the length of time which will be necessary for you to remain at the post.

The paymaster general is now taking measures for forming his settlements with the army. In his arrangement, the whole are to be included, and will undoubtedly extend to Fort Pitt.

The happy event of a general peace diffuses very universal satisfaction. With great sincerity, I return you my congratulations on the occasion, and beg you to accept my thanks for the good wishes which you apply personally to myself.

XXV.— IRVINE TO WASHINGTON.[2]

CARLISLE, *May* 8, 1783.

Sir:— Your excellency's favor of the 16th of April did not come to hand till this day. Agreeable to your desire, I will proceed to Fort Pitt immediately.[3]

I entreat your excellency will be pleased to give particular instructions respecting any measures you may deem proper for that garrison; as I have reason to fear it will otherwise come in late for a share of public notice.

Letters of a late date inform me that the savages have not done any damage in that quarter since the first of April.

---

[1] The secretary at war wrote Irvine, June 23, 1783, but the letter miscarried. (See Appendix B,— Jackson to Irvine, September 15, 1783.)

[2] This letter is the last one written by Irvine as commander of the western department to Washington which has been found,— one written as late as the 6th of September, 1783, unfortunately being lost.

[3] Irvine reached Fort Pitt on his third trip out, a little past the middle of May. On the first of July, because of the scarcity of provisions at his post,

XXVI.— WASHINGTON TO IRVINE.[1]

ROCKY HILL, *September* 16, 1783.

Sir:— Your letter of the 6th by Lieutenant Rose has been duly received.

As the secretary at war had undertaken to furlough all that part of the army which lay south of the Delaware, I was much

---

he furloughed most of the troops for a few days, and afterward continued the furloughing for some time, in rotation. From the fifteenth of May to the eighteenth of July, there was but one maraud of savages into the western settlements. From the last mentioned date to the time of Irvine's final departure from Pittsburgh, comparative quiet reigned throughout the western department. On the twenty-sixth of September, he received a letter from the assistant secretary at war notifying him that as soon as a detachment of troops arrived which were then on their way, he would be relieved from command at Fort Pitt, which he so much desired. He was authorized to furlough as many of his garrison at once as consistent with safety. This he did, turning over the remainder to one of his captains, and on the first day of October started for his home in Carlisle.

[1] This letter of Washington ended the official correspondence between him and General Irvine during the revolution. The latter, the day before his departure, was presented with the following address:

"PITTSBURGH, *September* 30, 1783.

"To Brigadier General INVINE,

"Commanding at Fort Pitt and its Dependencies.

"*Sir:*— The inhabitants of Pittsburgh having just learned that you intend to retire from this command to-morrow, would do injustice to their own feelings if they did not express their thanks to you, and their sense of your merit as an officer. During your command in this department, you have demonstrated that amidst the tumults of war, the laws may be enforced and civil liberty and society protected. Your attention to the order and discipline of the regular troops under your command, as well as to the militia, your regard to the civil rights of the inhabitants, the care you have taken of the public property, and your economy in the expenditure of the public money, we have all witnessed. This conduct, we assure you, has given general satisfaction to a people who, before your time, were, unfortunately for them, much divided, but now united.

"As you are now about to quit the military life (in which your ability and integrity have been so conspicuous), we wish you all possible happiness, and that your fellow citizens may long enjoy your usefulness in civil life, in which we doubt not you will deserve their utmost confidence.

"We regret that we were not sooner informed of the time you intended to set out, as we are confident the whole country would have, with pride, joined us in this or a more animated and better drawn-up address.

surprised on the receipt of your letter, to find that business so irregularly conducted at Fort Pitt; but, on inquiry at the war office, the difficulty seems evidently to have originated from circumstances that could not have been foreseen, the particulars of which you will be fully informed of by Major [W.] Jackson, assistant secretary at war, and which, I hope, will be perfectly satisfactory to you.

"We sincerely wish you health and a happy meeting with your family and friends at Carlisle;—and are, with great esteem and respect, sir, your obedient and very humble servants,

"John Ormsby,
Devereux Smith,
David Duncan,
Daniel Elliott,
Samuel Ewalt,
George Walker,

Joseph Nicholson,
Samuel Sample,
Alexander Fowler,
William Christy,
John Hardin,
William Amberson."

GENERAL IRVINE'S REPLY.

"FORT PITT, *September* 30, 1783.

"*Gentlemen:*— Accept my sincere thanks for the address, however flattering, handed me by you on behalf of the inhabitants of the town of Pittsburgh. Conscious of the rectitude of my intentions, I am happy that they have met with your approbation. This testimony of your satisfaction is to me a most pleasing reward for the anxious moments I have passed. I have ever felt disposed to sacrifice personal considerations for the benefit not only of the public, but for that of every individual connected with my local command.

"Your concurrence in all the measures which I adopted to facilitate the public service, deserves my most unfeigned acknowledgments. I have the honor to be, with great regard, gentlemen, your most obedient servant,

"W. IRVINE."

APPENDIX A.

IRVINE TO THE PRESIDENT OF CONGRESS.

I.

PHILADELPHIA, *October* 3, 1781.[1]

Sir:—I am sorry to be under the necessity of troubling your excellency to inform you that I have it not yet in my power to proceed to Fort Pitt, not being able to obtain the small supply of cash which congress was pleased to direct a warrant issued in my favor for.

This information I think it my duty obliges me to give, lest the objects for which I am ordered there may be lost. I can assure your excellency no unnecessary delay shall be made the moment I have it in my power to proceed. I have, therefore, to request the further orders of congress.

II.

FORT PITT, *December* 3, 1781.[2]

Sir:—Agreeable to the directions of congress, I have arranged the troops here in such a manner as to retain no more officers than sufficient for the number of men.[3] The whole are now re-formed into four companies, namely: the seventh Virginia regiment, commanded by Colonel Gibson, into two;

---

[1] Irvine directed this and the following letter to the president of congress, simply. The incumbent, at that date, was Thomas McKean, of Delaware. He was superseded on the 5th of November, 1781, by John Hanson, of Maryland.

[2] This letter is, to a great extent, anticipated by Irvine's letter to Washington of the day previous (ante, p. 72).

[3] This, it will be noticed, was in accordance with the instructions of congress, directing him "to arrange the troops which compose the garrison of Fort Pitt and its dependencies in such manner as to retain no more officers than are absolutely necessary for the number of non-commissioned officers and privates at these posts." (Ante, p. 72, note 1.)

and the late eighth Pennsylvania, also into two. The latter I have styled a detachment from the Pennsylvania line, and have directed the supernumerary officers to repair forthwith to join their respective regiments in the line. I have dismissed several civil staff officers.[1] The only one retained is Mr. Samuel Sample, who has been doing the duty of quartermaster ever since Mr. Duncan was put under arrest.[2] I am of opinion some person to act in that department is indispensably necessary; and having no cause to fault Mr. Sample's conduct, have continued him until the pleasure of congress is known.[3]

I am sorry to inform the honorable, the congress, that General Clark's expedition has failed. He got no further than the rapids of the Ohio, whence a number of his men has returned here. Several of his detached parties are killed or taken, particularly a Colonel Lochry, with about one hundred men, all volunteers, except a company commanded by Captain Stokely, raised by Pennsylvania for the defense of Westmoreland county. This party, on its way down after the main body, was ambuscaded at the mouth of the Miami river, and it is said was all cut to pieces.[4] These misfortunes have thrown the people of this country into great consternation, especially of Westmoreland county, where the loss of so many of their best men has thinned and weakened their frontier

---

[1] Irvine was, by congress, authorized and directed, it will be remembered, to arrange the staff departments within his command, so as to retain no more officers or persons in those departments than the service absolutely demanded. (Ante, p. 72, note 1.)

[2] David Duncan. He attended to Michael Huffnagle's (the contractor's) business at Fort Pitt. (Ante, p. 81, note 1.)

In March, 1781, Duncan was appointed by the supreme executive council of Pennsylvania, a commissioner of purchases for the county of Westmoreland. His duty was to supply the garrison at Fort Pitt and state troops called out for the defense of the border. Being charged with speculating in public funds, he had been put under arrest, but, it appears, was soon after released. He had previously resigned.

[3] Mr. Sample's office was that of acting assistant quartermaster. He was an old resident of Pittsburgh, having kept a public house there as early as 1770.

[4] See Appendix G,— Irvine to Moore, December 3, 1781.

exceedingly. Many are preparing to retreat to the east side of the mountain early in the spring.

It is a prevailing opinion, and I fear too well founded, that the savages and British at Detroit will be so elated with the miscarriage of General Clark and others, that they will, in all probability, visit this post, or at least harass the whole frontier country, in the spring.[1] I assure your excellency we are ill-provided for their reception. Fort Pitt is a heap of ruins. It never was tenable when in best repair. There is a much better position about four miles down the river, at the mouth of Chartiers creek, where a redoubt could be built at a small expense,— I am certain much smaller than to repair Fort Pitt. Besides, there are many advantages attending keeping a garrison there, which give it a preference to this place.

As I believe re-formations and arranging the troops were the first objects congress had in view by sending me here, that being now nearly accomplished, and little danger to be apprehended of an attack during the winter,— I request congress will be pleased to permit me to go down the country as far as Carlisle for the months of January and February. If your honorable body thinks proper to continue me on this command, I will return in March, or as soon as they please to direct. However, I flatter myself they will not insist on my continuance without allowing me a few more regular troops. If I had five hundred in addition to the few here, I could probably, with the aid of the militia, afford effectual support to the country, by being able to act on the defensive. But I am persuaded it would answer a much better purpose if we could act offensively. There is great necessity, in my opinion, for adopting speedily some regular plan for action, or this country had better be entirely evacuated and given up at once; as there are at present but small prospects of saving the few troops and stores that are here should the enemy push us in April. I think proper measures could be better concerted by my being present either with congress or General Washington;

---

[1] The savages, in fact, did "harass the whole frontier country in the spring" of 1782; and, owing to very mild weather in February, their visits were much earlier than usual. (Ante, p. 99, note 2.)

as there are many things which on such occasions can not be so well committed to paper. However, I shall submit to the pleasure of congress, and in the meantime wait here for orders, which I beg by the return of the express, who I have directed to wait your excellency's commands.

APPENDIX B.

CORRESPONDENCE WITH THE CONTINENTAL BOARD OF WAR;[1] ALSO WITH THE SECRETARY AT WAR[2] AND HIS ASSISTANT.[3]

I.—IRVINE TO THE BOARD OF WAR.

PHILADELPHIA, *September* 25, 1781.

Gentlemen: — I received this morning a resolution of congress directing me to repair forthwith to Fort Pitt to take the command of that garrison.

As I believe this measure has been recommended by your honorable board, I must request you will please to reconsider the matter. I consider it lays me under great hardships which I am well convinced you did not intend; however, the facts are that it will be taking on me a command that is in no

---

[1] On the 12th of June, 1776, congress appointed a committee of five of its own members to be known as the board of war and ordnance. It was the duty of the board to keep a full register of the army; a regular account of the state and disposition of the troops in the respective colonies; and a full account of all war material belonging to the United States. The board was to send all dispatches and monies from congress to the colonies and armies; and it had charge of the raising, fitting out, and dispatching of all the land forces. It had the care, also, of all prisoners of war and the custody of all papers coming into its possession by order of congress or otherwise. In short, it had a general supervision of all matters appertaining to the land forces.

The board had been abolished previous to the date of the above letter; but the members were requested to continue to transact its duties until assumed by the secretary at war; which officer was not elected for over a month subsequent; hence, the necessity that Irvine should address his letter to the board of war.

[2] Major General Benjamin Lincoln was elected by congress on the 30th of October, 1781, as secretary at war, superseding the continental board of war and ordnance in office about a month afterward, and serving until the 29th of October, 1783, when he retired with a vote of congress acknowledging his highly meritorious services. The reason why the three following letters were directed to the board of war was because when written, Irvine had not yet received information of Lincoln's entering upon the duties of his office.

[3] W. Jackson.

degree adequate for an officer of my rank and that there are neither money nor materials to put the few troops there in a respectable situation. I hope neither congress or the board will expect that I should shut myself up there with a command not superior to a major's. I believe there are great irregularities and abuses committed and that some arrangements are absolutely necessary. I consider myself under obligations to your honorable board in placing such confidence in me as to think me a suitable person to make these arrangements, but I flatter myself the resolution may be altered so far as respects my remaining there.

The board, I hope, will also consider that my traveling there, if no troops go, will be attended with a heavy expense. I must necessarily take a number of horses and attendants, all of which must be, in the present situation of affairs, defrayed as a private person at tavern expense. Either some money must be advanced on account, or a few months' pay will be indispensably necessary for me.

I am informed the few troops there are in a most deplorable situation, for want of money and in fact every necessary of life. Should I go there, they will of course look up to me for relief. I hope, therefore, that at least one month's pay may be provided for them; and such clothing as can be spared them should be instantly forwarded, otherwise the winter setting in will prevent their getting them. There are now some few articles of clothing at Carlisle for that garrison, which the quartermaster cannot forward for want of money.

II.— IRVINE TO THE BOARD OF WAR.

FORT PITT, *December* 3, 1781.

Gentlemen: — I do myself the honor to transmit copies of my orders for the purpose of arranging the troops here, and also respecting provision, which I hope will meet the approbation of your honorable board.[1] I have struck off two commis-

---

[1] The following are the orders referred to: —

[I.]

"FORT PITT, *November* 10, 1781.

"The troops formerly of the eighth Pennsylvania regiment are no longer to be considered as a regiment, but a detachment from the Pennsylvania line,

Appendix B. 159

saries, one forage master, and one Indian interpeter. There remain yet Mr. [Alexander] Fowler and his clerk, who says he is yearly appointed by congress auditor of accounts, with three rations per day for himself and one for his clerk; and that he has not yet received a dismissal either from congress or the auditor general. I request express directions respecting this man; and if he is to be struck off, an order to him to deliver all the stationery on hand; as I am informed he has a pretty good stock. When this is done there will not be a man on the civil staff except Mr. Samuel Sample, who has been doing the duty of quartermaster ever since Mr. [David] Duncan was put under arrest. As I think there is an indispensable necessity for some person to act in that department, I have continued him till further orders. I have also struck off or rather changed the title of ten *artificers* and now call them fatigue men. Any person to look at the place and be told that a number of artificers were employed, I believe they would rather imagine they were pulling down than building up or repairing. Such a complete heap of ruins to retain the name

---

and for the present to be arranged into two companies and commanded by Lieutenant Colonel [Stephen] Bayard; the different companies to be commanded by the following officers, namely: 1st company — Captain Clark, Lieutenants Peterson and Reed; 2d company — Captain Brady, Lieutenant Ward and Ensign Morrison.

"Lieutenant Crawford will do duty of adjutant to the detachment and Lieutenant Neily the duty of quartermaster, until further orders. The non-commissioned officers, drummers, fifers and privates, are to be divided into two companies as equally as the case will admit of, and Colonel Bayard will make the arrangement as soon as possible.

"Captain Joseph Lewis Finley doing the duty of major of brigade, and Captain John Finley that of deputy judge advocate, will continue in these offices and remain at this post, until further orders. All the other officers of the Pennsylvania line will repair to the regiments they are respectively arranged to as soon as they can with any degree of convenience. They will leave all accounts respecting in any manner the pay, clothing or retained rations of the men, commissioned officers and privates, in the hands of those officers hereby ordered to take charge of them. The retiring officers will please to call upon the general before their departure, who can inform them of the rendezvous of the different regiments.

"Colonel Gibson will arrange his regiment as directed by a former general order and send such officers into Virginia as he can at present spare. He will also please to send a trusty sergeant of his regiment with the Maryland troops,

of a post, I believe cannot be found in any other place. The stores are also nearly exhausted. When you see the returns (which I have directed the commissary of military stores to send), you will be able to determine whether the causes assigned for the issues are proper. But as I consider this does not lie with me to decide on, shall, for the present, say no more on this subject.

I have written to congress and the commander-in-chief, in which I have given my opinion that Fort Pitt is not tenable and that a redoubt could be built within four miles, at Chartiers Creek, at a less expense than would repair this place; that it has many advantages as a position. I have also asked leave of congress to go down the country for two months, and mentioned that I could concert proper measures for the defense of this country better by being present with congress, the board of war, or the commander-in-chief; as there are many things which cannot be so well committed to paper.

The contractors have not supplied the troops tolerably with provisions. I have not been able to get half the things exe-

---

with directions to deliver them to the executive of the state they belong to, with all convenient speed.

"Such commissioned officers as think proper may draw two rations per day in future, when the state of the magazine will admit of it."

[II.]

"FORT PITT, *November* 12, 1781.

"All provision returns in future are to be signed by officers commanding corps and countersigned by the acting brigade inspector, except the commandant's issues at out-posts, and also excepting officers' messes in the garrison, whose orders may be issued in the first instance, but monthly digested into rations by the parties and contractor, to be finally certified by the brigade inspector before they can be deemed vouchers for the contractor.

"Officers commanding at out-posts are to be accountable for all provisions, military stores and public property of every kind; and when relieved, they are to deliver an inventory signed by themselves to the relieving officer, of every article in their charge. When they return to this post, they are to report any material occurrence during their command to the general or commanding officer, and also render an account of all stores expended, with the cause of such expenditure. All officers returning from patroling, excursions, or commands of any kind, are to make similar reports. The brigade inspector will direct the issues for the friendly Indians. He will receive instructions from the general from time to time, how many are to be allowed provisions, and also who in the staff department are to draw rations."

cuted that I intend, being frequently three or four days without a mouthful. You will see by my letter to Mr. Duncan, who does the contractor's [Michael Huffnagle's][1] business here, and his answer to me of this date, what the prospects are;[2] though I fear he over-rates matters, especially if I am to judge from past promises, few which are complied with. I must here take the liberty to report my opinion to the board, which is — that if the contract was even complied with in the fullest extent, it is not an extensive plan enough; as the detachment can never amount to one hundred where there are only two hundred men. But suppose even the militia called out and posted by twenties at ten different places, I do not see how they are to be fed.

The service here is very different from most other places. The contract might do at a stationary garrison, but this is not the case here, as more than half the men are always on one

---

[1] Ante, p. 81, note 1.

[2] Neither of these letters have been found. The following throws some light upon the nature of the contract and the difficulties in the way of its fulfillment:

"PHILADELPHIA, 20 *December*, 1781.

"*Sir:*— I having contracted with the honorable Robert Morris, Esquire, financier-general, for the supplying of the post of Fort Pitt with provisions, I propose to supply the militia and ranging company for Westmoreland county, the ration to consist of the same articles as for the continental troops, and to be paid for at the same rate, which is eleven pence half penny for every ration, in gold or silver,— to be delivered at Hannastown and Ligonier; and twelve pence per ration at Rook's block house;— that the lieutenant or oldest sub-lieutenant of the county countersigning the orders of the officers to be sufficient vouchers for settlement; that the supreme executive council [of Pa.] will settle with me every three months; that if any provisions shall be taken by the enemy, having an escort which is to be granted by the lieutenant upon proper application of the contractors, shall be paid for as rations issued; if any magazine shall be taken, to be paid for in like manner, the contractors having proper vouchers to produce for such quantity so taken; that the supreme executive council are to advance me one hundred pounds in gold or silver.

"I shall be obliged to you to mention these proposals to council, as it will be easier for me to supply them than any other person, my having the contract for the continental troops. Your most obedient, humble servant,

"MICH. HUFFNAGLE.

"The Honorable Christopher Hays, Esqr. [member of council from Westmoreland county, Pennsylvania]."

command or other. I fear the contract cannot be fulfilled without an ample supply of cash. Not a man in the whole country has credit for one hundred pounds.

As there were no subaltern officers here belonging to the Pennsylvania line except four who, by mistake, were left out of the arrangement last year, I was under the necessity of retaining them here — at least till others from the line can be ordered here in their stead, which cannot be well done now before the spring. It is very hard on these gentlemen, as they thought themselves continued. They are deserving men. If they cannot be again re-admitted into the line, I would propose that congress make some such resolution as this in their favor: "WHEREAS, Lieutenants Reid, Peterson, Neily, and Ensign Morrison, officers in the Pennsylvania line, were by mistake left out of the arrangement in October, 1780,— *Resolved*, If they cannot be admitted again into the line with propriety, that they be entitled to every emolument granted to other retiring officers agreeable to an act of congress of the 21st of October, 1780; and if they cannot be admitted again into the line, that the commanding officer of the Pennsylvania line be directed to relieve them as soon as possible with other officers, and that they be entitled to full pay for the time they have done or shall do duty." It would I think not only be unjust but cruel not to allow them some such [relief] as the foregoing. I request the honorable, the board, will be pleased to have some steps taken respecting them.

I had no other shift for a partial supply of forage than to order the quartermaster to barter a few old cast horses and other useless articles,[1] but this is so small it will not last long.

---

[1] The order was directed to the acting assistant quartermaster, Samuel Sample, at Fort Pitt, and was in these words:

"FORT PITT, *November* 12, 1781.

"*Sir:*— You are hereby authorized and directed to dispose of all unnecessary and cast horses, the property of the United States, and other articles belonging to the quartermaster's department at this post and its dependencies that are unfit for service or are likely to become so by decay or such as cannot be repaired at small expense to the public.

"Your articles of sale must be either for ready cash — specie — or forage, equivalent for the sum agreed for. In the execution of this business, I make

Wood and coal are much more difficult to be had here than is generally imagined. It takes three teams kept very busy to supply these articles.

In 1780, it was ordered by congress that General Washington should employ such a number of express riders and post them at such places as he thought proper. He directed one to remain here, but I cannot find that there ever was any such a person; if there was, he was kept in the quartermaster's employ and not under the direction of the commanding officer. However, there is no doing without one. I have been obliged, in this instance, to send a soldier and find him with money to bear his expenses. I hope you will direct Colonel [Samuel] Miles [deputy quartermaster] to refund that, and give the man as much as will bring him back. I beg also you will give orders for establishing one here.

I have also enclosed a return of the troops and of the military stores.

III.—Irvine to the Board of War.

Fort Pitt, *December* 13, 1781.

Gentlemen:— This will be handed to you by Ensign Tannehill, paymaster of the 7th Virginia regiment, who (as there is no deputy paymaster here) carries the muster and pay rolls of his own regiment and also of the Pennsylvania detachment, the officers of which wish him to receive their pay. The officers in the first instance agree to defray Mr. Tannehill's expenses, but hope the honorable, the board, will allow him reasonable expenses, as the rest of the army receive their pay clear. I know it may be answered that if they had patience they would be done so by, too. But their necessities are extreme. Few officers are able to do duty for want of

---

no doubt you will do your utmost for the good of the public. Indeed, great economy is necessary in every department.

"The amount of these sales must be appropriated for procuring forage indispensably necessary for the support of the garrison. This information I think proper to give you that you may arrange matters accordingly. I am, sir, your obedient, humble servant.

"Wm. Irvine, B. Gen'l."

clothing. When there was a paymaster and remnant of paper money in his hands, it was of no use, as no kind of paper currency passed in this part of the country for many months past; so that the depreciation the Pennsylvania troops received has been of no value to them; and the Virginia regiment never received any. In short, they conceive themselves totally neglected, and that the main army wants for nothing; but, on the contrary, are firmly of opinion they live in the greatest luxury. As for the soldiery, the enclosed petty piece will show what disposition they are in, which was some time after my arrival taken off the fort gate.[1] I have made strict inquiry for the author, but without effect. I apprehended this disposition has been encouraged by part of Colonel Rawlings' regiment being detained here long after orders had arrived for their being sent off to Annapolis. They were not sent at all, but broke off, marched down in a body to the governor, who, it is said, received them kindly, without even a rebuke; which, under their circumstances, was probably right, as they were doubtless in a most miserable situation; the cause of which should, in my opinion, be enquired into, as the tendency and evil effects are evident. For whether they were received or not in the manner above, the report among the troops here is so, and they believe it.[2]

I need not urge the necessity there is for at least some months' pay being sent to the troops here, as your honorable board must be well convinced of the propriety of the whole army being on the same footing as near as possible. Indeed, if practicable, those here should be relieved, particularly the Pennsylvanians; as they are only a detachment. I wish Colonel Gibson's regiment could be filled up and another sent

---

[1] This "petty piece" not found.

[2] "The Maryland corps [part of Rawlings' regiment] is at present stationed upon the frontier of Westmoreland, but it appears by recent information, that they are determined to march to Maryland to apply for clothing, of which they are quite destitute."— Col. Daniel Brodhead to Pres't Reed, from Fort Pitt, Aug. 23, 1781.

"The Marylanders have in a body deserted from their posts on the frontier of Westmoreland county and marched to the other side of the mountains."— Same to same, August 29, 1781.

to relieve the Pennsylvania detachment in the spring. They never will be good for much, as long as they remain here. As for Colonel Gibson, I think he should continue as long as troops are kept in the district. No man knows this country better, nor any man, I believe, the Indian country so well.

IV.— IRVINE TO THE BOARD OF WAR.

FORT PITT, *December* 14, 1781.

Gentlemen:—Since I closed my letter of yesterday, Mr. Duncan, one of the contractors, has been with me, and reports that he has been deceived and disappointed by several persons, who engaged to procure flour for him; that he has not now an ounce on hand; and that as the river will in all probability freeze this night, the transportation of about six thousand weight he has at Redstone [now Brownsville, Pa.] will be impracticable;— that if Mr. Huffnagle, the principal contractor, does not soon come up, or send an immediate supply of cash, he will not be able to go on with the business, even for the time he promised in his letter to me on the subject, a copy of which I enclosed to you the 2d instant. I am obliged to give entire credit to his report. Colonel Gibson's and my private credit hath already procured a considerable quantity of flour for them. We borrowed about enough this morning for three days, which is the last I know of can be obtained in the same way.

I am sorry to be under the necessity of giving your honorable board so much trouble in a business which you had reason to think you had now done with. Yet I think it incumbent on me to give you the earliest and best accounts in my power, that you may not be unapprised of what is too likely to be the consequence. I really fear the few troops that are here must disband; and I would not feel so unhappy under this apprehension if I foresaw a possibility of saving the stores,— by saving them I mean a mode of conveying them into a more interior part of the country. Perhaps matters may take a more favorable turn than I imagine. I can only promise that every exertion and expedient in my power shall be made use of.

V.— MAJOR GENERAL BENJAMIN LINCOLN [1] TO IRVINE.

WAR OFFICE, *Philadelphia*, December 21, 1781.

Dear Sir:— I have considered the several matters contained in your letter of December 3, and return you my thanks for the different arrangements you have made at your post, all which I entirely approve of. With regard to Mr. Fowler, the auditor of accounts, I cannot see the least necessity for his services and shall therefore send him the order you desire. The commander-in-chief will write you on the subject of removing your post or not, that business having been referred to him by congress. I am sorry to observe that any difficulties have arisen in supplying you with provision. I have consulted Mr. [Robert] Morris [superintendent of finance] on the subject and he has promised that it shall be remedied and that a supply of cash shall be sent on to you.

With respect to the four Pennsylvania officers, it gives me pain that any deserving officers should be excluded from the service, but I see no possibility of their being again admitted into the line, as you must know the state has already a proportion of officers double to that of the troops; nor do I see the necessity of a special resolution in their favor. They must naturally fall in with the rest of the supernumerary officers. I see no reason why they should not be entitled to every emolument allowed them as well as to full pay for the whole time they may remain in actual service. I will give the necessary orders for their being relieved as soon as possible.

When Mr. Morris shall have sent you the money, every difficulty with respect to forage will be obviated. It has been thought proper to abolish all stationary express riders; if, therefore, you have occasion for one, you must procure a man and furnish him with money out of the supply which will be sent you.

---

[1] Secretary at war.

Appendix B.

VI.—LINCOLN TO IRVINE.

WAR OFFICE, *December* 26, 1781.

Dear General:—I enclose you a copy of the orders regulating the issues of provision at the several posts supplied by contract.

You will please to observe that after the 1st of January, the officers are not to draw any rations, but are to pay for such articles as they draw from the contractors at the same rates as the troops are supplied; and to enable them to do this, they will be paid their subsistence money. However, as the officers are not yet furnished with the money, they must settle their accounts with the contractors at the end of the month and pass proper receipts, to entitle them to receive pay from Mr. Morris.

Mr. Michael Huffnagle, the contractor for your post, will deliver you this and will also deliver you one hundred printed victualing returns.

I would wish to furnish you with a copy of the contract, but really a multiplicity of business prevents it. I must therefore take the liberty of referring you to Mr. Huffnagle for a copy, and must also refer him to you for a copy of the inclosed orders.

VII.—LINCOLN TO IRVINE.

WAR OFFICE, *January* [1782].[1]

Sir:—I have before me your letter of the 13th ultimo mentioning the great necessity the officers at Fort Pitt are in for want of money and clothing.

It is a distressing circumstance that it is not now in the power of the United States to pay the army; but it is as true as it is unfortunate. We have, however, better times in view. The states are doing every thing in their power to make the situation of the army easy. Matters are reducing to a system. All partial payments are at an end, and the financier hopes before long to make a payment to the whole army. In the

---
[1] The date, except the month, is torn off the original.

meantime it becomes the duty of every officer to study contentment himself and endeavor to cultivate the same temper among the soldiery; for unless this is done, we may in this last stage of the war, when every thing wears the face of success, do an act which will render every exertion ineffectual.

The soldiers will be fully clothed; and this should quiet them for a little time. Some clothing will also be sent up for the officers sufficient to furnish each with a suit, for which they will be charged, and they may be assured that in future the smallest and most distant post occupied by the United States will have the same attention paid them as the rest of the army.

VIII.— IRVINE TO LINCOLN.

CARLISLE, *March* 17, 1782.

Sir:— I will set out from this place for Fort Pitt to-morrow morning. As I had the commander-in-chief's orders to pay some attention to the recruits and troops of the Pennsylvania line at this post, beg to inform you that they are without clothing and arms. The clothing I believe is preparing for them; but to fit them for marching, I think arms and accoutrements should be immediately sent on here. However, as this is only a matter of opinion, I submit it to you. I believe the general intends they shall march under Colonel Richard Butler, to join the southern army, except a proportion of the recruits [who are to march] to Fort Pitt. I have written on this subject to his excellency by his command.[1]

P. S.— The numbers, when all are collected, will I think amount to about three hundred rank and file.

IX.— IRVINE TO LINCOLN.

FORT PITT, *April* 30, 1782.

Sir:— I wrote you some days since by a certain Montour, captain of Delaware Indians;[2] I did not like to explain by him my reasons for sending him.

---

[1] See Irvine to Washington, March 17, 1782, ante, page 96.
[2] The letter of Irvine has not been found. The "John Montour" he speaks

Appendix B.

He seemed anxious to be either employed[1] or to go with his wife into the Indian country for a place of safety, as he termed it. The fact is I was suspicious of his fidelity; but he is so cunning that no hold could be laid on him. This, however, is the worst place he could possibly be in, if he meant to go off, being perfectly acquainted with all the Indian country and at Detroit. He was in the British interest and service before he joined us. I suppose the best way to manage him will be to amuse him with expectation of being employed in service; or, perhaps, he might render service joined with the Oneidas. You will be better able to judge how he should be disposed of, when you see and converse with him. It must have been very ill-judged to give such fellow a commission.[2]

---

of was a son of Andrew Montour, a half-blood Indian, and a man of information and education, but a great savage. His father, whose Indian name was Sattelihu, was the oldest son of Madame Montour, a French-Canadian woman, and Robert Hunter, an Oneida chief. Andrew was a captain of a company of Indians in the English service in the Old French War, and rose to be a major. John had a captain's commission at date of the above letter.

[1] The following will give an idea how he desired to be employed:

"To the most excellent James [William] Irvine, brigadier general commanding the western department and Fort Pitt, etc.:

"The petition of us, the subscribers, humbly showeth to your excellency that we want revenge upon the savages for the injury they have done unto our brother soldiers here of late; and if your excellency will grant us, your petitioners, privilege to go into the Indian country, we shall endeavor to acquire as many scalps from our enemy and make such discoveries as can be made; which we think we are capable of going through with. Now, through your excellency's grace and usual goodness, we hope to have our request granted.

"Pittsburgh, April 13, 1782. [Signed.] John Montour, captain. Lewis Williams, James Clarke, William Warton, Joseph Coleman, John Gladwin,— soldiers belonging to the Pennsylvania line. N. B.— To be supplied with ammunition sufficient."

[2] The following is the order issued by Irvine to Montour, sending him to the secretary at war:

"*Sir:*— The desire you express to serve with the northern army, and other reasons, induce me to grant your request. You will, therefore, proceed to Philadelphia with all possible dispatch, where you will wait on the secretary at war for orders. Given under my hand at Fort Pitt, April 16, 1782.

"WM. IRVINE, B. Gen'l."

X.—Irvine to Lincoln.

Fort Pitt, *May* 2, 1782.

Sir:— I do myself the honor to inclose you Lieutenant Colonel Wuibert's report to me of the situation and circumstances of this post, the ground, houses around it, etc., in which he has not discovered any thing but what I was before well acquainted with.[1] The officer who preceded me in command had great contention respecting his occupying some houses, particularly Major Ward's,* who brought a civil action against him, and several others brought tedious suits.[2] This

---

* I believe no person has obtained a legal right for the orchard. It is part of what is called a proprietary manor, the property of Mr. Penn. But when Lord Dunmore took into his head to extend Virginia to this place, Ward and others might probably have obtained grants from him. As it is now well known to be in the state of Pennsylvania, I suppose his grants are not worth a farthing. Be this as it may, I have no right to determine anything respecting the claimants of private property, as twenty others claim it as well as Ward.

---

[1] This report has not been found. As to its author, see p. 34; also, Appendix M, — Wuibert to Irvine, no date.

[2] Major Edward Ward was the person spoken of. He was a half brother of Colonel George Croghan, and an old resident of Pittsburgh. The officer referred to by Irvine as his (Irvine's) predecessor who had " great contention " with Ward, was Colonel Daniel Brodhead. The following extract from a letter written by the latter, dated at Fort Pitt, October 28, 1781, throws light upon these "contentions:"

"On the 27th of June, 1779, I did myself the honor to address a letter to the honorable board of war, respecting the range of this and neighboring garrisons; and, on the 23d of July following, the United States, in congress assembled, passed an act regulating the manner of taking it, and satisfying the persons interested, etc.

"Previous to my receiving this act of congress, I was honored with two letters from the board of war, directing me to act, in this case, according to custom and usage. In consequence, I ordered some of the troops to be posted in a house occupied by Messrs. [Edward] Ward and [Thomas] Smallman, and for so doing, process from the court of Yohogania [county, Va.; which court and county afterward became extinct] was immediately issued against me.

"On the 27th of February, 1780, I informed the honorable board of war by

same Ward *claims* what was formerly called the King's Orchard, which lies immediately adjoining and encircles three bastions of the fort. This I have enclosed with a slight fence and use it as a pasture for the public and officers' horses. This man is teasing me to promise him a certain rent, which I can not with propriety do.[1]

letter, of the proceedings of that court; and, on the 18th of April following, congress passed an act declaratory of the intention of that honorable body to support me in the execution of my duty at this post. This last act was shown to the court of Yohogania, and I expected their proceedings would close against me. But I have since seen their record, whereby it appears that they proceeded to judgment, and awarded damages, etc., but no writ of outlawry has been issued, although I did persevere to deny their jurisdiction.

"The court of Westmoreland has now taken up this matter, and many actions are commenced against me for trespasses, etc., for having presumed to act agreeable to my instructions and my conscience, because the legislature of Pennsylvania has not, in compliance with the act of congress, passed a law in favor, or agreeable to their recommendation; and lately an inquisition was held, to turn me out of my quarters, on a suggestion of a forcible entry and detainer, whereby I have been under the necessity of attending Hannastown court; and otherwise considerable expenses have accrued and costs have been awarded."

[1] From the following certificates, it seems that Ward was desirous to save all his legal rights, whatever they might be, and that Irvine was disposed to gratify him in that particular:

[I.]

"This is to certify whom it may concern that about thirty-four acres of ground adjoining Fort Pitt, formerly called the King's Orchard and Gardens, are occupied and inclosed for the use of the garrison; and that I prevented Major Edward Ward and other claimants from erecting buildings or making any kind of improvements thereon. Given under my hand at Fort Pitt, August 3, 1782. WM. IRVINE, B. Gen'l."

[II.]

"FORT PITT, *June* 9, 1783.

"I do certify that the orchard and gardens formerly called the King's, containing about forty acres and one hundred apple trees, have been enclosed and occupied for public use during my command at this post; and that I prevented Major Ward and others, who lay claims to it as private property, from erecting buildings or making any kind of improvements thereon, namely: from November, 1781, to this date. WM. IRVINE, B. Gen'l."

In 1777, Ward's deposition was taken at Pittsburgh, a part of which was in these words: "The deponent further saith that upon the evacuation of Fort Duquesne, by the French, on the approach of the British army, General Forbes, by one of the deputy agents of Indian affairs, made request to the

As to the houses, I have not yet pulled any of them down, but mean in case of any intelligence of the approach of an enemy to set fire to them. Ward's is an old wooden building, which was formerly a redoubt, but has been carried from the place it formerly stood on, and now built house-fashion. It is not worth much though he sets a high value on it. Irwin's house was also a redoubt, but it is now environed by the other houses of the town of Pittsburgh. It is certain that if it is meant to occupy this place any length of time (as would appear the intention by the commander-in-chief and your orders to me), that these houses and several other obstructions should be instantly removed. In case of emergency, I will not hesitate a moment to do it, but these people think it hard to have it done as long as they are not apprehensive of danger. I assure you, sir, this is a very troublesome command, sufficiently so without being obliged to quarrel with the inhabitants. I could wish you would take these points into consideration and instruct me respecting them.

If any troops should be sent to this quarter or any excursion made, some few tents, at least bell tents, would be necessary. I did not make any demand of this article from the quartermaster general, as I at that time thought them unnecessary for garrison duty. The few troops here are the most licentious men and worst behaved I ever saw, owing, I presume, in a great measure, to their not being hitherto kept under any subordination, or tolerable degree of discipline. I will try what effect a few prompt and exemplary punishments will have. Two are now under sentence and shall be executed to-morrow.[1] They not only disobeyed their officer (who com-

---

chiefs of the Six Nations for permission to re-establish a fort at the same place, for the purpose aforesaid, and to prevent the French from returning, which was granted. A fort was built and garrisoned [Fort Pitt], which continued in possession of the British troops till the year 1772, when it was evacuated by them and taken possession of by deponent, who occupied the same till taken possession of by Captain John Conolly, in 1774, with the Virginia militia."

[1] John Phillips and Thomas Steed. The former, it will be remembered, was pardoned by Irvine.

As a matter of interest to the Masonic Fraternity in the West, and to

manded at Fort McIntosh), but actually struck him, and it is supposed would have killed him, had he not been rescued by two other soldiers.

XI.—LINCOLN TO IRVINE.

WAR OFFICE, *May* 15, 1782.

Sir:— I have been honored with your letters of the 30th ultimo and of the 2d and 3d instant. I am fully in opinion with you that no promise of rent could be made under the present state of the title to the orchard, so called. Nor do I think you should hesitate one moment whenever it becomes expedient to take down the old buildings. Should a movement in your quarter be thought on, every necessary will be forwarded. Prompt and exemplary punishment will, I am persuaded, soon restore that discipline which ill-timed lenity ever subverts.

As the officers you mention have long since been deranged[1] and have for some time past quitted actual service, it would be best they should settle all their accounts with the public at the same time. I dare not assure them that money can be advanced, but I will endeavor that on a settlement equal justice shall be done them with other officers in similar circumstances.

Congress having determined to reduce the number of officers to the absolute necessities of service, Mr. Farrell, deputy conductor of military stores at your post, can no longer be

---

show that Irvine was disposed to treat kindly the soldiers who behaved well, it may be mentioned that on the 15th of the previous month, the following officers under his command sent Gen. Irvine a petition, which was granted, asking the privilege of secretly meeting together as a most ancient society, the first and third Monday evenings in every month, except on occasions of emergency: J. H. Lee, sergeant major, Pa. detachment; Thomas Wood, sergeant major, 7th Virginia regiment; Simon Fletcher, quartermaster's sergeant, Pa. detachment; William Semple, sergeant; John Harris, corporal; Matthew Fout, sergeant; Michael Hanley; Matthew McAfee, corporal; John Hutchison; Martin Sheridan; John Kean; J. Williams, sergeant 7th Va. regiment.

[1] The writer's meaning is, that they did not come in under a certain new arrangement.

retained in service. You will please, upon the receipt of this letter, to inform him thereof and desire him to prepare the whole of his accounts for settlement.

You will please to direct the commanding officer of your artillery [1] to take charge of all the military stores, which is certainly a part of his duty. Such assistance as he may want must be afforded by some of the other officers, of whom I observe there is a great proportion to the number of men at the post.

XII.— LINCOLN TO IRVINE.

WAR OFFICE, *May* 30, 1782.

Dear Sir:— It seems to be the wish of congress that the Indians mentioned in your letter to General Washington,[2] an extract of which has been laid before them,[3] should be kept at Fort Pitt; as they can there be supplied as cheap as any where else, unless they reside within the limits of some contract. They also wish that the soldiers might be employed in assisting to build huts for the Indians. If huts cannot be built, and the state of the garrison is such that they cannot be kept longer under cover of it, I wish to have your opinion how they can be removed;— to know their number, ages, sex, and ability to travel; whether they can travel without wagons; if not, where they can be obtained, what number will be necessary, and how a guard can be furnished. On your report will rest the final determination of this matter.

XIII.— IRVINE TO LINCOLN.

FORT PITT, *July* 1, 1782.

Dear Sir: — My letter of the 16th of June informed you of the defeat of a body of volunteer militia who went against Sandusky [under Col. Wm. Crawford]. That disaster has not abated the ardor or desire for revenge (as they term it) of

---

[1] Major Isaac Craig.
[2] See Irvine to Washington, 20 April, 1782, ante, pp. 104-106.
[3] That is, before congress.

these people. A number of the most respectable are urging me strenuously to take command of them, and add as many continental officers and soldiers as can be spared; particularly the former, as they attribute the defeat to the want of experience in their officers. They cannot, nor will not, rest under any plan on the defensive, however well executed; and think their only safety depends on the total destruction of all the Indian settlements within two hundred miles; this, it is true, they are taught by dear-bought experience.

They propose to raise by subscription, six or seven hundred men — provision for them for forty days, and horses to carry it, clear of expense to the public, unless government, at its own time, shall think proper to reimburse them. The 1st of August is the time they talk of assembling, if I think proper to encourage them. I am, by no means, fond of such commands, nor am I sanguine in my expectations; but rather doubtful of the consequences;— and yet absolutely to refuse having anything to do with them, when their proposals are so generous and seemingly spirited, I conceive would not do well either; especially, as people generally, particularly in this quarter, are subject to be clamorous, and charge continental officers with want of zeal, activity, and inclination of doing the needful for their protection.

I have declined giving them an immediate, direct answer, and have informed them that my going depends on circumstances; and, in the meantime, I have called for returns of men who may be depended on to go, the subscription of provisions, and horses. The distance to headquarters is so great that it is uncertain whether an express could return in time with the commander-in-chief's instructions. As you must know whether any movements will take place in this quarter,— or if you are of the opinion it would, on any account, be improper for me to leave the post, I request you would write me by express. But, if no answer arrives before, or about the 1st of August, I will take for granted you have no objection, and that I may act discretionally.

Should it be judged expedient for me to go, the greatest number of regular troops fit to march will not exceed one hundred. The militia are pressing that I shall take all the continentals along and leave the defense of the post to them; but this I shall by no means do. If circumstances seem to require it, I shall throw in a few militia with the regulars left — but under continental officers.

P. S.— The sooner I am favored with your ideas on the subject the better, particularly if you have objections to the plan; as, in that case, I would not give the people the trouble to assemble.

XIV.— LINCOLN TO IRVINE.

WAR OFFICE, *July* 10, 1782.

Dear Sir:— I have been honored with your favor of the 21st of May and 10th of June. There are no resolves of congress relative to your post. Should there be any or such as your troops are interested in, I will forward them.

I would send for your amusement some resolves, but my assistant and secretary are both sick and absent from office.

XV.— IRVINE TO LINCOLN.

FORT PITT, *July* 16, 1782.

Sir:— This moment I have received an account that Hannastown,[1] the county town of Westmoreland, was burned last

---

[1] "By provision of the act [erecting the county of Westmoreland] the courts were to be held at the house of Robert Hanna till a court house should be built. Hanna's settlement was on the old Forbes road, about thirty miles east of Pittsburgh, and about three miles northeast of the present county town, Greensburg. Robert Hanna, a north-county Irishman, had early opened a public house here, and near him had soon been commenced a settlement prosperous for those times. If we except the region immediately contiguous to Fort Ligonier, and the region about the forks of the Ohio [Pittsburgh], the settlement about Hanna's was, at this date [1773], the most flourishing in the county. After the courts had been appointed for here, the place was further stimulated. It was the first collection of houses between Bedford and Pittsburgh dignified with the name of town. It, at no time, contained more than perhaps thirty log cabins, built after the primitive fashion of those days, of one story and a cock-loft, in height, with clap-board roofs, and a huge mud chimney at one end of each cabin. These, scattered along the narrow pack-

Saturday afternoon by a large body of Indians, some say three hundred, others only one, with some mounted.[1] That place is about thirty-five miles in the rear of Fort Pitt, on the main road leading to Philadelphia, generally called the Pennsylvania [Forbes] road. The Virginia [Braddock's] road is yet open, but how long it will continue so is uncertain, as this stroke has alarmed the whole country beyond conception. Should the country be evacuated on the south side of me, I know not what the consequence will be, having no magazine of provision, indeed barely supplied from day to day. I cannot at present write more particularly, as I am not yet certain whether the enemy are not in force in the neighborhood. I have sundry reconnoitering parties out, but the bearer, a Mr. Elliott, who promises to forward this from Lancaster county, where he lives, could not be prevailed on to wait their return.

XVI.— LINCOLN TO IRVINE.

WAR OFFICE, *July* 24, 1782.

Dear Sir:— I have been honored with your two letters of the 1st and one of the 5th instant.[2] Your letter of the 1st, in which you speak of a proposed expedition to Sandusky, met General Washington here. Immediately on the receipt of it, I conversed with the general on the subject of the expedition — at that moment there was a rumor that Charleston was evacuated; this induced the general to suspend giving his opinion on the matter until it could be ascertained whether Charleston was evacuated or not. If it had been, he would have ordered the troops at Carlisle to your assistance, under Colonel [Rich-

---

horse track among the monster trees of the ancient forest, was that Hannastown, which occupied such a prominent place in the early history of Western Pennsylvania, where was held the first court west of the Alleghany [mountains, and] where the resolves of May 16, 1775 [in opposition to the tyrannical acts of Great Britain], were passed."— G. Dallas Albert, in Dr. Wm. H. Egle's *History of Pennsylvania*, pp. 1153, 1154.

[1] Ante, p. 140, note; see, also, Appendix G,— Irvine to Moore, same date as the above letter.

[2] Only one of Irvine's letters here referred to, that of the 1st of July, 1782, has been found. (Ante, page 174.)

ard] Butler. He has since little or no reason to suppose the report true; he, therefore, yesterday determined not to send those men from Carlisle, lest they should be called for by General [Nathaniel] Greene.

It is impossible for me at this distance, and with my present information to judge of the propriety of your proceeding or not; your own judgment must determine you when all circumstances are combined. If you should succeed it will be a pretty stroke indeed.

I have only to add, if your movements are such as can be justified on military principles (I presume you would not attempt a movement upon any others, however strongly urged by those who wish the expedition to go forward at every hazard), whether you succeed or not, you will be justified by all good men.

XVII.— IRVINE TO LINCOLN.

FORT PITT, *July* 25, 1782.

Sir:— The incursions of the Indians on the frontier of this country will unavoidably prevent the militia from assembling so soon as the 1st of August. Indeed, I begin to entertain doubts of their being able to raise and equip the proposed number this season; however, I am requested to meet all the militia officers on this subject the first of August, when the business will doubtless be determined on or given up for the present.

I have written to [John Moylan] the clothier-general and sent him accurate returns of the clothing received and issued at this post since my arrival, and also articles remaining on hand, together with an exact estimate of what will be indispensably necessary this fall;— linen overalls and other summer clothing which were promised to be forwarded have been entirely neglected, which has been attended with many inconveniences and evil consequences. Two hundred regimental suits came up last November. Circumstances rendered it proper to deliver them at that time, which I believe was much earlier in the season than the main army received theirs; add to this they were quite too small and of a bad quality,— they are now entirely worn out; so that if the clothier-general should not think of sending our proportion early in the fall and any accident should prevent their arrival before winter sets in, the men will absolutely perish; particularly as transportation is so tedious to this place, and in winter impracticable.

These are the reasons I give you this trouble; as I apprehend some neglect or mistake may happen without your direction. Two hundred suits, with some shirts and shoes, would be sufficient with those on hand.

Enclosed is a return of the friendly Delaware Indians at this post. About a dozen pack-horses would be enough to transport their children and baggage, which is not heavy at present;— they are entirely naked, poor wretches! But as to a guard, I know not how that is to be obtained. In the disposition of mind the people are now in, five hundred men would not guard them over the mountains; so I presume they are likely to remain where they are as long as the populace choose to let them live. I assure you they are troublesome company for a commanding officer. No reasoning can persuade the people of this country, but that an officer who will protect an Indian at all, on any account or pretence, must be a bad man. However, this shall by no means deter me from protecting them as long as it is the pleasure of congress it shall be done. If they are to remain here, I beg you will direct some winter clothing sent for them. They are perpetually teasing me; indeed, it is a shame to see them.

The soldiery have been all summer kept close to duty and extreme hard fatigue in repairing the fort. So much is yet to be done that little of their time can be spared to build Indian huts. Upon the whole, I believe the best thing to be done, when the weather begins to set in cold, would be to set them into a piece of woodland, as near the fort as possible;— let them keep guard for themselves, and give information if likely to be attacked. If you approve of this plan, I will execute it if possible. The reasons against keeping them in the garrison are so numerous and evident that I need scarce trouble you with them [two of the principal, however, are their uncommon filthiness, and that they would consume more fuel than all the garrison beside].[1]

XVIII.— LINCOLN TO IRVINE.

WAR OFFICE, *August* 16, 1782.

Sir:— By the enclósed resolves[2] you will observe that congress are attentive to the safety of your post. Such articles of military stores as you now want or may hereafter have occasion for, you will please to draw for on the store at Carlisle. If you should not find a sufficient supply there, I wish to have a particular return of such articles as are necessary to the security of your post, and they shall be forwarded with all possible despatch.

XIX.— IRVINE TO LINCOLN.

FORT PITT, *August* 23, 1782.

Sir:— I am honored with your favor of the 24th of July. I did expect to have gone on the excursion spoken of before this time, but a variety of accidents and obstructions have intervened. It is not yet entirely laid aside; the 10th September is the day now appointed for the last effort.

I intended transmitting you returns of the militia ordered out by me for the defense of the frontier, but notwithstanding I have taken an infinity of pains to collect them, I have hitherto found it impossible. Indeed, the detached situation they

---

[1] The words in brackets are, in the original, attempted to be erased, but are legible.

[2] These resolves, which were passed on the 8th of August, were in the following words:

"*Resolved*, That it be recommended to the states of Pennsylvania and Virginia immediately to draw out and order to Fort Pitt, each state one hundred and fifty men properly officered and accoutred, to be under the orders of the commanding officer of that post, to enable the said officer more effectually to cover and protect the country.

"That the secretary at war and superintendent of finance take order that proper magazines be laid up in the said post, which may enable the commanding officer, in case the said post should be invested by the enemy, to render it tenable until relieved."

are in renders it difficult for the officers to get them in; add to this, they are all to be taught how to make them, not having been formerly demanded. The requisition on Washington county was for one hundred and sixty; and on Westmoreland, sixty. The first has generally had about half the number out, and the latter nearly their full complement continually out. I have studied economy scrupulously in every instance, and think the pains I have taken has had some effect.

XX.— LINCOLN TO IRVINE.

WAR OFFICE, *September* 2, 1782.

Sir:— I have been honored with your favor of the 23d ultimo. Your state are planning two expeditions against the Indians. A committee is gone to General Washington to consult him on the subject and to solicit his aid. How far they will succeed I know not. I think it is probable something will be done.

I have ordered a quantity of ball to Carlisle. Powder we have there, and paper for cartridges. Should you want, you will direct your order there. Peace is talked of,— how far we may depend on it, I am quite at a loss to say. You will learn from the papers all the information we are possessed of.

XXI.— LINCOLN TO IRVINE.

PHILADELPHIA, *September* 7, 1782.

Sir:— I have only time to mention to you that an expedition is agreed on to Sandusky. You will be requested to command it. It is proposed to send twelve hundred men made up as followeth, viz.:

To be detached from Fort Pitt	150
Rangers of this state	60
The militia ordered by congress to be raised by this state and the state of Virginia	300
Part of Hazen's regiment [1]	200
Volunteers from your part of the country	490
	1,200

[1] This regiment was stationed at Lancaster, Pennsylvania.

At the same time an attempt will be made against the Genesee towns;[1] nine hundred men will be sent there. The state [Pennsylvania] have borrowed money enough to execute these designs. You will hear more fully on the matter in a few days. I expect the two movements may be made by the eighth of October.

XXII.— IRVINE TO LINCOLN.

FORT PITT, *September* 12, 1782.

Sir:— I received your favor of the 16th August and also letters from the governors of Virginia[2] and Pennsylvania,[3] acquainting me of the requisition of congress on each for one hundred and fifty men to be sent here, and their having ordered them accordingly. They have not yet arrived, and everything has been so quiet in this quarter since the beginning of August, and the season so far advanced, besides the difficulty of getting provision for them, that I now almost wish they may not come.

But as I did not know what information you might have got of the enemy's intention against this post from some other quarter, I could not think myself at liberty positively to countermand their march.[4] Immediately, however, on receipt of the governors' letters, I wrote them how matters stood here.[5] If they do come up, I shall not detain them longer than the exigency of affairs may require.

---

[1] Villages and settlements of the Seneca Indians upon the Genesee river, in western New York.

[2] See Appendix H,— Harrison to Irvine, August 21, 1782.

[3] Not found. It was dated the 13th of August. See Appendix G,— Irvine to Moore, September 9, 1782.

[4] The following is an extract from the *Pennsylvania Packet* of the 5th of September, 1782 (No. 933), under the Richmond (Va.) head of August 24th:

"Certain accounts are . . . received of an expedition being intended against Fort Pitt by the British and their Indian allies. From the rigorous measures adopted by this state [Va.] and Pennsylvania, we have reason to hope their designs will be effectually counteracted and at the same time will convince the public of their real views in holding out the idea of peace."

[5] See Appendix G,— Irvine to Moore, September 9, 1782; also Appendix H,— Irvine to Harrison, September 3, same year.

XXIII.—Irvine to Lincoln.

Fort Pitt, *September* 12, 1782.

Sir:— This[1] will be handed to you by Mr. Perry, who informs me he has some intention to contract for supplying the troops at this post with provision. He has requested me to write you, more by way of introduction than a recommendation, as he says he can obtain sufficient security for any engagements he may enter into. All I know of the man is that he is possessed of considerable property, and I believe has as much credit in this country as any other man.

XXIV.—Lincoln to Irvine.

War Office, *September* 14, 1782.

Dear Sir:— Congress have agreed that the recruits of Pennsylvania and part of Hazen's regiment shall be employed on the two expeditions undertaken by this state, which I mentioned to you in my last letter. Two hundred of General Hazen's will be sent to join you. The executive of this state[2] informs me that they will order sixty of their rangers to Fort Pitt. I hope with those troops, those you can spare from the fort, the three hundred lately ordered to you by congress, and the volunteers of your country, you will have a respectable force; and that the expedition against Sandusky may be undertaken with rational hopes of success.

The state are making every preparation for procuring a supply of horses and sacks for removing the flour and other necessary stores. The beeves will travel with the troops. The eighth of October is fixed on as the day for marching from the places of rendezvous, namely: Fort Pitt and Muncy at Wallace's place,[3] on the west bank of the Susquehanna. I

---

[1] The previous letter, on the back of which, in the original, a note was written introducing Mr. Perry, was inclosed in the above. It will be seen that their dates are the same.

[2] That is, of Pennsylvania; the continental war office being located in Philadelphia.

[3] Now Muncy, Lycoming county, Pennsylvania.

have some reason to hope that General Washington will order, at the same time, some troops up the Mohawk river. You will, I doubt not, be making every preparation in your power, the moment you get this information. I will forward some ammunition to Carlisle, where you may secure a supply.

XXV.— LINCOLN TO IRVINE.

WAR OFFICE, *September*, 27, 1782.

Dear Sir: — From late accounts forwarded by his excellency, General Washington, we learn that the Indians are all called in;[1] this has induced the resolution to lay aside the expeditions I mentioned to you in my last.

XXVI.— LINCOLN TO IRVINE.

PHILADELPHIA, *October* 30, 1782.

Dear Sir: — I have been honored with your private letter of the 8th instant. What number, or whether any of the general officers will retire, is yet uncertain; however, as you will have nearly one brigade in your state, and as a general officer will probably be kept at Fort Pitt, I suppose both you and General Wayne will be continued in service, but this is mere private opinion.

I know too well how little officers have received not to be fully convinced that you must have spent much of your private fortune; and my own experience has taught me what are the expenses of two families; but I conceive matters are in too unsettled a state for you to think of removing your family at present. But I am of opinion you may with great safety visit your family as you propose; and it is probable that when you are at Carlisle, I shall have it in my power to write you more fully.

---

[1] Ante, p. 135, note 2.

XXVII.—Lincoln to Irvine.

War Office, *October* 30, 1782.

Sir:—I have been honored with your two favors of the 8th instant. I have written to General Greene that if he should think proper to retain any of the troops of this state [Pennsylvania] with him in South Carolina and not all of them, that he would select one complete regiment and officers to command it; and that the other officers and men should return to this state. I cannot therefore fully arrange your line until I hear from General Greene.

I think you may retain your present aid [Lieut. John Rose]. You will do it until we know what is done by the General [Washington] with the main army. We are so exceedingly at a loss respecting the designs of the enemy, that I am not sufficiently informed to make any observations on the latter part of your letter. Before you receive this, you will know that the proposed expedition is laid aside — for that the Indians are called in.

XXVIII.—Lincoln to Irvine.

War Office, *December* 14, 1782.

Sir:—I have been honored with your letter of the 28th of October. Before you receive this, the clothing will, I hope, have reached Fort Pitt. I expect we shall soon have it in our power to make the troops a handsome payment. An extract from your letter to me respecting the new settlers, was laid on the table of congress. The expedition mentioned in a former letter from you, will in my opinion be laid aside; as the present state of our finances forbid the prosecution of it.

XXIX.—Irvine to Lincoln.

Fort Pitt, *January* 1, 1783.

Sir:—Confined to my room by a severe attack of the rheumatism, it was not in my power to acknowledge sooner the receipt of your letters. I flattered myself with the hopes of obtaining before this time an answer to my letter from his excellency, General Washington, and his leave to go down the country. But favored with your consent, I fear the state of my health will hardly permit me to venture on this journey before the month of February. I think it necessary to acquaint you of this circumstance, as your orders would not meet me in Carlisle at a time when you might expect it by the permission asked and granted.

As the present arrangement of the army might affect the officers of this garrison in such a manner as to reduce all three field officers here present, I must request you to order whoever should supply their places to repair to this post before my departure from here. Besides different other reasons, it would be highly inconvenient and inadvisable, that the command, in my absence, should devolve upon any body inferior to a field officer. The clothing destined for this garrison [should be received before the] season sets in severe; and the [destitute soldiers, in such a] situation, are much exposed to its [inclemency].

XXX.— LINCOLN TO IRVINE.[1]

WAR OFFICE, *March* 22, 1783.

Dear Sir: — I was by Mr. Rose honored with the receipt of your favor of the 6th. I have communicated to him by way of answers to various questions he laid before me all I have to say of a public nature. Such is the present state of affairs, that I could not move for his promotion with any probability of success. Congress, at least many of them, are hourly looking for the arrival of the messenger of peace.

Mr. Rose mentioned to me your wish to have my private sentiments respecting the removal of your family to Fort Pitt. Such a measure in the present state of things I think could not be advised; for the moment there is peace, each state will, in my opinion, be left to keep up or not, as they shall judge proper, garrisons within themselves. Should this be the case, your

---

[1] This letter was directed to General Irvine at Carlisle, Pennsylvania, where he was then visiting his family, he having reached home the 4th. (See p. 53.)

stay would not be long at that post as a continental officer. However, before the weather will permit you taking this journey with your family, we shall be freed probably from our present painful suspense.

XXXI.— IRVINE TO LINCOLN.

CARLISLE, *April* 16, 1783.

Sir:— I have this day received letters by express from Lieutenant Colonel Bayard, the commanding officer in my absence at Fort Pitt, informing me that the savages have lately killed and taken a number of families at nearly the same time in many different places of the country as well on the frontier of Virginia as Pennsylvania.[1] Not less than seventeen persons are said to be killed and scalped in a small settlement on Wheeling creek. The whole number mentioned to be killed and taken exceeds thirty.

I am of opinion that nothing short of a total extirpation of all the western tribes of Indians, or at least driving them over the Mississippi and the lakes, will insure peace. It is probable that congress will think proper to give some instructions under these circumstances. If they should, you will no doubt recollect that the terms of enlistment of the regular troops end with the British war. I also beg to inform you that the contract for supplying provisions being limited to the post of Fort Pitt, will not answer for covering the country even on the defensive plan. I could therefore wish your instructions on this head as soon as may be, if my return to that place is thought necessary, which, however, I will postpone till I receive your answer, unless his excellency's (General Washington's) letter, which I daily expect should direct my immediate return.

My aid-de-camp told me you had no objection to my getting a non-commissioned officer and six dragoons with me. If I am to go up [to Pittsburgh], I hope you will please to order them to this place in time to set out with me.

---

[1] See Appendix M,— Bayard to Irvine, 5 April, 1783.

XXXII.—LINCOLN TO IRVINE.

WAR OFFICE, *May* 3, 1783.

Sir:— Mr. [Ephraim] Douglass, who will have the honor of presenting this letter,[1] is charged with a message to the Indian nations on the frontiers of the United States. You will be pleased to afford him every assistance which will contribute to render his mission speedy and effectual.[2]

---

[1] This letter was directed to Irvine at Fort Pitt although he was at Carlisle. However, he soon left for Pittsburgh, reaching their previous to the arrival of Douglass.

[2] On a report of the secretary at war of the United States to congress on the 1st of May, 1783, to whom had been referred a letter from President Dickinson of the supreme executive council of Pennsylvania to the delegates of that state, covering one from General Irvine to him on the continuation of Indian hostilities in the vicinity of Fort Pitt, that body

"*Resolved*, That the secretary at war take the most effectual measures to inform the several Indian nations, on the frontiers of the United States, that preliminary articles of peace have been agreed on, and hostilities have ceased with Great Britain, and to communicate to them that the forts within the United States, and in possession of the British troops, will speedily be evacuated; intimating also that the United States are disposed to enter into friendly treaty with the different tribes; and to inform the hostile Indian nations, that unless they immediately cease all hostilities against the citizens of these states, and accept of these friendly proffers of peace, congress will take the most decided measures to compel them thereto.

"*Ordered*, That the secretary at war transmit the proceedings of congress herein, with copies of President Dickinson's and General Irvine's letters, to the commander-in-chief and to the commissioners for Indian affairs in the northern department."

The secretary at war appointed Ephraim Douglass, a prominent citizen of the western department, a resident of Westmoreland county (of that part which soon became Fayette), to visit the western tribes under the foregoing resolution; and issued to him early in May, 1783, proper instructions for his guidance in the performance of his duties. He also wrote the above letter to be presented to the officer commanding at Fort Pitt. For further information as to his visit, see Appendix M,—Douglass to Irvine, June 7 and July 6, 1783.

XXXIII.— LINCOLN TO IRVINE.

PORT TOBACCO, *June* 23, 1783.

Sir:— It is the pleasure of congress that furloughs[1] should be offered to all the men engaged for the war with a proportion of officers. As the men who compose the garrison at Fort Pitt are men under this description, it becomes necessary they should be relieved. The officer [Captain Joseph Marbury] who will have the honor of delivering this letter commands a party who will take possession of the fort on your withdrawing the present garrison.[2] I wish the gentleman who has the care of the military stores would continue his charge of them until farther orders.

The men who belong to the line of Pennsylvania, you will please to order to Carlisle. Should any of your men live between Fort Pitt and Carlisle who wish to receive their furloughs before they arrive there, you will please to give them written ones. On their arrival at Carlisle they will find three months' pay in Morris's notes, payable in six months from their date.

The men belonging to Virginia you will please to order to Winchester unless any of them should incline to receive their furloughs before they arrive there. In that case, I wish they also might be indulged. On their arrival, they will receive the same pay as those of the line of Pennsylvania.

---

[1] The following was the form of furloughs, or discharges, used at that period:

These are to certify, that the bearer hereof, *Jeremiah Barmon, soldier* in the *second Pennsylvania regiment*, having faithfully served the United States *seven years and nine months*, and being enlisted for the war, is hereby discharged from the American army. *Given at Fort Pitt, September 30, 1783.*

Wm. Irvine, B. Gen'l.

Registered in the books of the regiment [in this case, of the detachment]. *J. Crawford, Lieut. 3d Penn'a regiment*, adjutant.

[FORT PITT, *September* 30,] 1783.

The within [the above] certificate shall not avail the bearer as a discharge until the ratification of the definitive treaty of peace; previous to which time, and until proclamation thereof shall be made, he is to be considered on furlough. *Wm. Irvine, B. Gen'l.*

[2] This letter was detained, causing Irvine a great deal of anxiety and trouble.

XXXIV.— IRVINE TO LINCOLN.

FORT PITT, *July* 18, 1783.

Sir:— Various reports respecting new arrangements of, and settlement with the army, have reached this place; among others that all the troops for the war are conditionally discharged and have received four months' pay; though I do not mean to pay any regard to reports, yet circumstances are so strong in favor of the truth of some of them I begin to persuade myself that your orders or dispatches to me have miscarried (nothing official has come to hand since my aid-de-camp left you in March, except a letter from his excellency, the commander-in-chief, dated the 16th April, directing me to return immediately to this post), as I cannot suppose you would omit at least advising me of such material changes.

It may probably be necessary to acquaint you that such of the non-commissioned officers and privates as have a residence in this country, expect a final settlement here; and it has been repeatedly indispensably so for me to assure them that they would be treated, in all respects, exactly as every part of the army. In this I not only looked on myself justifiable, but that a contrary conduct would have been criminal, as it would have implied a doubt of the justice of congress or the states.

Accounts in an obscure and indirect way of the late turbulency of the troops at Philadelphia have also arrived here, yet this garrison have hitherto continued in perfect subordination and good order, but I can scarce flatter myself they will long remain quiet after hearing all the rest of the army are at liberty. Under these circumstances without advice or orders, I presume you will conceive I must be not a little embarrassed, and that I naturally wish for instructions as soon as possible.

If a time cannot be fixed for final settlement, it will be very agreeable to me even to be able to assure the men when they will be settled with, and what mode will be adopted for warning them to assemble for this purpose, if it can be done with propriety.

I am told it is determined to keep this post garrisoned on

the peace establishment; if so, I presume a relief will soon arrive, and think it probable you will refer the commanding officer to me for advice in particular cases, notwithstanding I conceive this will be my duty without any such reference. I entreat you to be so good as to be explicit in your instructions to myself, particularly respecting the time for me to give up the command of the post.

I yet keep an officer and only ten men at Fort McIntosh, merely to take care of the works; a small garrison for this place of one hundred men cannot well afford any for that post. Pray, what is to be done in this case; is it to be demolished or left standing; or might it not be prudent to put a family or two in it, to save it from accidental or wanton destruction? It is on the west side of the Ohio, thirty miles down from this place, and the same distance advanced towards the Indian country. If it should happen that I cannot keep the regular troops together till I receive instructions, I intend calling in about thirty militia only in the present tranquil state, to guard the stores and post. In this last case, will it be proper for me to leave the place in charge of a careful captain till the new garrison arrives? These queries are more numerous and prolix than I could wish, but hope you will not think them unnecessary or improper.

Scarcity of provisions laid me under a necessity of furloughing most of the troops on the 1st instant for a few days,—which I continue in rotation. The person who does the contractor's business informs me he cannot long procure this small supply for want of money which he says his principals do not furnish him with.

There is some cash subject to my orders, but not enough to pay the non-commissioned officers and privates one month, exclusive of officers, who are also distressed for subsistence, especially since the contractor cannot supply them with provision. I have also indulged as many officers with leave of absence as could be spared, but this only serves such as have connections in this country, who are few. No officers of the Virginia line have ever been sent to relieve those who ought to have retired last January, which is peculiarly hard on those gentlemen.

No Indian incursions have been made since the middle of May, then only in one instance. I have no accounts from Mr. Douglass or those with him with the flag since his departure. I therefore am of opinion he has been well received. I beg the favor of you to direct either this letter, or a copy of it, to be transmitted to his excellency, General Washington. I would by no means give you this trouble, but for an apprehension of my directing a wrong route to him; some pretend to say he will soon be at the Bath in Virginia.[1]

XXXV.— LINCOLN TO IRVINE.

WAR OFFICE, *August* 4, 1783.

Sir:— I have been favored with the receipt of your letter of the 18th ultimo. The letter which I had the honor to address to you on the 23d of June, by the officer [Capt. Joseph Marbury] commanding the detachment intending to take possession of Fort Pitt when your garrison should retire, would inform you of the arrangements which were taken in pursuance of the resolves of congress directing the troops enlisted for the war to be furloughed.[2]

The accounts of the army are committed to the paymaster general for settlement, who is vested with special powers for this purpose. You will be informed, I presume, by that officer, or by the commanding officer of your line, in what manner the accounts are to be made up and finally adjusted.

Your expedient of granting furloughs in routine to economize provision was perfectly prudent and proper.

---

[1] This letter is given as copied by Irvine. It is differently arranged from the original, though the substance is the same.

[2] These resolutions passed congress May 26 and June 11, 1783. They instructed the commander-in-chief to grant furloughs to the non-commissioned officers and soldiers in the service of the United States, enlisted to serve during the war, who were to be discharged as soon as the "definitive" treaty of peace was concluded, together with a proportionable number of commissioned officers of the different grades.

As the peace establishment is not yet resolved on, it is impossible to say what will be done with Fort McIntosh; although I do not conceive it will be continued as a garrison. Your proposition of permitting a family to reside there will, I think, answer the purpose of preventing accidental injury to the works and have future good consequences should circumstances render it necessary to re-occupy the post.

Should you apprehend any risk from an incomplete or, rather, an insufficient garrison being left at Fort Pitt, you will be pleased to carry your intentions respecting a call of thirty militia into effect until a re-enforcement arrives.

The commander-in-chief is expected to visit congress soon. Your letter will be shown to him when he arrives.

XXXVI.— IRVINE TO LINCOLN.

FORT PITT, *August* 17, 1783.

Sir:— Enclosed are returns of the stores at this post.[1] They are well-assorted, packed, and safely stored in such a manner as to give little trouble to whatever officer may have them in charge hereafter. I suppose there will be little alteration before my departure, as the expenditures have been very trifling for many months past. I intend taking receipts for the whole from my successor, which I will transmit to the war office.

Nothing remarkable has occurred since my letters of the 18th July and 4th of August,[2] except that great numbers of men have crossed the Ohio, and have made actual settlements in different places from the Muskingum to the Wabash. This will, in all probability, renew the Indian war.[3]

---

[1] These "returns" not found.
[2] The letter of Aug. 4, 1783, has not been found.
[3] The crossing over of inhabitants of the west to the Indian side of the Ohio, to form settlements, commenced some time before; but as the Delawares had not yet become, as a nation, hostile to the United States, the Fort Pitt commander, Col. Daniel Brodhead, in order to preserve peace with that tribe (as they claimed the lands adjoining the Ohio), determined to drive off the intruders. His action is best described in his own words:

"I received a letter [on the 9th of October, 1779] from Col. Shepherd, lieu-

I anxiously wish to be relieved, particularly as I conceive my continuance here, under present circumstances (at least as far as has come to my knowledge), can be of little or no use to the public.

P. S.— The Virginians were paid when discharged, one month in specie, with three in notes; as the cash in my hands will not reach to pay the Pennsylvanians exclusive of the officers' subsistence, I hope an addition in specie will be sent with the notes; both of which, as well as discharges, the men are

---

tenant of Ohio county [Virginia], informing me that a certain Decker, Cox and company, with others [all from Yohogania and Ohio counties], had crossed the Ohio river and committed trespasses on the Indians' lands, wherefore I ordered sixty rank and file to be equipped, and Captain Clark of the 8th Pennsylvania regiment proceeded with his party to Wheeling, with orders to cross that river and to apprehend some of the principal trespassers and destroy their huts. He returned without finding any of the trespassers, but destroyed some huts. He writes me the inhabitants have made small improvements all the way from the Muskingum river to Fort McIntosh and thirty miles up some of the branches. I sent a runner to the Delaware council, at Coshocton [site of the present town of that name], to inform them of the trespass and assure them it was committed by some foolish people, and requested them to rely on my doing them justice and punishing the offenders, but as yet have not received an answer."— *Brodhead to Washington, from Pittsburgh, October 26, 1779.*

The emigration across the Ohio made little headway until after the Delawares were driven from the valleys of the Tuscarawas and Muskingum, in the spring of 1781. It then began to increase. Towards fall of that year, meetings were held in different places "for the purpose of concerting plans to emigrate into the Indian country [for the emigrants] there to establish a government for themselves." (Appendix G,— Irvine to Moore, Dec. 3, 1781.) By the next spring, the movement had received quite an impetus. Ambition, on the part of a few; to acquire cheap lands, on the part of many; seem to have been the inciting causes. (Ante, p. 109.) From that time until the date of Irvine's letter there had been, apparently, *no relaxation* in the emigration; for in August "great numbers of men" had crossed the Ohio and made "actual settlement," as expressed by him.

The Indian war was indeed renewed — after a number of years; or, rather, the revolution, so far as the United States and the western savages were concerned, was continued; for peace was never fully established between the two until the treaty at Greenville in 1795. Great Britain, during all this time, was covertly hostile to the United States, aiding and abetting the Indians in many ways. It was not until after Wayne's victory and Jay's treaty that the Northwest enjoyed complete immunity from savage aggressions.

impatient for. They have repeatedly been informed by report that they are the only men, for the war, who are unpaid and held in service.

XXXVII.— W. Jackson[1] to Irvine.

PRINCETON, *September* 15, 1783.

Sir:— In the absence of General Lincoln, who is on a visit to Massachusetts, I have the honor to acknowledge the receipt of your letter by Lieutenant Rose.

The secretary at war's letter of the 23d of June not having reached you, accounts for your want of intelligence respecting the measures which had been taken for relieving, paying, and furloughing the troops composing your garrison. The causes which delayed the march of the troops [Captain Joseph Marbury's company] from Maryland having been sometime removed, I hope they will have arrived before you receive this letter; lest any unforeseen circumstance should have happened to prevent them, I have furnished Lieutenant Rose with a copy of that letter and I have taken measures for procuring, to send by that gentleman, Mr. Morris' notes for the three months' pay which have been given to the rest of the army. It may be of service to the soldiers that they should know that these notes pass current as ready money in the stores at Philadelphia.

Should you deem it perfectly consistent with the safety of the post and the security of the public stores, to furlough a part of your garrison before the Maryland detachment arrives, you are at liberty to do so.

I regret exceedingly that circumstances should have made it necessary for you to continue so long in command at Fort Pitt, which, on several accounts, must militate with your convenience. But I am confident in the persuasion that Captain Marbury, with his detachment, must very soon arrive to take possession of the post.

I enclose an order to the contractors at Carlisle to supply such provisions as you shall find it expedient to grant certificates for to the troops of your garrison when on their return

---

[1] Assistant secretary at war.

to Philadelphia. These supplies may be likewise granted to those soldiers whose homes are distant from Carlisle; it is intended that a sufficiency should be supplied to subsist them to their respective places of abode.[1]

Your letter which mentions an apprehension of the Indian war being renewed by the settlements which are made and making between the Muskingum and Wabash has been laid before congress and is referred to a committee.[2]

---

[1] "The contractors for Pennsylvania will please to issue, on the orders of Brigadier General Irvine, such provisions as he shall draw for, to subsist the soldiers composing the garrison of Fort Pitt to their respective homes when furloughed. W. JACKSON, Assistant Secretary at War.
"WAR OFFICE, *September* 15, 1783."

[2] Congress soon took action in the matter, issuing a proclamation prohibiting and forbidding "all persons from making settlements on lands inhabited or claimed by Indians, without the limits or jurisdiction of any particular state." The following was the text:

"By the United States in congress assembled. A proclamation.

"Whereas, by the ninth of the articles of confederation, it is among other things declared, that 'the United States in congress assembled have the sole and exclusive right and power of regulating the trade, and managing all affairs with the Indians not members of any of the states; provided, that the legislative right of any state within its own limits be not infringed or violated.' And whereas, it is essential to the welfare and interest of the United States, as well as necessary for the maintenance of harmony and friendship with the Indians, not members of any of the states, that all cause of quarrel and complaint between them and the United States, or any of them, should be removed and prevented; therefore the United States in congress assembled, have thought proper to issue their proclamation, and they do hereby prohibit and forbid all persons from making settlements on lands inhabited or claimed by Indians without the limits or jurisdiction of any particular state, and from purchasing or receiving any gift or cession of such lands or claims, without the express authority and directions of the United States in congress assembled; and it is moreover declared, that every such purchase or settlement, gift or cession, not having the authority aforesaid, is null and void, and that no right or title will accrue in consequence.

"Done in congress, at Princeton, this twenty-second day of September, in the year of our Lord one thousand seven hundred and eighty-three, and of our sovereignty and independence the eighth.

"ELIAS BOUDINOT, President.
"CHARLES THOMSON, Secretary."

No attention whatever was paid to this proclamation. The consequence was that the settlements increased continually — so rapidly indeed that in less than two years the United States found it necessary to drive off the settlers by

P. S.— You are at liberty to make such arrangements in delivering over the stores to Captain Marbury as you shall find force. To that end, the commissioners of Indian affairs, on the 24th of January, 1785, instructed Lieut-Col. Josiah Harmar, of the first American regiment, to employ such force as he might judge necessary "in driving off persons attempting to settle on the lands of the United States." In obedience to these instructions, that officer detached Ensign John Armstrong with a party of twenty men furnished with fifteen days' provisions to perform the task.

On the 1st day of May, Col. Harmar wrote the president of congress, from Fort McIntosh, that "Ensign Armstrong, having marched with his party as far down as opposite Wheeling, which is about seventy miles from hence, pursuing the course of the river, and having executed his orders (excepting a few indulgences granted on account of the weather), returned on the 12th ultimo." The colonel thus continues: "I have the honor of inclosing to your excellency his report, with sundry petitions, handed him by the settlers; likewise the opinion of some reputable inhabitants on the eastern side of the river, with respect to them. On the 20th ultimo, I received the inclosed representation, signed by sixty-six of them, praying for a further indulgence of time, and informing me that they had sent on a petition to congress on the subject. In answer to which, I thought it most expedient to grant them one month from the 21st ultimo to remove themselves, at the expiration of which time parties will be detached to drive off all settlers within the distance of one hundred and fifty miles from this garrison, which, in my present situation, is all that is practicable. The number of settlers lower down the river is very considerable, and, from all accounts, daily increasing. I would, therefore (before I proceed further in this business), beg to know the pleasure of your excellency and your particular orders upon the subject."

The report of Ensign Armstrong was, in substance, that he marched down the Ohio, March 31st; crossed the Little Beaver on the 1st of April; dispossessed one family at that place; other families at Yellow Creek, at Mingo Bottom, or Old Town, at Norris's Town, at Haglin's, or Mercer's Town, and at a place opposite Wheeling; that he arrested a man named Ross, who seemed to be obstreperous, and sent him to Wheeling in irons; that he was threatened by a man named Charles Norris, with a party of armed men, but upon showing his authority there was no further offensive demonstration; and that at Mercer's Town he had learned that Charles Norris and John Carpenter had been elected justices of the peace and had acted as such.

The "opinion of the respectable inhabitants" was explained by Ensign Armstrong to his colonel:

"As the following information through you to the honorable the congress may be of some service, I trust you will not be displeased therewith. It is the opinion of many sensible men (with whom I conversed on my return from Wheeling) that if the honorable the congress do not fall on some speedy method to prevent people from settling on the lands of the United States west of the Ohio, that country will soon be inhabited by a banditti whose actions are a disgrace to human nature.

most expedient. If the officer who now superintends the stores should not continue, may I request that you would in-

"You will in a few days receive an address from the magistracy of Ohio county, through which most of those people pass, many of whom are flying from justice. I have, sir, taken some pains to distribute copies of your instructions, with those from the honorable the commissioners for Indian affairs, into almost every settlement west of the Ohio, and had them posted up at most public places on the east side of the river, in the neighborhood through which those people pass. Notwithstanding they have seen and read those instructions, they are moving to the unsettled countries by forties and fifties. From the best information I could receive, there are at the falls of the Hockhocking upwards of three hundred families; at the Muskingum, a number equal.

"At Moravian Town there are several families and more than fifteen hundred on the rivers Miami and Scioto. From Wheeling to that place there is scarcely one bottom on the river but has one or more families living thereon. In consequence of the advertisement by John Emerson, I am assured meetings will be held at the times therein mentioned. That at Menzon's or Haglin's town, mentioned in my report of yesterday, the inhabitants had come to a resolution to comply with the requisitions of the advertisement."

The following is "the advertisement" alluded to:

"ADVERTISEMENT.

"*March* 12, 1785.

"Notice is hereby given to the inhabitants of the west side of the Ohio river that there is to be an election for the choosing of members of the convention for the framing a constitution for the governing of the inhabitants, the election to be held on the 10th day of April next ensuing, viz.: one election to be held at the mouth of the Miami river, and one to be held at the mouth of the Scioto river, and one on the Muskingum river, and one at the dwelling house of Jonas Menzons, the members to be chosen to meet at the mouth of the Scioto on the twentieth day of the same month.

"I do certify that all mankind, agreeable to every constitution formed in America, have an undoubted right to pass into every vacant country, and there to form their constitution, and that from the confederation of the whole United States congress is not empowered to forbid them, neither is congress empowered from that confederation to make any sale of the uninhabited lands to pay the public debts, which is to be by a tax levied and lifted [collected] by authority of the legislature of each state.   JOHN EMERSON."

The "representation" mentioned by Col. Harmar in his letter to the president of congress, was to the effect that the settlers desired to act consistent with their duty to their country and the commands of the legislature, and asked for indulgence in time for removing their families and effects. The petitioners asked delay until they could hear from their papers which they had forwarded to be laid before congress. Colonel Harmar replied, allowing the indulgence mentioned in his letter, but notifying them that his orders were peremptory.

form Captain Marbury that he must appoint an officer to take charge of them,— that officer to be responsible to him, he himself having the general superintendency.[1]

On the 1st of June, Col. Harmar wrote the secretary of war in these words: "The honorable the commissioners for Indian affairs . . . left me instructions to drive off all surveyors or settlers on the lands of the United States; in consequence of which, a party has been detached, who drove them off as far as seventy miles from this post. The number lower down the river is immense, and, unless congress enters into immediate measures, it will be impossible to prevent the lands being settled.

"I have written, some time since, upon the subject, requesting particular orders how to conduct myself, as it is out of my power to sweep them further than the distance of one hundred and twenty or one hundred and fifty miles from hence. This is a matter of so much importance, that perhaps you may judge it necessary to remind congress of it."

The letter was referred in congress to a committee, who brought in a report approving the conduct of Colonel Harmar; also authorizing him to remove his troops, and take post at or near the Ohio, between Muskingum and the Great Miami, " which he shall conceive most advisable for further carrying into effect the before mentioned orders," and appropriating six hundred dollars for the purpose of transporting the troops and their baggage. It was under this order that Fort Harmar was erected near the mouth of the Muskingum.

At the commencement of October, Gen. Richard Butler, passing down the Ohio to hold a treaty with the Indians at the mouth of the Miami river, found settlements at intervals on the Indian side of the Ohio from the mouth of Yellow creek well nigh opposite that of the Great Kanawha. Butler did what he could on his downward trip to warn off the persistent settlers, giving orders to one of the army officers who was also to descend the river to the Muskingum, " to pull down every house on his way," some of those recently demolished having already been rebuilt by the determined bordermen.

But, was the "course of empire" which had so persistently taken "its way" beyond the Ohio, *completely* arrested by the United States authorities? Were *all* the settlers from " Little Beaver " to the " Wabash " driven off ? These are questions for the future historians of "the territory northwest of the river Ohio" to answer — if they can. But this much is certain: no constitution for governing the inhabitants was framed; the new state scheme beyond the Ohio came to naught.

[1] This letter was received by General Irvine at Fort Pitt on the 26th of September — only four days before his final departure from that post. See Appendix M,— Irvine to Marbury, October 1, 1783.

APPENDIX C.

CORRESPONDENCE WITH THE SUPERINTENDENT OF FINANCE.[1]

I.— MORRIS TO IRVINE.

OFFICE OF FINANCE, *March* 6, 1782.

Sir:— I have examined the letters and accounts which you submitted to my inspection, relative to supplies furnished at Fort Pitt by Mr. [John] Irwin, the deputy commissary general of issues. In consequence, I have directed Mr. Swanwick to pay you the sum of two hundred dollars to purchase the seven thousand three hundred and ninety-three pounds of flour and eight hundred and eighty-four pounds of beef mentioned in that account; and I will direct the quartermaster to forward the salt.

I must request, sir, that whoever you may employ to purchase those articles, be directed to make out proper and regular accounts of the transaction with proper vouchers to pass at the public offices, and that they may be duly transmitted to me in order to have the same adjusted.

II.— MORRIS TO IRVINE.

OFFICE OF FINANCE, *March* 6, 1782.

Sir:— The letter which you wrote to the honorable secretary at war the 20th ultimo, has been laid before me and the contents duly considered. The uncertainty of the militia ser-

---

[1] Robert Morris was superintendent of the finances of the United States, at the above date. He was born the 20th of January, 1734, in Liverpool, England. He came to the United States at the age of thirteen. In the course of time, he engaged in commercial pursuits in Philadelphia. At the close of the year 1775, he was sent to congress from Pennsylvania. He was unanimously elected by that body general financier, on the 20th of February, 1781, and continued in office until September 30, 1784. He died in great pecuniary embarrassment, in Philadelphia, May 8, 1806.

vice you mention appears to be so great that I know not how any regular and permanent provision can be made for the supplies, when they are called to act beyond the bounds of the post at Fort Pitt. I must request, therefore, that when any are called out for continental purposes and employed where the present contract cannot provide for them, that you will yourself enter into engagements for supplying them with provisions on the most frugal terms practicable, and I will cause those engagements to be complied with.

III.— IRVINE TO MORRIS.

FORT PITT, *April* 29, 1782.

Sir:—When I arrived at this post, the contractors' stock of provisions was nearly exhausted and not a shilling or credit to purchase any more. Under these present circumstances, I could not think of any other alternative than to lend them three hundred pounds which I found could be spared out of money I drew from the quartermaster general, for a few weeks, as we could go on in the mean time. They promised to repay it by the tenth of May, as they thought one of them could be back from Philadelphia by that time. They have sent a person into Virginia to buy beef cattle; should he fail, I know not what we shall or can do. There is no beef in this country. These people neglected their business entirely in not laying up salted pork in the winter, which might have been done with great ease. Should any more troops come up, they will not be able to supply them unless money is advanced them. I could not get a single person in the whole country who would undertake to provide provisions for one hundred and sixty militia, even for the term of one month; indeed, no man has credit sufficient. I am greatly nonplussed on this account, as this number is indispensably necessary to be kept up on the frontier of Washington county to keep the whole county from flying. Mr. Huffnagle has engaged with [the supreme executive] council [of Pennsylvania] to find the militia of Westmoreland for the present. The number I have called from that county is only sixty-five. The whole of the militia ordered out by me amounts (including officers) to two hundred and sixty; but as I presume they will never be quite complete, I count on about two hundred rations daily. They are at present billeted, but this by no means answers, nor can it be done long. Since I came up, I have given permits to ten boats for New Orleans and Kentucky, loaded with flour. I believe none of them carried less than thirty tons. I am informed ten or twelve more are to be down in one fleet of a much larger size. I think there will not much flour be left in the country by the middle of May. By that time or the first of June, the mills cease for want of water. I wish some of these adventurers may not fall into the hands of the enemy. It is reported (but I know not by what authority) that the British have again taken possession of the Illinois country; if so, they will undoubtedly make a post at the mouth of the Ohio; these boats will be a great object for them. Should any such event actually have taken place, I will advise the adventurers thereof and shall also take the earliest opportunity of acquainting you.

IV.— IRVINE TO MORRIS.

FORT PITT, *May* 2, 1782.

Sir:— I did myself the honor to write to you the 29th ult. Since that time the contractors have got up from Virginia thirty head of cattle, purchased with the money I lent them, which will not last more than thirty days for the present garrison. If one of these gentlemen is not up here with money to purchase more before the expiration of that time, I cannot say what the consequences may be. The troops are not in a temper to bear much hunger, though they have been pretty well tried too frequently. For seven days together the latter end of April, they had not an ounce of meat. As Mr. Duncan will hand this to you, he can inform you what their prospects are, and whether they can do the business or not. This, however, I think incumbent upon me to repeat, that they cannot without ready money procure provisions even for a day.

Inclosed are vouchers for the money you gave me to pay for provisions, borrowed for the use of the public by Mr.

John Irwin; this business has been transacted on the best terms I could. The balance shall be disposed of as you think proper to order.

V.— IRVINE TO MORRIS.

FORT PITT, *May* 9, 1782.

Sir:— I have contracted with a Mr. Thomas Parkison to provide provisions for the militia of Washington county who may be drawn out into actual service.[1] The price for a ration the same as the contractors for this post have, which is the lowest I could get anybody to undertake it for. I gave Messrs. Huffnagle and Duncan the preference, but they asked

---

[1] The contract was as follows:

"Article of agreement indented and concluded on at Fort Pitt, this 3d day of May, 1782, between William Irvine, Esq., brigadier general (by authority invested in him by the Honorable Robert Morris, Esq., superintendent of finance), of the one part, and Captain Thomas Parkison, of Washington county, state of Pennsylvania, of the other part, witnesseth:

"That said Parkison for the consideration hereinafter mentioned doth hereby for himself, his executors and administrators, promise and agree to, and with General Irvine, to furnish and issue rations to the militia of the county aforesaid, called out into actual service by order of General Irvine and stationed at the following places, namely: at Montour's bottom, Yellow creek, Mingo bottom, and Wheeling or Grave creek; the ration to consist of one pound of flour and one pound of fresh beef or pork or three quarters of a pound of salt meat. Two quarts of salt are to be issued to every hundred rations of fresh meat. And General Irvine agrees on his part to allow said Parkison eleven pence half penny for every such ration issued by him, and is to use his best endeavors with the superintendent of finance to procure money for the payment of the same at the end of two months from the commencement of the issue, which is to be the tenth instant.

"Said Parkison's vouchers for rations issued are to be returned signed twice every week by commissioned officers commanding the company or parties; which provisions and weekly returns are to be examined and compared by a field officer on duty having charge of the militia then in service; whose certificate [must also be obtained] and also that of the county lieutenant or sub-lieutenant that so many militia of said county were in actual service at that time by the general's order — for the number of days of whatever month,— the returns and certificates to be dated and clear, which certificates and returns or duplicates must be lodged with General Irvine.

"For the true performance of the above agreement, said Captain Thomas Parkison doth bind himself, his executors and administrators (in case of fail-

twice that sum. Mr. Parkison has engaged to do the business on his own credit for two months, to commence the tenth instant. On the tenth of July, I have promised him a payment which will enable him to go on as long as we shall want militia for this campaign. I hope you will direct measures to enable me to comply with this engagement. I cannot yet ascertain exactly the number of rations Mr. Parkison will have to issue, but think they will not exceed one hundred daily. I will take every possible precaution to prevent unfair practices in this business. Mr. Huffnagle at present supplies the militia of Westmoreland county, under a contract made with [the supreme executive] council [of Pennsylvania], but as I have called sixty men from that county into actual service, I presume the feeding them will ultimately become a continental charge.

VI.— IRVINE TO MORRIS.

FORT PITT, *May* 10, 1782.

Sir:—I did not receive your letter of the 4th of April till yesterday by Mr. [John] Canon.[1] I shall always be happy in having it in my power to render service to the United States in any line. I will appoint the agent you mention for inspecting and receiving flour, etc., as soon as I see a probability of that business being worthy of attention; till then such an appointment would be unnecessary expense. At present I am sorry to inform you that the people of this country seem little disposed to pay taxes in any mode ; and I fear Mr. Canon will either find himself much disappointed in his expectations

---

ure), in the penal sum of three hundred pounds specie, to be paid unto the Honorable Robert Morris, Esq., superintendent of finance, in behalf of the United States.

"In witness whereof, we have hereunto set our hands and affixed our seals this 3d day of May, 1782.

"THOMAS PARKISON, [SEAL.]
"WILLIAM IRVINE. [SEAL.]

"Signed, sealed, and delivered in the presence of

"JOHN ROSE."

[1] For a biographical notice of Canon, see Appendix J,— Marshel to Irvine, July 12, 1782, note.

respecting flour, or he meant to deceive, which I will not undertake to say.[1] Be this as it may, I am of opinion it would be best to receive every ounce that is offered, whether in casks, as you direct, or not, as I look on it in a manner as clear gain. Under this idea, would it not be best also for me to authorize Mr. Parkison to receive common flour from the inhabitants, provided it does not exceed the quantity of rations he may have to issue, as it will be some time before any can be got in (the county commissioners having only met yesterday for the purpose of laying a tax)? Your instructions to me on

---

[1] What these expectations were may be inferred from the subjoined letter:
"OFFICE OF FINANCE, *Philadelphia*, April 4, 1782.

"*Sir:*— As you have frequently represented how convenient and agreeable it would be to the inhabitants of Washington county to pay the amount of their taxes assessed by the late supply bill in flour delivered at Fort Pitt at the market price, and as I am not only disposed to accommodate them but think such deliveries may be of use to the United States, I do hereby agree to receive any quantity of good, sound, sweet and merchantable flour which the inhabitants of Washington county may send to that post, packed in casks fit for transportation; the said flour to be delivered to Brigadier General Irvine, or to such person as he may appoint to receive it, the quality to be inspected, approved, and the price of flour and casks fixed by such person; and, in case of dispute about the quality or price of any parcel of flour offered at Fort Pitt in consequence of this agreement, then the said person shall choose one arbitrator, an honest, capable man, the party offering the flour shall choose another, these two shall choose a third, and the three shall determine whether the flour is merchantable or not. If adjudged merchantable, they shall also say what price is to be paid for the same, never exceeding the market price. If adjudged unmerchantable, it is not to be received on account of the United States.

"The whole deliveries are not to exceed in value the amount of the quota of taxes assigned to Washington county, namely: eight thousand and seventy-five pounds and one shilling, Pennsylvania currency; and for the amount of every parcel or quantity of flour received for the use of the United States, General Irvine will give a certificate to me of the quantity of flour and the amount thereof, which may be transmitted to the state treasurer, and I will receive the same from him as so much money on account of the taxes of Washington county.

"You will ever find me disposed to serve and oblige the faithful citizens of the United States in every instance which consists with my duty.

"ROBERT MORRIS.

"P. S.— Every cask of flour must be branded with the miller's name or mill-brand, and be well coopered. R. M.

"JOHN CANON, Esq., representative in assembly for Washington county."

that head shall be as punctually complied with as possible. I am further of opinion that every species of provision should be received, provided any of the contractors will accept of it at the prices which it may be received at.

The seasons for transporting flour from this country to New Orleans are from the middle of February till the first of June; and from the first of November till the last of December; at other times the river is either too low or frozen. A boat which will carry forty tons costs about forty pounds; five men with a super-cargo are enough to work the boat. One super-cargo might do for a number of boats, being practicable to keep in fleets. Boatmen generally get from three to four pounds per month.

VII.—Morris to Irvine.

Office of Finance, *May* 29, 1782.

Sir:—I have been honored with your several favors of the twenty-ninth of April and of the ninth and tenth instant. I read to the contractors so much of the first as related to them, and although they did not absolutely confess but rather sought to evade the charge, I could clearly perceive that it was well founded. I have paid them fully and therefore they must repay the money advanced to them; and I hope you will take care that they comply exactly with their contract.

I am glad that you gave permission to the boats to carry down flour. The opening of a market for that article is the sure and certain means of rendering it plenty and cheap there hereafter. I am very sorry, however, to find that the people are so unwilling to pay taxes when their immediate preservation, as well as interest, are so deeply concerned; but I hope they will learn better and thereby avoid the disagreeable consequences which might ensue. Mr. Canon, from his manner of speaking to me, did, I believe, expect that the taxes would have been paid in the manner I mentioned to you, but whether he was himself deceived or meant to deceive me, the fact is equally disagreeable.[1] I heartily approve your idea of receiv-

---

[1] Further developments showed conclusively that Mr. Canon was acting in the utmost good faith.

ing whatever provisions may be offered and hope that something considerable may be done in that way.

Your contract with Mr. Parkison shall be carried into effect on the part of government. It will be necessary that you transmit a certified copy of it to me; and I will thereupon certify the previous authority given to you and my assent, after which the whole shall be recorded in the proper offices. When Mr. Parkison has made the issues, the mode of doing which you will point out to him, his accounts and vouchers must be sent to the treasury, and the amount being certified to me, shall be paid.

I pray, sir, that you will accept my sincere thanks for your care and attention. Be assured of every support in my power.

VIII.— IRVINE TO MORRIS.

FORT PITT, *July* 5, 1782.

Sir:— The bearer, Mr. Wilson, goes to Philadelphia with the contractors' accounts for May and June. I have brought them to a strict account as to what their prospects are for a regular supply in future. They acknowledge they have doubts of being able to procure supplies till Mr. Wilson returns, unless he is very speedy. I believe they have not money and am certain they cannot get credit; so that I have every reason to fear the worst consequences.

Should they fail altogether, I have no alternative at present but to try to obtain a temporary supply on my own credit; but as this is a business I do not wish to have anything to do with, and am sensible I should not interfere, except in a case of the most urgent necessity, I shall be much obliged for your directions how to act. I do not expect any considerable supply on account of taxes before the last of October, if even then. I have written council [the supreme executive council of Pennsylvania] on this subject to inform them of the disposition of the people; and have urged several officers of civil government to make immediate representations, whom it will come most properly from; but I fear some of them are tainted with a desire to promote setting up a new state.

IX.— IRVINE TO MORRIS.

FORT PITT, *August* 22, 1782.

Sir:— Mr. Wilson returned without an answer to my letter of the 5th of July. I presume it may not be unnecessary to inform you that Messrs. Huffnagle and Duncan seem undetermined whether they will enter into a contract for the ensuing year or not; Mr. Huffnagle rather positively told me he would not.

There is not the smallest prospect of provision being got in for taxes. The county commissioners or assessors have not done anything towards laying a tax. I am sorry to give you so much trouble in this business, but think it highly proper you should be apprised of it.

X.— IRVINE TO MORRIS.

FORT PITT, *August* 23, 1782.

Sir:— This will be handed to you by Mr. Thomas Parkison, together with his accounts and vouchers, for rations furnished the militia of Washington county, under my orders, and also a copy of his agreement with me.

The nature of the service the militia are employed on, particularly being so far detached and in such small parties, renders it altogether impracticable to obtain either returns or certificates so accurate as I could wish and alluded to in the contract; yet I am persuaded from many concurring circumstances, the number of rations he charges has been fairly issued, namely: five thousand two hundred and sixty-one. I am certain more men have been out on duty than he has charged rations for, many of whom have been fed by frontier inhabitants at whose houses they were quartered. Every possible step has been taken to prevent fraud in this business, and I am of opinion the endeavors have been successful.

I hope I shall not be under a necessity of keeping any militia out longer than the first of October. The whole expense will be small when compared with that of former years; and I flatter myself not less real service has been performed.

XI.— Morris to Irvine.

Office of Finance, *September* 5, 1782.

Sir:— I have received your several letters of the 5th July and 22d and 23d of August. I had intended answering the first by Mr. Wilson, who brought it. I was, by the time of his setting out, incapacitated from doing it. I am very sorry to find the state of the country you are in, to be such as you represent it, but I conceive your representations are correct and require the serious attention of government.

Mr. Parkison's accounts are in the hands of the proper officers and will be duly attended to. I am very much obliged by your attention to the public business. I am persuaded that it has been very great and useful. I know not as yet what determination will be taken with respect to the savages in your quarter, but I hope no more militia will be found necessary, for they create a very great expense and answer very little purpose. And what aggravates the matter still more is the consideration that after all many of the inhabitants of that country, as we are lately informed, only wait a favorable moment to disown the government they now sue to for protection.

XII.— Morris to Irvine.

Office of Finance, *October* 3, 1782.

Sir:— Your favor dated at Fort Pitt, on the 12th of last month, has been delivered by Mr. Perry. Colonel [Ephraim] Blaine [1] having assumed the contract for supplying the troops at Fort Pitt until the first of January next, I have proposed to Mr. Perry to join him in it, expecting from his influence and credit beneficial results.

---

[1] For notice of Col. Blaine, see Appendix M,— Blaine to Irvine, April 2, 1783, note.

XIII.— IRVINE TO MORRIS.

FORT PITT, *January* 1, 1783.

Sir: — A tedious fit of the rheumatism has prevented me acknowledging the receipt of your letter of the 7th of October, 1782, however anxious I was to state to you an account of the sum transmitted to me by the council of Pennsylvania, subjected to your orders.

As the first intimation of any expedition I received, I was urged to use the utmost exertions to march on a certain day fixed. The orders countermanding the execution of these operations and your letter, did not arrive for a long time afterwards. Under such circumstances, the council of this state could justly not expect that money destined for a piece of service so much pressed should remain unappropriated in my hands for such a length of time. By a cautious assiduity — by a lucky combination of circumstances — by transferring such purchases of provisions as were actually paid for to the contractor at the original cost,— the expenses incurred have been comparatively trifling.

The messenger from council, Colonel Carnahan, delivered me fourteen hundred eighty-two pounds five shillings and a penny, and the cash now in my hands amounts to twelve hundred twenty-four pounds six shillings and ten pence. I am, besides, possessed of obligations on the contractor for two hundred thirty-six pounds seven shillings, which sum you will please to deduct from the payment due Colonel Ephraim Blaine, for the supplies furnished this post for November and December, 1782. The state of Pennsylvania, consequently, will receive credit for fourteen hundred and sixty pounds, thirteen shillings and ten pence. I shall transmit to the council an account of the other unavoidable expenses.

This transferring the purchases of provisions to the contractor did prove a fortunate accident to this garrison. It prevented a total want, which to anticipate would not have been in his power, being destitute of ready cash. Our situation with respect to provisions still continues critical. The quantity of meat laid in will supply this post eighteen or twenty days, and flour is procured with the utmost difficulty, as the temporary exigencies call for it. The arrival of Mr. Alex'r Blaine last night, removes this uneasiness in some measure,—having had no previous intimation by whom this post would be supplied with provisions in future.

I am in hopes the state of my health will permit me to undertake a journey to Carlisle in the beginning of February. Should you intend to give any orders upon me for the money in my hands, I beg to be favored with them before that time.

XIV.—IRVINE TO MORRIS.

FORT PITT, *January* 17, 1783.

Sir:—John Pierce, Esq., paymaster general, informs me in a letter dated November 29, 1782, which I received yesterday, that in consequence of his application to you for the subsistence of the officers at this garrison to be ordered from the money in my hands, he had received a draft on John Swanwick for five hundred thirty-eight dollars and twelve-ninetieths, dated November 20th, 1782, payable to him or his order on the 31st of December last. As this order does not particularly specify the money in my hands, and as I am in doubt for what purposes you might intend it, I shall defer complying with his demand until the middle of February next, against which time your orders will easily reach me, if you think proper to countermand the payment being made by me.

By this measure, I expect to prevent occasioning unnecessary trouble, in case you approve of it. I also wish not to thwart your views; but the urgent necessities of the officers, particularly those who, by the new arrangement of the army, are obliged to give up their commands, are such that I think it unavoidable to satisfy the demand and impossible to put off the payment beyond the time mentioned, as they then at farthest must return to their respective homes. Nor can I persuade myself that the difference could be material where the money is reserved; and I should rather be inclined to think that this sum, if it is kept unappropriated by me, may be rendered of more immediate use whilst retained in your own hands. Your silence on this head will convince me of your approbation, in which case you will please to remark that the amount of the sum mentioned for the subsistence of this post is to be deducted from the amount of the cash remaining in my hands, as delivered to you in my letter of January 1st.

Unacquainted with the terms upon which the garrison is supplied with provisions by the present contractor, I could wish to be furnished with a copy of his contract.

XV.— Morris to Irvine.

Office of Finance, *March* 14, 1783.

Sir:— I have received your several letters of the first January, 12th of February and 6th of March. Lieutenant Rose is now engaged in settlement of the accounts, which will, I suppose, be speedily adjusted. Whatever balance may be found due will be payable to Mr. Hilligas by you on a warrant in his favor. You will discharge that by buying the bills of the paymaster at Fort Pitt on the paymaster general, or the orders I may have issued on Mr. Swanwick and which you shall find in that quarter. These can be remitted to me. I will cause receipts to be made on the warrant above mentioned so as to fully adjust the matter.

As to the object of contingencies which your aid mentioned to me, the proper mode is for you as commander in the department to issue your special warrants on the paymaster, mentioning in them the service for which they are issued. The other matters he was charged with being in the war department, I directed him to apply to General Lincoln, who will, I dare say, do anything which shall be proper. Before I close this letter, permit me to express the sense I entertain of your attention to the public service and interest. Accept my thanks for them, together with the best wishes for the speedy and perfect re-establishment of your health.

XVI.— IRVINE TO MORRIS.

FORT PITT, *September* 6, 1783.

Sir:— The balance of the public money, subject to your order remaining in my hands, after a settlement at your office, amounted to two thousand seven hundred and twenty-six dollars, seventy-ninetieths, specie. Lieutenant Rose will present you the bills drawn on the paymaster general for the payment of the troops and the subsistence of the garrison, amounting in full for the sum mentioned. For the final adjustment of the matter, you will please to order receipts to be given on a warrant in favor of Mr. Hilligas as directed by you in a letter dated the 14th of March, 1783.

APPENDIX D.

JOHN PIERCE, PAYMASTER GENERAL, TO IRVINE.

I.

PHILADELPHIA, *January* 12, 1782.

Sir:—The superintendent of finance has agreed to pay the officers' subsistence money, at the end of each month, which I shall forward to your department as it becomes due. You will oblige me by desiring any trusty officer who may come this way, and will return, to call on me, as I am fearful my opportunities may not be frequent for sending it. I wish also that the musters may be taken for every person entitled to receive pay or rations as early as possible at the end of each month and transmitted to me in this city. I have given into Mr. Tannehill's hands the money for the rations for January, who will want the musters for that month before he can make a payment.

As to pay, I am not instructed to say when it may be expected, but can assure you that the troops at Fort Pitt will have the same attention paid them as the rest of the army.

You will oblige me by informing me who would be a proper person to consign my business to in the department. Mr. Tannehill appears to me a proper person, but as I am unacquainted with him and you have an opportunity of observing his conduct, I wish you would please to write me on the subject.

II.

PHILADELPHIA, *May* 30, 1782.

Sir:—I have sent by the bearer, three months' subsistence agreeable to your estimate for the troops at Fort Pitt. Had money been plenty here a larger supply would have been forwarded. Another regulation has taken place in regard to subsistence, which I suppose you have received. As your situation is so distant, I think it cannot take place before the 1st of June. I am much obliged for the estimate, and will thank you for another when I again send on money.

When money is sent on for the pay of the troops, I shall take measures proper for the purpose; but the allowance to Mr. Tannehill, for his present trouble, I cannot ascertain. It will be best for him to make a reasonable charge in addition to his other pay and obtain your certificate; as you are best acquainted with the trouble of the business. Congress will not admit of any *establishment* for the purpose.

III.

PHILADELPHIA, *September* 2, 1782.

Sir:— In answer to yours of the 23d ultimo, I beg leave to inform you that our treasury is so far exhausted that it will not be possible to transmit your garrison any subsistence money at this moment, but shall endeavor to do it soon. Are you not mistaken that there is not more money in your chest than will pay August? The balance which appears to be on hand with Mr. Tannehill is now six hundred and twenty-one dollars, which will amount to more than three months' subsistence. I have stated the particulars of my account current with Mr. Tannehill and inclosed it to him, which you can advert to for your satisfaction.

IV.

PRINCETON, *September* 16, 1783.

Sir:— Lieutenant Rose having represented the difficulties attending the settlement of the Pennsylvania troops at Fort Pitt, unless some person be authorized to transact the business for that detachment, I conceive that, as the regiments at headquarters are allowed agents by the commander-in-chief, for the same purpose, it will be highly necessary and proper that an agent whom the troops can confide in should also be appointed by the officers, to represent that detachment to settle their accounts at Philadelphia, receive their certificates and distribute them to the respective claimants.

I think it very proper that this agent should examine and receive the vouchers of the several regimental paymasters whose accounts are connected with this settlement, and request that you will please to signify this to that person so appointed; and I do hereby authorize him to call to account such regimental paymasters and will be bound by his transactions on this occasion, provided the same shall be agreable to the existing resolves of congress. I shall send any farther necessary instruction on the first application.

APPENDIX E.

CORRESPONDENCE WITH THE DEPUTY[1] AND ASSISTANT QUARTERMASTER GENERAL.[2]

I.—MILES TO IRVINE.

PHILADELPHIA, *March* 12, 1782.

Sir:—I have written Mr. Duncan to deliver to the person you shall appoint to receive them, all the quartermaster's stores under his care and to dismiss all the persons employed by him, as soon as the stores are delivered. I shall, therefore, be obliged to you to appoint some suitable person for this purpose (but pray let him be a person capable of keeping his own accounts, to prevent the expense of a clerk). Some of the gentlemen of the line, I doubt not, will accept it for a small addition to their pay, which I shall leave you to fix; and as you are a judge of the suitableness of the respective gentlemen, and as the person will act under your immediate direction and inspection, I can rest assured that no improper appointment will be made. All I am anxious for is, to have the business done with economy and punctuality.

II.—MILES TO IRVINE.

[PHILADELPHIA, *April* 3, 1782.]

Sir:—By the bearer, Andrew Adam Seitz, are sent six hogsheads of clothing, one hundred axes, and five hundred weight of rod iron.[3] The other articles will be sent as fast as

---

[1] Samuel Miles.
[2] Samuel Hodgdon.
[3] "Rec'd the 3d of April, 1782, of Samuel Miles, deputy quartermaster, one box containing one hundred axes and five hundred weight rod iron, which I promise to deliver to the commanding officer at Fort Pitt, and for which I have duplicate receipts of this tenor and date. ANDREW ADAM SEITZ."

"Rec'd 3d April, 1782, of J. S. Howell, deputy clothier general, six pack-

wagons can be procured. The roads have been so bad that no wagons could be got sooner.

III.— MILES TO IRVINE.

PHILADELPHIA, *April* 16, 1782.

Sir:— There are three wagons loaded with a variety of stores, some public and some private, for the officers of the garrison [at Fort Pitt]. Inclosed is a receipt for what was loaded out of my office. Mr. Wister and the other persons concerned have, I suppose, sent receipts for the stores sent by them.[1]

I wish those three wagons might, if possible, be loaded back. If there are any loading of any kind, either private or public, I shall be obliged to you for procuring it for them, for their pay is to be the same, whether they return loaded or empty. Whatever they bring, therefore, will be a saving of so much.

IV.— MILES TO IRVINE.

PHILADELPHIA, *May* 4, 1782.

Sir:— I have purchased (by order of Mr. Morris) thirty-two bushels of salt, to pay a number of persons for provisions supplied the garrison of Fort Pitt some time ago. The bearer, Benjamin Tell, has it in charge, contained in eight barrels. I have enclosed a list of the persons' names to whom it is to be distributed, with the quantity each is to receive, and I must beg the favor of you to put it into the hands of some trusty person, for distribution, who must take receipts from the persons that receive it, for their respective proportions, which receipts (as soon as the whole is delivered) I must beg you will be so obliging as to transmit to me, that I may close the account of the salt, as it is separate from the other transactions of my department.

---

ages of clothing . . . which I promise to deliver to Brig. Gen. Irvine for the use of the troops under his command stationed at Fort Pitt, having signed three receipts. ANDREW ADAM SEITZ."

[1] See the two receipts just mentioned.

The whole quantity to be delivered is 31¼ bushels; the remaining three pecks will I hope make up any deficiencies that may happen by measuring it out in small quantities.[1]

Mr. Tell has also in charge the public team purchased for the use of the post at Fort Pitt, which has been detained here for want of a driver.

V.—MILES TO IRVINE.

PHILADELPHIA, *May* 23, 1782.

Sir:—I received a few days ago a letter from Mr. Hughes, your brigade quartermaster, acquainting me that he cannot nor will not do the duty of quartermaster at Fort Pitt, unless

---

[1] "Account of salt due the following persons for beef, flour, pork, etc., purchased by Colonel John Gibson's orders for the use of the troops in the western department since the first of August, 1781, to the 20th of October, following:

	Bushels.	Pecks.
"To David Rankin, for three beef cattle. (Three bushels paid by Gen. Irvine)	5	2
" Edward Cook, for 16 hundred weight flour	4	
" Mr. Wells, for 1,000 weight flour	2	2
" Col. Carman and Company, for 8 hundred do	2	
" Henry Spear, for 1,000 weight of do	2	2
" Richard McMachan, balances for beef	2	2
" Van Camp, for 4 hundred of flour	1	
" B. Cuykendall, for 2 hundred weight of do		2
" Thomas Roberts, for one bullock	1	1
" Mr. White, for one hundred weight of flour		1
" Jacob Bausman, for 4 hundred pounds beef	2	
" Mr. Moore, for one bullock	1	3
" Sam'l Sample, one bullock	2	2
" Mr. Downing, for one bullock	2	2
" Robert Lawdon, for 2 hundred weight flour		2
	31	1

" I do certify that I have purchased, received and delivered the above quantity of beef and flour to John Irwin, D. C. Gen'l of Issues, and as my receipts are given to the different persons to be paid in salt; and as there is no continental salt here, I beg that Gen'l Irvine will use his influence, if possible, to obtain the quantity of salt, so as I may be able to pay off the debts according to contract.   SAM'L SAMPLE.

"I do certify that I received of Mr. Samuel Sample beef and flour to the full amount of the within account for the use of the continental troops.

"FORT PITT, *October* 30, 1781.   GEO. WALLACE, A. C. I."

he can receive his pay regularly every month. This is a thing impossible for me to promise, as I am sure I shall not have it in my power to fulfill such an engagement. He also tells me that he cannot perform the business without, at least, one clerk.

It is possible I may be mistaken with respect to the business of the post. But according to my idea of it, I cannot conceive that a clerk can be necessary. It is undoubtedly right that he should have a suitable number of persons to do the laboring part, but I should think one man would readily do all the writing, as well as direct the business. However, you, sir, who are on the spot, are certainly a better judge of this matter than I can possibly be at this distance. I shall, therefore, thank you to make such arrangements as you will find absolutely necessary, which I shall, as far as it depends upon me, readily agree to, and do all in my power to support.

VI.— MILES TO IRVINE.

PHILADELPHIA, *November* 28, 1782.

Sir:— Agreeable to your advice, I attempted to contract with Mr. Blaine for supplying your post with forage; but though he is willing to take the contract, he chose to defer it till his return to Fort Pitt, not knowing on what terms he could purchase hay and grain. I have therefore to request the favor of you to take this trouble for me; and to make the best contract you can with Mr. Blaine, at so much per ration, which (agreeable to the new plan in the quartermaster's department to take place the first of January next) is fourteen pounds of hay and ten quarts of oats or other grain equivalent, for all the horses entitled to forage at your post as well the officers' as public teams.

As you are fully acquainted with the situation of the country, you are much better qualified to fix the price with Mr. Blaine than I can possibly be at this distance. I shall therefore make no other apology for troubling you with the business; and shall, if necessary, confirm any contract you think proper to make for the purpose. I hope when this contract is made, it will not be requisite for me to appoint any person to do the duty of quartermaster at Fort Pitt. If wood is to be purchased, it can, I doubt not, be contracted for to be delivered at the garrison, and the other duties can be but trifling.

I have little prospect of furnishing another team this fall. I should have written you more fully by this opportunity, but have been in daily expectation of finishing the contract with Mr. Blaine till within this hour, when he informed me he could not fix the price till his arrival in your country, and is just now ready to set out. From the same cause, also, I have been prevented from obtaining an order from Mr. Morris for you, appropriating part of the moneys in your hands to the purchase of forage. But there cannot, possibly, I should suppose, be any reasonable objection to it, or of furnishing Mr. Blaine with the same proportion of cash on the contract for forage that he has received on that for provision.

I received your letter of September ———, but hurry of business and want of opportunity prevented my answering it; that of July did not come to hand. Four wagons with clothing for your garrison, set out from here yesterday.

VII.— Irvine to Miles.

Fort Pitt, *January* 1, 1783.

Sir:— Your favor of the 28th of November was delivered to me yesterday by Mr. [Ephraim] Blaine. He purposes to furnish forage either in bulk, at a certain advance for his trouble, or to issue it by the ration, which he thinks he cannot afford to furnish under one shilling three pence. This, at present, is not so unreasonable as it may appear, compared to the prices of forage below, since grain and hay have considerably advanced during the winter; and I am certain it could not be furnished here much cheaper this season. To contract for forage I think at any rate the most eligible method; but I am quite at a loss to determine which of these proposals to prefer. I am so much the more diffident to enter into any engagements with Mr. Blaine upon his conditions, as he finds himself unable to engage in the business unless he receives at least one hundred pounds advanced in cash.

However, in confidence, to come to a reasonable conclusion with you and to receive in advance the sum mentioned, Mr. Blaine enters upon the engaging of forage, as soon as our present stock is exhausted, and leaves you the choice of his proposals. He expects you will communicate to him your definite answer without delay; and you should obtain orders from the financier general [Morris] upon me for the sum demanded, as it is positively not in my power to advance him any money at all without it. You will please to forward these in a manner that they may reach me here in the beginning of February, at which time I expect to go down the country.

The clothing you mention has not arrived. The impracticability of the roads detains the wagons on your side the hills; and I am told their different loads have been repacked and are forwarded on pack-horses. I fear a great deal will be lost and more spoiled.

VIII.— HODGDON to IRVINE.

PHILADELPHIA, *March* 22, 1783.

Sir:— I have, in company with your aid, just seen Mr. Morris and settled the matter relative to the forage delivered at Fort Pitt. He requests that you will settle with the contractors up to the first of April, either by ascertaining the number of rations actually issued from the commencement of the supply, or the quantity of each kind of forage received during the time of the supply. In either case, your judgment will be conclusive and the account immediately admitted. When the amount is known, a draft will be given the quartermaster general therefor and the vouchers taken by you received in payment. That the whole matter may appear to have fallen under his notice and direction, this mode is thought the most eligible.

I wish you to still take the trouble of insuring a future supply. Being on the spot and having perfect knowledge of every circumstance, your interference will prevent mistakes and their train of consequences. I will undertake to comply with any engagements in this business you may find it necessary to make. I rely on your goodness to indulge me and serve the public in this particular. Any officer you think essentially necessary to conduct the quartermaster's business, I wish you to appoint. When the capacity in which he acts is known, it shall be confirmed and a suitable allowance made for his services. The secretary at war thinks proper to postpone the transporting the several articles in your returns until others may be procured and the roads more settled.

IX.— HODGDON TO IRVINE.

PHILADELPHIA, *April* 15, 1783.

Sir:— I have received your letter of the 3d instant, and noted its contents. Peace being unquestionably settled, renders an appointment in the quartermaster's department at Fort Pitt unnecessary; on which account, I am glad you have suspended it, and am also much obliged for your attention to the procurement of forage absolutely necessary for the garrison. The mode I exceedingly approve. You will please to request Captain Zingly to keep a particular account of sales and disbursements, that nothing may perplex the business on final adjustment of the accounts for supplies furnished the post.

As Captain Emes is already in charge of the public stores at Carlisle, I shall empower him to receive and make sale of such horses and wagons as may chance to arrive there; and to give receipts to the persons who make the delivery; and particularly to call on all officers contiguously situated for any horses they may have in possession. All received will be sold at Carlisle — as I am with you in sentiment that it will be most for the interest of the public. If a new appointment was necessary, your recommendation would insure it to Mr. Postlethwait, having previously heard that he was an active, intelligent and honest man.

X.— Hodgdon to Irvine.

PHILADELPHIA, *September* 19, 1783.

Sir:— The two wagons at present employed at your post can be no longer necessary, as the garrison is so much reduced. In future, the commanding officer is at liberty to hire the small portion of transportation that may be wanted. No hauling except wood can create any expense, and as the command is not entitled to forage, it would be double the expense to support public teams merely for this service. You will therefore dispose of those you have, in the manner you think most likely to accommodate the removal of your officers and men.

I wish you to direct the person last employed by you as quartermaster to make out his account and you to certify the time and value of his services, after which I will do my endeavors to have him paid. The wood for the use of the garrison is to be cut as usual near the fort, the proprietor in common with others will receive a reasonable compensation.

APPENDIX F.

CORRESPONDENCE WITH JOHN MOYLAN, CLOTHIER-GENERAL, AND JACOB S. HOWELL, HIS DEPUTY.

I.—Jacob S. Howell to Irvine.

Philadelphia, *December* 17, 1781.

Sir:— I received your favor of the 2d instant by express, and am pleased to hear the clothing arrived safe. I have received a supply of cloth from the eastward and shall [take the earliest time] to furnish you with the . . . also with shirts, shoes and overalls. [You will] therefore be pleased to send an officer in a month or six weeks from this time to receive and take charge of the clothing. No delay will be made on my part unless some unavoidable [accident should] happen to prevent his return.

II.—Howell to the Commanding Officer at Fort Pitt.

Philadelphia, *February* 19, 1782.

Sir:— Inclosed is Barney Hart's receipt for four boxes and two hogsheads clothing for the troops stationed at Fort Pitt, which you will please to receive and deliver them to the paymasters of the two regiments, proportionate to their wants, and acquaint me with the quantity issued to each. You will please to observe that I have sent some superfine cloth for officers, which is a very large proportion of the quantity in store. I wish it was in my power to send you more; but, as that is not the case, you must accept the will for the deed.

III.—Irvine to John Moylan.

Fort Pitt, *July* 25, 1782.

Sir:— I inclose you a return of clothing received, issued and . . . at this post since my arrival here. [It is because] the most necessary articles for the [men are] exhausted that I am under the necessity to make early application, and urge their being speedily sent on, for several reasons,— particularly the impracticability of the roads late in the year. I therefore request you not to postpone forwarding the clothing for this garrison until the supplies of the whole army are collected. The transportation here is so tedious by its distance and the troops are so bare by receiving their regimentals so early last fall — an indulgence enforced by necessity — that they will not only suffer but perish should we be disappointed in our expectation of an early supply.

The total want of linen overalls this summer has exposed the soldiers to numberless inconveniences. To prevent a similar distress next summer, I insert linen overalls and shirts in an inclosed return of clothing wanted again this winter, which is calculated with the utmost precision by the number of our effectives. As you must still retain on hand our proportionary quota of linen overalls for this year, I wish you would forward them with the rest of the clothing in the fall. We should have the use of them the next proper season. The clothing promised the Indians has been entirely neglected. I am obliged to furnish them with blankets and shirts specified in the return.

IV.— MOYLAN TO IRVINE.

PHILADELPHIA, *August* 11, 1782.

Sir: — I am favored with your letter by Captain Hughes. Perfectly sensible as I ever have been of the particular attention due to corps like yours so far remote from every source of supply, I beg leave to assure you that nothing on my part has been left undone to provide in time for the clothing of the troops under your command; but unfortunately in this as well as many other instances the means of conveyance have not kept pace with the exertions I have made since my arrival in this city. For proof of which exertions the appearance of those troops who have received their clothing is the best evidence I can appeal to.

The linen overalls with other articles appropriated for your detachment as well as the clothing promised the Indians, you must recollect were all in readiness about the time you left this place, and for the greater dispatch packed up agreeably to your directions in pieces to be made up by the garrison; but the application has been frequently made for the means of transporting them — here they still remain.

I have good hopes, however, that these goods with whatever may be allotted for the winter supply of your troops will be shortly forwarded to you. The amount of your return of clothing wanted can be easily procured, having actually on hand the most necessary articles it specifies. The necessity of sending them on in time to prevent the danger and delays of bad roads I shall take care to urge to the minister at war, and I have little or no doubt but he will cheerfully enter into your views.

V.— Moylan to Irvine.

Philadelphia, *November* 10, 1782.

Sir:— A severe indisposition which has confined me near four weeks to my bed and but a few days since permitted me to creep about, prevented an earlier reply to your favor of the 12th September. I now have the pleasure to inform you that in the course of this week, if wagons can be procured, we shall forward to your address a supply of clothing for the troops under your command, to the full extent of the return you made me. For your better information I shall subjoin a note[1] of such articles at foot hereof as we are packing up for that purpose. I sincerely wish they may reach you in time to screen the men from the severity of the approaching season.

Several occurrences have unavoidably delayed this supply, as well as the linen overalls and hunting frocks, which were in

---

[1] This note was as follows:

"[Note.] Two hundred coats, two hundred vests, two hundred pair breeches, six hundred shirts, fifty or sixty blankets, three hundred and sixty-four pair hose, two hundred and sixty hats, three hundred linen overalls, five Indian robes, eleven Indian robes alias guina cloths, two lbs. vermillion, seven hundred pair shoes, three hundred hunting frocks, twelve match coats, eighteen sergeant's coats."

readiness to send you some months ago. This delay, however, should not, I think, deprive your men of their just proportion of the articles of clothing which have been appropriated for them. I have therefore ordered them to be sent on with the other articles now preparing for their use. You will observe that the Indians have not been forgotten in this supply.

VI.— HOWELL TO IRVINE.

PHILADELPHIA, *November* 25, 1782.

Sir: — On the other side you have invoice and receipt[1] for twelve packages of clothing sent to your address for the use of the garrison at Fort Pitt, under your command, which I hope will arrive safe and give pleasure to you and comfort to your troops.

The articles for the Indians contained in the package you will be pleased to have taken out and appropriated accordingly. I am sorry you have not had this supply earlier in the season, but means for transportation could not sooner be obtained.

---

[1] This invoice and receipt are purposely omitted as being of little general interest.

APPENDIX G.

CORRESPONDENCE WITH THE GOVERNORS OF PENNSYLVANIA.[1]

I.— IRVINE TO WILLIAM MOORE.[2]

FORT PITT, *December* 3, 1781.

Sir:— I am sorry to inform your excellency that this country has got a severe stroke by the loss of Colonel [Archibald] Lochry[3] and about one hundred ('tis said) of the best

---

[1] William Moore and John Dickinson.

[2] William Moore was president of the supreme executive council of Pennsylvania and governor *de facto* as well as *de jure* of that state, from the 14th of November, 1781, to the 7th of November, 1782. The letter was directed to the supreme executive council, as Irvine had not heard who had been elected chief executive.

[3] From the *Pennsylvania Packet*, 12 March, 1782: "Extract of a letter from Kentucky, dated December 6, 1781. 'It is but lately that the fate of Colonel Loughrie [Lochry] and his corps of Pennsylvanians, who were to do duty to the westward under the command of General Clarke [George Rogers Clark], has been publicly known. The rendezvous of the brigade was appointed to be at Wheeling. Col. Loughrie, whose regiment was composed of fine riflemen, happened to be something in the rear, but despatched a messenger to the general, informing him of his situation and strength, at the same time requesting that in case he could not wait until he came up, to leave him a supply of provisions. The general pushed forward, leaving a few men with the provisions for the Pennsylvanians and orders for them to follow to the mouth of the Miame [Miami]; Loughrie followed, but the general went on to the Falls [Louisville]. During General Clarke's stay at Fort Pitt, the enemy at Detroit got intelligence of his preparations and designs; the [they] detached a force of about 600, mostly Indians, in order to make a diversion in the Kentucky country, and if practicable, to intercept the general coming down the Ohio. This force reached the mouth of the Miami time enough to give a fatal blow to the unfortunate Loughrie and his men, who, when they came to the appointed place of overtaking the other regiment, unsuspectingly landed, and were soon surrounded by the enemy, and the whole party, amounting to 140 men, were either killed or made prisoners. The particulars of this mortifying disaster we have from prisoners that lately made their escape from the Indians.'"

men of Westmoreland county, including Captain Stokely[1] and his company of rangers. They were going down the Ohio on General Clark's expedition. Many accounts agree that they were all killed or taken at the mouth of the Miami river,— I believe chiefly killed.[2] This misfortune, added to the failure

[1] Thomas Stokely. He was among the captured and afterward returned to his home. He was in command, at the time, of a company of state troops, called rangers.

"I am now on my march with Captain Stokely's company of rangers and about fifty volunteers, from this [Westmoreland] county. We shall join General Clark at Fort Henry [Wheeling], on the Ohio river, where his army has lain for some weeks past, as it was most expedient to have the boats there, the water being deeper from [that point] to where he intends going than from Fort Pitt there."— Lochry to Pres't Reed from "Miraile's Mills, Westmoreland, Aug. 4th, 1781."

[2] The following is the British official report of the affair:

"CAMP NEAR THE OHIO, *August* 29, 1781.

"*Sir:*— The 26th you had enclosed an account that Captain Brandt [the Mohawk Indian chief, Thayendanegea, or Joseph Brant] and George Girty, with the Indians, advanced upon the Ohio, had taken one of Clark's boats after having passed down the river in the night. Not thinking themselves in number sufficient to attack him, and having found by his orders to Major Craigcroft [Major Charles Cracraft] that more troops were to follow under the command of a Colonel Lochry, [they] lay in wait for them, attacked and took the whole, not allowing one to escape. Agreeable to a return, it appears there has been thirty-seven killed, amongst whom is Lochry, their commandant, with some officers.

"This stroke, with desertions, will reduce Clark's army much, and if the Indians had followed advice and been here in time, it is more than probable he would have been now in our possession with his cannon.

"The prisoners seem to be ignorant of what his intentions are. Perhaps loss may oblige him to change his measures. However, we shall endeavor to keep the Indians together, and watch his motions. His first intention was to penetrate to Sandusky through the Indian country, from whence the troops from Fort Pitt were to return home and he to Kentucky.

"We are with great respect, sir, your most obedient and most humble servants, A. THOMPSON,
"ALEX'R McKEE.
"To Major DE PEYSTER [commanding at Detroit]."

Extract from a letter written by General Frederick Haldimand to Sir Henry Clinton, dated Quebec, 29th Sept., 1781: "I have received a dispatch from Detroit with an account of a stroke made by Joseph Brant upon the Ohio. . . . Major De Peyster informs me he is not without hopes that a large body of Indians detached for that purpose may yet fall in with Mr. Clark's main body, which it was expected would consist of 1,500 men, including a

of General Clark's expedition,[1] has filled the people with great dismay. Many talk of retiring to the east side of the mountain early in the spring. Indeed, there is great reason to apprehend that the savages and perhaps the British from Detroit will push us hard in the spring; and I believe there never were posts, nor a country, in a worse state of defense; notwithstanding, I am well informed there have been sundry meetings of people at different places, for the purpose of concerting plans to emigrate into the Indian country, there to establish a government for themselves. What the result of their meetings was I cannot say; and, as I do not intend to interfere in civil matters, I have not taken any notice of the affair.[2]

---

body from Augusta county in Virginia and a draft from the settlements in Kintuck [Kentucky]. The war in that country is, on our part, entirely defensive, except by scouting parties constantly employed to prevent the encroachments of settlers and to harass the frontiers, which I encourage as much as possible."

[1] [From General George Rogers Clark to the governor of Virginia, dated at Fort Nelson (Louisville), October 6, 1781:] —" We should have made a much better figure this campaign had it not been for an act passed empowering your excellency to stop the expedition. It seems it alarmed the country. The Greenbrier militia returned; the drafts in this country dispersed; great numbers returned to Virginia that were for the enterprise. It had equally as bad an impression on the Monongahela country; as the report happened about the time of rendezvous, and proved an excuse for numbers that otherwise would have joined the camp. . . . Captain [Isaac] Craig and company of artillery return to Pittsburgh, anxious for a second attempt in the Indian country."

[2] To " emigrate into the Indian country there to establish a government," as expressed by Irvine, was a statement somewhat alarming to Pennsylvania; for such schemes had been rife in the west for a considerable time, as was well known to the authorities of that commonwealth. The plan contemplating a new state in the Indian country was one thing; that of forming a new government which should take in the "disputed territory," quite another. There were several schemes all proposing to include not only the last mentioned but more or less territory beyond; and all arising from the same causes, namely: a "divided allegiance," insufficient protection from the savages, and the zeal of a few who hoped to further their own ambitious designs.

The desire for change was stronger with the Virginians than Pennsylvanians in the trans-Alleghany country, as events had already foreshadowed the extension of the boundary line farther westward than the former had generally been led to believe it would be located; hence, the greater number of supporters of "new state schemes" lived in what (as claimed by Virginia) had

From what observations I have been able to make, I am of opinion there are many obvious reasons that no time should be lost in running the line between Virginia and Pennsylvania. Civil government will never be fairly established till then, nor even the militia drawn out with regularity for their own defense.[1] I have no reason as yet to complain of the people for the refractory, ungovernable, loose manners generally ascribed to them. I assure you, sir, my pity for their situation is rather excited than wrath or indignation kindled. I have good grounds to believe that the settlements at Kentucky and the Falls will break up;—in which case, I fear a number of adventurers who talk of going down to New Orleans with flour will be killed or taken. Council may depend during my stay here that no exertions in my power shall be wanting in everything that may tend to the welfare of the state or protection of the inhabitants as far as consistent with my duty as an officer of the United States.

P. S.— Please to excuse the omission of personal address. We have not heard here who has been elected president [of the supreme executive council].

---

been the county of Yohogania. However, severe laws passed by Pennsylvania against attempts at forming new governments that should include any of her territory, and the employment of judicious means to enlighten the people of the west as to the fallacy and danger of opposing them, proved effectual in stamping out all designs for the building up of new states any portion of which should come within her boundaries.

[1] The attention of Washington was called to the same subject by Irvine the day previous (ante, p. 80).

"This country (I mean west of the Monongahela) has ever been considered by a majority of its inhabitants, to be within the state of Virginia; and it has been under that jurisdiction, without controversy, since the year 1774. But, on the publication of the agreement made between the commissioners for the two states, Virginia and Pennsylvania, at Baltimore, 1779, a report immediately followed that the line would be run without procrastination, in consequence thereof; this produced a relaxation amongst the officers (particularly in the military line) knowing that such an agreement would include the whole, or nearly so, of Yohogania county, and by that means the whole country was thrown into perfect anarchy and confusion."—*Dorsey Pentecost to Pres't Reed, July 27, 1781.*

II.—MOORE TO IRVINE.

IN COUNCIL, PHILADELPHIA, *December* 17, 1781.

Sir:—Your letter of the third of the present month has been read in council.

The loss of Colonel Lochry with his men and the distressed state of the post under your command and the country around it, gave us great pain; yet we hope from your vigilance and ability that every possible exertion will be made to protect the inhabitants as far as their exposed situation will admit of. It has been suggested to the general assembly that the best and perhaps cheapest means of protecting the frontiers will be found in the invasion of the Indian country. How far this may be prudent and practicable remains yet to be decided upon. Perhaps the disposition of the people of Westmoreland county to emigrate into the Indian country may be diverted and applied to this end. Be this as it may, it will be certainly proper to endeavor to fill up your battalions with as many men as can be obtained in that county; for which purpose, we shall send you two hundred and fifty pounds to begin with, and request that you will, as opportunity offers, communicate your success in recruiting, and the prospect which lies before you. You may depend on our giving you the earliest information of what may be done here, respecting the frontiers.

With respect to the line between this state and Virginia, every measure, on our part, has been taken to have had a temporary line run the last summer; but it has failed of being effectual by some omissions of the commissioners appointed on the part of that state; and it seems to be impracticable by the season, and perhaps unnecessary now to push that measure, as preparations are making for running in the spring, a permanent line founded upon astronomical observations.

We have long suspected that the representation of the state of things in Westmoreland has been colored by party resentments, which we hope will subside, and that harmony be obtained among the good people of that county, which is so very essential to their interest and safety. You will render the most acceptable service, at once to the county and to the state, by using your influence to effect so desirable a purpose; and the favorable representation you have made of their dispositions, affords a pleasing expectation that this may be in your power, and we have no doubt of your attention to an object so important to the command you are entrusted with, and so highly honorable to effect.

III.— MOORE TO IRVINE.

IN COUNCIL, *December* 29, 1781.

Sir:— Our assembly rose last night, having spent most of their time about a contested election; and, I am sorry to add, have done but little in regard to supplies for carrying on the war this year. However, they have adjourned to the second Monday in February, when, I hope, their attention will be turned from party disputes to the public service.

I have sent you under care of Messrs. Meason and Proctor, representatives for Westmoreland and Washington counties, the sum of five hundred pounds, specie, for the purpose of recruiting the Pennsylvania troops under your command.[1] Nine pounds specie are allowed for each recruit, to serve during the war, now raising here; six pounds specie are allowed to each recruit to be raised in the ranging companies, to serve during the war. The council repose confidence in you to raise the men on the best terms you can; and when this money is expended, your orders on us will be met with due honor, for any number of recruits you may engage.

The gentlemen are just going off, and I have only time to add that I wish you health and happiness, and success in the recruiting business.

---

[1] The following is an extract from the proceedings of the supreme executive council of Pennsylvania:

"IN COUNCIL, PHILADELPHIA, *Saturday, December* 29, 1781.

"An order was drawn on the treasurer in favor of John Proctor and Isaac Meason, Esquires, for the sum of five hundred pounds specie, to be forwarded to Brigadier General Irvine, for the purpose of recruiting the regiment stationed at Fort Pitt for the defense of the western frontiers, for which he is to account."

Appendix G.

IV.— MOORE TO IRVINE.

PHILADELPHIA, *January* 7, 1782.

Sir:— I wrote you a few days since by Messrs. Proctor and Meason, two of our assembly men, from Westmoreland county, who had an order on the treasurer of Lancaster county for five hundred pounds specie to be delivered you for the purpose of recruiting. From their information and the gentlemen of the council for the western frontiers,[1] we are in hopes you will be able to get a considerable number of recruits. As it is difficult for want of opportunities, as well as hazardous, to send you money hence, if you can get any persons in your parts to advance specie for drafts on council, for the purpose of recruiting, you may be assured of punctuality in honoring them, having laid by in the treasury, separate and apart from all monies, a considerable sum for the purpose of recruiting only. We have begun this business here under the superintendence of Colonel [Richard] Humpton [of the sixth Pennsylvania regiment], who has sent recruiting parties into most of the counties of the state. Our line[2] is very thin. General Washington is very desirous of having a respectable army in the field by the first of March. I hope we shall not be behindhand with our sister states in their complement of men, and that every exertion will be used for that purpose.

V.— IRVINE TO MOORE.

CARLISLE, *March* 17, 1782.

Sir:— I find, notwithstanding the precautions taken by the honorable, the council, and the vigilance of the recruiting officers to prevent British deserters and prisoners entering into our service, that several have perjured themselves and are actually in service,— some of whom are now in confinement,

---

[1] Matthew Jack, of Westmoreland, and Dorsey Pentecost, of Washington county, were the "gentlemen of the [supreme executive] council for the western frontiers," at that date.

[2] That is, the Pennsylvania line; consisting of the various regiments, in the continental service, belonging to that state (ante, p. 97, note 2).

at this place, for that crime. It is difficult to determine what punishment should be inflicted, or what steps would be most likely to deter those fellows from such conduct. As the crime does not properly come under military law, I beg leave to suggest a mode to your excellency, which, in my opinion, is the most likely to put an entire stop to such pernicious practices.

If council will think proper to order all such put in jail and direct the state attorney to prosecute them for perjury and the law rigorously executed as the crime may deserve, I think a few examples of cropping, pillory, etc., with a publication of the reason for such punishment over the state, will have a good effect. However, as this is only opinion, and I thought it my duty to give council information on the subject, I submit the matter to your excellency. Gavin Miller, a British prisoner of war, is under this predicament,— was enlisted by Lieutenant Jones of the second regiment. I have ordered him into close confinement in Carlisle jail till your excellency's pleasure respecting him shall be made known to the commanding officer at this post. I proceed immediately on my way to Fort Pitt.

VI.—MOORE TO IRVINE.

IN COUNCIL, PHILADELPHIA, *April* 13, 1782.

Sir:— The council have received information through various channels that a party of militia [1] have killed a number of Indians, at or near Muskingum,[2] and that a certain Mr. Bull[3] was killed at the same time. The council being desirous of

---

[1] That is, Washington county militia — not volunteers, as were those who soon after went upon the Sandusky expedition, under Col. Wm. Crawford (ante, p. 113; also p. 118 and note).

[2] Reference is here had to the "Gnadenhuetten affair" — the killing of the Moravian Indians by the men under Colonel David Williamson a few weeks previous, upon the Muskingum; that is, upon what is now known as the Tuscarawas, in the present Tuscarawas county, Ohio (ante, pp. 67, 99).

[3] Joseph Bull, son of a white man of the same name, but whose mother was an Indian woman. The father was known among the Moravian Indians as Schebosh; that is, *running water*.

receiving full information on a subject of such importance, request you will obtain and transmit to them the facts relative thereto, authenticated in the clearest manner.[1]

[1] How the governor and council of Pennsylvania came into official possession of the above facts, the following will show:

[I.]

"Relation of what Frederick Leinbach [a Moravian] was told by two of his neighbors, living near Delaware river, above Easton, who were just returned from the Monongahela:

"That some time in February [1782], one hundred and sixty men living upon Monongahela set off on horseback to the Muskingum [that branch now called the Tuscarawas], in order to destroy three Indian settlements of which they seemed to be sure of being the towns of some enemy Indians.

"After coming nigh to one of the towns [Gnadenhuetten], they discovered some Indians on both sides of the river Muskingum. They then concluded to divide themselves into two parties, the one to cross the river and the other to attack those Indians on this [the east] side. When that party got over the river, they saw one of the Indians coming up towards them. They laid themselves flat on the ground, waiting till the Indian was nigh enough, then one of them shot the Indian and broke his arm; then three of the militia ran towards him with tomahawks. When they were yet a little distance from him he asked them why they fired at him, he was Minister Schebosh's (John Bull's) son, but they took no notice of what he said, but killed him on the spot. They then surrounded the field, and took all the other Indians prisoners. The Indians told them that they were Christians and made no resistance. When the militia gave them to understand that they must bring them as prisoners to Fort Pitt, they seemed to be very glad. They were ordered to prepare themselves for the journey, and to take all their effects along with them; accordingly, they did so [prepare]. They were asked how it came they had no cattle. They answered that the small stock that was left them had been sent to Sandusky.

"In the evening, the militia held a council, when the commander of the militia [David Williamson] told his men that he would leave it to their choice either to carry the Indians as prisoners to Fort Pitt or to kill them, when they agreed that they should be killed. Of this resolution of the council, they gave notice to the Indians by two messengers, who told them, that, as they had said they were Christians, they would give them time this night to prepare themselves accordingly. Hereupon, the women met together and sung hymns and psalms all night, and so did likewise the men, and kept on singing as long as there were three alive.

"In the morning the militia chose two houses, which they called the slaughter houses, and then fetched the Indians, two or three at a time, with ropes about their necks, and dragged them into the slaughter houses, where they knocked them down; then they set these two houses on fire, as likewise all the other houses. This done, they went to the other towns [New Schœn-

VII.—IRVINE TO MOORE.

FORT PITT, *May* 2, 1782.

Sir:—I did not receive till yesterday your excellency's favor of the thirteenth of April. I will make minute inquiry bruun and Salem], and set fire to the houses, took their plunder, and returned to the Monongahela, where they kept a vendue among themselves. . . ."

[II.]

"*Sir:*—I received this afternoon a letter of the Reverend Nathaniel [Seidel], bishop of the united churches of the brethren, residing at Bethlehem [Pa.], dated the 5th instant. He informs me that the same day a melancholy report [see the foregoing 'Relation'] was brought to him by one Mr. Leinbach, relative to a murder committed by white men upon a number of Christian Indians at a place called Muskingum [upon the branch now known as the Tuscarawas]. He continues in his letter that the same Mr. Leinbach is to proceed the next day to Philadelphia, in order to give congress information how he came to the knowledge of that event, so that congress, unless it had already a better account of the affair than he can give, might, upon his report, take some measures with respect as well of the mischief already done as more which might be done, and thus prevent the total extirpation of a congregation of Indians converted to the faith of Jesus Christ, and the judgments of Almighty God against our dear country, which stands much in need of His divine protection. The bishop desires me to give attention to Mr. Leinbach's report (I have done it), and to direct him where he should make his addresses. I make bold, sir, to address him to you, and to beg the favor that you introduce him, if possible, this night, with the delegates of the state of Virginia, from whence, it is said, the mischief originated, and to-morrow morning with congress.

"Your humanity, sir, gives me confidence to use the freedom to trouble you this day—the day set apart for the service of men to their God—about a cause which is most properly His own. The tragic scenes of erecting two butcher-houses or sheds and killing in cold blood ninety-five brown or tawny sheep of Jesus Christ, one by one, is certainly taken notice of by the Shepherd, their Creator and Redeemer. I am, with particular respect, sir, your most obedient, humble servant, L. WEISS [Moravian Att'y].

"SUNDAY, 7 *April*, 1782. To CHARLES THOMSON, Esquire, secretary of congress. By [favor of] Mr. FREDERICK LEINBACH."

[III.]

"*Sir:*—The enclosed intelligence [Leinbach's 'Relation,' previously given] was communicated to congress on Monday last. For your further information respecting the channel of intelligence, I beg leave to send you a letter I received on Sunday from Mr. L. Weiss. It is the desire of congress that your excellency and the honorable council would be pleased to cause inquiry to be made into this matter. . . . CHAS. THOMSON [Sec'y of Congress].

"*April* 9, 1782. His excellency, WILLIAM MOORE, Esq., president of the state of Pennsylvania."

into the matter you require and transmit the best accounts I can obtain as early as possible [of the "Gnadenhuetten affair"]. In the meantime, I beg to refer you to the bearer hereof, Mr. David Duncan, whose business leads him pretty much abroad, and I am persuaded he can give a tolerable general account.[1]

VIII.— IRVINE TO MOORE.

FORT PITT, *May* 3, 1782.

Sir: — Immediately on receipt of your excellency's letter of the 13th of April, I wrote to Colonel [James] Marshel,[2] who ordered out the militia[3] to go to Muskingum [to that branch now known as the Tuscarawas],[4] for his and Colonel

---

[1] The first published account of the progress of the expedition to the "Muskingum," is to be found in the *Pennsylvania Packet* of April 16, 1782, and in the *Pennsylvania Gazette* of the next day. It is as follows:

"A number of men, properly provided, collected and rendezvoused on the Ohio, opposite the Mingo bottom [the Mingo bottom already spoken of as just below what is now Steubenville, Ohio], with a design to surprise the above towns [previously described as 'Indian towns upon the Muskingum']. The weather was very cold and stormy, the [Ohio] river high, and no boats or canoes to transport themselves across. These difficulties discouraged some, but 160 [about 100] determined to persevere, and they swam the river, in doing of which some of their horses perished with the severity of the cold. When they got over, officers were chosen, and they proceeded to the towns on the Muskingum [that is, to the branch of that stream now known as the Tuscarawas]."

[2] Irvine's letter to Marshel has not been found.

[3] That Marshel, who was lieutenant of Washington county, had authority to order out the militia, the following will show:

"IN COUNCIL, PHILADELPHIA, *Tuesday, January* the 8th, 1782.

"*Ordered*, That the lieutenants of the counties of . . . Westmoreland and Washington be authorized and empowered to call out such and so many militia, according to law, as they may judge necessary for repelling the enemy."

[4] This letter establishes the fact that the men who went to the "Muskingum" were not only *militia*, but that they were *ordered out* by the highest military authority of Washington county. Marshel had become tired of "volunteer plans." (See Appendix J,— Marshel to Irvine, November 20, 1781.) The *Pennsylvania Packet* of April 16th (No. 872) and the *Pennsylvania Gazette* of the next day have this to say concerning the origin and object of this expedition to the "Muskingum:"

"In a late paper we gave an account that a woman and three children had been carried off by the savages from their habitation near Fort Pitt; and in

[David] Williamson's report of the matter.[1] Colonel Williamson[2] commanded the party. Inclosed you have their letters to me on the subject, by way of report.

<blockquote>
our paper of the 9th[6th]inst. we mentioned an advantage being gained over those Indians. By a gentleman who arrived here [Philadelphia] on Saturday last [April 13th, 1782], from Washington county [Pennsylvania], we have the following particulars: That on the 17th [10th] of February last, the wife and three children of one Robert Wallace, an inhabitant on Raccoon creek (during his absence from home), were carried off by a party of Indians. Mr. Wallace, on his return home in the evening, finding his wife and children gone, his house broke up, the furniture destroyed, and his cattle shot and laying dead about the yard, immediately alarmed the neighbors, and a party was raised that night, who set out early the next morning; but unfortunately a snow fell, which prevented their following, and they were obliged to return. About this time [day unknown], a certain John Carpenter was taken prisoner from the waters of Buffalo creek in said county [Washington], and another party had fired at a man, whom they missed, and he escaped from them. These different parties of Indians, striking the settlements so early in the season, greatly alarmed the people, and but too plainly evinced their [the Indians'] determination to harass the frontiers; and nothing could save them [the frontier people] but a quick and spirited exertion. They therefore came to a determination to extirpate the aggressors and, if possible, to recover the people that had been carried off."
</blockquote>

Michael Huffnagle writing from Hannastown, March 8, 1782, says: "The savages last Sunday three weeks took into captivity two families upon Raccoon and Short creeks below Pittsburgh. I am afraid the first good weather we may expect a stroke upon some of our frontiers here." The following is confirmatory of the fact of the early visitations of the savages:

"The intelligence which has been received from the frontiers of the state respecting the ravages of the Indians, and the murders which they have committed at this early season, leaves no room to doubt of their determination to exert their utmost power to distress us during the year, and confirms the accounts we had received from Fort Pitt, Washington [county], etc., of the combinations formed by them for that purpose."—*Pres't Sup. Ex. Coun. to Gen. Assem., April* 2, 1782. (See also, p. 99, note 2, and p. 155 and note thereto.)

[1] It will be observed that, in the above letter, the declaration of General Irvine that Colonel Marshel "ordered out the militia [of Washington county] to go to Muskingum" is unequivocal; and that, for that reason, he wrote to him for his official "report of the matter," and for that of Colonel Williamson, who commanded the party. But why "go to Muskingum" (that is, to that branch of the river now known as the Tuscarawas)? Leinbach (ante, p. 235, note) answers the question: "In order to destroy three Indian settlements of which they [the militia] seemed to be sure of being the towns of some enemy Indians [that is, warriors — Marauding Indians]."

[2] For a notice of David Williamson, see Appendix M,— Williamson to Irvine, June 13, 1782, note.

I have inquiries making in other quarters; — when any well authenticated accounts come to my knowledge, they shall be transmitted.

IX.— IRVINE TO MOORE.

FORT PITT, *May* 9, 1782.

Sir:— Since my letter of the third instant to your excellency, Mr. Pentecost[1] and Mr. Canon[2] have been with me. They and every intelligent person whom I have conversed with on the subject,[3] are of opinion that it will be almost impossible ever to obtain a just account of the conduct of the militia at Muskingum.[4] No man can give any account except some

---

[1] Dorsey Pentecost; a resident of Washington county, Pennsylvania, and, at the above date, a member of the supreme executive council of his state. His home was about six miles a little to the east of north of the present town of Washington, the county seat of that county.

[2] John Canon; a prominent citizen of Washington county, at the above date, and a member of the assembly. (For a notice of him, see Appendix J,— Marshel to Irvine, April 2, 1782, note.)

[3] Among those talked with by Irvine was John Carpenter, who had escaped from the savages, as hereafter mentioned. (See *Cincinnati Commercial*, May 24, 1873.)

[4] The following official letters sent by Pentecost to Moore give information concerning the "Gnadenhuetten affair:"

[I.]

"PITTSBURGH, *May* 8th, 1782.

"*Dear Sir:*— I arrived at home last Thursday, without any particular accident. Yesterday I came to this place; have had a long conference with General Irvine and Colonel Gibson, on the subject of public matters, particularly respecting the late excursion to Kushocton [the Tuscarawas]. That affair [killing the Moravian Indians] is a subject of great speculation here,— some condemning, others applauding the measure; but the accounts are so various that it is not only difficult, but almost, indeed entirely impossible to ascertain the real truth. No person can give intelligence but those that were along; and, notwithstanding there seems to have been some difference amongst themselves about that business, yet they will say nothing; but this far I believe may be depended on, that they killed rather deliberately the innocent with the guilty, and it is likely the majority was the former. I have heard it insinuated that about thirty or forty only of the party gave their consent or assisted in the catastrophe. . . .

"It is said here, and I believe with truth, that sundry articles were found amongst the [Moravian] Indians that were taken from the inhabitants of

of the party themselves; if, therefore, an inquiry should appear serious, they are not obliged nor will they give evidence. For this and other reasons, I am of opinion further inquiry into the matter will not only, be fruitless, but, in the end, may be attended with disagreeable consequences.

Washington county, and that the [Moravian] Indians confessed themselves that, when they set out from St. Duskie [Sandusky], ten warriors came with them, who had went into the settlements, and that four of them were then in the [Moravian] towns, who had returned. If those [Moravian] Indians that were killed were really friends, they must have been very imprudent to return and settle at a place they knew the whites had been at, and would go to again, without giving us notice and, besides, to bring warriors with them, who had come into the settlements and after murdering would return to their towns and of course draw people after them, filled with revenge, indignation, and sorrow for the loss of their friends, their wives, and their children. . . .
"DORSEY PENTECOST."

[II.]

"PITTSBURGH, May 9, 1782.

"*Dear Sir:*— Since writing the letter that accompanies this, I have had another and more particular conversation with General Irvine on the subject of the late excursion to Kushacton [the Tuscarawas]; and, upon the whole, I find that it will be impossible to get an impartial and fair account of that affair; for, although sundry persons that were in [the] company may disapprove of the whole or every part of the conduct [of those engaged in the killing], yet from their connection they will not be willing, nor can they be forced to give testimony, as it affects themselves. And the people here are greatly divided in sentiment about it; and on [an] investigation may produce serious effects, and at least leave us as ignorant as when we began, and instead of rendering a service may produce a confusion and ill-will amongst the people; yet I think it necessary that [the supreme executive] council [of Pa.] should take some cognizance or notice of the matter and in such a time as may demonstrate their disapprobation of such parts of their conduct as are censurable; otherwise, it may be alleged that [the Pennsylvania] government, tacitly at least, have encouraged the killing of women and children; and in a proclamation of this kind, it might be well not only to recommend but to forbid that, in future excursions [expeditions], that women, children, and infirm persons, should not be killed,— so contrary to the law of arms as well as Christianity.

"I hope a mode of proceeding something like this would produce some good effects and perhaps soften the minds of the people; for it is really no wonder that those who have lost all that is near and dear to them, go out with determined revenge and extirpation of all Indians. . . .
"DORSEY PENTECOST."

It has been mentioned that "a certain John Carpenter" was captured by the savages previous to the militia being called out by Marshel "to go to Muskingum" (ante, p. 239, note 4). He afterwards escaped from his captors.

A volunteer expedition is talked of against Sandusky, which, if well conducted, may be of great service to this country. If they behave well on this occasion, it may also, in some meas-

---

Carpenter's report as published in the *Pennsylvania Packet* of April 16th, 1782, was as follows:

"The person above mentioned [John Carpenter] to have escaped from the enemy says that he was taken by six Indians, two of which called themselves 'Moravians,' and spoke good Dutch [German] and were the most severe and ill-natured to him. He was taken to the above towns [previously mentioned as 'Indian towns upon the Muskingum'] and from thence four of the above Indians [who had captured Carpenter] set out with him for St. Duskie [Sandusky]. The second day of their march, in the morning, he was sent out for the horses, when he left them, and being a good woodsman came off clear, and got to Fort Pitt [reaching the settlements before the militia started for the "Muskingum"].

"While at Muskingum, the two Moravian Indians learnt [taught] him an Indian song, which they frequently made him sing, by way of insult, and afterward interpreted to him in obscene language; and he [Carpenter] left them [the two Moravian Indians] at Muskingum, where they stayed in order to go out with the next party against our settlements."

The following contains additional particulars of Carpenter's escape:

"A man of the name of John Carpenter was taken early in the month of March, in the neighborhood of this place [Wellsburgh, Brooke county, West Virginia]. There had been several warm days, but the night preceding his capture there was a heavy fall of snow. His two horses which they [the savages] took with him, nearly perished in swimming the Ohio. The Indians as well as himself, suffered severely with the cold before they reached the Moravian towns on the Muskingum [that is, the branch now known as the Tuscarawas]. In the morning after the first [2d] day's journey beyond the Moravian towns, the Indians sent out Carpenter to bring in the horses which had been turned out in the evening, after being hobbled. The horses had made a circuit and fallen into the trail by which they came the preceding day, and were making their way homeward. When he overtook the horses and had taken off their fetters, as he said, he had to make a most awful decision. He had a chance and barely a chance, to make his escape, with a certainty of death should he attempt it without success; on the other hand the horrible prospect of being tortured to death by fire, presented itself, as he was the first prisoner taken that spring; of course, the general custom of the Indians of burning the first prisoner every spring, doomed him to the flames. After spending a few minutes in making his decision, he resolved on attempting an escape, and effected it by way of Forts Laurens, McIntosh, and [Fort Pitt] Pittsburgh. If I recollect rightly, he brought both his horses home with him. This happened in the year 1782."— Doddridge's *Notes* (new ed.), pp. 263, 264. Compare, in this connection, the *Cincinnati Commercial*, May 24, 1873, as to Carpenter's capture and escape. This was the same Carpenter previously mentioned (ante, p. 197, note) as a new state justice of the peace.

ure, atone for the barbarity they are charged with at Muskingum.¹ They have consulted me and shall have every countenance in my power, if their numbers, arrangements, etc., promise a prospect of success.

Another kind of expedition is also much talked of, which is to emigrate and set up a new state. This matter is carried so far as to advertise a day of general rendezvous (the 25th instant). A certain Mr. J—— is said to be at the head of this party. He has a form of constitution actually written by himself for the new government. I am well informed he is now on the east side of the mountain trying to purchase or otherwise provide artillery and stores. A number of people, I really believe, have serious thoughts of this matter; but I am led to think they will not be able, at this time, to put their plan into execution.

Should they be so mad as to attempt it, I think they will either be cut to pieces or they will be obliged to take protection from and join the British. Perhaps some have this in view; though a great majority are, I think, well meaning people, who have at present no other views than to acquire large tracts of land.

As I thought a knowledge of these intentions might be useful to the executives of Pennsylvania and Virginia, the emigrants being now subjects of both states, I have written to the governor of Virginia on the subject also.¹

Mr. J—— has been in England since the commencement of the present war. Some people think he is too trifling a

---

¹ The expedition here spoken of is the one which marched against Sandusky under Col. Wm. Crawford. It has been supposed by some, owing to the loose wording of the paragraph, that the same men who took part in Williamson's expedition were also those who afterward marched against Sandusky; but Williamson's men, as we have seen, numbered only about one hundred who crossed the Ohio, and were exclusively of Washington county militia (ante, p. 236, note 1); while the volunteers against Sandusky numbered four hundred and sixty-eight and were from Washington and Westmoreland counties, Pennsylvania, and from Ohio county, Virginia. (See Appendix J,—Marshel to Irvine, May 29, 1782.)

¹ See Appendix H,— Irvine to Harrison, April 20, 1782. It is evident from what Irvine says that he refers to the establishing of a new state beyond the Ohio, in the Indian country. (Ante, p. 109.)

being to be worthy of notice. Be this as it may, he has now many followers; and it is, I think, highly probable that men of more influence than he are privately at work. J——, it is said, was once in affluent circumstances — is now indigent — was always open to corruption. I have no personal knowledge of the man; and have this character of him in too general terms to be able to assert it is genuine.[1]

No considerable damage has been done by the savages since my arrival here last. The whole of killed and captured that I have any account of amounts only to six souls. I think they must be either preparing for a great stroke or apprehensive of a visit from us.[2]

X.— Moore to Irvine.

In Council, Philadelphia, *May* 30, 1782.

Sir:— Your favors of the 2d, 3d and 9th of the present month, with the representations made by Colonel Williamson and Colonel Marshel,[3] have been read in council and shall be immediately laid before congress[4] as a matter of high impor-

---

[1] That any of those favoring the scheme had intentions of taking protection from, and joining the British, is possible but very doubtful; that some engaged in the movement were stimulated by prospects of preferment, is probable; but that a great majority had, as Irvine expresses it, "no other views than to acquire large tracts of land," or, perhaps, of obtaining cheap lands, is quite certain.

[2] There is another copy, evidently the first draft of this letter, extant, in the handwriting of Irvine, which is different'y arranged and somewhat differently worded from the above.

[3] The fact that the letters of Marshel and Williamson here referred to, and which had been obtained by Irvine, were the *official reports* of the expedition that resulted in the killing of the Moravian Indians — "the Gnadenhuetten affair" — naturally awakens an interest in their recovery; all efforts, however, in that direction have thus far been fruitless.

[4] The two letters were sent by the governor to the Pennsylvania delegates in congress, as the following proceedings show:

"In Council, Philadelphia, *Monday, June* 3, 1782."

"The council took into consideration several letters from General Irvine, respecting a proposed emigration from western parts of the state, and respecting the killing of a number of Indians at Muskingum [on the branch now known as the Tuscarawas] . . . and thereupon

"*Ordered*, that the letters from General Irvine of the third and ninth inst.

tance to the reputation of this state, and to the general interest and honor of the United States.¹ We request that you will continue your inquiries on this subject and transmit us such information from time to time as may come to your knowledge tending to elucidate this dark transaction.²

The proposed immigration appears to be a dangerous measure; and if the circumstances which you mention respecting

---

[*ult.*], with the representations of Colonels Marshel and Williamson, be laid before congress, and that they be transmitted to the delegates of the state in congress for that purpose."

Virginia, also, took measures to inquire into the "Gnadenhuetten affair," as the following from the *Pennsylvania Packet*, June 11, 1782 (No. 896), shows:

"RICHMOND, VA., *June* 1 [1782].

"Reports from our northwestern frontier mention some very daring inroads of the Indians, who, it is said, have cut off several families settled upon the branches of the Monongahela. . . . We learn that [the Virginia] government have appointed persons [Colonel William Crawford and another] to inquire into the circumstances of the late massacre of the Moravian Indians at the Muskingum towns, which we have great reason to fear has been a very unjustifiable aggression."

¹ These words only tend to increase the anxiety to know the particulars of "the representations" made by Marshel and Williamson concerning the "Gnadenhuetten affair."

² In a message sent the general assembly of Pennsylvania by President Moore, August 14th, following, he says: "We had great reason to apprehend a severe blow would be aimed at the frontiers by the Indians. Our fears, in this respect, have been but too well justified by events that have since happened, and there is reason to believe that the blow has fallen with redoubled force, in consequence of the killing of the Moravian Indians at Muskingum [upon that branch now known as the Tuscarawas], an act which never had our approbation or countenance in any manner whatever." The report of the committee of the assembly upon so much of his message as related to the killing of the Moravian Indians was made the next day, as follows:

"Your committee are of opinion that an inquiry, on legal principles, ought to be instituted respecting the killing of the Moravian Indians, at Muskingum — an act disgraceful to humanity and productive of the most disagreeable and dangerous consequences.

"*Resolved*, therefore, that this house will give every support in their power to the supreme executive council toward prosecuting an inquiry respecting the killing of the Moravian Indians at Muskingum."

Nothing further, however, was ever done in an official way, either by the United States, Pennsylvania or Virginia, "tending to elucidate the dark transaction."

Mr. J—— can be ascertained, he ought to be secured as a British emissary employed to inveigle away our citizens and place them in a situation which must compel them to put themselves under the protection of the British as the only means by which they can be secured from the ravages of the Indians. Such an event would afford a plausible story, which the British would seize with avidity and represent at every court in Europe as an instance of submission to them on the part of America;— a story which might be extremely injurious to America, and such as no man who has a due regard to his country would give a countenance to by any act of his.

The recruiting service is of so much importance that we cannot forbear to inquire anxiously what success you have in it and to request you will transmit to us a return of the recruits you have obtained as early as possible.

As to the expedition you mentioned, we can only say, we confide in your zeal and prudence to direct the force which may be in your power in the most effectual manner for covering the frontiers.[1]

XI.— IRVINE TO MOORE.

FORT PITT, *July* 5, 1782.

Sir:— There have been many meetings in this county respecting taxes. It is said, and I fear with truth, that a great majority of the people are determined not to pay any in any mode. It is also said that they are advised to this by some of the first people of the country.

The running the boundary line has been again put a stop to by a party of men who call themselves Virginians. It seems

---

[1] The carefully prepared instructions issued by Irvine to the officer who was to command the expedition against Sandusky (p. 118, note); the sparing of his favorite aid-de-camp, John Rose, to act as his representative upon that enterprise; and the sending of one of his surgeons to accompany the volunteers into the wilderness; show conclusively that he exercised not only the proper zeal but great prudence in directing, so far as it was in his power, the force afterward commanded by Col. Wm. Crawford, "in the most effectual manner for covering the frontiers," in hopes that it would give ease and safety to the inhabitants thereof.

the commissioner on the part of Virginia did not attend. Mr. McClean has been with me to ask my advice how to proceed, and to know whether I could spare any continental troops to assist. I could not well spare them; besides, on maturely considering the circumstances, I was of opinion it would not be proper for me to enforce the business with continental troops on the part of Pennsylvania; particularly as the commissioner from Virginia did not attend. I might be charged, perhaps, with promoting a quarrel between the two states. I therefore advised Mr. McClean to call on Colonels Cook [lieutenant of Westmoreland county], and Marshel [lieutenant of Washington county], and get them to assist him in representing fully to council this transaction, as well as the supposed cause of such conduct, and to bring if possible into view the principal secret actors in this and other (I think treasonable) acts. I believe this is done or will be in a few days. I also saw Colonel Marshel, who informed me he was collecting qualifications for this purpose.[1] I think Colonel Marshel is one of

---

[1] In August, 1763, Charles Mason and Jeremiah Dixon, of London, England, were selected by Lord Baltimore and the Penns to complete the boundary line between the provinces of Maryland and Pennsylvania. They were both eminent surveyors. The line they run has received their names — "Mason and Dixon's line;" figuratively, the dividing line between the northern and southern states of the Union.

Mason and Dixon's line was extended in 1767 to a point a little west of what is now Mount Morris, in Greene county, Pennsylvania; but this was a proceeding wholly independent of Virginia; and it was the intention of Pennsylvania to have extended the line to what was considered the southwest corner of the state. The surveyors, however, were stopped by the Indians at the point just mentioned. In 1781, for the sake of settling the minds of the people and preventing further disputes among the borderers, a temporary line was proposed to be run by common surveyors from the termination of Mason and Dixon's line, to a point twenty-three miles distant, that being the extent of five degrees, by common computation, from the Delaware river, which was the limit west of Pennsylvania. To run this temporary line, Alexander McClean was appointed in 1781, on the part of Pennsylvania. But his labors were interrupted. He was re-appointed in April, 1782, as shown by the following extract from the proceedings of the supreme executive council of Pennsylvania:

"PHILADELPHIA, *April* 6, 1782.

"*Ordered*, That Alexander McClean, Esquire, be appointed on the part of Pennsylvania, to run the line between this state and Virginia agreeably to in-

the most active, zealous supporters of government in this country.

This moment Dr. Knight[1] has arrived, the surgeon I sent with the volunteers to Sandusky. He was several days in the hands of the Indians, but fortunately made his escape from his keeper, who was conducting him to another settlement to be burned. He brings the disagreeable account that Colonel Crawford and all the rest (about twelve to the doctor's knowledge) who fell into their hands, were burned to death in a most shocking manner;[2] the unfortunate colonel, in particular, was over four hours in burning. The reason they assign for this uncommon barbarity is retaliation for the Moravian affair. The doctor adds, that he understood those people [the Moravian Indians] had laid aside their religious principles, and

---

structions to be given him for that purpose and that his appointment be under the seal of the state." Thereupon, a resolution of the Virginia house of delegates was passed as follows:

"IN THE HOUSE OF DELEGATES,
"*Saturday*, the 1st of *June*, 1782.

"*Resolved*, That the governor be empowered and required to appoint a surveyor who shall with such person or persons as may be appointed by the state of Pennsylvania, extend Mason and Dixon's line from the western termination thereof 23 miles due west and mark the same; and from thence to run and mark a meridian line to the Ohio river to answer the purpose of a temporary boundary; and that the governor do order out such a number of the militia as may be necessary for a guard during the time the said surveyor shall be running and marking the said line."

This was agreed to June 6, 1782, by the senate; but too late for the surveyor appointed to reach the mouth of Dunkard creek, where Mr. McClean had gathered his stores, and where on the tenth of that month a party of horsemen, about thirty in number, appeared on the opposite side of that river and opposed his beginning the survey. (See Appendix J,—Marshel to Irvine, June 15, 1782.) However, in November following, in conjunction with Joseph Neville, a surveyor appointed by Virginia, he finished the temporary line; the permanent one to the Ohio not being completed until 1785.

[1] By this it will be seen that Irvine made a mistake in the date of Knight's arrival, in his letter to Washington of July 11th (ante, p. 126). It should have been July 5th.

[2] In Irvine's letter to Washington (ante, p. 126), written seven days later, when Dr. Knight had somewhat recovered from his sufferings in the wilderness, his account is much more accurately given than in the above. All the prisoners then known by the doctor to have suffered death, except Crawford, were tomahawked.

have gone to war; that he saw two of them bring in scalps whom he formerly knew.[1]

The people generally seem anxious to make another trial, and press me to take command of them. Their proposals are to raise volunteers, provisions and horses, by subscription, at their own expense, without making any charge against the public, unless they should hereafter think proper to reimburse them. They also promise to obey orders, etc. The first of August is the time talked of to march. I have not yet determined whether to go or not, but in the meantime I am getting in returns of men, horses and provision subscribed. The arrangement made for covering the frontier has hitherto answered well; not more than four or five have been killed the two last months that I have heard of; but I much fear I shall not be able to keep the militia out much longer for want of provision.

I will, next opportunity, transmit a return of the Pennsylvania troops at this post and the attestations of the recruits.

XII.— IRVINE TO MOORE.

FORT PITT, *July* 16, 1782.

Sir:— Enclosed is a copy of a letter which is the best account I have been able to get of the unfortunate affair related in it.[2]

The express sent by Mr. Huffnagle through timidity and other misconduct, did not arrive here till this moment (Tuesday, 10 o'clock), though he left Hannastown Sunday evening, which I fear will put it out of my power to come up with the enemy, they will have got so far if they please; however, I

---

[1] How completely is now reversed what has for years been considered as one the facts of western history, viz.: that the object of Crawford's expedition was to murder the remnant of the Moravian Indians upon the Sandusky. We find, instead, the enterprise directed wholly against "enemy Indians," and that some "Moravians" gone back into heathenism, actually fought against the Americans, on that occasion.

[2] It is probable that the letter referred to by Irvine was one written by Michael Huffnagle to him, hereafter given. (See Appendix M,— Huffnagle to Irvine, July 14, 1782.)

have sent several reconnoitering parties to try to discover whether they have left the settlements and what route they have taken.¹

[1] Huffnagle soon after wrote the following to Moore:

"FORT REED, *July*, 1782.

"*Sir:*— I am sorry to inform your excellency, that last Saturday, at two o'clock in the afternoon, Hannastown was attacked by about one hundred whites and blacks [Indians]. We found several jackets, the buttons marked with the king's eighth regiment. At the same time this town was attacked, another party attacked Fort Miller, about four miles from this place. Hannastown and Fort Miller, in a short time, were reduced to ashes, about twenty of the inhabitants killed and taken, about one hundred head of cattle, a number of horses and hogs killed. Such wanton destruction I never beheld,— burning and destroying as they went. The people of this place behaved bravely; retired to the fort, left their all a prey to the enemy, and with twenty men only, and nine guns in good order, we stood the attack till dark. At first, some of the enemy came close to the pickets, but were soon obliged to retire farther off. I cannot inform you what number of the enemy may be killed, as we see them from the fort carrying off several.

"The situation of the inhabitants is deplorable, a number of them not having a blanket to lie on, nor a second suit to put on their backs. Affairs are strangely managed here; where the fault lies I will not presume to say. This place being of the greatest consequence to the frontiers,— to be left destitute of men, arms, and ammunition, is surprising to me, although frequent applications have been made. Your excellency, I hope, will not be offended my mentioning that I think it would not be amiss that proper inquiry should be made about the management of the public affairs in this county; and also to recommend to the legislative body to have some provision made for the poor, distressed people here. Your known humanity convinces me that you will do everything in your power to assist us in our distressed situation. I have the honor to be your excellency's most obedient, humble servant,

"MICH. HUFFNAGLE.

"His Excellency, William Moore, Esq'r, Pres't, Philadelphia."

The following is an extract from a letter written by Ephraim Douglass at Pittsburgh, July 26, 1782:

"My last contained some account of the destruction of Hannastown, but it was an imperfect one — the damage was greater than we knew, and attended with circumstances different from my representation of them. There were nine killed and twelve carried off prisoners, and, instead of some of the houses without the fort being defended by our people, they all retired within the miserable stockade, and the enemy possessed themselves of the forsaken houses, from whence they kept a continual fire upon the fort from about twelve o'clock till night, without doing any other damage than wounding one little girl within the walls. They carried away a great number of horses and everything of value in the deserted houses, destroyed all the cattle, hogs, and

I fear this stroke will intimidate the inhabitants so much that it will not be possible to rally them or persuade them to make a stand; nothing in my power shall be left undone to countenance and encourage them. But I am sorry to acquaint your excellency, there is little in my power — a small garrison scantily supplied with provision, rarely more than from day

poultry within their reach, and burned all the houses in the village except two; these they also set fire to, but fortunately it did not extend itself so far as to consume them; several houses round the country were destroyed in the same manner, and a number of unhappy families either murdered or carried off captives — some have since suffered a similar fate in different parts — hardly a day but they have been discovered in some quarter of the country, and the poor inhabitants struck with terror thro' the whole extent of our frontier. Where this party set out from is not certainly known; several circumstances induce the belief of their coming from the heads of the Alleghany or toward Niagara, rather than from Sandusky or the neighborhood of Lake Erie. The great number of whites known by their language to have been in the party, the direction of their retreat when they left the country, which was toward the Kittanning, and no appearance of their tracks, either coming or going, having been discovered by the officer and party which the general ordered on that service beyond the river, all conspire to support this belief."

The letter which follows contains information also upon the same subject:

"PITTSBURGH, *July* 30, 1782.

"*Dear Sir:*— I have taken the liberty of writing you the situation of our unhappy country at present. In the first place, I make no doubt but you have heard of the bad success of our campaign against the Indian towns [Crawford's campaign against Sandusky], and the late stroke the savages have given Hannastown, which was all reduced to ashes except two houses, exclusive of a small fort [Reed], which happily saved all who were so fortunate as to get to it. There were upwards of twenty killed and taken, the most of whom were women and children. At the same time, a small fort [Miller] four miles from thence, was taken, supposed to be by a detachment of the same party. I assure you that the situation of the frontiers of our county is truly alarming at present, and worthy our most serious consideration. . . .

"I make no doubt but you will be informed of a campaign that is to be carried against the Indians by the middle of the next month. General Irvine is to command. I have my own doubts. I have the honor to be your humble and obedient servant, DAVID DUNCAN.

"Honorable [James] Cunningham, Esq'r, Member of Council from Lancaster, Philadelphia."

The following extract from a letter written by General Irvine to Washington on the 27th of January, 1788, shows the origin of the attack upon Hannastown, and that the enemy came from the "heads of the Alleghany," as Douglass surmised: "In the year 1782, a detachment composed of three

to day, and even at times days without — add to this that, in all probability, I shall be, in the course of a few days, left without settlers in my rear to draw succors from. I have not time to add [more], having found a Mr. Elliott who is instantly setting out for Lancaster, from whence he promises to forward this.

XIII.— IRVINE TO MOORE.

FORT PITT, *July* 25, 1782.

Sir:— The destruction of Hannastown put the people generally into great confusion for some days. The alarm is partly over, and some who fled are returning again to their places; others went entirely off. I have got the lieutenant of the county [Colonel Edward Cook] and others prevailed on to encourage some of the inhabitants to re-occupy Hannastown, by keeping a post or small guard there.[1]

Inclosed are duplicates of the attestations of all the men enlisted here. The success in recruiting was so bad and the men also ordinary, that I thought it most prudent to desist. Several of those enlisted turned out to be deserters, one in particular [James Gordon] from our own line, whom I instantly executed, which I hope will deter others. Perhaps before winter some few better men may be got. Mr. Huffnagle informed me he had provided some provision (on a contract with [the supreme executive] council) for a ranging company and some militia ordered by Colonel Cook,[2] — and being in

hundred British, and five hundred Indians, was formed and actually embarked in canoes on Lake Jadaque [Chautauqua Lake], with twelve pieces of artillery, with an avowed intention of attacking Fort Pitt. This expedition . . . was laid aside in consequence of the reported repairs and strength of Fort Pitt, carried by a spy from the neighborhood of the fort.

"They then contented themselves with the usual mode of warfare, by sending small parties on the frontier, one of which burned Hannastown." (Ante, p. 140, note 8.)

[1] Hannastown continued to be occupied for some time after in a limited way.

[2] It will be seen from the following extract from a letter of Edward Cook, lieutenant of Westmoreland county, to the governor of Pennsylvania that he used every expedient to aid those who suffered by the attack upon Hannastown:

"WESTMORELAND COUNTY, *September* 2, 1782.

"*Sir:*— It may be necessary to inform your excellency that upon an applica-

extreme pinch for cash applied to me; and, as there was no immediate purpose the recruiting money could be applied to, I let him have one hundred and thirty-seven pounds. He promised to bring me your excellency's order or replace the money, neither of which has been done. I beg to have your excellency's pleasure in the matter, that in case you should not think proper to place it to his account and give me credit, I may immediately look to him for it. The remainder shall be either kept till a proper time to begin recruiting again, or disposed of as you think proper to direct.[1]

XIV.— Irvine to Moore.

Fort Pitt, *August* 28, 1782.

Sir:—I have been repeatedly informed that a certain Mr. ———, an attorney, has been one of the chief advisers of the people of this country against paying taxes, and that at a numerous meeting, he publicly recommended opposing the collectors by violence. I presume this has already been represented to your excellency by some civil officers, as a justice of the peace of Washington county was my principal informant, who I, at the time, told should have all the military under my command to assist, if necessary, to support the civil authority. No application has ever been made to me for any such purpose. My reason for troubling your excellency with

---

tion made to me by some of the distressed inhabitants of Hannastown and the vicinity thereof, I have allowed them to enroll themselves under the command of Captain Brice and draw rations for two months, upon their making every exertion in their power to keep up the line of the frontiers.

"The ranging company, consisting of about twenty-two privates and two officers, is stationed at Ligonier for the defense of that quarter."

[1] From the following, it appears that Irvine again loaned him about the same amount of the money belonging to the state:

"Fort Pitt, *August* 22, 1782.

"Received and borrowed from Brigadier General William Irvine, one hundred and thirty-two pounds and eight shillings, specie (money belonging to the state of Pennsylvania), which we promise to pay to General Irvine the first day of October next or bring an order from [the supreme executive] council [of Pa.] on him for that sum. Mich. Huffnagle,
"David Duncan."

this account of ———'s conduct at present is, that I understand he is about to leave this country immediately, and means to go to Philadelphia, and also expects admittance in the supreme court.

XV.— Moore to Irvine.

In Council, Philadelphia, *September* 4, 1782.

Sir:— The situation of affairs on the frontiers have engaged the serious attention of both the council and general assembly, the result of which has been a conference with some of the delegates of congress, in which it has been agreed to propose to his excellency, General Washington, to carry three expeditions into the Indian country: one from Fort Pitt; one from Northumberland, into the Genessee country; and one toward Oswego, from such place as the general shall think most practicable.

In order to have this business forwarded in the most decisive manner, General Potter[1] on the part of council and Colonel [Robert] Magaw[2] on the part of the general assembly are gone to headquarters to determine on this proposal, and are expected to return within a few days.

What will be the general's sentiments and determination on this subject it is not possible, at present, to determine; yet it seems to be proper to give you this hint, of which you will make such use as you may find occasion; and you may depend on the earliest information upon the return of the commissioners from headquarters.[3]

---

[1] Major General James Potter, at that date vice president of the supreme executive council of Pennsylvania.

[2] For notice of Col. Magaw, see Appendix M,— Magaw to Irvine, September 10, 1782, note.

[3] See Magaw to Irvine, just cited, for a full description of the visit of the commissioners to General Washington and the result of their conference.

XVI.— IRVINE TO MOORE.

FORT PITT, *September* 9, 1782.

Sir:— I have to acknowledge the receipt of your excellency's favor of the 10th [13th] of August.[1] Matters have been so quiet in this quarter since the beginning of August, that I could almost wish the militia may not come up; it will be fatiguing to them and expensive to the public. But I could not think myself at liberty to countermand them, not knowing the true cause of their being ordered.[2]

XVII.— MOORE TO IRVINE.

IN COUNCIL, PHILADELPHIA, *September* 18, 1782.

Sir:— An expedition from Fort Pitt being agreed on, and the orders relative thereto of course transmitted to you by the secretary of war, we now transmit to you an estimate of the expense for your information of the idea entertained here

---

[1] Not found. It is evident from what follows and from the tenor of a subsequent letter to the secretary at war (Irvine to Lincoln, September 12, 1782, ante, p. 82) that it gave Irvine information that one hundred and fifty militia from the counties of York and Cumberland were to be sent to Fort Pitt. The letter of Irvine to Lincoln, just mentioned, and the proceedings of the supreme executive council of Pennsylvania, an extract from which is given in the note following, fix the date of the letter from Moore to Irvine as of the 13th of August, instead of the 10th, as mentioned above.

[2] The following is an extract from the proceedings of the supreme executive council of Pennsylvania of August 13th, 1782:

"The council took into consideration a resolve of congress of the 8th instant recommending to the states of Pennsylvania and Virginia immediately to draw out and order to Fort Pitt, each state one hundred and fifty men, properly officered and accoutred, to be under the orders of the commanding officer of that post, to enable the said officer more effectually to cover and protect the country. That the secretary at war and superintendent of finance take order that proper magazines be laid up in the said fort, which may enable the commanding officer, in case the said post should be invested by the enemy, to render it tenable until relieved; and thereupon,

"*Ordered*, That the lieutenant of the county of York, and the lieutenant of the county of Cumberland, do immediately furnish seventy-five men from each of the said counties, according to law, and send them forthwith to Fort Pitt."

respecting it, and some kind of rule on that head. We are sensible of the difficulties attending this business, and the absolute necessity of the utmost expedition being used, and therefore authorize you to appoint such persons to procure the provisions, pack-horses, and stores, as you may judge most capable of the extraordinary exertion which in this case is required. This the council think the importance of the object and their confidence in your prudence and integrity will justify; and, in order to give you the fairest opportunity the nature of the case will admit of, we transmit to you by Mr. [John] Carnahan the sum of fifteen hundred pounds.[1] The state engages to pay the expense in the first instance, and for this purpose will forward the money to you from time to time as they perceive it will be necessary; but the council hope it will not exceed the estimate now sent to you.[2]

Whoever shall be appointed by you for these purposes will be required to procure clear vouchers of their expenditures and to make clear distinctions between the rations issued to the continental troops and those issued to the militia; and so of all other expenditures. I wish you success in the arduous task before you.

XVIII.—MOORE TO IRVINE.

IN COUNCIL, PHILADELPHIA, *October* 5, 1782.

Sir:—The council sent you by Mr. Carnahan, the sum of fifteen hundred pounds, for the purpose of forwarding the expedition into the Indian country. This expedition being

---

[1] The following is an extract from the proceedings of the supreme executive council of Pennsylvania, of September 18, 1782:

"An order was drawn on the treasurer in favor of John Carnahan, Esquire, for fifteen hundred pounds specie, to be paid by him to Brigadier General Irvine at Fort Pitt, for providing provisions, pack-horses, stores, etc., for the expedition carrying on against Sandusky towns."

[2] This was the estimate sent Irvine: "Expense of an expedition to Sandusky—1,200 men for 30 days:

"36,000 rations, at 10d., £1,500; 180 horses, at 3s, £1,080; 160 sacks at 10s., £80; 20 drivers, 30 days, at 3s. 9d., £112; 2 horse masters, at 7s. 6d., £30; 13 kegs, £3."

now laid aside,[1] you will please to pay the money to the order of Robert Morris, Esq., superintendent of finance, who engages to account for it here, agreeable to the order of general assembly appropriating the whole sum of which this is a part. You will also please to give council the earliest account of the payment of the superintendent's drafts, in order that the money may be charged to him, and the whole business immediately be closed.

XIX.—IRVINE TO MOORE.

FORT PITT, *October* 8, 1782.

Sir:—I am honored with your excellency's two letters of the 4th and 18th of September; the last, by Mr. Carnahan with the money, did not arrive here till the 5th instant. This delay and the detachment of Gen. Hazen's regiment not coming at the time proposed will unavoidably prevent my moving so soon as was intended. I have sent an officer express[2] to meet and hasten General Hazen's men, and though I am not certain what day they can arrive, take for granted, if at all, they will be here before the 20th; and, as the business would be impracticable later, have fixed on that day to march from Fort McIntosh, a post thirty miles advanced of this place.

Sixty rangers are counted to me as part of the men for the expedition. These I am not yet informed where they are to come from. Three hundred militia ordered by congress from below the mountain are also counted. These are not only so

---

[1] On the 28th of September, 1782, the [supreme executive] council received a letter from Washington, dated 23d of that month, expressing his opinion that the expeditions into the Indian country should be declined—the council thereupon ordered that they should be given up; also,

"*Ordered*, That the lieutenants of . . . Westmoreland and Washington counties call out no more militia after the expiration of the time of those now in service; his excellency, General Washington, having received intelligence that the British have called in all the savages, and that no more parties are to be permitted to be sent out against the frontiers." (As to the savages having been called in, see pp. 128, note; 135, note 2; and 184.)

[2] One of the officers constituting this "officer express" was John Rose. (See Appendix J,—Marshel to Irvine, October 21, 1782; also, Appendix K,—Irvine to Cook, October 10, 1782.)

far short of the number, but so few of them are fit, or in any manner clothed or equipped for such service, that most of them would be a dead weight or incumbrance; add to this, their term of service is nearly expired. I must therefore depend solely on the few regulars and what volunteers can be raised on this side the mountain. If about six hundred actually assemble, I am determined to make the attempt, particularly as I have some reason to hope General Clark will co-operate with us, if this last delay does not prevent it; as I had concerted measures with him that he should attack the Shawanese at the same time I did Sandusky. One of the expresses to him was wounded on his way down the river and narrowly escaped falling into the enemy's hands. I have sent another to him since that time, and a third since I received your last dispatches, in order to halt him a few days till I could get ready.

The estimate will be found in general too low, and several things omitted which cannot be dispensed with. The calculation for a horse to carry two hundred [weight] is too high;[1] however, you may depend I will spare no pains to have the business done on the lowest terms. I have appointed Mr. John Irwin, of Pittsburgh, the principal agent. If you should think proper to send any money in my absence, you will be so good as to address it to him subject to my orders. It would not be possible to procure the supplies in so a short time on any other plan than to purchase provisions from the volunteers which they had collected for their own use on the original plan of carrying the expedition. I mean, therefore, to order the whole to the place of general rendezvous; there have the whole appraised, and pay for it in bulk. Though some unavoidable waste will take place, yet I hope, on the whole, it will come within the price the rations are estimated at. The greatest difficulty with me is the uncertainty of the quantity, which cannot be ascertained till the whole is collected, but there is no alternative.[2]

---

[1] In the estimate sent Irvine the number of horses is put down at 180, and the rations (pounds) at 36,000, making 200 for each animal. (Ante, p. 257, note 2.)

[2] Two letters known to have been written by Irvine to Moore (or Dickinson).

XX.—IRVINE TO DICKINSON.[1]

FORT PITT, *January* 1, 1783.

Sir:—Inclosed I transmit to your excellency an account of a sum of money delivered to me by Colonel Carnahan and intended toward defraying the expenses of an expedition against the Indian settlements on Sandusky. You will easily convince yourself that, notwithstanding every preparation being adequate to the exertions necessary, and notwithstanding the delay of the orders countermanding my march, the expenses incurred are inconsiderable. I am in hopes even of putting off the kegs at no disadvantage.

A balance of the money sent me for the purpose of recruiting the Pennsylvania line remains in my hands. I expect your excellency's orders in what manner to dispose of it. The different trials have all proved unsuccessful, not only in the number of recruits, but with respect to the objects themselves.

XXI.—IRVINE TO DICKINSON.

FORT PITT, *June* 3, 1783.

Sir:—My anxiety to arm council against insidious men, to see infamous combinations against the interest of the state checked, jealousies between the civil and military subside, peace and harmony restored among all ranks,— will, I flatter myself, be an apology for this intrusion.

I am informed that companies are formed and plans laid in Philadelphia and other places for purchasing on their own

---

dated respectively 27th and 29th of October, 1782, have not been found. A brief outline of them, however, has been preserved. That of the 27th referred to the fact that additional expenses had been incurred for the defense of the frontiers. The one dated the 29th spoke of 'people settling beyond the Ohio north, within the boundaries of Pennsylvania; mentioning also, it seems, the fact of their intention to divide the state and form a new one.

[1] On the 7th of November, 1782, John Dickinson was elected president of the supreme executive council of Pennsylvania (becoming thereby the governor in fact and in law of the state) in place of Moore, whose term of office had expired.

terms, large tracts of the prime lands which are appropriated by law for the redemption of officers' and soldiers' certificates.

From anything I can learn, it will require great vigilance and a decisive line of conduct in the executive authority to prevent baneful effects, particularly as I have reason to believe those companies intend connecting themselves with the surveyors; and I am certain the military will keep a watchful eye on the whole of this transaction. If, therefore, the surveyors should by any finesse mistake or otherwise break over the bounds prescribed by law, troublesome turbulencies may ensue.

A mode occurs to me which I think will avoid the latter, namely: for council to order the whole tract laid off as bounded by law, previous to a single survey being made (except the reserved tracts), and this not to be done by any surveyors who are or may be appointed to districts within the tract; at least, without being joined by some person under the immediate order of council, who may perhaps judge it expedient to appoint some military officer for this purpose. There are sundry young gentlemen of the line well qualified for such business.

I am of opinion that the tracts reserved for the state at Forts Pitt and McIntosh should be laid off and some person appointed to take care of them, particularly at Fort Pitt, previous to the troops at this post being discharged; otherwise, the timber will be destroyed and land abused. I presume some person may be got to take charge of it for such privileges as will not injure the place — but from an indirect information only.

I have been led insensibly to advise [these measures] which I hope you will attribute not to arrogance but to zeal.[1]

---

[1] Irvine had, for a considerable period, zealously guarded the country beyond the Ohio and Alleghany, within the bounds of Pennsylvania, from intrusive settlers, as the following order shows:

"ORDER, FORT PITT, *February* 25, 1783.

"Any person who shall presume to ferry either men or women over the Ohio or Alleghany rivers or shall be found crossing over into what is generally called the Indian country between the Kittanning and Fort McIntosh without a written permit from the commanding officer at Fort Pitt, or orders for that purpose — until further orders shall be treated and prosecuted for holding or

XXII.— DICKINSON TO IRVINE.

IN COUNCIL, *July* 3, 1783.

Sir:— We are obliged to you for the communication in your letter of the 3d last; and have given such instructions to the surveyor general as we hope will be of use in preventing the mischief apprehended.[1]

We should also be glad if you would procure due care to be taken of the two tracts appropriated to the state, and prevent the timber from being destroyed.[2]

---

aiding others to correspond with and give intelligence to, the enemy. This order to be in force until civil government thinks proper to direct otherwise."

The country north and west of the Ohio and Alleghany rivers, to the western line of the state, as afterward determined, was claimed and occupied by different tribes of Indians, whose title thereto was extinguished by deed to the state from the chiefs of the Six Nations, for the sum of five thousand dollars, at the treaty of Fort Stanwix (now Rome), New York, October 23, 1784; and by deed from the chiefs of the Wyandots and Delawares, for the sum of three thousand dollars at a treaty held at Fort McIntosh (now Beaver, Pennsylvania), January 21, 1785.

[1] The general assembly of Pennsylvania, by their resolve of March 7, 1780, promised certain donations of land to be laid off to their officers and soldiers at the end of the war; and after that, by a particular law, appropriated the lands belonging to that state, which lay westward of the Alleghany and Ohio rivers, for that purpose and for the object of redeeming certificates of depreciation. The letter of Irvine of June 3 (not found), undoubtedly gave information of trespassers settling upon these lands. The governor, by a proclamation dated July 31, 1783, warned all persons from locating thereon.

[2] Instructions for H. Lee and John McClure from Brig. Gen'l Irvine:

"You are to take immediate charge of the fort, buildings and public property now remaining at the post of McIntosh for and in behalf of the state of Pennsylvania (except two pieces of iron cannon and some water casks, the property of the United States) and three thousand acres of land reserved for the use of said state. When the tract is surveyed you will attend and make yourselves acquainted with the lines; in the meantime you will consider it extending two miles up and down the river, and two miles back. You will take care that no waste is committed, or timber cut down or carried off the premises, and prohibit buildings to be made or any persons making settlements or to reside thereon, or from even hunting encampments; nor are any more families to be permitted than your own to live in the barracks or any part of the tract. In case of necessity for re-occupying the post for the United States, you are to give up the fort to the orders of the commanding continental officer at this place, retaining only such part of the buildings as may be neces-

We wish to do everything we can for the benefit of the state and for rendering justice to the officers and soldiers, and therefore should certainly appoint some military gentlemen to act in conjunction with the surveyor, if we had the power.

sary for you to live in. But if the troops should be so numerous as not to afford room for you, you will, in that case, occupy the buildings without the works or build for yourselves on some convenient place. But you will on no account whatever quit the place without orders from the executive council of Pennsylvania or their agent, so to do, whose directions you will hereafter obey in all matters relative to said post and tract of land. In case of lawless violence, or persons attempting to settle by force, or presuming to destroy anything on the premises, you will apply to Michael Huffnagle, Esquire, or some other justice of the peace for Westmoreland county.

"For your care and trouble in performing the several matters herein required, you may put in grain and labor any quantity of ground not exceeding one hundred acres, and keep or raise stock to the number of fifty head of horned cattle and eight horses. You will govern yourselves by these instructions until the pleasure of the honorable council is signified to you; and you will give up peaceable possession to them or their order whenever they think proper. Given under my hand at Fort Pitt, September 23, 1783.

"WM. IRVINE, B. Gen'l.

"We severally engage to conform to the foregoing instructions to us by General Irvine.
H. LEE.
"JNO. McCLURE.

"Witness, JOHN ROSE."

Instructions from Brigadier General Irvine to James Boggs:

"FORT PITT, *September* 30, 1783.

"You are to take charge of the tract of land opposite Fort Pitt reserved for the use of Pennsylvania, and not suffer any waste or destruction to be done of timber, or cut or carried off the premises except what is herein mentioned. You will on no account allow roads to be made through the tract, or landing places other than the old one formerly used by Indian traders and lately by the garrison. You will cautiously avoid giving offense to the commandant at this post; and if any trespasses are committed or violence used you will lodge regular complaint to Michael Huffnagle, Esq., or some other justice of the peace for Westmoreland county.

"You are, for your trouble and care, allowed to clear land and raise crops so as not to exceed one hundred acres and you may keep stock not to exceed twenty horned cattle and six horses. You are not to permit any buildings whatsoever to be erected, except for the use and convenience of your own families. You may, however, allow the troops of this garrison to cut and carry off firewood, if the commanding officer finds it expedient to take from them, but you must keep and render an account to council of the quantity so taken. You will also hereafter govern yourselves by such orders or instructions as you may receive from his excellency the president of the state; and you will

The measure would in all probability be advantageous; and we should be pleased if your prudence would avail itself of your situation to secure the Pennsylvania line against the

---

render peaceable possession when required by him or the lawful agent of the honorable the council, or take such lease as they shall think proper.
"WM. IRVINE.

"I engage to act conformably to the above instructions from General Irvine.
JAMES BOGGS.

"Witness, DAVID DUNCAN.

"N. B.— Until the tract is surveyed, it is considered to extend two miles down the Ohio river and two miles up the Alleghany and two miles back."

The "tract," it seems, was in a state of nature, not very inviting, if we are to judge of it from its appearance subsequent to this date, as depicted by the surveyor of it in a letter to the governor and council of Pennsylvania, from Washington, that state, written February 19, 1788. The writer says:

"This country has never experienced a winter more severe. The mercury has been at this place 12 degrees below the extreme cold point. At Muskingum 20, and at Pittsburgh, within the bulb or bottle. The difference may in part be accounted for by the inland situation of this place, and greater or lesser quantities of ice at the others. It has been altogether impossible for me, until within these few days past, to stir from the fireside.

"On Thursday last, I went with several other gentlemen to fix on the spot for laying out the town opposite Pittsburgh, and at the same time took a general view of the tract and find it far inferior to my expectations, although I had been no stranger to it. There is some pretty low ground on the River Ohio and Alleghany, but there is but a small proportion of dry land, which appears anyway valuable, either for timber or soil; but especially for soil. It abounds with high hills, and deep hollows, almost inaccessible to a surveyor. I am of the opinion that if the inhabitants of the moon are capable of receiving the same advantage from the earth which we do from their world — I say, if it be so — this same famed tract of land would afford a variety of beautiful lunar spots, not unworthy of the eye of a philosopher.

"I cannot think that ten acre lots, on such pitts and hills, will possibly meet with purchasers unless, like a pig in a poke, it be kept out of view. Would it not be more of advantage to the state if the legislature would alter the law that a town and a reasonable number of outlots, for the accommodation of the town, be laid out, the remainder of the land to be laid out in 200 acre lots — fronting the river when practicable — and extending back so as to include the hilly and uneven ground which might be of some use to a farm; I cannot but believe that Colonel Irwin and Colonel [Alexander] Lowrey, both members of the assembly, and who know the land well, will, on consideration, be of the opinion with me, that small lots on sides of those hills, can never be of any use but as above mentioned. Perhaps council may think proper to lay the matter before the legislature. I shall go on to do the business as soon as the weather will admit; and, before I shall have pro-

schemes of those projectors who prefer their own gain to more generous considerations.

ceded farther than may accord with the plan here proposed, I may have the necessary information whether to go on as the law now directs or not.

"I have the honor to be, your excellency's and the Hon. council's most obedient servant, DAVID REDICK."

APPENDIX H.

CORRESPONDENCE WITH BENJ. HARRISON, GOVERNOR OF VIRGINIA.

I.—IRVINE TO HARRISON.

FORT PITT, *April* 20, 1782.

Sir: — In obedience to the ordinance of congress of the 24th of September last, and also the commander-in-chief's instructions, for making arrangements with the continental troops under my command, combined with the militia on the west side of the Laurel Hill, in the states of Virginia and Pennsylvania, I wrote the lieutenants of Monongalia and Ohio counties[1] to attend a general meeting at this post the 5th instant, of the lieutenants and field officers whose opinions I wanted respecting the mode of defense, the number of men necessary, and several other matters. Colonel [David] Shepherd [lieutenant of Ohio county, Virginia] attended and informed me he had nothing in his power — most of the men in his district being now enrolled in Pennsylvania. Colonel [John] Evans [lieutenant of Monongalia county, Virginia] did not attend, but wrote me that the number of effective men in his district did not exceed 300; that they were so scattered as to form a frontier of eighty miles; and begged of me in the most earnest manner to assist him with men, arms, ammunition, etc.

The frontiers of Virginia and Pennsylvania are so connected that very few more men would guard both than each will require if they act separately. For this reason, I wanted a junction of the whole and intended to detach as circumstances should require. As at present I cannot expect any from Virginia I am making such arrangements as that part of the Pennsylvania militia will cover some of Virginia; but this mode I fear will not long be complied with on the part of

---
[1] See Appendix M,—Irvine to John Evans, March 28, 1782.

Pennsylvania, as they will think hard to be obliged to guard Virginians. The Virginians on the other hand complain that they have not an equal share of protection and expect that I will cover them with continental troops. I need not enumerate to your excellency many reasons which put this entirely out of my power. The council of Pennsylvania have directed their civil officers to order out, agreeable to law, such numbers of militia from time to time as I may think proper to demand. The Virginia civil officers on this side the Hill say they have no such instructions from your excellency, consequently I cannot draw them out except as volunteers, who rarely render much service. I flatter myself you will excuse this trouble when I assure your excellency that as well from inclination as duty, I wish to give assistance and support to the inhabitants of both states in proportion to the support I receive from civil authority; and that as a continental officer I have no local attachment.

Here I will take the liberty to observe as matter of opinion that unless measures are taken very soon to run the boundary line between Virginia and Pennsylvania and a regular administration of civil government takes place in both states, everything will be in utter confusion. New governments are much talked of being set up. I am told this scheme is carried so far that a day is appointed (by advertisement) to meet for the purpose of emigrating to establish a new government.* I am instructed by his excellency, General Washington, that he would give direction for a proportion of recruits of the Virginia line being sent to this district; but as Colonel Gibson will write your excellency on this subject, I need not trouble you.

This will be handed to your excellency by Lieutenant Thomas, who is an intelligent gentleman and can give you every necessary information respecting the affairs of this country.

---

* A certain Mr. J———, who, 'tis said, is not long from *England*, is at the head of the emigrating party, and some say has actually a form of a constitution for the new government ready written.

II.—HARRISON TO IRVINE.

IN COUNCIL [VA.], *May* 22, 1782.

Sir: — Your favor of the 20th ult., by Lieutenant Thomas, came safe to hand. Orders have been long since sent hence to the counties of Augusta and Hampshire to send to Monongalia seventy men to assist in guarding the frontiers of that county. These troops I expect will probably be stationed at or near Tygart's Valley and the West Fork. As these posts are at too great a distance from you, I suppose it would be improper to remove the men from them, though I perfectly agree in opinion with you that it would be generally better to place the whole defense of that country under one commander; for which reasons orders are now sent to the commanding officers of Monongalia and Ohio [counties], to furnish so many men as they can spare to assist you;[1] though there is one great obstruction to your plan, which is, that as our law now stands the militia of this state cannot be removed out of it. The assembly may probably make some alteration in the law; if they do, I shall advise you of it.

Measures are taking for running the boundary line between the two states, and I expect commissioners will meet for that purpose at the extremity of the Maryland line on the 10th day of July next, which I hope will quiet the people and reconcile them to the present governments.[2]

---

[1] See Appendix M,— John Evans to Irvine, June 30, 1782.

[2] Concerning this paragraph, Gen. Irvine in a letter to Alexander McClean, of Uniontown, Pa., afterward wrote:

"'Measures are taking for running the boundary line between the two states and I expect commissioners will meet for that purpose at the extremity of the Maryland line on the 10th day of July next, which I hope will quiet the people and reconcile them to the present governments.'"

"The above is extracted from Governor Harrison's letter to me, dated 22d May, 1782; but whether he made a mistake in the date, and intended June, but made it July, or whether there has been a mistake originally in the time proposed for meeting, I know not."

III.— Harrison to Irvine.

Virginia Council Chamber, *August* 21, 1782.

Sir:— On a requisition from congress to assist you with one hundred and fifty men, I have ordered seventy-five from each of the counties of Frederick and Berkeley to join you at Fort Pitt. I expect they will obey the order with cheerfulness, but if they do not and should halt at the boundary line, I have no power to compel them to go over it. I therefore recommend it to your consideration whether it would not be better to employ them in this country (where I think they may be usefully stationed to prevent the incursions of the Indians) than to order them into Pennsylvania, at the hazard of being disobeyed.

I have been exceedingly alarmed by a letter from the continental secretary of war, received yesterday by express, informing me of an intended attack on your fort, and the danger he thought it was in of falling into the hands of the enemy; as such an event would be attended with the most distressing circumstances as well to the frontier inhabitants of this state as of Pennsylvania, I have thought it my duty to take such steps as may be necessary for the relief of the fort in case it should be invested, and have therefore issued orders to the several counties most convenient to hold seventeen hundred men in constant readiness to march at the shortest notice for that service, and have appointed General Edward Stevens [1] to the command of them, to whom you will please to give notice if your apprehensions of being invested should continue.[2]

---

[1] See Appendix M,— Stevens to Irvine, August 25, 1782.

[2] Extract from the *Pennsylvania Packet*, 5 Sept., 1782 (No. 933):

"Richmond (Virginia), August 24. Certain accounts are . . . received of an expedition being intended against Fort Pitt by the British and their Indian allies. From the vigorous measures adopted by this state and Pennsylvania, we have reason to hope their designs will be effectually counteracted, and at the same time will convince the public of their real views in holding out the idea of peace."

IV.— IRVINE TO HARRISON.

FORT PITT, *September* 3, 1782.

Sir:— I am honored with your excellency's letter of the 21st of August. About the middle of July, appearances threatened an investiture of this place or a total destruction of the settlements on this side of the mountains. Hanna's, a county town, was attacked and burnt, about twenty were killed and taken there and in the vicinity. Wheeling was, at the same time, in some degree blockaded; a large body of Indians kept skulking about it for five or six days. In short they appeared in all quarters, and the alarm and consternation of the inhabitants were as great as can be conceived.[1]

Since the beginning of August all has been perfectly quiet. I have not heard of a single person being killed, nor scarce of an Indian being seen. I am not apprised of any late infor-

---

[1] Extracts from newspapers of 1782, relative to the attack on Hannastown:

[I.]

"Philadelphia, July 30. From Westmoreland county, 16 July. On the 13th a body of Indians came to and burnt Hannastown, except two houses. The inhabitants having received notice of their coming, by their attacking some reapers who were at work near the town, fortunately (except 15 who were killed and taken) got into the fort, where they were secure."— *Pennsylvania Packet*, 30 July, 1782 (No. 917).

[II.]

"Richmond, Aug. 17. By our last accounts from the northwestern frontier we learn that the Indians have lately destroyed Hannastown and another small village on the Pennsylvania side, and killed and captured the whole of the inhabitants."— *Pennsylvania Packet*, 27 Aug., 1782 [No. 929].

[III.]

"Extract of a letter from Fort Pitt, dated Sept. 3: 'From the middle to the last of July, the Indians have been very troublesome on the frontiers of this country — Hannastown was burned, several inhabitants killed and taken, and about the same time Fort Wheeling [Henry] was blockaded for several days; for two weeks the inhabitants were in such consternation, that a total evacuation of the country was to be dreaded [feared]; but since the beginning of August matters have been more quiet, and the people have again, in a great degree, got over their panic.'"— *Pennsylvania Packet*, 1 Oct., 1782 [No. 944]; *Salem Gazette*, Oct. 17, 1782.

mation respecting the designs of the enemy against this place, except what your excellency's letter contains, and I am entirely at a loss to know whether the secretary at war grounds his fears on the alarming accounts received from here or on intelligence received from another quarter. If the one hundred and fifty militia come on from Berkeley and Frederick, I will employ them as you advise (on the frontiers of their own state). But from the present calm state things are in, I would almost wish they would not come, particularly on account of feeding them, which is almost impossible. As congress have demanded them, and may be possessed of information unknown to me, I dare not positively countermand their march, but really their coming will embarrass me much.

I have been some time meditating and preparing for an excursion into the Indian country, which, if accomplished, will, I hope, nearly put an end to the Indian war in this quarter. My troops on this occasion are chiefly to be volunteer militia of the country, who propose not only to equip and feed themselves but also to provide provision for such continental troops as I shall be able to take from the post. I am more sanguine in this business, having last night received an express from General Clark in order to concert measures for a descent from his quarter at the same time.[1]

---

[1] Extract from the *Pennsylvania Packet*, Oct. 1, 1782 (No. 944):

"Richmond (Virginia), September 21. Late accounts from the northwestern settlements contradict the report formerly published of an action between our people and the Indians at the mouth of Wheeling.

"We hear an expedition is intended against the Indian towns on the waters of Lake Erie, the people in the neighborhood of Fort Pitt having been extremely irritated with the injuries received from those savages."

APPENDIX I.

WILLIAM DAVIES, VIRGINIA SECRETARY AT WAR, TO IRVINE.

I.

WAR OFFICE, VIRGINIA, *April* 12, 1782.

Sir:— The incursions of the Indians into the county of Monongalia[1] and the number of the inhabitants they have killed, have induced government to order a company from Hampshire to march to their relief, to be under the immediate command of Colonel Evans [lieutenant] of Monongalia. The defense of these people being a continental as well as state object, I have desired Colonel Evans to maintain a correspondence with you, not doubting of your readiness to co-operate in repelling the common enemy, as far as may be consistent with the more particular duties of your command at Fort Pitt. From the knowledge I have of your character, and the small acquaintance I had the honor to have with you in the army, I have taken this liberty more explicitly to address you, as I hope the people will meet with a more speedy and efficacious assistance from you in their present distress than the urgency of their circumstances can admit from a dependence upon government, who are so far removed from them; and in this ap-

---

[1] In October, 1776, the northwestern part of Virginia — then known as the District of West Augusta — was divided into three counties: Yohogania, Ohio, and Monongalia. (Ante, p. 24, note 2.) Before the date of the above letter, Yohogania county had become extinct, leaving only Ohio and Monongalia counties west of the western boundary line of Maryland. The north line of the latter county extended west from the western boundary of Maryland along the boundary line between Pennsylvania and Virginia to the dividing ridge whence the waters flowed east into the Monongahela and west into the Ohio. West of this ridge (which in its southerly course divided the two counties) was Ohio county, extending to the Ohio river and including the whole of what is now known as the "Pan-handle." The present counties of Ohio and Monongalia in West Virginia are remnants of the original ones just mentioned.

plication, I have a firmer confidence in your ready attention to it from the reflection that one Virginia regiment composes a part of your command. The people of Monongalia are distressed for ammunition as well as a few arms, both of which in the low state of our finances we find it extremely difficult to forward them. If therefore you have any to spare, particularly ammunition, it will be serving them essentially, and shall be replaced as soon as it can be forwarded; and as two or three hundred weight will be sufficient, or indeed half that quantity, I am in hopes it can be spared by you without inconvenience.

I am also to beg your assistance towards the support of General Clark,[1] so far only as to facilitate the transportation and safe conduct of a quantity of military stores forwarded from Richmond and other places for the support of the inhabitants down the Ohio, as well as to enable him, if practicable, to act offensively against the Indians. The stores are forwarded under the care of a Mr. Carney, whose principal difficulty will be in procuring boats, an escort, and provisions for them. If you can afford him any assistance in either of these points you will be rendering a very essential service to the exposed inhabitants of the new country, and perhaps enable General Clark to make such a diversion against the Indians below as may have a happy influence in securing the dependencies of Fort Pitt in peace and quietness.

II.

WAR OFFICE, VIRGINIA, *May* 1, 1782.

Sir:—I had the honor to address you some time since on the subject of supplies to General Clark. You will find by the enclosed extract the dangerous situation in which that country stands. I fear with all our exertions, we shall not be able to afford assistance in proper time. The letter from General Clark did not reach me until last Saturday. I am therefore very uneasy about his present situation. A guard of fifty men is thought sufficient by government, but how to get

---

[1] General George Rogers Clark, then at Fort Nelson (Lou'sville), Kentucky.

them is the question. If any persons will go down under the command of the officers entrusted with the stores, the government of this state will allow them the pay of militia, both for going and coming and for their provisions. This offer may be accepted by many, who are desirous of going to that country. We are also put to great inconvenience for boats, and I fear without your assistance we shall suffer. It would delay us too long to wait till boats could be built for transporting our stores. Our principal dependence must therefore be in hiring them, upon condition of paying for them altogether should they not return by a certain reasonable period. Upon this subject, I have also written Colonel Crawford[1] and Major [John] Hardin[2] and have sent the latter thirty pounds specie for that purpose, and should that be insufficient, his draft should be immediately honored as far as fifty pounds in the whole. But, sir, I must depend greatly upon your assistance in this matter, as I fear without it, we shall not be able to get the boats.

May I hope for an answer to this or my former letter? The business is of consequence, and as such I have taken the liberty to submit it to you.

III.

WAR OFFICE [VA.], *May* 22, 1782.

Sir:— Agreeable to the direction of his excellency in council, I have the honor to inform you of the steps taken for the defense of the frontiers. Several orders have, from time to time, been issued according to the various circumstances of our affairs in that quarter. Upon a representation of their distresses, orders were issued for one company of militia from Hampshire to march to Monongalia [county], and be disposed of as

---

[1] Col. Wm. Crawford. Whether the letter reached him before setting out upon the expedition against Sandusky in which he lost his life, is unknown; probably it did.

[2] Of the 13th Virginia regiment, formerly. He had a son John Hardin, Jr.; they were a branch of the celebrated Hardin family of Kentucky, of which there were officers in the revolution, in the war of 1812, and in the war with Mexico.

Colonel Evans should direct, and an officer and twenty privates from Augusta were ordered to be stationed at Tygart's Valley. The Hampshire men were to be relieved by a company formed from Rockingham and Augusta and the ensign and twenty [men] were to return without relief at the end of two months. In addition to these detachments, it was afterwards found necessary to order a re-enforcement of thirty-one rank and file from Augusta, including the ensign and twenty [men] before mentioned, and nineteen rank and file from Rockingham, to rendezvous at Tygart's Valley, under the immediate orders of Lieutenant Colonel Wilson, but subject to the general direction of Colonel Evans, and to be relieved after performing a tour of two months by the counties of Shenandoah, Frederick, and Berkeley, and the company first ordered from Hampshire will therefore return without relief at the expiration of their tour. There have likewise been subsequent orders [issued] to the county lieutenants of Augusta and Rockingham for twenty-two rank and file to be furnished by the first, and thirteen rank and file from the latter, to be stationed at such places as the commanding officer of Augusta should think proper for the defense of his county, and to be relieved after performing a tour of two months [duty], by the militia of Rockbridge.

I have informed Colonel Evans of the order of his excellency that the defense of the frontier should be subject to your directions in future, and have requested him to furnish such portions of his militia as you may think necessary to call for.[1]

IV.

WAR OFFICE, *August* 22, 1782.

Sir:— I acknowledge the receipt of your favor of the 25th of May and am much obliged to you for the assistance you have kindly afforded towards the transportation of the stores for General Clark. The unfortunate affair of Colonel Craw-

---

[1] See Appendix M,— Col. John Evans to Irvine, June 30, 1782.

ford will, I fear, greatly encourage the enemy and be attended with unhappy consequences, unless timely guarded against.

In consequence of a representation of the designs of the enemy against your post, government have directed that orders should issue for the immediate march of seventy-five men properly officered from Frederick and the like number from Berkeley [counties, Virginia]. A body of seventeen hundred men are also ordered to be in constant readiness to march at a moment's warning to your relief should the enemy actually attempt the investiture of your fort. To enable you the more readily to assemble this number of men, I enclose you the appointment made agreeably to which orders have been issued to the different county lieutenants. Happy in having opportunity to contribute to the strength and security of your garrison, I would request you to inform me of anything in my department in which I can assist you, and beg you freely to command me.

APPENDIX J.

CORRESPONDENCE WITH THE LIEUTENANT OF WASHINGTON COUNTY, PENNSYLVANIA.

I.—IRVINE TO JAMES MARSHEL.[1]

FORT PITT, *November* 18, 1781.

Sir:—I did not intend to call for any militia this winter if it could possibly be avoided. But the continentals are here so few and they so illy provided for, and, in short, so irregular and in every respect so unlike soldiers, that it is absolutely necessary to draw them as much together as the nature of the service will admit, to try to new model and arrange them be-

---

[1] James Marshel,—for so he spelled his name during the last half of his life — obtained rights to about 1,500 acres of land in what is now Cross Creek township, Washington county, Pennsylvania, between 1776 and 1778. He was born in the north of Ireland, Feb. 20, 1753, and came west from that part of Lancaster county which is now Dauphin, in that state. In 1779, when the Presbyterian congregations of Buffalo and Cross Creek called Rev. Joseph Smith, then of York county, as their first pastor, Adam Poe and Andrew Poe signing the call, it being difficult to find a person to bring the minister from "over the mountains," Marshel offered 200 acres of his land to any one who would do so. The offer was accepted and the removal made by Capt. Joseph Scott, who received the land; and it has descended direct to its present owners, his grandsons, J. M. K. Reed, Esq., and his brother John C. Reed. For a time, Marshel was an elder in the Buffalo church.

In the boundary controversy, he was an ardent Pennsylvanian, and in the bitterness engendered made enemies of several of those who favored the Virginia jurisdiction,—the controversy affecting the politics of his section for years after the boundary was established. When Washington county was erected in 1781, he was commissioned county lieutenant, holding that office at date of the above letter; also recorder of deeds and register of wills. He was again elected recorder and register, serving from 1791 to 1795.

Col. Marshel in 1795-6 advertised all his lands in Washington county for sale, and removed to Brooke county, Virginia, where he resided until his death, March 17, 1829. He left the following surviving children: John, who settled in Washington, Pa.; Robert, who settled in Ohio; a daughter, who married Mr. McCluny; and two other daughters, who died unmarried at an advanced age.

fore next campaign. This being the state of facts, I am compelled to call on you, to order a few militia for the defense of the post of Wheeling.[1] It is now garrisoned by a continental officer and fifteen privates. The same number of militia is the most I wish you to order. Indeed, I am of opinion that fewer would do during the winter; as I think there can be nothing more necessary than barely to keep a look-out, take care of the post, and give an alarm to the inhabitants in case of danger.

If you are of the same opinion, and can accomplish it, I propose that you engage one discreet, intelligent subaltern officer with six or seven men, to take charge of the post, by the first of December at farthest, and to remain there until the first of March unless sooner discharged or relieved; they to be allowed for it as having served a tour of militia duty, and every other emolument and allowance agreeable to law. If you approve of this scheme, I request you will lose no time in putting it into execution.[2] But if inconvenient, then you are to order out, agreeable to law, one subaltern, one sergeant, one corporal and fifteen privates. When they are ready to march, they are to come to me for instructions.[3]

[1] In July, 1774, soon after the commencement of hostilities in Lord Dunmore's war, Major Angus McDonald arrived over the mountains with a considerable force of Virginia militia, to take part in the conflict against the savages. He went down to the mouth of Wheeling creek, where, subsequently, the whole force, under the immediate command of Lord Dunmore, rendezvoused. A stockade fort was there erected under the joint direction of McDonald and Captain William Crawford; it is now the site of the city of Wheeling, West Virginia. The post was first called Fort Fincastle. Its name, after the commencement of the revolution, was changed to Fort Henry, in honor of Patrick Henry, governor of the state. It was several times assailed by the enemy during the revolution but never taken.

[2] The idea of General Irvine in "this scheme" was, to induce Marshel to fill up the post at Wheeling after relieving the continentals, who constituted its garrison, with volunteers, if he could well do so. This he preferred to making a "call" for the requisite number of militia, which, in reality, was a draft. But Marshel, as will be seen in his reply, was "tired out with volunteer plans."

[3] Extracts from the minutes of the supreme executive council of Pennsylvania:

"IN COUNCIL, PHILADELPHIA, *Monday*, *October* 8, 1781.

"A letter from his excellency the president of congress of this day was re-

I have ordered the bearer to wait one, or two days at most, for your answer, which I request by him, whatever your determination may be.[1]

II.— Marshel to Irvine.

Washington County [Pa.],[2] *November* 20, 1781.

Sir:— I am this moment honored with your favor of the eighteenth, and am sorry I cannot comply with your requisition for engaging a number of men for the defense of Fort Wheeling, as I am fairly tired out with volunteer plans; besides, I have received orders from [the supreme executive] council [of Pa.][3] to call out the militia according to

---

ceived and read, inclosing a resolution of congress of the twenty-fourth of September last, appointing Brigadier General William Irvine to the command of the continental post of Fort Pitt."

"In Council, Philadelphia, *Thursday, October* 11, 1781.

"The council took into consideration a resolve of congress of the twenty-fourth of September last, appointing Brigadier General Irvine to the command of Fort Pitt; and thereupon,

"*Ordered*, That agreeably to the said recommendation (ante, p. 72, note 1), the lieutenants of the counties of Washington and Westmoreland be ordered to call forth agreeably to law, upon his requisition, such militia as may be necessary for that post and the protection of the country."

[1] Marshel, as lieutenant of Washington county, received his appointment from the supreme executive council of the state on the 2d of April, 1781. By virtue of his office, he had a general supervision over military affairs of the county; or, in other words, over everything appertaining to the militia therein (ante, p. 12, note 1). His sub-lieutenants after December 24, 1781, were: William McCleery, William Parker, George Vallandigham and Matthew Ritchie.

[2] Very likely this, the first letter of Marshel to Irvine, was written at his house in what is now Cross Creek township, Washington county, on the farm now owned by Thomas McCorkle, Sr.

[3] These "orders," directed to the lieutenants of Westmoreland and Washington counties, were in the following words:

"In Council, Philadelphia, *October* 11, 1781.

"*Sir:*— You will perceive by the inclosed resolve of congress (ante, p. 72, note 1), that Brigadier General Irvine is appointed to repair forthwith to Fort Pitt and take upon him the command of that garrison. The council is disposed to pay a due respect to the regulation of congress, and to afford General Irvine all the assistance in their power. You are, therefore, hereby ordered to call forth agreeable to law, upon his requisition, such militia as may be necessary for the defense of that post and the protection of the country."

law on your order. I shall, therefore, order out according to class, the number of militia you have demanded and order the officer to wait upon you for instructions.[1]

III.—MARSHEL TO IRVINE.

WASHINGTON COUNTY, *November* 26, 1781.

Sir:—The bearer hereof is the officer who is to take the command of the militia I have drafted[2] for the post at Wheeling. I have, therefore, directed him to wait upon you for orders. You will please to dismiss him with all possible dispatch that he may attend the rendezvous at Catfish Camp [now Washington, Washington county, Pa.], on Thursday, the 29th inst.[3]

---

[1] This ordering out of the militia upon Irvine's requisition, was not in lieu of, nor did it in any manner interfere with the drafting of the militia to serve under the orders of the lieutenant of the county. In the one case, they were supplied with arms, ammunition and provisions by the United States; in the other, by the state. On the 5th of April following, this regulation was changed (ante, p. 104 and note 1). Irvine then took charge of all matters concerning the defense of the frontier.

[2] By this it will be seen that when Marshel ordered out any desired number of militia, for whatever service, he did so by drafting, and from a particular class; that is, from those not exempt because of having served on previous tours. (See, also, his previous letter.)

[3] The detachment ordered out was under the command of Lieutenant John Hay. Irvine's instructions to that officer were as follows:

"FORT PITT, *November* 28, 1781.

"*Sir:*—You will proceed with the detachment under your command to Wheeling, there to relieve the garrison of continental troops [consisting of one officer and fifteen privates], taking on yourself the charge of the post. I do not apprehend any danger of an attack during the winter season of any considerable number of the enemy, notwithstanding you ought to be vigilant and guard against being surprised, which a few skulking savages might affect if you should be found off your guard, and which could not fail of bringing disgrace on you and might be attended with fatal consequences to the inhabitants of the settlements, the protection of whom is the main object of your being posted there. You will also see that no waste takes place of any public property; suffer no person to pass down the river without a permit from the commandant at this place; stop and secure all suspected persons, giving me the earliest notice in your power; and you will also inform me from time to time of every material occurrence.

Appendix J. 281

IV.— IRVINE TO MARSHEL.

FORT PITT, *January* 10, 1782.

Sir:— You will please to order one subaltern, one sergeant and fifteen privates, to relieve Lieutenant [John] Hay and his garrison at Fort Henry, or Wheeling, in such time as you will judge they will with certainty reach that post by the 1st day of February.[1] You will be so good as to direct the officer you

"You will take an inventory of all public stores from the officer you relieve; and when you are relieved deliver a similar one, taking a receipt from the relieving officer.

"In case of an attack you will maintain your post to the last extremity, giving the earliest notice to the country that they may come to your support; or to me by express if in your power.

"Any provisions you procure for your party shall be paid for by the contractors here, on your certificates addressed to me, provided it does not amount to more than the allowance for the number of men. In procuring provisions by barter of Yates you will doubtless make the best bargain in your power. I have entire confidence in your prudence and vigilance. I am, dear sir, your humble servant, WM. IRVINE,
"B. G. Commanding Fort Pitt and Dependencies."

[1] That Marshel was fully able to comply with General Irvine's requisition, the following letter to William Moore, governor of Pennsylvania, is evidence:

"WASHINGTON COUNTY, *February* 4, 1782.

"*Sir:*— By this opportunity I have made return of the officers of this county, although the whole is not yet commissioned as will appear by the return inclosed. The officers and privates of the seventh company in the first battalion refuse to become subjects of this state [Pennsylvania]. The greatest part of the other officers elected, and not yet commissioned, objects to taking the oath of allegiance until the line is run. This difficulty I hope council will cause to be removed as soon as possible. The field officers of the first battalion were not elected by ballot, as the law directs, on account of a large mob that prevented those who were disposed to comply with the law from doing it in that manner, although they were, on the day appointed for election, elected verbally by a great majority, and therefore are commissioned.

"I have the pleasure of informing your excellency that I have been fully able to comply with your order in calling forth the militia agreeable to law, on General Irvine's requisition. The only difficulty we are under at present is the want of provision for the militia when in actual service, the contractors not being able to purchase more than is necessary for the regular troops. No doubt this difficulty will also be removed in due time.

"JAMES MARSHEL, L. W. C."

In this connection, it may be noted that the battalion of Colonel David

send, to take a copy of my instructions to Lieutenant Hay, for his government.[1]

V.— IRVINE TO MARSHEL.

FORT PITT, *March* 29, 1782.

Sir:— When your letter of yesterday to Colonel Gibson [2] came to hand, I was just about to send mine to you, by express. I now take the opportunity of Captain Smith. The object of my command in this quarter is to countenance and protect the people by every possible means (with propriety) in my power.

Though I am not so well acquainted with the present intended plan [3] as I could wish, or indeed would be necessary

---

Williamson (the 3d) is not mentioned in Marshel's letter. As a matter of fact, also, it may here be stated that Colonel Williamson, at that date, had received and accepted his commission from Marshel as colonel of his battalion, and taken the oath of allegiance. It is likewise certain that the latter looked upon Williamson as his "right hand man" in all matters of importance connected with his office of county lieutenant. (See letter No. VII following.)

[1] On the sixteenth of January, as already mentioned (ante, p. 84, note 2), Gen. Irvine left Fort Pitt to confer with congress on the state of affairs in the west, leaving Colonel John Gibson in temporary command of the post. Previous to his starting, he wrote Marshel of his intended trip, notifying him that Col. Gibson would command in his absence, and that he should "order out such numbers of militia (not exceeding sixty) for one tour" of a month's duration, as the colonel might require. (See first letter of Appendix K, which is the same as the one sent Marshel, substituting the name of the latter for that of Col. Edward Cook.) It is known that Gibson conferred with Marshel during Irvine's absence as to public affairs, particularly as to the garrisons established on the frontiers of Washington county and the number of men allotted to each. (See Marshel's next letter.)

[2] Not found. It was doubtless written to Colonel Gibson under the impression that Irvine had not yet returned to Fort Pitt.

[3] This "intended plan" was a proposed expedition from Washington county against the Wyandots upon the Sandusky. The enterprise was very quickly given up; but the scheme was laid so soon after the "Gnadenhuetten affair" that a message received at Bethlehem, Pennsylvania, to the effect that 600 men were to meet on the 18th of March to go to Sandusky, was construed by the Moravians there to mean "for the purpose of cutting off the remainder" of the Moravian Indians at that place. (See Appendix M,— Seidel to Irvine, April 11, 1782.) Of course, there was no such purpose in the minds of those planning the expedition. When, however, Crawford's expedition *did* go to the Sandusky, the same was said of it — "to murder the remnant

for me, yet I cannot think of letting any good opportunity
slip, or which may be thought so by people (who have, I hope,
duly weighed matters) for a nicer point of formality or eti-
quette. I therefore send you an order by Captain Smith on
the officer commanding at Fort McIntosh for ammunition and
flints. There the principal stock of these articles are, which
is at present in my power. I hope it may be obtained in due
time. I sincerely wish the party success.

VI.— Marshel to Irvine.

Washington County, *April* 2, 1782.

Sir:— I have been honored with your favors of the 28th
and 29th ult.,[1] with the greatest satisfaction to find you were
disposed to supply us with ammunition, although we have not
been able to execute the proposed plan. I am under the disagreeable necessity of informing you that the principal post
on the river, namely, the mouth of Yellow creek,[2] has been
evacuated for some days for want of provision, which I am
afraid will prevent my attendance at Fort Pitt on Friday next,
being obliged to fill up that station, and supply them with
provision as soon as possible in order to prevent the frontier
in that quarter from breaking. However, I shall most heartily
concur in any plan that may be adopted for the good of the
country; and as soon as matters are on any tolerable footing
in this county, I will do myself the honor to wait upon you at
Pittsburgh.

---

of the Christian Indians," there; and this has ever since been constantly reiterated in current histories of the west; until, finally, the publication in
another work *(Crawford's Campaign against Sandusky)* of Irvine's instructions to the commander of that expedition (see, also, note on p. 118 of this
book), and much other positive testimony, showed its utter fallacy.

[1] That of the 28th not found; but see a similar one, Appendix K,— Irvine
to Cook, of the same date.

[2] That is to say, "opposite the mouth of Yellow creek." This stream, a
tributary of the Ohio, flows into that river on the right, on what was then the
Indian side of the Ohio, fifty-five miles by water below Pittsburgh. It was at
or near this point, which is on the east side of the Ohio, that the killing of
Logan's (the Mingo chief's) relatives took place on the 30th of April, 1774.

I have ordered a number of the field officers of this county to attend at the time and place appointed in your letter to me of the 28th of March, for the purpose therein mentioned.[1] I have also requested James Edgar, Esq., one of our representatives, to attend as aforesaid. Should he attend, I could wish he might be admitted to sit in your council.[2] Colonel

---

[1] Ante, p. 104, and note.

[2] James Edgar, then a prominent citizen of the western department, was a native of York county, Pennsylvania, where he was born of Scotch-Irish ancestry, November 15, 1744. His father subsequently removed to North Carolina, but young Edgar remained on his farm until the outset of the revolution. By the committee of York county he was chosen a member of the provincial conference of June 18, 1776, and elected by the people to the convention of July 15, following. He was a member of the assembly, 1776-7, from his native county; of the provincial council of safety from October 17 to December 4, 1777, when he took his seat in the supreme executive council, an office he filled acceptably until February 13, 1779. In the autumn of this year, he removed to Westmoreland county, Pennsylvania, in that part which afterward became Washington county. Upon the organization of the latter county, he was appointed one of the justices July 15, 1781, and, along with John Canon, was representative of the general assembly of the state, at the date of the above letter. He was admitted to take part in the council held by Irvine on the 5th of April.— Adapted from Wm. H. Egle, in *Penn. Mag. of Hist. and Biog.*, Vol. III, p. 324.

John Canon, the other representative (he was not, however, at the council), came to what was afterward Washington county, as early as 1774. In February of that year, he and Henry Taylor were appointed by the Westmoreland county court to view a road from the Gist settlement on the Youghiogheny river to Paul Froman's mill on Chartiers creek — the place afterward occupied by Dorsey Pentecost,— within a few miles of the place where Canon afterwards founded the town of Canonsburgh. Canon at once appears as a partisan of Virginia, in the boundary controversy, and was a justice of her Yohogania county court. This court was continued until August, 1780, though the boundary compromise was made in 1779; and, on the organization of Washington county, in 1781, Canon was appointed one of the sub-lieutenants under James Marshel as county lieutenant. In 1784, he was commissioned a justice of the Washington county courts, which position he occupied until his death. In 1782, he was, as we have seen, a representative in the general assembly of his state (ante, p. 205, note), having been elected the fall previous.

Canon had acquired Virginia rights to three several tracts of land adjoining each other and together containing over 1,000 acres, in Chartiers Valley, about eight miles north of Washington and about twenty miles south of Pittsburgh, on one of which he laid the town of Canonsburgh, where he lived till he died. He, with other public-spirited citizens, brought about the estab-

[John] Gibson will be able to imform you the number of garrisons on the frontier of this county, together with the number of men allotted to each, as agreed upon by us in your absence. Maj. [James] Carmichael[1] will report to you the situation of each garrison, except the one at [opposite] the mouth of Yellow creek, at which place there were thirty men, besides eight invalids left at some of the frontier houses, which number I expect to have again at that place in a few days; but how long we shall be able to continue them, I know not, as we have never yet been supplied by government with one article to support the militia in actual service, except the ammunition we have received from your garrison. However, this is most certain, that unless an expedition be carried against some of the principal towns early this summer, this country must unavoidably suffer. But if, at your council, it is thought best not to carry an expedition early in the summer, I shall expect that the number of militia called out for the protection of the country will be justly proportioned in the different counties. But I flatter myself that an expedition will be promoted, and that we shall be able to raise our full quota in this county. About the 15th of May next appears to me to be a proper time for the rendezvous.[2]

---

lishment in that town of a high school, which in 1791 was organized as an academy, he donating the lot and erecting the building. In 1794, the academy was incorporated by the state legislature, and Canon made one of the trustees. He died in the latter part of 1798, just before that institution was made Jefferson college, long afterward an influential institution of learning. Canon was an active, intelligent and gentlemanly man. He died when but little past the meridian of life, leaving a widow and several children. Mrs. Canon was eminently pious, friendly and generous. Her house was the seat of hospitality, the favorite resort of Christian ministers and serious students.

[1] James Carmichael should not be confounded with John Carmichael. The last mentioned had, previously to 1775, settled in what is now Franklin township, Fayette county, that state, then Westmoreland county, on the waters of Redstone creek, about eight miles from Col. Cook's, where he erected a mill. He was elected a member of the constitutional convention of 1776, and of the general assembly in 1777. He died in 1796, leaving a widow and two sons, James and Thomas.—Wm. H. Egle, in *Penn. Mag. of Hist. and Biog.*, Vol. III.

[2] This was an official foreshadowing of Crawford's campaign against Sandusky.

VII.— MARSHEL TO IRVINE.

WASHINGTON COUNTY, *April* 4, 1782.

Sir:— The bearer hereof, Colonel Williamson,[1] is now prepared for a voyage down the river with about 30,000 weight of flour; but, from a real love to his country, proposes not only to carry an expedition against Sandusky, with the militia of his county together with what volunteers might be raised in Westmoreland, but also to advance such part of the above flour as might be necessary on the occasion, on condition it would be replaced in the fall or paid for in cash. I find it much more difficult to supply our militia in actual service with provision than I expected,[2] and that the people in general on the frontier, are waiting with anxious expectation to know whether an expedition can be carried against Sandusky early this spring or not. I could therefore wish that Colonel Williamson would be countenanced in this plan, if, with propriety, it can be done.

P. S.— Colonel Williamson will be able to give you a true account of the situation of our frontier at present.

VIII.— MARSHEL TO IRVINE.

CATFISH [now Washington], *May* 1st, 1782.

Dear Sir:— Since I wrote you by Mr. Kerr, your express arrived with the disagreeable intelligence of the desertion of

---

[1] David Williamson, colonel, at the above date, of the 3d battalion of Washington county militia, was, it will be remembered, present at the meeting at Fort Pitt called by General Irvine for the 5th of April, 1782 (ante, p. 104, note 1). His project against Sandusky was not a new one. Ever since the Wyandots had taken up the hatchet against the border, the destruction of their villages was "a consummation devoutly to be wished." To that end a number of schemes had been laid; but, for various reasons, all had proven abortive; until now the whole frontier were "waiting with anxious expectation to know whether an expedition" could be "carried" against that most prolific hive of mischief to the border. (For a biographical notice of Williamson, see Appendix M,— Williamson to Irvine, June 13, 1782, note.)

[2] That is, in service under his orders as lieutenant of the county; not such as had been drafted and put under General Irvine's orders; but, by the arrangement made the next day at Fort Pitt between Irvine and the principal field officers of the militia and others, this was changed (ante, p. 104, note 1).

some of your troops. I have used every method in my power to alarm the inhabitants of this county, and to encourage the apprehending suspected persons.¹

Since I had the honor of consulting you on the expediency of an expedition against Sandusky, I have met with the officers and principal people of this county and find that, in all probability, we shall be able to carry the expedition; I therefore request you will send by the first opportunity such instructions to the officer who may be appointed to command as you may think proper.

The bearer, Captain Thomas Parkison, a gentleman of credit and considerable property, will undertake to supply the militia in actual service at 11½d. per ration; which I believe is as low as any person can undertake it for. I could wish this gentleman might be employed, as he can be depended upon for the fulfilling any engagement he may enter into [ante, p. 203].

P. S.— You will please to forward by your express, Captain [John] Hughes' letter to council.² Monday, the 20th inst., is appointed for the general rendezvous at the Mingo Bottom [on the east side of the Ohio].

---

¹ Ante, p. 112. On the 1st day of June, Irvine issued the following order: ". . . The general would fondly flatter himself that he will not be much troubled with the trial of deserters, or disobedience of orders, in the future; but lest any should remain so abandoned as to desert, he thinks proper to give this notice, that it is his determination to give positive orders to all officers or parties who shall be sent after them, to put to death all deserters, whatsoever, in the same manner as they would or ought the common enemy of the United States. . . At the same time that he is determined to keep up vigorous discipline, he will not cease to be the friend of the faithful soldier." (See, in this connection, p. 119, note 1.)

² The following is an extract from the proceedings of the supreme executive council of Pennsylvania:

"PHILADELPHIA, *Dec.* 27, 1781.

"The council taking into consideration the appointing officers for the ranging company for the county of Washington,

"*Resolved*, That John Hughes, Esq., be appointed and commissioned to be captain of a company of rangers to be raised in the county of Washington."

Captain Hughes' letter to Moore, mentioned above, was as follows:

"CATFISH CAMP, WASHINGTON Co., *May* 1st, 1782.

"*Sir:*— As Colonel Marshel has informed me that an express for Philadel-

IX.— MARSHEL TO IRVINE.

WASHINGTON COUNTY, *May* 11,[1] 1782.

Dear Sir:— Agreeable to your requisition of the 6th ult., I have called out a number of the militia of this county, to relieve those on duty, and directed [Lieutenant] Colonel Val-

---

phia is to set out to-morrow, I take the opportunity to let your excellency in council know that there is no possibility of raising men in this country upon the principles council have thought proper to order. My officers and myself have been as industrious as circumstances could possibly admit. I conceive the only mode would be to class the county for eighteen months men, which would be two campaigns, or any other term the council should think necessary. This is the sentiment of the better kind of people in this country as well as my own.

"There are many other reasons that hinder the officers in the recruiting service, as having not cash except such as are for that service and no provision made here for their subsistence, that renders them under these disadvantages. Please your excellency in council to consider these grievances that I have laid down, and I make no doubt but they will be remedied. . . .

"JOHN HUGHES,
"Captain Washington Rangers."

[1] It will be seen by a reference to pages 233 and 239, ante, that, on the first day of May, Irvine wrote Marshel for his report of the expedition that went to the Tuscarawas— "Williamson's expedition;" that he received Marshel's reply and transmitted it (with the one received from Colonel Williamson) on the third of May to Moore; and that neither the letter of Irvine to Marshel nor the replies thereto have been found. This hiatus in the correspondence will, it is feared, never be filled.

Various relations, besides the one received from the secretary of congress (ante, p. 238, note), had reached the supreme executive council concerning the "Gnadenhuetten affair" before the letters of Marshel and Williamson were forwarded. The first published account of what transpired upon the "Muskingum" after the arrival of the militia, is to be found in the *Pennsylvania Packet* of April 16, 1782, and in the *Pennsylvania Gazette* of the next day. This account, after mentioning that the Indians had collected a large quantity of provisions to supply their war-parties, says:

"They [the militia] arrived at the town [Gnadenhuetten] in the night, undiscovered, attacked the Indians in their cabins, and so completely surprised them, that they killed and scalped upwards of ninety (but a few making their escape), about forty of which were warriors, the rest old men, women and children. About eighty horses fell into their hands, which they loaded with the plunder, the greatest part furs and skins, and returned to the Ohio, without the loss of one man, and at the place where they chose their officers they held a vendue. And in order to prevent the inhabitants from bidding against

Appendix J.

landigham[1] and Major White[2] to wait upon you for instructions. You will please to order to them such quantity of arms as can be spared; flints will also be wanted for the use of the militia on the frontiers, but much more so for the expedition; therefore, I have sent the bearer for such number of flints as can be spared, in order that the party that goes on the expedition may be supplied first. Please to send by the bearer such instructions to the officer who may be appointed to command as you may think proper to give.

X.— Marshel to Irvine.

Washington County, *May* 29, 1782.

Dear Sir:— I have the honor to inform you that on Saturday last, about five hundred men[3] (including officers) set out for Sandusky, under the command of Colonel [William] Crawford. A perfect harmony subsisted among officers and men, and all were in high spirits,— no accident of any consequence

---

the adventurers, they divided the spoil equally between officers and men, first reimbursing those who had lost their horses in swimming the river."

Before the foregoing appeared in the Philadelphia papers, several reports were circulated east of the mountains concerning the "Gnadenhuetten affair." One was to the effect that one hundred and sixty militia from the Ohio had destroyed two Delaware Indian towns and killed ninety-five Indians; another that the militia had killed ninety-nine Moravian Indians, namely: thirty-three men and sixty-six women. A third ran as follows: "The Moravian Indian congregation at Sandusky is butchered by the Scotch. They came and told them they must prepare directly for death. The Indians requested but an hour's time for this purpose, which was granted. They went to their meeting house to join in prayers to the Lord. After the hour had passed,. they [the militia] fell upon them and butchered all of them in cold blood, in the meeting house, and then set the house on fire." (See, in this connection, Appendix M,— Seidel to Irvine, April 11, 1782— post, p. 358, note 4.)

[1] George Vallandigham (grandfather of Clement L. Vallandigham, the late noted Ohio politician) was, at the above date, lieutenant colonel of the second battalion of Washington county militia; also one of the sub-lieutenants of the county, under Marshel.

[2] John White, a justice of the peace at that date, living in Strabane township, Washington county, Pennsylvania.

[3] The number which actually marched was four hundred and sixty-eight, but a few of these returned before reaching the Tuscarawas.

happening either in crossing the river or during their stay at the Mingo bottom [on the west side of the Ohio].

I have not yet ascertained with exactness the number of men from the different counties, but I believe they are nearly as follows, namely: Westmoreland,[1] about one hundred and thirty; Ohio [county],[2] about twenty; and Washington,[3] three hundred and fifty. Mr. Rose, your aid-de-camp [ante, p. 117], was very hearty when I left him. His services on this occasion have endeared you much to the people of this county, and given general satisfaction to the men on the expedition.

A report prevails in the country that Britain has acknowledged our independence. I could wish to be informed of the truth of this report. I have been asked by a Presbyterian minister and some of his people to request you to spare one gallon of wine for the use of a sacrament. If it is in your power to supply them with this article, I make no doubt you will do it, as it cannot be obtained in any other place in this country. Mr. Douglass or the bearer will apply for it.[4]

---

[1] Mostly from that part which afterward became Fayette county, Pennsylvania.

[2] Ohio county, Virginia, included, at this date, the whole of the territory now in West Virginia known as "the Pan-handle," and a considerable area to the south of it.

[3] Washington county, Pennsylvania, in 1782, was bounded north by the Ohio river, east by the Monongahela, south and west by Virginia. All of Pennsylvania west of the Laurel Hill not included within those boundaries constituted Westmoreland county, at that date (ante, p. 50); but Fayette county was formed from the latter the next year.

[4] No doubt the wine was sent if the general had it to spare. He was exceedingly accommodating to the country people as well as to the citizens of Pittsburgh. His watchful care over the rights of the latter, when in the least intruded upon by the soldiery, the following petition and order will show:

[I.]

"PITTSBURGH, *May* 29, 1782.

"The humble petition of a part of the inhabitants of the town of Pittsburgh most humbly beggeth: That your honor will be pleased to take it into consideration, that several of the officers, and soldiers of this town have of late made a constant practice in playing at long bullets in the street that goes up by the brew-house and that a number of children belonging to us, who are dwellers on the same street, are in danger of their lives by the said evil practices,— we therefore hope (since we have no civil magistrate to apply

XI.—Marshel to Irvine.

June 11, 1782.

Dear Sir:— This moment came to hand the enclosed letter,[1] by which you will learn the unhappy fate of our little army [under Colonel Crawford]. What the consequences may be, God only knows. I would fondly hope that matters are not quite so bad as they are represented; as men who quit an

---

to) that your honor will condescend to put a stop to such practices in the street, by your own special orders. And by your honor's endeavors we are forever bound to pray and shall forever remain, sir, your honor's most obedient, humble servants to serve. [Signed] John Bradley, Thomas Girty [brother of Simon], William Brady, John Jewry, James McLelland. [Directed] To the Hon. Wm. Irvine, Esq., Brig. Gen. Com. W. D."

[II.]

"Fort Pitt, *May* 31, 1782.

"Sundry inhabitants of the town of Pittsburgh having petitioned General Irvine to prohibit the officers and soldiers from playing long bullets in the streets and set forth the great danger the lives of the children are in, by such practices,— he, therefore, in the most express terms forbids it being done in future. At the same time, he thinks it a favorable occasion to recommend to the troops not to incommode or disturb the people of the town with their company too frequently. They can find other places and modes to amuse themselves than in dram shops, which, in the end, will be pleasanter and more advantageous."

[1] The letter received by Marshel was as follows:

"Cross Creek Mills, 11th *June*, 1782.

"*Sir:*— Last night nine men arrived at the Mingo Bottom [on the east side of the Ohio river], who give us the disagreeable news of our army under the command of Colonel Crawford being defeated on Tuesday last about one mile and a half from the upper Sandusky town. They attacked our men about twelve o'clock [Tuesday, June 4th]. The battle lasted until Wednesday night. On Tuesday, they killed four of our men and wounded about twenty. On Wednesday they did but little damage, but were re-enforced by a great number of Indians. Wednesday night, our men left the ground, and Thursday in the afternoon were attacked again, when the nine men quit the army in the beginning of the battle and cannot tell how it went. They were in distress for victuals, and I expect they will all be in want that have the luck to return.

"Sir, I have written in haste and confusion. From your humble servant,

"Edmond Polke, Major 4th Battalion.

"P. S.—Sir, please to send some men to our fort as soon as possible, as I fear it will break. To Col. J. Marshel [and] Col. Wm. Coverly."

army in time of action generally represent matters worse than they really are, in order to save their own credit. Besides, the event of the battle on Thursday, is not yet known to us.[1]

---

[1] Six days after the date of the above letter, Dorsey Pentecost wrote to Governor Moore of Pennsylvania as follows, concerning the information gleaned by him of the expedition against Sandusky:

"WASHINGTON COUNTY, *June* 17th, 1782.

"*Dear Sir:*—By a person who is now here, on his way to the head of Elk, I have just time to tell you that on the 25th of last month 478, some say 488 men, mounted on horses, set out under the command of Colonel Crawford, for Sandusky. They were discovered at the Muskingum [Tuscarawas], and from there, all the way out, spies were kept on them. The Sandusky people collected the Shawanese and the light dragoons from the British posts, between Sandusky and the post at Detroit. They attacked our people in the plains of Sandusky, near the Sandusky river, Tuesday was a week last. The battle continued two days. The first day was very close and hot work, the second day was at long shot only. On the night of the second day, our people retreated, and the Indians broke in on them in the retreat and routed them; however, about two hundred stuck together and brought off all the wounded, except three, which were left on the ground. The next day, the Indians attacked our people in the rear, but were repulsed with considerable loss on their side. They then pursued their retreat with success and unmolested to the Ohio. I met the men at the Mingo bottom [on the west side of the Ohio] last Wednesday [June 12th], about thirty-five miles from my house, and collected the information I send you.

"There are about twenty wounded (few dangerous) and about half that number killed. There are a good many missing, amongst whom are Colonel Crawford and a number of other valuable men; but as the scattered parties are coming in daily, I have hopes of them. As the people were much confused when I met them, I could not get the information requisite. What little I got was from Major Rose, aid-de-camp to General Irvine, and who went as aid to Colonel Crawford. I hope the general will give you a particular account, as he will receive it from the major. I am told that the Indians were much superior to our people [in numbers]; that, in the engagement, they suffered greatly; and that Colonel Crawford strongly recommended to return before they got to the town, alleging that our people were too weak [to attack the enemy], as the Indians had early intelligence of their coming; but he was overruled by the rest of the officers. . . .

"DORSEY PENTECOST."

On the 6th of July following, Major William Croghan of the Virginia line wrote from Fort Pitt to William Davies, Virginia secretary at war, as follows, concerning the Sandusky expedition:

"*Dear Colonel:*— . . . About six weeks ago five hundred volunteers of this country commanded by (our old) Colonel William Crawford went on an expedition against the Indian towns. The men were cowardly; no more than

I shall be as expeditious as possible in raising a party of men to secure their retreat across the [Ohio] river, should they be pursued so far.

---

about one hundred having fought the Indians, who came out from their towns to meet them [this is an error]. The firing continued at long shot with rifles for near two days. The second evening our party broke off and retreated in the most disorderly manner. Colonel Crawford and a few others, finding the men would pay no attention to orders, were going on coolly in the rear, leaving the road in case the Indians should pursue, until the second day, when they thought they might venture on the road; but before they had marched two miles, a body of Indians fell in between them and the rear of the party, and took them prisoners.

"We had no certainty of this unhappy affair until yesterday, when Doctor Knight, who was taken with Crawford, came into the garrison, in the most deplorable condition man could be in and be alive. He says that the second day after they were taken, they were carried to an Indian town, stripped and then blacked, and made to march through the Indians, when men, women and children beat them with clubs, sticks, fists, etc., in the most cruel manner.

"Colonel Crawford and the doctor were confined together all night. The next day, they were taken out, blacked again, and their hands tied behind their backs, when Colonel Crawford was led by a long rope to a high stake, to the top of which the rope about the colonel was tied. All around the stake a great quantity of red hot coals were laid, on which the poor colonel was obliged to walk barefoot, and at the same time the Indians firing squibs of powder at him, while others poked sticks (on fire) into every part of his body; thus they continued torturing him for about two hours, when he begged of Simon Girty, a white renegade, who was standing by, to shoot him, when the fellow said, 'don't you see I have no gun?' Some little time after this they scalped him, and struck him on the bare skull several times with sticks, and being nearly exhausted he lay down upon the burning embers, when the squaws put shovelfuls of coals on his body, which, dying as he was, made him move and creep a little; the doctor was obliged to stand by to see this cruelty performed.

"When the colonel was scalped they slapped the scalp over the doctor's face, saying this is your great captain's scalp; to-morrow we will serve you so. The doctor was to be served in the same manner in another town some distance off (from this place), and on his way to his place of torment he passed by the place where Colonel Crawford's dead body had been dragged to and burned, and where he saw his bones. The doctor was guarded by but one Indian. On the way, the Indian wanted a fire made and he untied the doctor, ordering him to make it; the doctor appeared willing to obey, was collecting wood till he got a good chunk in his hand with which he gave the Indian so severe a blow as leveled him. The Indian sprung up, but seeing the

XII.— MARSHEL TO IRVINE.

June 11, 1782.

Sir:— Since morning I have been riding through the country in order to raise men, but find a general scarcity of arms and ammunition; therefore request you may dispatch by water such quantity of both as you may think necessary, especially ammunition.

XIII.— MARSHEL TO IRVINE.

FROM MR. DOUGLASS', *June* 15, 1782.

Dear Sir:— On my way to this place I met with Mr. Ormsby,[1] who informs me that Mr. [Alexander] McClean,

---

doctor seize his gun ran away; the doctor could not get the gun off, otherwise would have shot the Indian.

"The doctor steered through the woods, and arrived here the twenty-first day after he left the Indian, having no clothes. The gun being wood-bound, he left it after carrying it a few days. For the twenty-one days, and two or three more while under sentence of death, he never ate anything but such vegetables as the woods afforded. None of the prisoners were put to death but those that fell into the hands of the Delawares, who say they will show no mercy to any white man, as they [the white men] would show none to their friends and relations, the religious Moravians. I believe, I have not told you that the whole of the five hundred who went out with Crawford returned except about fifty. W. CROGHAN.

"[P. S.] — Colonel Harrison and Mr. William Crawford, relations of Colonel Crawford, were likewise taken prisoners, but fortunately fell into the hands of the Shawanese, who do not kill their prisoners [afterward, they were tortured to death by the Delawares]."

[1] John Ormsby was an Irishman by birth. He had served some time in the British army; was subsequently a teacher; had traveled in several of the provinces, but finally came to Pittsburgh under Forbes, and helped build Fort Pitt. He was an industrious, enterprising man, and kept the first ferry over the Monongahela. He was in Pittsburgh during Pontiac's war and lost heavily, being then engaged in trade with the Indians. His epitaph is a condensed biography of the man. It reads as follows:

"On the 19th day of December, A. D. 1805, the remains of the venerable John Ormsby, aged 85 years, was interred, agreeably to his desire, with the ashes of his beloved wife [in Trinity churchyard, Pittsburgh]. Mr. Ormsby may truly be styled the patriarch of the western Ormsbys. He migrated to Fort Duquesne about the time the British took possession of it, at which time

Colonels [Christopher] Hays and [Benjamin] Davis, have actually failed in running the line on account of a party of Virginians (as they called themselves) making a little parade at a distance. This opposition no doubt will increase and their party become formidable if the line is not extended immediately and I should be afraid to attempt it again with militia. But if, with propriety, you can send twenty or thirty of your troops under command of an officer well affected to the state of Pennsylvania, I shall raise such number of militia as will be necessary to protect Mr. McClean in the execution of his office.[1]

XIV.— MARSHEL TO IRVINE.

WASHINGTON COUNTY, *June* 21, 1782.

Dear Sir:— Your favor of the 17th I have received. I thought to have been in Fort Pitt to-morrow on purpose to meet with, or hear from Mr. [Alexander] McClean, that some plan might be laid to extend the line; but it appears to me clearly from your letters, that, as a continental officer, you cannot interfere on account of the failure of the artist on the part of Virginia; therefore, I have given over the matter at present, or until a representation is made to the executive of this state; which, I am informed, is already done by Colonel [Edward] Cook, [Christopher] Hays and McClean; or, rather, that they,

---

he was commissary of provisions and paymaster of disbursements for the erection of Fort Pitt. Subsequently he entered largely into the Indian trade, and, in the year 1763, was plundered of all his property, his people murdered, and himself shut up in Fort Pitt during the siege. Mr Ormsby was a large stockholder in the Indian grant ["Indiana"], which would have remunerated him from all losses by the Indians, had not the revolution taken place. Notwithstanding, he was a staunch whig and gloried in our independence."

[1] This proposition Irvine declined for excellent reasons, given in a letter to Moore by the general, July 5, 1782 (ante, p. 248). Marshel was expressly authorized by Pennsylvania to order out as many of the militia as McClean might judge necessary for guards to the commissioners while running the temporary line. Thus far, however, aid had only been asked of Westmoreland county, as Washington had sent so many of her men under Crawford against Sandusky.

together with some others, met at Colonel Cook's[1] a few days ago for that purpose. But I am afraid they are not so well acquainted with the conduct of some of the principal ringleaders as perhaps some others are, which, as you observe, would be necessary to be known.

I make no doubt they have urged the necessity of Virginia being called upon to appoint a commission that will go into the business; but, as the saying is, in order to put the saddle on the right horse and that government may be better informed, I shall take some trouble in procuring such depositions as may be thought necessary to throw light on the subject. One I have already obtained, a copy of which (for your private satisfaction) is inclosed. I expect to have a number more of the same nature in a few days. Before I transmit them to council, or make any representation, I shall wait upon you at Fort Pitt, as soon as I am prepared.

Captain Cunningham with two classes militia of the 2d battalion will rendezvous at Mr. Ormsby's the 22d instant. You will please to order them such quantity of ammunition as you may think proper, as it will be inconvenient to supply them from the Mingo Bottom [on the east side of the Ohio]. These two classes are designed for the two upper stations on the river, and are rendezvoused at Mr. Ormsby's on purpose to escort the provision to their respective stations. I wrote to Captain [Thomas] Parkison some time ago to have the provision ready at the time and place of rendezvous, which I expect he will do.

P. S.— Not having time at present to take a copy, I have sent the original deposition, which you will please to preserve until the rest are collected.

XV.— Marshel to Irvine.

Washington County, *June* 24, 1782.

Sir:— Your letter by express I have just now received and am astonished at the conduct of Captain Cunningham. I see

---

[1] For the location of Col. Edward Cook's house, see Appendix K,— note to first letter.

no other remedy but to call upon the same men to rendezvous again, which I have directed Captain Cunningham to do, and appointed Saturday, the 29th inst., for the rendezvous at Mr. Ormsby's; which I apprehend is as soon as they can be collected. I conceive neither Captain Cunningham nor any of the party can have the remotest thought of being excused a tour of duty on account of any service they have already done; therefore I will depend upon them serving this tour.

XVI.— Marshel to Irvine.

Friday Morning, July 2, 1782.

Sir:— By different expresses from Colonels [William] Parker[1] and [David] Williamson, I am informed with certainty that the enemy at Glenn's Bottom have crossed over the river to their own side; that the party first discovered at the Mingo Bottom [on the east side of the Ohio], continue there. I am therefore of opinion that their main body is at that place. Colonel Williamson has marched to Coxe's fort,[2] about four miles below the Mingo Bottom, at which place I have directed him to stay until further orders. Colonel [Thomas] Crooks[3] is gone to Wheeling. I have also directed him that if he apprehended no danger in leaving that post for a few days, to form a junction with Colonel Williamson. To-morrow, I intend marching whatever men may rendezvous in this quarter to Richard Well's fort, which is within five miles of the Mingo Bottom, at which place I intend to stay, if circumstances will admit, until I hear from you; and shall expect, if you think it necessary, that a number of your troops will march to our assistance as soon as possible.

---

[1] Col. Parker was, at that date, a sub-lieutenant of Washington county, Pennsylvania.

[2] Coxe's fort was in the vicinity of what is now Wellsburgh, county-seat of Brooke county, West Virginia,— in the "Pan-handle."

[3] Crooks, at this date, was colonel of the fifth battalion of Washington county militia. He was a resident of Bethlehem township, that county, and a justice of the peace therein.

XVII.— MARSHEL TO IRVINE.

CATFISH, *July* 4, 1782.

Sir:— Repeated application has been made to me by the inhabitants on the south line of this county, namely: from Jackson's fort[1] to Buffalo creek,[2] and I am at a loss to know what to do.[3] The people declare they must immediately aban-

---

[1] This fort was a short distance southwesterly from the present Waynesburgh, county-town of Greene county, Pennsylvania. It was then in Washington county, the former being set off from the last mentioned county in 1796.

[2] Buffalo creek rises in what is now East Findley township, Washington county, Pennsylvania, flowing westerly into the Ohio.

[3] The following petitions, sent to Irvine by citizens of Washington and Westmoreland counties, show, in a clear light, the dangers and trials of the borders from the time of his first meeting, at Fort Pitt, with the field officers of the militia and some of the principal citizens of the west, to the 14th of July, 1782:

[I.]

"To the Honorable General Irvine, commandant on the western waters:

"Your humble petitioners showing forth our situation since the year 1777, that we have lived in a state of anarchy. We were in great hopes that your honor would have supported us that we could have lived at our own homes; but lately, learning that the station is evacuated, we expect nothing else but that the Indians will be immediately amongst us. Therefore, we, the subscribers, have met this day at the house of John McDonald. At the risk of our lives and fortunes, with the assistance of Almighty God, we are determined to make a stop here the ensuing summer. We look upon it prudent to use the means as well as prayers. Therefore, sir, to you we look for aid and assistance, as we are but few in number, not able to repel the enemy. Therefore, we look to you for men, ammunition and arms.

"We know that provision is scarce, therefore we will find the men that are sent to us, only allowing us rations-pay. The number of men we request is ten. McDonald, last Tuesday, waited on Colonel James Marshel, our county lieutenant, requesting him for some assistance of men, powder and lead. His answer was he could not furnish him with either.

"*Sir:*— We understand that George Vallandigham is to sit in council with you to-morrow, who was a sufferer as well as we, and has lately left his place of abode and took his refuge near Colonel [John] Canon's. Pray, sir, ask of him our present situation. [Signed] Wm. Littell, Joshua Meeks, John Robb, James Littell, James Baggs, John Hull, Thomas Moon, John McDonald, John Reed, Wm. Anderson.

"N. B.— The situation of McDonald's place is pleasant, lying and being on a knoll or advantageous piece of ground for any garrison. We the sub-

don their habitations unless a few men are sent to them during harvest. They also declare their willingness to submit to,

scribers observing that the states must have receiving and issuing stores, it is our opinion that according to McDonald's promise, we think it the best place for said stores. McDonald's promises are that the states shall have, without cost, his still-house, hogsheads, his cellar under his new house, together with the lowest story of his spring house, without price or fee to the states. We have appointed Joshua Meeks and John McDonald to lay our petitions before your honor. April 5, 1782."

[II.]

"JOHN DODDRIDGE'S STATION, *April* 20, 1782.

"To his excellency, General William Irvine, commander of the western department.

"*Sir:*—The dangerous situation that our frontiers at present seem to be in obliges us, your humble petitioners, to beg for your assistance at such a difficult time as it now is. Our case is such as follows, namely: We, the inhabitants near Mr. Alexander Wells' mill, are very unhandy to any other mill and daily open to the rage of a savage and merciless enemy, notwithstanding the great care that hath already been taken for our safety by placing guards on the river. The inhabitants that live near enough the mill to fort there look upon themselves not of sufficient force to guard the mill and carry on any labor to support their families. They will, therefore, undoubtedly break off, unless your excellency will please to grant them a few men to guard the mill. Unless this is done we must also break ground, as the mill is not only our main support in regard to bread for our families, but likewise in furnishing us with flour for every expedition that we are called to go upon. Their going off will expose us to another front side open. Therefore, we, your humble petitioners, pray that, if it is in your power to help us at such a difficult time, you will not be negligent in doing as much as possible. [Signed] Samuel Teter, Henry Nelson, James Scott, Philip Doddridge, Charles Stuart, John Comley, Walter Hill, Benjamin Pursle, Morris West, Thomas Shannon, John Marical, Michael Hough, Sen., John Carpenter, James Newell, William McClimans, Aaron Sackett."

[On the same day a like petition was sent in from the following persons living near Well's fort — George Brown, John Baxter, Matthew Fouke, Samuel Naylor, John Sappington, Sen., John Sappington, George Naylor, and, on the next day, a similar one from the following persons of Hoghland's station, near Alexander Well's mill: George McColloch, William Logan, John Biggs, Benj. Biggs, Zach. B ggs, Charles Hedges, James Andrews, Wm. Harrison, Sen., Nicholas Rodgers, Solomon Hedges, Joseph Hedges, Silas Hedges, Joseph Hedges, Jr., Isaac Meek, Wm. Bonar, D. Hoghland.]

[III.]

"To his excellency, General Irvine, commander-in-chief of the western department.

"*Dear Sir:*—We, the inhabitants, who live near Mr. Alex. Wells' mill, being very unhandy to any other mill, and daily open and exposed to the rage of a

and supply the men on the faith of government. If you approve of sending a few men to this frontier, you will please to

savage and merciless enemy, notwithstanding the great attention paid by the general to our frontiers, and ordering men to be placed on the river,—yet those inhabitants who live near enough the mill to fort there, find ourselves unable to guard the mill and carry on labor for the support of our families; and so, of consequence, cannot continue to make a stand without some assistance. And it is clear that if this mill is evacuated many of the adjacent forts, at least seven or eight, that now hope to make a stand, must give up; as their whole dependence is on said mill for bread as well as every expedition from these parts. And scouting parties that turn out on alarms are supplied from here. Therefore, we, your humble petitioners, pray you would order us a few men to guard the mill — so valuable to many in these parts in particular and the country in general. May 2, 1782. [Signed] James Edgar, Henry Graham, David Vance, Arthur Campbell, Joseph Vance."

[Nine days after, another and similar petition was sent in from the inhabitants of Charles Wells' and other stations lying near Mr. Alex. Wells' mill. It was signed by Charles Wells, Charles Wells, Sen., William Hervey, James Miller, Henry Hervey, John McCormick, James McGuire, Baldwin Pierson, David Cox, Francis McGuire, William Sparks, Geo. McCoy, Thomas Smith. Another of like tenor was sent in on the 14th of May by the inhabitants of Mingo Bottom Fort and the vicinity of Alex. Wells' mill. It was signed by Edmond Polke, Richard Elson, Edmond Baxter, William West, Jacob Walter, Geo. Otter, Leonard Head, Zach. Fowler, John Decker, Luke Decker.]

[IV.]

"WASHINGTON COUNTY, CROSS CREEK SETTLEMENT, *May* 18, 1782.

"We, your petitioners, have been several weeks in actual service on these waters and on the waters of Buffalo creek and finding the distressed situation of the frontier inhabitants by the daily incursions of the savages which we are fully of opinion the river guards cannot prevent, and as there are nine or ten forts that are constantly depending on Alexander Wells' mill for grinding where they are served and their work with speed dispatched, we are entirely sensible that it is necessary and requisite that your excellency send a guard of seven, eight or nine men, to be stationed at said mill for their safety and to the satisfaction and encouragement of the forts adjacent. We, your petitioners, do reside in the interior parts of the country, though at present in the service of your excellency with all possible punctuality. [Signed] Benjamin White, captain; Albert Ramsey, captain; Nathan Powel, lieutenant. To his excellency, Brig. General Irvine."

[V.]

"To the honorable Brigadier General Irvine, commanding the troops in the western department.

"The petition of the frontier inhabitants of Brush creek most humbly showeth:— That, since the commencement of the present war, the unabated fury of the savages hath been so particularly directed against us, that we are, at

order the bearer such quantity of ammunition as you may think proper.

last, reduced to such a degree of despondency and distress that we are now ready to sink under the insupportable pressure of this very great calamity. That from our fortitude and perseverance in supporting the line of the frontier and thereby resisting the incessant depredations of the enemy, our bravest and most active men have been cut off from time to time, by which our effective force is so greatly reduced that the idea of further resistance is now totally vanished. That the season of our harvest is now fast approaching, in which we must endeavor to gather in our scanty crops, or otherwise subject ourselves to another calamity equally terrible to that of the scalping-knife,— and from fatal experience, our fears suggest to us every misery that has usually accompanied that season. That we are greatly alarmed at the misfortune attending the late excursion to the enemy's country [Crawford's expedition against Sandusky]; as we have every reason to believe that their triumphs upon that occasion will be attended with fresh and still more vigorous exertions against us.

"In this perilous situation, sir, we submit our case to your consideration and beg that it may be applied to the feelings of humanity and benevolence, which we firmly believe you possess. Wherefore we humbly pray for such an augmentation of our guard through the course of the harvest-season as will enable them to render us some essential service. But, as we know from experience that no certain dependence can be placed on the militia upon these occasions, as some failure may probably happen on their part through the course of the season,— and as we have hitherto been accustomed to the protection of the continental troops during the harvest season, we further pray, that we may be favored with a guard of your soldiers, if it is not inconsistent with other duties enjoined on you. But particularly we pray, that whatever guard may be allotted for us in future, may be ordered into the inhabited stations along the frontier, where they can be of service, either in covering our working-parties in the fields, or protecting our defenseless families in our absence. And your petitioners as in duty bound shall pray. Brush Creek, June 22, 1782."

[This petition, so unexceptionably elegant in diction, as well as powerfully strong and clear in the points stated, is signed by nineteen borderers, mostly Germans. The document itself is in a bold and beautiful hand. It would be hard to find in all the revolutionary records of the west a more forcible statement of border troubles, in a few words, than this.]

[VI.] "*July* 14, 1782.

"*Sir:* — We, the inhabitants living on the Alleghany river, being much distressed on account of the Indians, cannot get our harvest in; and our grain is now suffering on that account. We humbly implore your honor, if it pleases you, to assist us about two weeks with eight or ten men as a guard for us while we reap and gather our grain, and we are in duty bound to pray. To Brigadier General Irvine, commanding officer." [Names torn off the original.]

XVIII.—MARSHEL TO IRVINE.

WASHINGTON COUNTY, *July* 17, 1782.

Dear Sir:— Yours of the 15th I have received by Mr. [Ebenezer] Zane, before the receipt of which I had ordered a draft for the post at Wheeling and directed Colonel [Thomas] Crooks to relieve Colonel [John] Marshall,[1] who is yet at that place, although I believe his party is very small at present. I understand few or none of the class ordered on duty with Colonel Crooks is gone out, but that they are associating to oppose taxation and prevent the sheriff collecting any more delinquent fines in that quarter. They have caused some of their officers to resign their commissions and threaten those who continue to act with tarring and feathering if they call upon them for any more militia duty.

Indeed every day new difficulties arise in calling out the militia of this county, and those who do turn out on their tours behave so exceedingly ill that I am many times put to a stand to know what to do. However, it will not do to give up while anything can be done. I have, therefore, called out another class for that post and expect some of them at least will be there in a few days. In the meantime, I have directed Major [William] Pollock to send a few of the militia from the Mingo Bottom [on the east side of the Ohio] to Fort Henry until the last draft arrives.

With regard to the meeting you recommend between Colonel [David] Shepherd and myself, I apprehend there will be no necessity for it. Colonel Shepherd appears friendly and well-disposed. Neither is there any dispute among the people as far as Ohio county extends; the whole of the opposition is from the inhabitants on the Monongahela river, who can have no pretense to claim protection from the government of Virginia, nor do I believe they are countenanced by any officer of that government. I rather think they are encouraged by the new state party.

---

[1] John Marshall, colonel 4th battalion, of Washington county militia, was a resident of Hopewell township, that county, a man of influence and a relative of the lieutenant of Washington county.

I can give but very little account at present of the disposition of the people of this county in carrying the expedition [proposed against Sandusky, this time to be commanded by Irvine in person]. We have had one meeting of part of the officers of the county, at which I informed them of the principles on which you would go and to which they unanimously agreed, and seemed very anxious to carry it on your plan or rather the plan proposed by Westmoreland people; the only difference I find is, about the time of rendezvous. Those of the inhabitants I have talked with on the subject seem to think the 1st of August rather too soon; but that difficulty can be easily removed with the more sensible part of the people; and, in order to come as near the time proposed as possible, I have appointed the 1st day of August for the officers to meet at Catfish Camp to make report of the number of volunteers raised and equipped in their respective districts, at which meeting (as I expect it will be general) I could wish you would attend, which I think would add new life to the expedition. I am almost certain it would be attended with good consequences. It will also be a good opportunity of exposing the narrowness of soul of those who prefer their private emolument to the public good.[1]

Maj. [William] Pollock this day informed me of the late expedition against Hannastown,[2] etc.; a particular account of which (as I received it from him), I have written to the officers of this county, and again urged the necessity of an expedition by every argument that appeared to have any weight. What effect it may have I know not at present.

If a like stroke is made upon us as has been made on Westmoreland, we should be at a loss for ammunition; and if you should judge it proper to deposit a quantity in some safe place in the county, I shall send for it as soon as I known your determination.

---

[1] Gen. Irvine visited Catfish either on that day or just before, but the particulars of his journey are wholly unknown.

[2] That is, the attack on that place by the enemy (ante, pp. 140, note, 176, 250).

XIX.—MARSHEL TO IRVINE.

[No date.][1]

Dear Sir:— Your favor of the 18th, I have received. I am much surprised indeed at the account you have received from [John] Slover [pilot to the expedition against Sandusky]. The intelligence he gave me was bad, but nothing equal to what he has reported to you. He told me that the Indians expected we would carry another expedition against them this summer, and that, at their council, they had determined on two expeditions, one of which was designed against Wheeling; the other, they were not fully determined whether this country or Kentucky should be the object; that, in the meantime, they would keep out spies on our frontier in order to watch our motions and take a prisoner to know our determination. He did not mention a word to me either of their number or of bringing artillery. He said the Indians informed him that the night our people left the field at Sandusky, there were some British troops from Detroit within a few miles of them (I think seven); that they had two field pieces and one mortar. This I think is nearly what he told me on his arrival.[2] With

---

[1] The above letter was written about the 20th of July, 1782.

[2] John Slover, one of the guides upon the expedition under Crawford against Sandusky, after his arrival on the frontier and while on his way to Fort Pitt, seems to have had an interview with Marshel. It is evident also from the above letter that what he told him was in brief what he had heard and seen in the wilderness up to the time of his escape from the savages as afterward given more fully to Irvine, and at considerable length to H. H. Brackenridge, who wrote out his narrative (ante, p. 128, note). He gave to the latter, however, no information concerning the presence of British troops on the Sandusky (as he mentioned to Marshel and Irvine) or relative to artillery being brought so near the battle field; at least, nothing is said of either in his published account; nevertheless, his relation concerning them was strictly true.

The following from "The Short Biography of John Leeth" (pp. 15, 16) is, probably, the only account extant of incidents transpiring at Upper Sandusky immediately before the arrival of Crawford's army; it has information also concerning the bringing of cannon by the rangers:

"The spring following, I was married to a young woman, seventeen or eighteen years of age, also a prisoner to the Indians, who had been taken by them when about twenty months old. I was then in my twenty-fourth year. Our place of residence was in Moravian Town [Gnadenhuetten] for about two years; about which time Col. Williams [Col. Daniel Brodhead], an American

regard to his character, I am altogether unacquainted; but I
think there is reason to suspect his veracity.¹ I could wish he

officer, took possession of Coshocton [in the spring of 1781]; and shortly after,
the British and their Indian allies took Moravian Town, with me, my wife and
children, and all the Moravians, prisoners and carried us to [Upper] Sandusky.

"After arriving at [Upper] Sandusky, the British would not suffer me to
trade on my own footing and for myself; but five of them having placed their
funds into one general stock, employed me to attend to their business for
them; and two of them being my old employers, they gave me the same
wages as before. Whilst in this employ, Cols. Williams [Williamson] and
Crawford marched with an army against Sandusky, at which time I was
closely watched by the Indians and had to make my movements with particular regularity, though I had spies going to and fro by whom I could hear every
evening where the army was encamped, for several days.

"One evening I was informed the army was only fifteen miles distant [near
the present village of Wyandot, Wyandot county, Ohio], when I immediately
sent the hands to gather the horses, etc., to take our goods to Lower Sandusky.
I packed up the goods (about £1,500 worth in silver, furs, powder, lead, etc.)
with such agility that by the next morning at daylight we started for Lower
Sandusky. I also took all the cattle belonging to the company along. After
traveling about three miles, I met Capt. [Matthew] Elliott, a British officer;
and, about twelve miles farther on, I met the whole British army, composed
of Col. Butler's Rangers [a company from Detroit, under the command of
Capt. William Caldwell]. They took from me my cattle and let me pass.

"That night I encamped about fourteen miles above Lower Sandusky, when,
just after I had encamped and put out my horses to graze, there came to my
camp a man who was a French interpreter to the Indians [Francis Le Vellier].
'Well,' said he, 'I believe I will stay with you to-night and take care of
you.' I told him he could remain there for the night, but I intended starting
early in the morning. Next morning, after we had got our horses loaded
ready to start and the Frenchman had mounted his horse, we heard a cannon
fire at Upper Sandusky. The Frenchman clapped his hand to his breast and
said, 'I shall be there before the battle is begun;' but, alas, poor fellow! he
got there too soon. Without fear or any thought but victory he went on to
where a parcel of Indians were painting and preparing for battle; put on a
ruffled shirt, and painted a red spot on his breast, saying,—' Here is a mark
for the Virginia riflemen;' and shortly after marched with the Indians to
battle, where in a short time he received a ball in the very spot and died
instantaneously.

"I arrived at Lower Sandusky on the second day, and remained there three
days to hear the event. At length the Americans under Col. Williams
[Williamson] stole a retreat on the Indians who were gathering around them
in great numbers; but Col. Crawford, with most of his men was taken by
them. They tomahawked all his men and burnt him alive."

¹ Slover's character was that of an honorable man as already explained
(p. 129, note).

might be checked, for the reports he spreads in the country have a most evil tendency.

XX.— MARSHEL TO IRVINE.
July 30, 1782.

Dear Sir:— This moment came to hand the inclosed circular letter.[1] The account Mr. [Samuel] McColloch gives, no doubt is true; therefore I have directed Colonel [Matthew] Ritchie, sub-lieutenant, to send for such quantity of ammunition as you may think proper to spare. The timely intelligence of the enemy's approach, I think is a very lucky circumstance. The frontier forts are all alarmed as far as the Mingo Bottom [on the east side of the Ohio], and I expect by this evening we shall have a considerable number of men on the frontier. I could wish this alarm might not prevent the proposed meeting at Catfish.

XXI.— MARSHEL TO IRVINE.
Friday Morning, August 2, 1782.

Dear Sir:— I have just now been informed by express that a small party of Indians have been discovered at the Mingo Bottom [on the east side of the Ohio] yesterday morning; that they continue about the fort, and that a party (supposed to be large) on the other side of the river has been heard cutting wood both above and below the fort; that some of their party on this side the river took a canoe from the fort last night and has it lying in view on their own shore.

The same express also informs me that the trail of the party which crossed at Glenn's bottom, near Wheeling, has been discovered coming into the settlement up Buffalo creek. They are now supposed to be near Ramsey's fort.

Although I have not yet ascertained with certainty either the situation of the enemy or of our militia, yet I have thought it best to inform you of the circumstance, as perhaps

---

[1] From Major Samuel McColloch. See Appendix M,— Bayard to McCleery, August 4, 1782, note.

Appendix J. 307

you may think proper to move down the river as far as the Mingo Bottom immediately. Should this be your determination, I could wish to be informed by this express.¹

XXII.—IRVINE TO MARSHEL.

FORT PITT, *August* 10, 1782.

Sir:— An address was handed me this day signed by the principal inhabitants of the frontier on the waters of Buffalo and Tenmile.² Though I do not think there is so much danger as they apprehend, yet, if they run, the consequence is the same, and I do not wish any more breaches made in the settlements. I hope the present intelligence will soon put the people into better spirits. I would be glad to countenance every part of the country, and think a little time will persuade

---

¹ Irvine complied with Marshel's request. On Sunday morning following, he marched with a party of regulars "toward the Mingo Bottom." See Appendix M,—Bayard to McCleery, August 4, 1782.

² Tenmile creek empties into the Monongahela on the left, at Millsboro, Washington county, Pennsylvania. The following is the address referred to,—the original, which is before me, being in the beautiful handwriting of the noted Thaddeus Dod:

"WASHINGTON COUNTY, *August* 7, 1782.

"May it please your honor:

"We, the inhabitants of the frontiers on the headwaters of Tenmile and Buffalo creeks, in the county of Washington, finding our dangers and distresses still increasing upon us through the disorderly state of our public affairs and the continual alarms from the encroachments of the savages, are driven to the necessity to apply to you and humbly to implore your assistance.

"We shall not pretend to dictate to you as to the manner of affording us aid, nor shall we trouble you with a long detail of our calamities. As to our circumstances, we shall refer you, sir, to the bearer hereof [Van Swearingen], whom we confide in as being fully acquainted therewith. We are not insensible of the difficulties of granting assistance to us, which arise from the opposition to the lawful authority of the state, but as we have ever been and still desire to be in subjection to the authority, we humbly hope and request that we might not be indiscriminately punished for the faults of those who, living out of danger themselves, feel not the necessity of proper regulations in our country. We, therefore, without taking up any more of your attention, subscribe ourselves, sir, your most humble servants. Thaddeus Dod, David Dille, Patrick Allison, Demas Lindsly, Thomas Atkinson, John Dickinson, Samuel Dickerson, Samuel Magon, Jno. Craig."

them to determine on remaining on their places. You will therefore call out one officer and twenty men, to range on that quarter for two weeks only (for the present); by that time the people will be able to get in their grain and hay, and probably affairs may put on a more favorable appearance. I should be glad for several reasons, that an active, good officer could be ordered on this service. Captain [Andrew] Swearingen will victual them, and I will direct Captain [Thomas] Parkison to take it into his accounts. The officer will therefore be directed to apply to, and make his arrangements with, Captain Swearingen respecting provisions and ammunition.

XXIII.— MARSHEL TO IRVINE.

WASHINGTON COUNTY, *August* 26, 1782.

Dear Sir:— By the inclosed resolutions you will learn the result of our last meeting at Catfish.[1] The meeting was general, and the officers and principal inhabitants who met on

---

[1] The following record of the proceedings of the meeting gives the resolutions mentioned by Marshel:

"At a meeting of the officers and principal inhabitants of Washington county, at Catfish Camp, on Thursday, the 22d of August, 1782, for the purpose of carrying an expedition under the command of Brigadier General Irvine against Sandusky or other Indian towns bordering on our frontier,

"*Resolved,* That each and every battalion Washington county militia shall furnish the quota of men, provision and pack-horses equipped for transportation hereunto annexed to each and every battalion respectively, namely:

	Men.	Horses.	Rations.
1st Battalion, commanded by Col. [Henry] Enoch	61	22	3,600
2d " " " " [Geo.] Vallandigham	165	62	9,900
3d " " " " [David] Williamson	140	53	8,400
4th " " " " [John] Marshall	140	53	8,400
5th " " " " [Thomas] Crooks	165	62	9,900
	671	252	40,200

"*Resolved,* That each and every person furnishing 200 rations (each ration to consist of 1¼ pounds flour and 1¼ pounds beef) and delivering the same at the time and place appointed by the commanding officer of each battalion, shall be exempted a two months' tour of duty under the law, in future, in lieu thereof that each and every person who shall deliver a good pack-horse

the occasion were unanimous in sentiment, except the infamous —— ——,[1] who labored all his might to set aside all law and government and depend wholly upon the virtue of the people for raising and equipping this county's quota of men. However, notwithstanding all his and other designing men's opposition, I have no doubt of raising and equipping the proposed number, about five hundred men (perhaps more), and that we shall be able to rendezvous at such place as you may appoint, by the 15th of September, which will be as soon as the people of this county can possibly be in readiness.

---

fit for the service, properly equipped with a halter, pack-saddle, lashing-rope and two kegs, or one good bag, and delivering the same as aforesaid, shall in like manner be exempted a tour as above mentioned.

"*Resolved*, That it be recommended to each company to choose three good men of their own body who shall be empowered to assess upon each and every delinquent person not furnishing as aforesaid his proportionable share of the expense of what provision and pack-horses may be necessary, in proportion to the value of his estate; and in case the company being legally called should refuse to choose such men, then the captain of such company shall, with the delegate elected to represent them in the council, choose the men as aforesaid; and when there is no representation, then in that case the captain shall call to his assistance his two subaltern officers and choose as aforesaid; provided, the same is effected on or before the 6th day of September next.

"*Resolved*, That if any of the said horses as aforesaid impressed or entered equipped and appraised, and proceeding on said expedition, be lost in said service, shall, unless paid for by government in the term of one year, be paid by the company in proportion to their estates.

"*Resolved*, That each captain keep a fair account of each and every person's subscription of provision and pack-horses in their respective districts; also a duplicate list of their subscriptions when delivered at the time and place appointed by the commanding officer of the battalion, which said duplicate list, or a certified copy thereof, shall be forthwith transmitted to the lieutenant or the sub-lieutenant of the district, in order as well to ascertain the person who complies with his subscription, as that they may be paid for or have discount with government for the same in the present or future taxes.

"*Resolved*, That each battalion deposit at one or more mills in their respective district, their quota of wheat on or before the 6th day of September next. Signed by order of the council,   JAMES MARSHEL.

"Test: WILLIAM POLLOCK, Clerk."

[1] This name, although given in the original letter, I have thought best to omit in this connection. The language of Marshel is perhaps stronger than the exigencies of the case demanded.

XXIV.— IRVINE TO MARSHEL.

FORT PITT, *August* 27, 1782.

Dear Sir:— Your favor of yesterday is now before me. The resolutions, I think, are very well; the execution is another thing. However, I trust you will not be mistaken notwithstanding. I expect you will furnish me with accurate returns of men, horses, and provision the soonest [time] possible, that I may actually depend on being assembled at the general rendezvous on the day I shall appoint. I presume you will be able to furnish me with these returns on the 8th of September at farthest, for, after that date, there will be full little time for my orders to circulate, appointing time and place. My final determination and orders shall therefore depend on them. The 15th will be late, but if you cannot be ready before, it must do. I expect [the lieutenant of Westmoreland county] Colonel [Edward] Cook's returns this night or to-morrow. I wrote you by Captain [John] Hughes yesterday, by which you will perceive I was apprised of the opposition you mention.

XXV.— MARSHEL TO IRVINE.

WASHINGTON COUNTY, *August* 29, 1782.

Dear Sir:— Your favors of the 26th and 27th inst. I have received, and am much obliged to you for your opinion respecting the plan for raising and equipping our quota of men in this county. I perceive you have been apprized of the opposition we have met with and that the account you had by report, of the resolutions entered into by the officers and principal people of this county, was not altogether true. Notwithstanding the plan is not so clearly and fully expressed in the resolves as I could wish, yet, if it is well executed, it will do; and at present I have no more doubt of its being carried into effect (at least so far as will answer the end) than I have of my own existence. It may be that I am too sanguine in my expectations; but I am willing to leave the general rendezvous to determine whether the gentlemen opposing or those executing the plan have the most influence in the county.

I have not only directed the field officers to appoint the place of rendezvous; [to name] suitable persons to superintend the pack-horses, stock, flour, assistant drivers, etc.; and to make returns on the 7th of September of the number of men, horses and rations that may be depended upon in their respective districts: but have also appointed the 13th of September, for their assembling as aforesaid, with every apparatus for the campaign (except salt), and to hold themselves in readiness to march on the morning of the 14th to the general rendezvous which I considered you would not appoint later than the 15th, and that the people of this county could not possibly be called to a general rendezvous before that time.

The returns you require shall be transmitted as soon as possible. All the companies in Colonels [David] Williamson and [John] Marshall's battalions that I have heard from have raised the full quota of men, pack-horses and provision assigned them: I expect the others will do the same.

I do not know whether you have thought how the men on the expedition are to be supplied with salt and camp kettles; for my part, I have not till lately; — the latter, in my last order to the field officers, I have mentioned, and requested them to procure as many as possible: the former I durst not mention for fear of disaffecting the people, although it is absolutely necessary, and it cannot be got by any other means.

We must yet call upon the different companies to supply themselves with that article; but, if possible, let it be done some other way.

Captain [John] Hughes informs me you require a troop of light horse from this county to consist of forty-five or fifty men; I have thereupon assigned each battalion its quota, and ordered them to be raised and equipped. If you have no objection, I propose that Captain Hughes and his officers take command of them during the expedition.

I have been thinking of some suitable persons to be appointed superintendents general of the pack-horses, etc., but cannot yet fix my judgment. It is likely at the general rendezvous I shall be better able to give my opinion with regard to these appointments.

XXVI.— MARSHEL TO IRVINE.

Thursday, September 12, 1782.

Dear Sir:— By an express this moment arrived from Wheeling I have received the following intelligence, namely: that a large trail, by supposition about two hundred Indians, was discovered yesterday about three o'clock near to that place. Captain Boggs who brought the account says that when he had left the fort about one mile and a half he heard the swivel at Wheeling fired and one rifle. He further says that Ebenezer McColloch from Vanmeter's fort,[1] on his way to Wheeling got within half a mile of the place shortly after Boggs left it where he was alarmed by hearing a heavy and constant fire about the fort, and makes no doubt the fort was then attacked.[2]

Boggs is now gone into the settlements to alarm the inhabitants and I am afraid will injure the expedition. As we have had so many false alarms this summer, I cannot think of making much ado about the present, until the truth of it is known with certainty. Notwithstanding, I should be inexcusable in not giving you the account as I have received it.

From what I can learn the people of this county are making every preparation in their power for the expedition, and I believe nothing will prevent us from raising and equipping nearly our quota, if the present alarm does not. As the time your last order had to circulate was very short, it is likely the men will not be all collected to the general rendezvous before the 19th. If anything material occurs on the frontier you may expect the earliest intelligence in my power.

---

[1] This fort was situated on the south side of Short creek, a few miles above its junction with the Ohio river, in Ohio county, Virginia. The land on which it was located belonged to the widow and heirs of Joseph Vanmeter, and was subsequently owned by his eldest son, Morgan Vanmeter. In 1847, it belonged to the heirs of George Mathews.

[2] See Appendix M,— Ebenezer Zane to Irvine, September 17, 1782.

XXVII.— MARSHEL TO IRVINE.

Sunday Morning, September 15, 1782.

Dear Sir:— You may depend upon it as matter of fact that a large party of Indians are now in our country. Last night I saw two prisoners [deserters from the enemy] who made their escape from Wheeling in time of the action, and they say the enemy consists of two hundred and thirty-eight Indians and forty rangers, the latter commanded by a British officer; that they attacked Wheeling fort on Wednesday night and continued the attack until Thursday night, at which time the above deserters left them. That fort, they say, was the principal object of the enemy; but it appears both from their account and the enemy's advancing into the country that they have despaired of taking it.[1] The deserters say that shortly before they left the enemy, that they had determined to give up the matter at Wheeling, and either scatter into small parties in order to distress and plunder the inhabitants, or attack the first small fort they could come at. The latter, I am this moment informed, is actually the case; that they have attacked one, Rice's blockhouse, on what is called the Dutch fork of Buffalo, and it's to be feared it will fall into their hands,[2] as only those have been called upon who are not going on the expedition; I am afraid they will not turn out as well as they ought to do.

If the enemy continue to advance in one body, the matter will become serious and perhaps require our whole strength to repel them; but if it can possibly be avoided, I could wish not to call upon a man that is going on the expedition.[3] Besides the battalion rendezvous is appointed as soon as the men could possibly be collected, unless the officers have made other

---

[1] See Appendix M,— Zane to Irvine, September 17, 1782.

[2] Rice's fort was about fourteen miles from Wheeling. Marshel's fears were not well founded. The fort was attacked, it is true, but the enemy were repulsed by a garrison of only six men, the Indians losing four of their warriors.

[3] That is, the expedition against Sandusky, then in contemplation by General Irvine.

appointments, as you will see by Colonel [William] McCleery's letter they have done in the first battalion. No doubt ammunition will be wanted on this occasion, a small quantity such as the bearer can carry will do.

P. S.— Should you think of joining the militia, Catfish Camp at present appears to me to be the most suitable place to establish your headquarters, at which place I shall order one battalion to rendezvous on Tuesday next; I mean those that are going on the expedition, as Catfish will be in their way to Fort McIntosh.

XXVIII.— IRVINE TO MARSHEL.

FORT PITT, *September* 15, 1782.

Dear Sir:— I received your favor of this date, and am under some difficulty to determine what is best to be done. I am prepared for marching to any point at a moment's warning. If the enemy should advance in force into the country, the repelling them will, beyond a doubt, become clearly a duty; but, on the other hand, if I do not go to the general rendezvous at the time appointed, every body who may assemble there and not find me, will immediately disperse; and if I should order the rendezvous to be postponed but one day, they will not obey a second summons in any time. Upon the whole, either the expedition must be given up entirely, and make an object of these rascals altogether, or we must keep going on with the expedition, at least, till the matter can be clearly ascertained whether the enemy are advancing or retreating.

If matters become so serious that the expedition must give way to immediate preservation of the country, I will march instantly to your quarter. In this, I will govern my movements by the intelligence I shall from time to time receive from you. If I do not, therefore, hear from you again before next Wednesday morning at six o'clock, I shall take for granted they have left the country, and will proceed to McIntosh.[1] On the other hand, should there be a necessity for

---

[1] This fixes the date as the 18th of September, for the assembling. From the following undated communication of General Irvine's, and without ad-

my aid, you will by all means advise me, and in the meantime let the people for the expedition go on assembling. I presume they will not collect much sooner at any rate. I will join whenever it may be adjudged most advisable.

XXIX.— Marshel to Irvine.

September 16, 1782.

Dear Sir:— The bearer is one of the deserters from the enemy in time of the action at Wheeling. Some people say the other deserters report this fellow is a villain. However, be that as it may, I think it best to send him to you that such order may be taken respecting him as you may think proper.

XXX.— Marshel to Irvine.

September 16, 1782.

Dear Sir:— About half an hour before the receipt of your letter of the 15th, I had dispatched an express to you, which I expect you will receive by the bearer.[1]

The enemy, I am in hopes, are dispersed; therefore, we shall go on with the rendezvous with all possible expedition, although it will not be in our power to be at McIntosh before the 21st; perhaps some may be there sooner.

XXXI.— Marshel to Irvine.

September 16, 1782.

Dear Sir:— A few minutes after I wrote you yesterday morning, I received an account of the enemy being within

---

dress, but evidently a copy of a circular letter sent to the county lieutenants, it is seen that the day fixed upon and the place for the general rendezvous, agree with the above: "Ample time having been given for the militia, volunteers and others, to prepare for the expedition, you will direct those of your county to assemble at Fort McIntosh on the 18th inst. with their several quotas of provisions, horses and other equipments; and I expect they will come there in such perfect order in every respect as that the whole will be able to take up the line of march the succeeding day. I am aware a number of difficulties will arise, but I am certain that they may all be surmounted by a determined people."

[1] The deserter from the enemy, who carried the previous letter; that is, the other one of this date.

one mile and a half of Wells' mill; that they had burnt a house and destroyed the family; in consequence of which, I immediately ordered the militia of the fourth battalion [Col. John Marshall's] as well those for the expedition as others, to rendezvous at my house, and the third [Col. David Williamson's] and fifth [Col. Thomas Crooks'] battalions to rendezvous at Catfish [now Washington, Washington county]. However, the alarm with regard to the house being burnt was false, notwithstanding at the time I had no doubt of it being true.

It now appears to me from every circumstance that the main body of the enemy is gone over the [Ohio] river and that a small party remains on our frontier to annoy us and prevent the others being followed. As part of the militia of this county — that for the expedition — has been ordered to rendezvous on this occasion and others who mean to go now live on the frontier, they cannot possibly rendezvous on the day appointed, nor do I know your determination at present, therefore can only order the men to hold themselves in readiness. If I have no other accounts from the frontier this day, I shall direct the volunteers for the expedition to return home and await marching orders, which I shall expect to receive from you.

XXXII.— IRVINE TO MARSHEL.

FORT PITT, *September* 18, 1782, 9 o'clock, P. M.

Sir:— I have this moment received dispatches from the [continental] secretary at war,[1] informing me that some regular troops are ordered from below to assist us in our intended expedition. I am therefore to beg you will immediately countermand the march of the volunters and others of your county till further orders. As soon as I am positively assured of the time the troops will be here, I shall give you the earliest notice. I hope the good people of your county will not think hard to be stopped, as the measure is designed for the best and to insure success if possible.

In the meantime, you will please to direct that they hold

---
[1] Lincoln to Irvine, September 7, 1782 (ante, p. 181).

themselves in perfect readiness to march at a moment's warning; and for this purpose, would it not be best to deposit the flour in some convenient place in each battalion, and also have the cattle pastured in parcels? As far as I am yet instructed, about the 6th of October will be the time for our next rendezvous. It must, however take place on a certain day, as it is intended also to favor an expedition from another quarter.[1] You shall hear from me soon again.[2]

XXXIII.— Marshel to Irvine.

Washington County, *October* 15, 1782,
5 o'clock, A. M.

Dear Sir:— Your favor of the 13th, only came to hand late last night, the express unfortunately took sick by the way; it is therefore out of my power to stop the militia of this county until they rendezvous in battalion. If they are sent home, I am clearly of opinion they can not be collected again this season even if the troops from below should arrive in a few days. Numbers of them have missed saving fall crops on account of holding themselves in readiness for the expedition; others are obliged to go over the mountains for necessary articles; and the season is so far advanced that almost every person in the country will be engaged in securing their corn, etc.; so that they will entirely lose sight of the expedition. To detain them at the battalion rendezvous would be a waste of time and provision at an uncertainty; besides I fear it could not be done. The militia of this county will not stay long at one place unless they are confined. Indeed I fear a delinquency in Westmoreland full as much as in this county, if not more so. Upon the whole, my opinion is that the matter must be given up for this season; but lest I should be wrong, will not throw out the remotest hint of it until I hear from you again. I shall direct the

---

[1] The expedition here referred to was one contemplated against the Genesee Indian towns.

[2] A similar letter was sent to Colonel Cook, lieutenant of Westmoreland county.

field officers to discharge their battalions until farther orders; in the meantime, take their opinion with regard to the disposition of the people, and if it appears that they can be rallied again, you may depend upon every exertion in my power if required.

P. S.— I shall write Colonel [David] Shepherd agreeable to your request.

I have all the cash in my hand I received from you except the price of the kegs and twenty-one pounds to Colonel [David] Williamson for cattle; •this I expect will be returned if required.

XXXIV.— MARSHEL TO IRVINE.

WASHINGTON COUNTY, *October* 21, 1782.

Dear Sir:— This will be delivered to you by Mr. Robert Wallace, who will also inform you of his intention of applying to his excellency, General Washington, in order to get his family exchanged. He will also give you his idea of the manner in which the exchange is to be effected, etc. Notwithstanding I have no great opinion of the practicability of his plan, yet if anything can be done for him in the line he proposes, I make no doubt you will put him on the right track or save him further trouble.[1]

I am anxious to know the reason why the troops have not come from below. I hope you will not forget (if Major

---

[1] Mention has been made of the capture of Robert Wallace's family (ante, pp. 99, 240). Wallace's wife, a son ten years old, another aged two-and-a-half years, and an infant daughter, constituted the family. Mrs. Wallace and her infant were, soon after the capture, tomahawked and scalped; but the two boys were taken to Sandusky, where the oldest died. The other was finally rescued by his father from the savages. A little over eight months had elapsed since the family were taken, to the date of the above letter; yet, from the words of Marshel, it is evident Wallace had obtained no knowledge of the death of his wife and infant daughter. This is a singular fact, as both were killed by the savages before they reached the Ohio. He had not learned, also, of the death of his eldest child, at the above date. It will be seen by reference to page 239, note 4, last line, that the killing of the wife and daughter was unknown upon the border when the militia started for "Muskingum."

[John] Rose[1] is returned) to write me by Mr. Wallace. I could wish that the cattle for which I paid Colonel [David] Williamson might be sent for as soon as possible. They are now at his house. He informs me they are troublesome to him, he not having pasture of his own.

XXXV.— MARSHEL TO IRVINE.

WASHINGTON COUNTY, *October* 25, 1782.

Dear Sir:— Your favor of the 20th with the inclosed I received yesterday evening, which will enable me, I hope, to satisfy the people who may ask me the reason why the expedition is stopped. Notwithstanding, it is very extraordinary indeed that you have received no official account of the expedition being laid aside. It may be the thoughts of peace being near, was the cause of this neglect. I sincerely wish with you that an honorable peace may soon take place; and, that no mistake may happen, at any rate nothing shall be wanting in my power to prepare either for peace or war.

The public arms in this county I shall order to be carried into Fort Pitt immediately. The cash remaining in my hands I have sent by Colonel [William] Parker with an account of my expenditures, but have not taken any receipts, as I intended to do this business at the rendezvous; therefore, have made you "Dr." in the account. The necessary vouchers, besides the delivery of the articles purchased, I shall transmit the first opportunity.

If an officer and about twenty-five men from you could be spared a few days as a guard to the sheriff of this county, it would enable him to collect the delinquent [militia] fines, which would be of infinite service to the county, and also prepare us for a settlement of public accounts. Colonel Parker will confer with you on the subject.

---

[1] Major Rose was one and Capt. Sam'l Brady the other of the "officer express" sent by Irvine eastward, to find out why the regulars expected at Fort Pitt, for the Sandusky expedition, were so tardy, and to hasten their march (ante, p. 134, note 2).

XXXVI.— MARSHEL TO IRVINE.

WASHINGTON COUNTY, *November* 1, 1782.

Dear Sir:— Colonel [Edward] Cook [lieutenant of Westmoreland county] applies to me for a few volunteers as a guard for the artists to run the state line. I expect to raise some for that service, but have not any ammunition to give them. Colonel [Thomas] Crooks also borrowed three pounds powder and four and one-half pounds lead, when he went to serve his tour at Wheeling, which was to be replaced. I am now called upon for it. If you will please to send me the above quantity, also five pounds powder and six or seven of lead, for the volunteers now going on duty, you will oblige [me].

XXXVII.— MARSHEL TO IRVINE.[1]

WASHINGTON, *May* 18, 1783.

Dear Sir:— Colonel [David] Williamson informs me that a large party of Indians have been discovered on Thursday last about twenty miles below Wheeling; that they have routed the land jobbers[2] on the other side of the [Ohio] river, and are expected to cross about the place they were first discovered. From every circumstance I can learn, it appears that the party is formidable and that they mean to strike in different places. What the consequence may be God only knows, for I do not believe that fifty volunteers can be raised in the county to repel them. At any rate, ammunition will be wanting for the frontier inhabitants if none else should be got to use it. You will please therefore to send by the bearer such quantity as you may think necessary. Should the alarm prove false, I shall take special care that none of it be wasted.

---

[1] This letter was written while Irvine was absent from Fort Pitt, at his home in Carlisle. It was directed,— "To General Irvine or, in his absence, Colonel Bayard, commanding Fort Pitt." It closed the correspondence between Marshel and Irvine.

[2] That is, the "new state" settlers (ante, p. 196, *et seq.*

APPENDIX K.

CORRESPONDENCE WITH THE LIEUTENANT OF WESTMORELAND COUNTY, PENNSYLVANIA.[1]

I.— IRVINE TO EDWARD COOK.[2]

[CIRCULAR.]

FORT PITT, *January*, 1782.

Sir:— I am to go down to Philadelphia on business connected with my command here; and, as I am not certain what time I may be detained there, I am apprehensive there may be an absolute necessity for calling out some militia before I

---

[1] Extract from the proceedings of the supreme executive council of Pennsylvania:

"IN COUNCIL," PHILADELPHIA, *Saturday, January* 5, 1782.

"The council took into consideration the appointment of a lieutenant for the county of Westmoreland, in the room of Archibald Lochry, Esquire, deceased; and Edward Cook, Esquire, sub-lieutenant of the said county, being recommended to the board as a proper person for said office: thereupon,

"*Resolved*, That Edward Cook, Esquire, be appointed lieutenant of the county of Westmoreland in the room of Archibald Lochry, Esquire, deceased, and that he be commissioned accordingly."

[2] Edward Cook was born Jan. 1, 1739, of English parentage, in the Cumberland valley, on the Conococheague, then in Lancaster, now Franklin county, Pennsylvania. His father was probably a farmer. Edward first made a prospecting tour across the mountains. In 1770, he removed to the "Forks of Yough" between the Monongahela and Youghiogheny rivers, now Fayette county. He first established a store, and afterward a line of pack-horses across the mountains. In 1776, he had completed and moved in a stone house, yet standing, where he lived and died. At an early day, he not only kept a store, but erected mills, farmed, had a still house, and owned slaves. He was a member of the committee of conference which met at Carpenter's Hall, June 18, 1776, and of the convention of July 15, following. In 1777, he was appointed by the general assembly one of the commissioners from Pennsylvania to meet those from the other states, which assembled at New Haven, Connecticut, November 22, 1777, to regulate the prices of commodities. In 1781, he was in command of a battalion of rangers for frontier defence, and was a sub-lieutenant of Westmoreland, 1780–1. On the the 5th of January, 1782, he was, as stated in the note immediately preceding this, made lieuten-

return, especially as this garrison must be employed in repairing the fort. Colonel Gibson will command in my absence, and will be the best judge when this necessity will arise.

On his requisition you will therefore order out such numbers of militia (not exceeding sixty) for one tour from your county, as he will call for, the tour not to be for a longer term than one month.[1] I hope to return by the first of March, before which time, I presume there will not be much danger of any damage being done; at the same time, I think it most prudent to take every proper precaution.[2]

---

ant of the county, in place of Archibald Lochry, deceased. This office he continued to hold until the erection of Fayette county, in 1783.

On the 25th of July, 1782, the supreme executive council "ordered that a special commission of oyer and terminer and general jail delivery, directed to the Honorable Christopher Hays and Dorsey Pentecost, Esquires, and Edward Cook, Esquire, be now issued to the counties of Westmoreland and Washington for the trial of divers persons now confined in the jails of the said counties charged with high crimes and misdemeanors." (See Appendix M,— Hays and Cook to Irvine, Dec. 25, 1782.) Col. Cook was one of the commissioners who laid out the present county-seat of Fayette county. He was appointed one of the justices of his county with jurisdiction (along with John Hoge, Thomas Scott and William Walter) including Washington county, on the 21st of November, 1786. He was made presiding judge of the Fayette common pleas, April 8, 1789. On the 7th of August, 1791, he became associate judge of Fayette under the new constitution. He was a man of influence, and during the excise troubles in 1794 was chosen chairman of the Mingo creek meeting, and was largely instrumental in allaying the excitement, and thus virtually ending the so-called Whisky Insurrection. He died November 28th, 1808. His wife was Martha Crawford of Cumberland, now Franklin county, sister of Col. Josiah Crawford. She was married to Edward Cook in 1770. She died in 1837, aged ninety-four years, in the old stone house, into which they moved, as she always said, in "Independence Year." It stands about two miles northeast of Fayette City, formerly Cookstown. Colonel Cook had but one child, James Crawford Cook, who was born in 1772, and died in 1848.

[1] Gibson exercised the authority conferred upon him by Irvine in making a requisition upon the lieutenant of Westmoreland for a number of militia to protect the frontier of that county. This was made necessary because of threatened marauds of the savages. Sixty were ordered out for one month's tour of duty, and stationed on the frontiers of Westmoreland.

[2] This was a circular letter, a like one having been sent to Col. James Marshel, lieutenant of Washington county. (Ante, p. 84, note 2; also, p. 282, note 1.)

II.— Irvine to Cook.

Fort Pitt, *March* 28, 1782.

Sir:— You are already acquainted with the resolution of congress and orders of the president and council of Pennsylvania respecting my command in this quarter;[1] in addition to which, I have received instructions from his excellency, General Washington.[2]

As making arrangements to cover and protect the country is the main object; and [as] it is to be done by a combination of regulars and militia, the business will be complicated; and [as there will be] a diversity of interests, I think it of the utmost importance that whatever plan may be adopted [it] should be as generally understood as the nature of the service will admit. You will conceive that, on this occasion, I shall stand in need of the counsel and assistance of some of the principal people of the country. I wish, therefore, to see you and at least one field officer of every battalion in your county, for which purpose, I request you will be pleased to warn such as you may think proper to attend at this post on Friday, the 5th of April next; punctually to the day will be necessary, as I have written to Colonel Marshel and others in Washington county also, to attend on that day.[3]

III.— Cook to Irvine.

April 8, 1782.

Sir:— I must request you to furnish those militia with arms, such of them as want that article, likewise ammunition. It will be necessary to send those to Carnahan's block house, in order to scout toward Ligonier, etc., where I expect they will be joined by a draft from the north side of the Youghiogheny.

Your honor will be pleased to give him [the bearer, Sergeant

---

[1] Ante, p. 72, note 1; also, p. 279, note 3.
[2] See Washington to Irvine, p. 94.
[3] Ante, p. 104 and note; also, p. 284.

John Ashcraft] the necessary instructions. I have not had time to order out the field officers to the conference agreeable to your request.[1]

IV.— Cook to Irvine.

At My House,[2] *April* 18, 1782.

Sir:— Last Thursday, the draft from the battalion in which I live (being the second) set out for their place of rendezvous at widow Myres'. They consist of about fifty men. I cannot tell whether the other company at Carnahan's block house is complete, but I have ordered Captain [Joseph] Beckett, who commands this draft, to detach from his so as to make them complete. I have instructed him in the mode of defense agreeable to the arrangement.[3] I furnished them with ammunition and expect they will obtain arms from those they relieve sufficient to equip them. Captain Beckett will take the first opportunity to give you a return of those under his command. I was not at home when the drafts from the fourth or upper battalion went along, being at court. I left orders for them to proceed to Carnahan's block house. Colonel [John] Pumroy of the first battalion [of Westmoreland county militia] is near Hannastown. I have sent orders to him to superintend the draft this month.

V.— Cook to Irvine.

May 26, 1782.

Sir:— I have received two letters from you since I have had the opportunity of answering.

I wrote to Colonel Pumroy, as I mentioned in my last, to take the command agreeable to the arrangement, which he has not attended to. Colonel [Charles] Campbell [sub-lieutenant

---

[1] See the letter of Irvine next preceding.

[2] About two miles northeast of the present Fayette City, Fayette county, Pa. It is still standing (ante, p. 321, note 2, last paragraph).

[3] From this, it will be seen, that Col. Cook had been informed of the arrangements agreed upon at the meeting at Fort Pitt, April 5th.

of Westmoreland county] wrote me that Pumroy would attend this month, and I understand he has not. In short, it appears that every thing is done by those people that they think will promote confusion and disorder. I never can hear that one man is gone from that quarter to the defense of the frontier. Those that were drafted for the defense this month have chiefly turned out volunteers on this [Crawford's] expedition [against Sandusky] and that is the reason why so few are from this quarter, which is the only part that has done any thing.

I have endeavored to do every thing in my power, and can get so little done to any purpose that my quiet and peace are so destroyed that life, in some measure, is burthensome. I have ordered Colonel [Benjamin] Davis [of the second battalion of Westmoreland militia] now to the frontier for what remains of this month and have ordered a few men more to re-enforce Captain [Thomas] Moore. Eight men are gone. I hope after this month there shall be less cause of complaint.

P. S.— Before I was done writing, Ensign Cooper came in and informs me that Pumroy has attended, but has not waited upon you nor made any report; upon which I have written to him and countermanded the order to Davis. Many thanks for your care about the fine.

VI.— COOK TO IRVINE.

AT MY HOUSE, *May* 29, 1782.

Sir:— There seems to be a general outcry against the payment of taxes over the whole country. The plea that is made use of against it is that there is not specie in the country sufficient to discharge the sum demanded; but if assurances could be given that Mr. Morris would take specific articles, such as provisions, etc., it is thought that it would ease the minds of the people and produce salutary effects. If it was in your power by circulars letter or by some means to give encouragement respecting that mode of discharging the tax, it is thought it would be of signal service.

At the request of some gentlemen, I have written to you; as

it is feared that the opposition will be so great that the matter cannot be effected; which will be a sensible injury to the public in general. If there is any other eligible mode, I would be glad to have the general's sentiments on the subject.[1]

VII.—Cook to Irvine.
May 30, 1782.

Sir:— There is a certain Benjamin Dye and a certain Henry Foster that are delinquents in the militia. Their fines are five pounds five shillings each. We are lately informed the price of common labor is rated at three shillings six pence by the assembly, which brings the fines to that sum.

P. S.— I am told it is a French boat those persons are gone or going with.

VIII.— Cook to Irvine.
June 10, 1782.

Dear Sir:— We are much distressed on account of the want of a few arms towards arming the guard for running the line. I am under the necessity of making or rather renewing the application on that score. If it is in your power to send only ten it will be a great help, and I will pledge my word for the delivery of them to your post again as soon as the guard returns.[2] I have thought that if you should think it advisable to send a few active officers and a few privates of the regular troops it would give a kind of sanction and weight to the matter.[3]

---

[1] Gen. Irvine had already corresponded with Mr. Morris concerning this matter (ante, pp. 204–207) so far as Washington county was concerned.

[2] Two days after the appointment of Alexander McClean, by Pennsylvania, as commissioner on part of that state to run the temporary boundary line, the lieutenant of Westmoreland county was authorized to furnish such number of militia of his county, as might be wanted as guards to the surveyors. Over one hundred were drafted but arms were wanting. For a supply — ten, if no more — Cook writes as above.

[3] Irvine declined sending any continentals upon that service for good reasons (ante, p. 248). The same request was afterward made by Marshel (see p. 295), who met with a like refusal.

Colonels [Christopher] Hays and [Benjamin] Davis are gone on and intend delaying a few days at the mouth of George's creek thinking that the opposition may perhaps scatter or subside; for we are well assured of an opposition by the inhabitants, who apprehend the running of the line will be a prelude to the taxes, which they have a most sovereign aversion to;[1]— at all events, if possible, send a few arms.

I have sent the copy of the two letters from Mr. Morris to Colonel McClean and expect they will be of service, and that he will make a good use of them. I will take care to have Mr. ———'s conduct inquired into.[2] This is not the first offense. I understand they are holding meetings in Washington county lately about a new state, which shows this is a most distracted country.

IX.— Cook to Irvine.

June 24, 1782.

Dear Sir:—In my last, I mentioned something of the anxiety of the people in general for another expedition. By the bearer hereof [Benjamin Harrison],[3] you will learn something of the truth of what has been asserted.[4] But it seems to be the general opinion that it will not do without General Irvine takes the command with what regulars can be spared. Indeed, it is wished that the whole could go, and garrison the posts with militia [that is, let the militia garrison the posts, while the regulars go upon the expedition].

[1] The reason for opposition to the running of the line on part of those who lived in the vicinity is thus made plain. When this letter was written, Cook did not know that the enterprise had been abandoned by McClean for the time; indeed, it was given up on the very day of his writing (June 10th).

[2] Concerning the man whose name is left blank at this point, Irvine, on the back of the above letter, wrote: "——— ———, an attorney of Virginia, formerly an active partisan, if not disaffected, as well as ——— ———." The last blank is filled with the name of the leader of the new state scheme (ante, pp. 109, 244).

[3] Then, or soon after, colonel of the 4th battalion Westmoreland county militia.

[4] Referring to proposals from some gentlemen of Westmoreland, to "carry" an expedition against Sandusky. (See next letter.)

If the general was to make a demand of the number of militia necessary, it is not doubted but they will be furnished, together with provisions and transportation for the regular troops. I have written this without waiting for an answer to my last as Captain [Benjamin] Harrison, in behalf of the people in his quarter, has requested me to write by him.

P. S.— It is also talked of that they will put themselves under the command of the continental officers so as to fill up the two regiments under your command.

X.— IRVINE TO COOK.

FORT PITT, *June* 26, 1782.

Sir:— Since my last by Mr. McClean, Captain Harrison arrived with your favor of the 24th, and other papers, proposals from some gentlemen in your quarter for carrying an expedition.[1] These people seem so much in earnest that I am led to think if other parts of the country are so spirited and patriotic something may probably be done; but as it will take some time to come to a proper knowledge of this matter, and that must be accurately done, there can be no harm in making the experiment. Captain Harrison proposes having a subscription taken from all the companies in your county similar to that he handed me from Captains Beall and Moore. If this was done and the whole transmitted to me, I would soon be able to determine whether it would be worth while to give the people the trouble of calling them together;— these, I suppose, may be obtained by the twentieth of July. If found sufficient to warrant an assembly, then the first of August would be as soon as they could well be got together.

I have no intimation of any system being on foot in Washington county for this purpose. It is said the people wish an expedition; but I am rather doubtful [of its accomplishment, as] they expect it done in a regular channel, namely: to be called out by law; then they will of course expect to be fur-

---
[1] See Appendix M,— Robert Beall and Thomas Moore to Irvine, June 23, 1782.

nished with all necessaries by the public. This is a business I have no authority for; nor could I promise positively to pay for a single pack-horse, until I receive instructions for that purpose from congress or the commander-in-chief; my present orders being to act on the defensive only. If, nevertheless, when the season is so far advanced (as I believe I mentioned in my last) that I shall not have a right to expect any regular effective force to carry offensive measures on a larger scale, I would, in that case, look on it justifiable for me to join with the people of the country, in making excursions into the enemy's country, particularly when they are so spirited as to propose doing it at their own personal risk and expense.[1]

XI.— COOK TO IRVINE.

AT MY HOUSE, *August* 9, 1782.

Sir:— We have hired five spies who are now out, who are to reconnoiter from Fort Crawford to the Kittanning, agreeable to what was proposed when with you. They are ordered to correspond with those you may send. They are to make the figure of the day of the month upon a tree in order to ascertain their meeting or appointing places, and leave a line under a stone at the root of the tree importing the nature of the discovery if they have made any.

I have had a meeting of the field officers and other principal inhabitants upon the subject of the expedition.[2] The plan agreed upon I will lay before the gentlemen who are to meet

---

[1] Ante, pp. 123, 175, 303.

[2] The following is a copy of the proceedings:

"At a meeting of the field officers and other respectable inhabitants of the county of Westmoreland at the house of Colonel Edward Cook, on Thursday, the eighth day of August, 1782, to consult on a plan for an expedition against the Sandusky Indian nations bordering on our frontier,— Colonel Christopher Hays, Esq., Colonel Alexander McClean, Colonel Benjamin Harrison, Captain Hezekiah McGruder, and Charles Foreman, Esq., were appointed a committee to form a plan for that purpose.

"1st. *Resolved*, That each battalion of the militia of Westmoreland county shall furnish their quota of men, provisions and horses, equipped

at Catfish Camp [now Washington, Washington county] the 15th instant. It is thought we cannot complete our plan before the 20th instant, so as to make returns.[1]

for transportation, hereunto annexed to each and every battalion respectively, namely:

			Men.	Rations.	Horses.
The 1st Battalion	Col.	John Pumroy	61	4,117	30
" 2d	"	Col. Benj. Davis	176	11,800	88
" 3rd	"	Col. Geo. Beard	122	8,235	61
" 4th	"	Col. Benj. Harrison	123	8,302	61
" 5th	"	Col. Theophilus Phillips	119	8,032	59

"The said provision, etc., to be deposited at such time and place in each and every battalion as the commanding officer shall appoint.

"2dly. *Resolved*, That the commanding officer of each and every battalion do exempt the militia from one month's service and each and every man that shall furnish and equip one horse sufficient for the said service at the time and place appointed for depositing said provisions.

"Provided always that the said expedition proceeds on or is carried into execution. And every horse so as aforesaid entered be adjudged and appraised by two indifferently chosen by each company of said battalion respectively.

"3rd. *Resolved*, That in case any of the said horses so as aforesaid entered and equipped, adjudged and appraised and proceeding on said expedition, be lost in said service, the lieutenant and sub-lieutenants of the county together with the members of this committee in conjunction with those whose names are hereunto annexed, do pledge themselves, their fortunes and honors for the payment of the said horses agreeable to the said appraisements. [Signed] Edward Cook, Alexander McClean, Benj. Davis, Christopher Hays, Charles Foreman, Nehemiah Stokely, Benj. Harrison, Hez. McGruder, Zadock Springer, Samuel Wilson, John Hughes, Thomas Warring, Paden Cook, Theophilus Phillips, Andrew Sinn."

[1] The following order issued to Lieut. Richard Johnson, the day previous to the writing of the above letter, exhibits Cook's watchful care over the northern settlements of his county:

"AT MY HOUSE, *August* 8, 1782.

"*Sir:*— You are to proceed with the militia under your command to Myres' Station where you will receive arms and ammunition either there or by applying either through the field officer or in person to the general. You will have to detach a few men to Reyburn's, Waltour's and Fort Barr. I cannot inform you of the number necessary to each. You will be directed by the strength of your party or the number you can spare; and in this matter you will consult the field officer who superintends the different stations. I am, sir, your most obedient servant, EDWARD COOK."

XII.— Cook to Irvine.

August 27, 1782.

Sir:— I thought to have been able to inform you something particular about the intended expedition. I am yet in the dark about it. I have had no return from the north side of Youghiogheny as yet; although I am of opinion that this county would furnish near five hundred men with provision and horses equivalent; that is, from what I have been able to learn, although I am obliged to build something on conjecture. Colonel Harrison is on his way to Colonel Marshel in order to investigate the state of matters there and will call upon you on his return.

P. S.— Sir: After I had sealed this letter I recollected this from Colonel [Charles] Campbell respecting spies he says he has hired, desiring me to acquaint you with them.[1] September 2, 1782.

XIII.— Irvine to Cook.

[CIRCULAR.]

[No date.][2]

The negro man who came in from the Shawanese town arrived at the Mingo bottom [on the east side of the Ohio], the 7th Aug., and was fifteen days on the way.

---

[1] The letter here referred to was as follows:

"*August* 27, 1782.

"*Sir:*— A return of Captain Hugh Martin's and Captain John McClelland's volunteers to go on the campaign and horses and rations: men, twenty-eight; rations, nineteen hundred and eight; horses, ten. Sir, these are all the returns that were made to me of this battalion. You will inform the general [Irvine] that I have hired six spies that keep a constant scouting from the Laurel Hill to Wasson's place on Crooked creek; and if he would order it so that the spies who go up the Alleghany and they, were to meet, he could have constant intelligence if any party of Indians would come in any part to strike the inhabitants. I am, sir, your humble servant,

"Cha's Campbell.

"To Colonel Edward Cook."

[2] Written about September 1, 1782.

He was examined minutely by me. The interesting and material parts of the intelligence he brings are as follow:

That last winter Capt. [Alexander] McKee[1] was busy arranging matters with the Indians to come against Fort Pitt in the spring ; but, in February, two deserters arrived at the [Shawanese] towns from Gen. Clark, who gave the information that Fort Pitt was put into such a state of defense as would render the reduction of it uncertain; but that the Falls [Louisville] were weak, and could easily be reduced. On this report, they changed their ground and determined to go against the Falls and continued in this mind till after Colonel Crawford's expedition. They then changed their ground once more and determined to reduce Wheeling. Mr. McKee actually marched for that purpose from the [Shawanese] towns [in what is now Logan county, Ohio] with one hundred rangers (British) as they are called [Capt. Caldwell's company], and about three hundred Indians.[2] A day or two after his departure runners came in who gave the information that Gen. Clark was approaching with a train of artillery and a large body of troops.

The alarm was universally given and expresses sent after McKee, who returned to the town [Wapatomica]. In the mean time Blue Jacket, the Shawanese chief, went himself to reconnoiter Gen. Clark. He returned in six days with a confirmation of the first report; on which McKee marched with every soul that could be collected; the negro thinks, in all about one thousand, but is of opinion that not more than one-

---

[1] Alexander McKee was a native of Pensylvania and early became a trader among the Indians, carrying on a large business from Pittsburgh in conjunction with Alexander Ross, from 1768 to 1772, when he became Sir William Johnson's deputy Indian agent, resident at that place. He was, upon the erection of Bedford county, made one of its justices; and, upon the creation of Westmoreland, his commission was extended for that county. Upon the breaking out of the revolution, he was suspected of tory proclivities and was put upon his parole; which was afterward renewed. Finally, in the spring of 1778, he fled (along with Matthew Elliott, Simon Girty and others) to the enemy, reaching Detroit at length, where he was continued in the Indian department. He had his headquarters, at date of the negro's leaving the Indian country, among the Shawanese.

[2] That McKee after Crawford's defeat left Lower Sandusky for the Shawanese towns is certain.

half of that number were active, real warriors; as there was a great number of boys, old men, and even women who marched.

Upon the whole he does not think more than seven hundred were fit to bear arms, in which number he includes the hundred English [Caldwell's company]. The [Shawanese] towns were quite evacuated except a few women and children and some prisoners. These were busily employed in packing up their effects to push towards Detroit, in case Gen. Clark should beat their warriors, of which they were exceedingly apprehensive. They were determined, however, to meet and fight him near the town [Piqua, on Mad river, six miles below the present Springfield, O.] he drove them from, two years ago, about forty miles from where they now live.

The tribes assembled on this occasion were the Shawanese, Delawares, Wyandots, Mingoes, Monseys, Ottawas and Chippewas, which include the whole on this side the Lake [Erie]. He adds that every man was there who was able to crawl. Before McKee returned [from his short march towards Wheeling] he detached forty warriors with two Frenchmen, with orders to watch our frontiers and give intelligence of our movements, particularly if an expedition was "carrying on their backs," as he termed it.[1]

From a variety of circumstances I am led to give credit to the negro's account, particularly his mode of escape and his having lived two years with Blue Jacket, as much in the character of a steward or manager as a servant; besides, the fellow tells a plain, connected history. As I apprehended a circulation of this account through the country may be both satisfactory and useful, I have troubled you with it. If you are of this opinion, you will please to let it be as generally known as possible.

---

[1] After the negro left, the enemy successfully invaded Kentucky and gained the battle of the Blue Licks, in August. In September, the expedition against Wheeling was renewed (Zane to Irvine, September 17, 1782, Appendix M), but it availed them little. Gen. Clark met the enemy, finally, at what is now Piqua, Miami county, Ohio, on the 10th of November, 1782, surprising and routing them. (See Clark to Irvine, November 13, 1782, Appendix M.)

P. S.— Mr. Slover was present when I examined the negro; he says he lived in the family with him at the town [Wapatomica] and thinks he may be depended on.[1]

XIV.— COOK TO IRVINE.

September 3, 1782.

Sir:— I herewith send you as accurate a return as I believe can be made.[2] I have struck off some that were actually returned, to make an allowance for lee-way; and if I can depend upon the returns made to me, which I think there is not the least doubt, you may rely on this. I have collected the returns of the second battalion from the captains myself; and inclosed you have two of the colonels' returns, which will show you how much I have allowed for lee-way, I have no return from the third battalion, but I have received a letter declaring their quota completed. I have allowed him [the colonel of said battalion] for lee-way fifteen men and ten horses.

I have hereby showed you how I have formed my judgment of the matter. I have also sent to the different battalions and have let them know that they may expect the rendezvous will be about the 15th instant, but that they shall hear from me when it is absolutely appointed or set.

XV.— COOK TO IRVINE.

September 9, 1782.

Sir:— I received yours dated this day, and will take every effectual measure in my power to have the militia assembled by the day appointed. There is a number of them speaking to me to enquire of the general if he can furnish them pistols, swords and carbines suitable for light horse or cavalry. I have been importuned to mention it, and you may take what notice you think proper of it.

---

[1] I have been able to verify almost all the particulars of this interesting and very valuable account of the transactions of the enemy in the Indian country during the first half of the year 1782. The negro's recital was singularly truthful and clear.

[2] " Return " not found.

XVI.— Cook to Irvine.

September 19, 1782.

Sir:— I received yours by express. Those I have seen of the volunteers promise to hold themselves in readiness by the time appointed to march again. And, for further encouragement, I have promised them a tour of duty for the disappointment; with which they seem well satisfied. I have sent out people and taken every opportunity to give them notice respecting your order. I think there will not be that tardiness which appears now, when the day is appointed again; as they will have their provisions, etc., in a collective situation.

XVII.— Irvine to Cook.

Fort Pitt, *October* 10, 1782.

Sir:— Sundry uncertain accounts have arrived here purporting that the regular troops are countermanded, and that a cessation of arms has taken place,— particularly that the Indians are to be restrained from committing depredations, and much more, which, as I have no official accounts, I can give no credit to. But as some circumstances favor these reports, and it is also said David Tate has dispatches for me on the subject, in order to gain as much time as possible [and to save the militia the trouble of assembling again if unnecessary],[1] I have sent Major Rose,[2] my aid-de-camp, to try to meet him, and with directions to communicate to you as much of the contents as may be necessary for your information and government. You will, therefore, please on this occasion to give full credit to whatever directions he may give in the matter as if coming from me.[3]

---

[1] These words in brackets, in another copy of the same letter, are omitted.
[2] See p. 261, note.
[3] This letter was addressed,— "To Colonel Cook or Colonel Marshel, lieutenants of Westmoreland and Washington counties."

XVIII.— COOK TO IRVINE.

AT MY HOUSE, *October* 11 (3 o'clock), 1782.

Sir:— I am under great difficulties occasioned by reports that Captain Brady has given out at Hannastown respecting a cessation of arms, and the regulars who were coming being stopped. It has spread over the whole country and produced a general stagnation with respect to the expedition. There is also a copy of a letter written by General Potter to Joseph Brady, horsemaster general, desiring him to retire, there being no further call for him on account of a manifesto published by Carlton, etc.

The account from Hannastown circulated by Captain Brady came so well authenticated that I have waited this whole day for a letter from you. I was out yesterday and bought seven beeves [1] and appointed a number of people to drive these cattle up by to-day. . . . To-morrow, I think at all events to go on the business again. I have three coopers at work making kegs; but if these reports are groundless you will please to write me pretty fully on the subject, as I will have to send over the whole again; for the reports have done much hurt. I have heard of Captain Brady's returning to you, and having heard no account, I begin to conclude it must be false. It is

---

[1] The following is the account receipted, for these cattle:

"Brigadier General Irvine,

"In account with Colonel Edward Cook,   *Dr.*

"For beef cattle purchased by his request for the expedition, namely:

	£.	S.	P.
One beef cow cost, purchased of Wm. Reed	7.	0.	0.
" steer from William Walker	6.	10.	0.
" small do. from James Sterret	3.	0.	0.
Two cows from Conrad	11.	0.	0.
One bull from Paul Shower	4.	0.	0.
Thirty-six kegs bought from sundry persons	3.	12.	0.
One cow from Ethan Ellis	5.	10.	0.
	40.	12.	0.

"Received the amount of the above account the 26th of October, 1782.

"EDW. COOK."

asserted to me beyond a doubt that the regular troops destined here are turned back. I am very impatient to hear from you.

P. S.— I wrote a hasty line to Mr. Reed about horses and referred him to you. I expected to have had an answer from him before now. I see no prospect of getting horses here other than those already engaged by the volunteers. Captain Lynn, whom we were speaking about, is gone down the country.[1]

---

[1] This letter was met by Colonel John Gibson, one of the "officer express" sent out to see what caused the delay in the coming up of the regulars who were expected for the Sandusky expedition. The letter was opened by him, and upon it he wrote:

"Saturday, 12 o'clock.
"I took the liberty of reading the letter and shall proceed on, having learned nothing further than what is contained in it. I am, dear sir, with respect. JNO. GIBSON, Col."

The following letter contains information concerning the subject written about by Cook to Irvine above:

"UNION TOWN, *October* 10, 1782.
"*Dear Sir:*— I have been waiting your orders these several days last past, and when come to hand I know not what to do. However, I will always act in duty as far as able. I have this morning seen a copy of a letter from General Potter to General Brady of the horsemaster department, acquainting him that General Carleton had issued a manifesto that the savages should no longer harass our frontiers; on which General Potter requested General Brady to retire, as his assistance will not be wanting. However that may be, I know not. The copy was certified by Parson Mitchell; and the bearer said he saw the original. Yet I could wish the expedition to proceed, as I am of opinion it is the only season to distress the savage nations.

"One of the gentlemen you mention to be applied to for assistance will be in town to-day. I shall make my address to him agreeably to your request, and doubt not of his ready assistance. Colonel Morgan I mean; who has ever shown himself ready on such occasions, and whose influence is great in his own country.

"For the particulars of the letter from General Potter, I refer you to the express, who heard it read. If it be possible I shall attend the first of November, agreeable to your request, to hear what they have to say. I am, sir, with sincere regard, your very humble servant, ALEXANDER McCLEAN.

"Colonel EDWARD COOK."

XIX.— IRVINE TO COOK.

FORT PITT, *October* 18, 1782.

Sir:— I received your letter by Sergeant Porter, and one last night from Colonel Marshel, which is full of despondency. Indeed, by all the accounts I can collect it would be vain to insist on bringing the few willing people to the general rendezvous, as there is not the most distant prospect that half sufficient would assemble. Under these circumstances, I think it would be most advisable to give up the matter at once and direct the provision etc. to be restored to the owners.

It is with the utmost reluctance I can prevail on myself to give up the point, but find there is no alternative; for if even the regular troops should yet come, I do not think enough of volunteers would turn out to join them. Would it not however be well to advise people generally to salt as much meat as possible this winter. If the war continues there is little doubt but they will get a good price for it in the spring; and if it should be peace, vast numbers of people will come into and travel through this country; so that there is no danger of a good [bad] market whatever happens.

I suppose the beeves you have purchased will not lose any thing for some weeks in pasture. As soon as you think there is danger of that, I beg you will be so good as to hire some person to drive them down here; charge the hire in the beef account; and as to the kegs, if they cannot be disposed of, you will please to direct them to be stored and branded.

XX.— COOK TO IRVINE.

October 19, 1782.

Dear Sir:— Yours of the 18th inst. by Sergeant Porter [is received]. I shall only mention for the present that Colonel [Christopher] Hays and myself mean to see you about Friday next.

XXI.—Cook to Irvine.

At the New Town,[1] *October* 30, 1782.

Sir:—Inclosed you have an advertisement respecting the new state.[2] I hear of a great many more going to improve lands on the north of the Ohio.[3] It is a matter of speculation among some gentlemen learned in the law whether those improvements may not make a title, or rather lay the foundation for one; as there is no express law prohibiting the settlement, and no retrospect laws can be made. If it be so, I think your officers and soldiers ought to go and mark by thousands; as the only way to fight a rascal is by his own weapons.

I would beg leave to repeat the request about the two masons. I have tried all I can to get them in the country but to no effect. Some time next week would answer.

XXII.—Cook to Lieutenant-Colonel Stephen Bayard.[4]

Hannastown, *May* 15, 1783.

Sir:—If it were possible to let the ranging company have eight pounds powder and sixteen pounds of lead, as they are entirely out of ammunition, it would be of great service, as it is not known what the danger may be.

---

[1] Laid out by Col. Cook and by him named Freeport. The name was subsequently changed to Cookstown, in honor of its proprietor; and again, by act of incorporation, to Fayette City. It is fourteen miles below Brownsville, on the Monongahela, in Fayette county. It was not settled for twelve years after the date of this letter.

[2] Beyond the Ohio, in the Indian country, in what is now the state of Ohio.

[3] Within the limits of Pennsylvania.

[4] Bayard was then in command at Fort Pitt. This was just before Irvine's return from Carlisle, upon his second visit.

APPENDIX L.

IRVINE TO HIS WIFE.

I.

FORT PITT, *November* 14, 1781.

My Dearest Love:—I wrote you by one Reed the other day, just informing you of my arrival here. You can easily conceive of my anxiety to hear from you. I hope some person will come up soon that will bring some account from you. We had some extreme bad weather on the mountain, yet I never felt less fatigued nor injured by a journey in my life.

It is truly distressing to see how this country is laid waste, and more so to hear the lamentations of widows for their murdered husbands and children and the husband for his wife and children.[1] The wagons arrived this day only, and we will go to house-keeping to-morrow. We have hitherto been at lodgings. Colonel Gibson talks of sending an Ohio pike, by way of curiosity, for you and Mrs. Callender to dine on. I would send some venison, but fear it would not keep — of which and wild turkey, we have great plenty. I have not now time to write Mrs. Callender, but mean to do so by an express about a week hence.

Colonel Brodhead, Bayard, and other officers, will leave this [post] in a week.[2] Every thing is perfectly quiet in this quarter, though not so down at Kentucky, where, it is said, the Indians are troublesome.

---

[1] By this it will be seen that the horrors of the western border war, conducted as it was, on the part of Great Britain, against men, women and children, at once made a deep impression upon the mind of General Irvine.

[2] Colonel Daniel Brodhead, Lieutenant-Colonel Stephen Bayard and others left, though on what day is uncertain; but Bayard returned to his command of the "detachment of the Pennsylvania line" at that post.

II.

FORT PITT, *December* 2, 1781.

My Dearest Love:— I am still in a doubtful state about my dear little girl,[1] never having heard any other account than what your letter contained by John Kerr . . . I hope the pike got safe [to Carlisle]. We have great plenty of them — venison and turkey and other pretty good living. We even have a pack of hounds and go frequently a hunting.

There is no appearance of Indians in this country at present, nor are the people under the smallest apprehension before April.

III.

FORT PITT, *December* 29, 1781.

My Dearest Love:— This day I expected my express, but there is, as yet, no account of him, but I hourly look for him. The bearer, Mr. Joseph Bull [Schebosh], is an elder of the Moravian Indian congregation, who, together with the ministers, converts, etc., had built a pretty town and made good improvements, and lived for some years past, quite in the style of christian white people; but were last fall taken prisoners by a party of Indians commanded by that infamous rascal, Matt. Elliott,[2] and carried away, to the number of one

---

[1] Anne, the youngest child. There were then but two children in the family. The eldest was a son — Callender, afterward father of Dr. Wm. A. Irvine, now of Irvine, Warren county, Penn. The children born subsequently, were William N., Armstrong, Elizabeth, Mary B., and a daughter who died in infancy; also, Rebecca, James and John W.: in all, ten.

[2] Matthew Elliot was an Irishman by birth. He had formerly resided in Pennsylvania, east of the Alleghany mountains, and early engaged in the Indian trade, headquarters at Fort Pitt. He was thus employed when hostilities began in 1774, between the Virginians and the Mingoes and Shawanese. He remained in the Indian country until after the battle of Point Pleasant and the marching of Lord Dunmore to the Scioto river, protected by the savages. He was, in fact, their messenger,— sent by the Shawanese asking terms of peace with the Virginian governor. After the ending of "Lord Dunmore's War," he again traded from Fort Pitt, with the Indians, beyond the Ohio.

hundred families from their fine farms, into the wilderness, where they are starving.[1] Mr. Bull is going down to Bethlehem to represent the sufferings of his people to the society of the Moravians.[2] I wish I could appoint a day to be with you, but that is impossible.

On the 12th of November, 1776, he made his appearance in one of the missionary establishments of the Moravians upon the Tuscarawas river, with a number of horse-loads of merchandise, also a female Indian companion, and a hired man, on his way to the Shawanese towns upon the Scioto. He left the next day, but was followed by a party of six warriors from Sandusky and made prisoner, his goods being distributed among the Indians. He was taken to Detroit, where he succeeded in convincing the commandant of that post of his tory proclivities; was given a commission as captain and sent back to Pittsburgh as a spy. Here he remained some time, poisoning the minds of such as would listen to his seductive words; and, subsequently, in company with Alexander McKee and Simon Girty, fled from Pittsburgh; making his way to the Delawares first; then, to the Shawanese; and, finally, to Sandusky and Detroit. This was in the spring of 1778. In August of that year, he was attainted of high treason by Pennsylvania.

As an officer in the British Indian department at Detroit, he served during the revolution, vibrating between that post and the country of the Ohio Indians.

[1] This is an account of the breaking up of the Moravian mission upon the Tuscarawas about the 1st of September, 1781, by a party of Indians from the Sandusky river, where the missionaries and their families were carried together with the Moravian Indians. These finally located in October of that year, it will be remembered, at a point a little over two miles south of the present county-seat of Wyandot county, Ohio, but on the opposite (east side) of the stream, where they prepared to spend the winter. (Ante, pp. 59, 60.) They were, however, in a starving condition.

[2] A number of Moravian Indians, led by Mr. Bull, were, because of the scarcity of provisions upon the Sandusky, permitted by the Wyandots, during the latter part of October, 1782, to return to the valley of the Tuscarawas, to gather some of the corn left standing in the fields by the missionaries and their Indians. After Mr. Bull and his party arrived in the valley, they set to work harvesting the crop; finally, all, except five of their number and their leader, after some hard labor, started back with about four hundred bushels of corn, reaching the Sandusky in safety. Not so the six who remained behind. A small party pursuing some hostile savages who had been raiding into the settlements, followed the tracks of the latter to the Tuscarawas, where, at New Schœnbrunn, Mr. Bull and his five "Moravians" were found and captured. "The generous and humane officer" commanding those in pursuit of the marauding Indians, "on finding that they [Mr. Bull and his five 'Moravians'] were not of the enemy," took them back with him.

IV.

Fort Pitt, *April* 12, 1782.

My Dearest Love:—I received your two letters by Captain [Major Isaac] Craig and Mr. Hughes; I am, therefore, in arrears in the letter way; but the fault is not in me, being [as I am] extremely anxious to inform you of my arrival here, but I have not had a single opportunity. I had very cold weather, though dry, and made a speedy march. I got up [here] the Monday [March 25, 1782] after I left you. One of my horses took lame and I was obliged to leave him about half way.

Things were in a strange state when I arrived. A number of the country people had just returned from the Moravian towns, about one hundred miles distant, where, it is said, they did not spare either age or sex. What was more extraordinary, they did it in cool blood, having deliberated three days, during which time they were industrious in collecting all hands into their churches (they had embraced Christianity), when they fell on them while they were singing hymns and killed the whole. Many children were killed in their wretched mothers' arms. Whether, this was right or wrong, I do not pretend to determine.

Things were still in greater confusion nearer home [meaning nearer Fort Pitt]; for, on the morning [of March 24th] before my arrival here, a party of militia attacked some friendly Indians, who were not only under our protection but several actually had commissions in our service—at the very

---

They afterward reached Fort Pitt, where Gen. Irvine set them at liberty; the "Moravians" being allowed to return to the Sandusky and Mr. Bull to Bethlehem, Pennsylvania.

The party that followed the trail of the retreating savages from the Ohio river to New Schœnbrunn, was under command of Capt. John Biggs. Mr. Bull and his fellow prisoners were first taken to Fort Henry; thence to Fort Pitt, where they were treated very kindly by General Irvine, and finally released, as just mentioned. (See Appendix M,—Seidel to Irvine, April 11, 1782; and the answer of Irvine, May 8, following.) The regulars who were relieved by Lieut. John Hay, of the Washington county militia (ante, p. 280, note 3), guarded the six prisoners to Fort Pitt, during the first week in December.

nose of the garrison, on a small island in the river — of whom they killed several,[1] and also made prisoners of a guard of continental troops, and sent Colonel Gibson a message that they would also scalp him. A thousand lies are propagated all over the country against him, poor fellow, I am informed. The whole is occasioned by his unhappy connection with a certain tribe, which leads people to imagine, for this reason, that he has an attachment to Indians in general. However false this reasoning may be, yet no reasoning will or can convince people to the contrary.[2]

People who have had fathers, mothers, brothers or children, butchered, tortured, scalped, by the savages, reason very differently on the subject of killing the Moravians [that is, the Moravian Indians], to what people who live in the interior part of the country in perfect safety do. Their feelings are very different.[3] Whatever your private opinion of these matters may be, I conjure you by all the ties of affection and as you value my reputation, that you will keep your mind to yourself, and that you will not express any sentiment for or against these deeds;— as it may be alleged, the sentiments you ex-

---

[1] As this event occurred on the 24th of March and the return of Williamson and his men from the Tuscarawas was considerable time before it is very plain that the two transactions had no connection whatever (ante, p. 102, note 1), a constant reiteration in western histories to the contrary notwithstanding.

[2] The following extract is from a deposition by John Sappington to be found in Jefferson's *Notes* (new ed., 1853), p. 268:

"I was intimately acquainted with General [John] Gibson, and served under him during the late war, and I have a discharge from him now lying in the land office at Richmond, to which I refer any person for my character, who might be disposed to scruple my veracity. . . . I do not believe that Logan had any relations killed, except his brother [at the killing of the Mingoes, June 30, 1774, at Baker's Bottom, opposite the mouth of Yellow creek]. Neither of the squaws who were killed was his wife. Two of them were old women, and the third with her child which was saved, I have the best reason in the world to believe was the wife and child of General Gibson. I know he educated the child and took care of it as if it had been his own."

[3] It is to be inferred from this language of Irvine that the killing of the Moravian Indians was not generally denounced by the suffering bordermen — by those who had "had fathers, mothers, brothers, or children, butchered, tortured, scalped, by the savages." But Col. Edward Cook (who lived however

press may come from me or be mine. No man knows whether I approve or disapprove of killing the Moravians.

I called a meeting of most of the principal militia officers. They were convened here last Friday. After long conferences, which lasted near two days, they parted seemingly pleased with the plans I proposed to adopt for the protection of the country and promised they would support me.[1] I have also been fortunate enough to suppress the mutinous disposition of the troops without blood-shedding. From all this, you will make yourself easy respecting my present safety.

Some people are killed and some taken, by the Indians, in almost every quarter. I lost five of my men, a few days since, who were wood-cutting and carelessly laid down their arms to load the wagon, when a party rushed on them. This was at a fort [McIntosh] we have thirty miles down the river.

Whether my mind may change or not, I cannot say, but from the state of things at present I would not consent for the

---

rather more "in the interior part of the country"), writing to the governor of Pennsylvania, on the second day of September following, says:

"I am informed that you have it reported that the massacre of the Moravian Indians obtains the approbation of every man on this side the mountains, which I assure your excellency is false; that the better part of the community are of opinion the perpetrators of that wicked deed ought to be brought to condign punishment; that without something is done by government in the matter, it will disgrace the annals of the United States, and be an everlasting plea and cover for British cruelty."

There was, also, a man in Pittsburgh, though not a suffering borderer, who wrote very freely to his friends in disapprobation of the killing of the Moravian Indians, as the following extract from one of his letters clearly shows:

"The Pennsylvania militia formed an expedition against the Indians about three months ago; but, instead of going against the enemies of the country, they turned their thoughts on a robbing, plundering, murdering scheme, on our well-known friends, the Moravian Indians, all of whom they murdered in the most cool and deliberate manner (after living with them apparently in a friendly manner for three days), men, women, and children; in all, ninety-three tomahawked, scalped and burned, except one boy, who, after being scalped, made his escape to the Delaware Indians (relatives of the Moravians), who have ever since been exceeding cruel to all prisoners they have taken."— *Major William Croghan to William Davies, Virginia Secretary at War, July 6, 1782.*

[1] Ante, pp. 104, 284, 323.

universe to your coming up [here]. If your sister [Mrs. William] Neill lives in the country this summer and you could accomplish taking the children with you, I should have no objection to your spending some weeks with her. . . Major Craig brought me two shirts.

V.

FORT PITT, *May* 1, 1782.

My Dearest Love:— I wrote you yesterday by Captain Vanlear. By him, I also wrote Mr. [William] Neill [Irvine's brother-in-law] on business of his.

I received advices two days ago by express from the commander-in-chief, which creates a kind of suspicion that it is more than probable I shall not be much longer at this place, at this time, than till the latter end of July. From that time, perhaps, I may be absent till the first of November. But this is as yet uncertain and undetermined. As to sending for you under these circumstances, I cannot think of it. . . This is the most wretched and miserable vile hole ever man dwelt in; and for a woman, of any credit, delicacy, or humanity, I never saw such another.

My time is employed in the best manner I can think of; sometimes, trying to bring into some order and discipline the rascally, abandoned troops; at other times, riding, walking, hunting; and at others, gardening. But this, Mr. Rose and his man Henry attend particularly to. I assure you we have a pretty good garden, such as would pass with you as tolerable. How elegant our peas are — thick and fine! and we have wild tongue-grass, asparagus, and a variety of fine greens in great abundance.

There is no school, which is another grand objection [to your coming], as this is the time your dear son [Callender] should not lose an hour. Perhaps things may take a favorable turn. I am heartily tired and almost worn down with people coming daily for protection and assistance.

VI.

Fort Pitt, *May* 10, 1782.

My Dearest Love:— I have nothing new since I wrote you by Mr. Duncan. I got your little pathetic letter by Mr. Ormsby.

How little, my love, you must reflect on the hardships and sufferings that thousands undergo, ten thousand fold more grievous than yours, if possible. Consider what anguish must the poor, wretched mother feel who has a tomahawk struck into her infant's head while in her arms; and what is yet worse, some have their infants carried off they know not where nor for what purpose. The most hope they can have is that they may be living, but for what purpose — why, at best, to be brought up as savages, which I think worse than death.[1]

When you think seriously of these things, and much more I might enumerate, [you will see your condition in a more favorable light]. I dare say you see daily instances of people — your neighbors around — who, on many accounts, are more distressed than yourself. You know no real want, except a separation from me. My labors and exertions in the cause of my country and particularly my endeavors at this moment to avert some of the evils I have now mentioned, from some hundreds of [people of] this country, — though I do not reap many benefits or emoluments [therefrom], the day must come when some of my family must reap the rewards due my toils, in one way or other. This, however, ought to be a consolation, that whether matters turn out well or not in the end, I have done for the best.

VII.

Fort Pitt, *May* 21, 1782.

My Dearest Love:— I received your letter by Mr. Reed and will write you by him when he goes again, which he says will

---

[1] The horrors of the western border war are, in these few words, strikingly and truthfully depicted.

be in about a week. I stand much in need of a pair or two of thread-stockings and gloves — none to be got here.

I had some intention last week to go with a party of volunteer militia against an Indian town [Sandusky] but have now given up thoughts of it.[1] Mr. Rose, however, marched this morning. The town [Upper Sandusky] is upwards of two hundred miles distant from this place. It will be near a month before he can possibly return.[2] In the mean time I will apply myself close to gardening and making improvements on a spot over the river, which I hope to procure for Callender — 'tis a lovely spot indeed.

VIII.

FORT PITT, *June* 15, 1782.

My Dearest Love:— It is long indeed since I heard from you. I have expected Mr. Duncan a fortnight. Mr. Rose returned last night from the expedition with the militia against the Indian town Sandusky, but was unsuccessful. They fought part of two days, but were obliged to retreat without destroying the town, but lost only about forty men killed, wounded, and missing. Mr. Rose's horse was wounded.[3] As I am not certain of a sure conveyance for this I will not add [any thing more].

---

[1] The enterprise here spoken of was the expedition under Colonel William Crawford. The following relates to this expedition:

"BEDFORD, *May* 18, 1782.

"*Sir:* . . . On my way from the Standing Stone, I met sundry persons who came from the Monongahela and Washington county; all of them agree in reporting that a party consisting of upwards of six hundred volunteers are going against Sandusky and are to meet to-morrow at Mingo Bottom [on the east side of the Ohio], in order to cross the [Ohio] on their way to that place."— *Benard Dougherty to Pres't Moore.*

[2] See letter following, as to the return of "Mr. Rose."

[3] This is the only place I remember ever to have seen this fact stated.

APPENDIX M.

MISCELLANEOUS CORRESPONDENCE.

I.— COLONEL JOHN GIBSON[1] TO IRVINE.

FORT PITT, *January* 28, 1782.

Dear General:— Your letter from Proctor's by Ensign Morrison, with the money therein mentioned, came safe to

---

[1] John Gibson was born at Lancaster, Pennsylvania, May 23, 1740. He received a classical education, and was an excellent scholar at the age of eighteen, when he entered the service. His first campaign was under General Forbes, in the expedition which resulted in the acquisition of Fort Duquesne — afterward Fort Pitt — from the French. He then settled at Pittsburgh as a trader. War broke out in 1763 with the Indians, and Gibson was taken prisoner at the mouth of Beaver in what is now Beaver county, Pennsylvania, together with two men who were in his employ. They were, at the time, descending the Ohio in a canoe. One of his men was immediately tortured at the stake, and the other shared the same fate as soon as the party reached the Kanawha. Gibson, however, was preserved by an aged squaw, and adopted by her in the place of a son who had been killed in battle. In 1764, he was given up by the Indians to Col. Bouquet, when he again settled at Pittsburgh, resuming his occupation of trading with the Indians.

In 1774, Gibson acted a conspicuous part in the expedition against the Shawanese, under Lord Dunmore; particularly in negotiating the peace which followed. It was upon this occasion, near the waters of the Scioto river, in what is now Pickaway county, Ohio, that Logan, the Mingo chief, made to him the speech so celebrated in history.

On the breaking out of the revolution, Gibson was the western agent of Virginia, at Pittsburgh. After the treaty held in the fall of 1775, at that place, between the Delawares and the representatives of the Shawanese and Senecas on the one part, and the commissioners of the American congress on the other part, by which the neutrality of the first mentioned tribe was secured, he undertook a tour to the western Indians in the interests of peace. Upon his return, he entered the continental service, rising, finally, to the command of the 13th Virginia regiment, at Fort Pitt, in the summer of 1778, he having previously seen service east of the mountains. He remained at that post from that date until the close of the war, having several times the chief command, though temporarily, of the fort and its dependencies. For his ser-

hand.¹ Agreeable to your instructions, I have delivered to each of them thirty-six pounds [sterling], and am in hopes they will be able to enlist a number of men.

Since you left us, nothing material has happened only that the pork from Hannastown, which Mr. Huffnagle had engaged, did not arrive, and we were for three days without a single ounce of meat. However, the country people begin now to bring it in pretty fast, and when Wilson [one of the contractors] arrives I am in hopes we shall be well supplied.

I have engaged [John] Small to saw the plank for the platform, and as soon as the weather permits I shall begin to make the repairs you pointed out to me.

You must have had a disagreeable jaunt down the country, as the weather was excessive cold and the roads very bad. I could have wished you had staid until the snow fell, as it made the roads much better; but I hope by this time you have overcome your fatigue and are happy in the enjoyment of your family and friends. Captain [Isaac] Craig will deliver you this, to whom I beg leave to refer for the news at Fort Pitt. Major [Frederick] Vernon and Captain [Samuel] Brady go with him.² Captain Carnahan is still here. *He talks* of setting off in a few days. I shall be happy to hear from you by every opportunity and especially if the match between Mrs. Callender and Colonel [Stephen] Bayard is broken off. Please present my most respectful compliments to Mrs. Irvine and family, Major Rose, and the gentlemen of Carlisle.³

---

vices, a Virginia military land warrant was issued before December 31, 1784. He remained in the west and was a member of the convention which framed the constitution of Pennsylvania in 1790; and, subsequently, was a judge of Alleghany county, that state; also a major-general of militia. He was secretary of the territory of Indiana until it became a state, and, by virtue of his office, was, at one time, its acting governor. He died at Braddock's Field, in Alleghany county, April 10, 1822. At the time of his death, he was a pensioner under the act of March 18, 1818.

¹ Not found. It was written by Irvine on his way over the mountains from Fort Pitt. Proctor's was on the old Forbes road, in Westmoreland county, Pa.

² Craig soon returned to Fort Pitt (ante, p. 343). Captain Brady also came back (ante, p. 319, note; also, p. 336).

³ This letter was directed to Irvine, at Carlisle. It will be remembered that

II.—Captain John Finley to Irvine.

Fort Pitt, *Saturday Evening, February* 2, 1782.

Dear General:— This evening we are informed that the troops which compose this garrison, intend to mutiny, and have appointed Monday next to put it into execution. It appears to be general throughout all the corps. Mr. Tannehill's

before leaving Fort Pitt, he placed Gibson in temporary command of the post (ante, p. 85, note). During his absence, the following orders were issued (at the dates therein given) by Gibson:

"Fort Pitt, *January* 16, 1782.

"Orders. Colonel Gibson commanding. The colonel-commandant requests the favor of the officers of the day and guards at dinner in future."

"Fort Pitt, *January* 26, 1782.

"Orders. The troops in this district will be mustered between the fourth [first] and fifth of next month. The officers commanding corps will have as many of their number present as possible. Officers commanding companies will have muster rolls made out to the first of Feb'y 1782. The artillery will be mustered on the first of the month; the 7th Virginia regiment on the second; and the Pennsylvania detachment on the fourth.   John Finley, S. I."

"A detachment will parade to-morrow morning at troop-beating for a command of two weeks. Detail:

S[ubaltern]. S[erg't]. D[rum]. R[ank and F[ile].
"Pennsylvania detachment — 1.   0.   0.   9.
"Lieutenant [Samuel] Reed for command."

"Fort Pitt, *January* 27, 1782.

"Orders. Captain Clark, commanding. A garrison court-martial will set to-morrow morning at ten o'clock for the trial of Richard Richards, matross in Captain [Isaac] Craig's company of artillery. Captain [Uriah] Springer will preside: members — Captain [James] Lloyd, Lieutenant Crawford, Lieutenant [Jacob] Coleman, Lieutenant [Henry] Dawson."

"Fort Pitt, *January* 30, 1782.

"Orders. Captain Clark, commanding. At a garrison court-martial whereof Captain Springer was president, Richard Richards, a matross in Captain Craig's company of artillery, was tried for being out of the garrison after tattoo beating and abusing an inhabitant of the town of Pittsburgh;— no positive evidence appearing against him in support of the latter part of the charge, the court acquit [him] of it, but find him guilty of being out of the garrison after tattoo beating and sentence him to receive fifty lashes on his bare back by the drummer of the garrison. The commandant approves the sentence; and it [the punishment] is to take place this evening at retreat beating."

not bringing money to pay them appears to be their reason for such conduct. They have been repeatedly told that you would bring money with you to pay them, but they will not believe it. I dread the consequences, and am afraid it will be attended with the loss of some lives should they attempt to march off, which I think they will do. The officers seem determined to use every strategem to prevent it, and put a stop to it before that time; and if they still persist, we must try what force we can collect to oppose them. I will write you more fully by Mr. Duncan; he intends to leave this post on the tenth instant. I am busy mustering and inspecting the troops, and hope will have the abstract ready to send by Mr. Duncan.

"FORT PITT, *February* 12, 1782.

"A muster roll of the corps belonging to this detachment for the month of January, 1782, [is] to be given to Mr. Tannehill immediately, that he may be enabled to draw the subsistence and settle the accounts of provisions, agreeable to the instructions of the paymaster general."

"FORT PITT, *February* 17, 1782.

"A detachment from the troops of this garrison [is] to parade this evening, with their packs for a command of two weeks. Lieutenant [John] Harrison will command the detachment:

"S[ubaltern]. S[erg't]. C[orporal]. D[rum]. R[ank].
" 0. 0. 1. 0. 7.— Detachment;
" 0. 0. 0. 0. 6.— Guard."

"FORT PITT, *February* 20, 1782.

"The shoes which are arrived for the department are, agreeable to the returns, to be divided as follows: to the 7th Virginia regiment, forty-six pairs; to the detachment Pennsylvania line, thirty-eight pairs; to Captain Craig's company, twelve pairs. The officers commanding corps are requested to be very particular in delivering them to such as are most employed on duty and fatigue.

"Notwithstanding the repeated orders to the contrary, the commanding officer is sorry to see so much remissness in attending the parade. He requests that particular attention will be paid by every one to the former orders issued by General Irvine, and that in particular the rolls may be called after tattoo beating, and that all such as are absent at any time at roll-calling may be confined."

"FORT PITT, *February* 22, 1782.

"A garrison court-martial is to sit to-morrow for the trial of such prisoners as may be brought before it. Captain Clark is appointed president; Captain [Benjamin] Biggs, Captain-Lieutenant [William] Martin, Lieutenant [John] Ward, and Lieutenant [Jacob] Springer, members."

I am apprehensive from the information which Mr. Tannehill gives me that I shall get no clothing. He tells me he could get but little satisfaction from General Lincoln. After making a return of the officers of every rank at this post, nothing but the muster abstract was handed to the clothier general, where I find I was mustered on command to join my regiment. I hope you will set the matter in a clear light to the minister at war, as he may not know that you ordered me to remain here.[1]

There must have been some mistake in the calculation of the officers' subsistence at this post; they have sent but 9d. ½ per ration, and we are obliged to pay the contractors eleven pence half penny per ration. I hope you will represent this matter to the paymaster general. Mr. Tannehill informs me he will write the first opportunity to Mr. [John] Pierce [paymaster general] concerning it. I will be happy to see you at this post again.

P. S.— Col. Gibson is apprehensive that the gentleman that carries this letter will delay on the road, and does not write, as he expects a speedier conveyance shortly.[2]

III.— GEORGE GIBSON TO IRVINE.

YORK, *February* 5, 1782.

Dear Sir:— Mr. Lowrey[3] is of opinion that it will be almost impracticable to make a wagon road from Sandusky to Detroit until the summer month begins, the country being

---

[1] The following is the order referred to:

"FORT PITT, *December* 15, 1781..

"Captain John Finley is appointed to do the duty of brigade major and inspector at this post and its dependencies till further orders, in the room of Captain Joseph [L.] Finley, who is ordered [as a supernumerary] to join his regiment in the line."

[2] This letter was addressed to Irvine at Carlisle.

[3] Alexander Lowrey, the son of Lazarus Lowrey. He was born in the north of Ireland, in December, 1727. His parents, with several elder children, came to America in 1729, and settled in Donegal township, Lancaster county, Pennsylvania. His father became an Indian trader, which occupation Alexander entered about 1748, in partnership with Joseph Simon of the town of

low, level and swampy, many small rivulets that disembogue into Sandusky river being in the spring swelled to large, deep streams. He is certain that it would be exceeding tedious and not to be done without much labor.

He lays down the following route: Embark the armament at Fort Pitt during the spring freshets. Go down the Ohio to

---

Lancaster,— the fur trade with the Indians being at that period quite lucrative. The connection with Mr. Simon, continuing for forty years, was finally closed and settled without a word of difference between them, with large gains resulting, over many and severe losses from Indian depredations on their trains and trading posts.

Mr. Lowrey was, from the first, outspoken and ardent for separation from the mother country. In July, 1774, he was placed on the committee of correspondence for Lancaster, and was a member of the provincial conference held in Philadelphia on the 15th of that month; and of that convened in Carpenters' Hall, 18th of June, 1776; also of the convention of the 15th of July following. He was chosen to the assembly in 1775, and, with the exception of two or three years, served as a member of that body almost uninterruptedly until 1789. In May, 1777, he was appointed one of the commissioners to procure blankets for the army. In 1776, he commanded the third battalion of the Lancaster County Associators, and was in active service in the Jerseys during that year. As senior colonel he commanded the Lancaster county militia in the battle of Brandywine. At the close of the revolution, Colonel Lowrey retired to his fine farm adjoining Marietta. Under the constitution of 1789–90, he was commissioned by Governor Mifflin justice of the peace, an office he held until his death, which occurred on the 31st of January, 1806. His remains lie interred in Donegal church graveyard.

Colonel Lowrey was married three times: first to Mary Waters, in 1752; next to Mrs. Ann Alricks, widow of Hermanus Alricks, of Cumberland county; and lastly, to Mrs. Sarah Cochran, of York Springs, in 1793. He left two sons and three daughters by his first wife. The sons settled near Frankstown, leaving numerous descendants. His daughter Elizabeth married Daniel Elliott, of Cumberland county, who afterwards removed to Pittsburgh, and was engaged in Indian trade with his father-in-law. The daughter Mary married John Hay, who also went to Pittsburgh. Margaret, the youngest, married George Plumer who was born in Westmoreland county, and represented that district in the legislature and in congress for many years. By his second wife, he had one child, Frances, who married Samuel Evans, of Chester county, but they lived and died on Colonel Lowrey's home-place. Mrs. Evans had sons and daughters, and was a woman of great force of character and intelligence.

Colonel Lowrey was a remarkable man in many respects, and his life was an eventful one, whether considered in his long career in Indian trade, a patriot of the revolution, or the many years in which he gave his time and

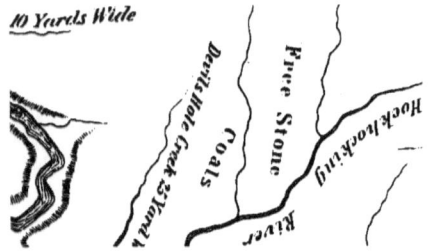

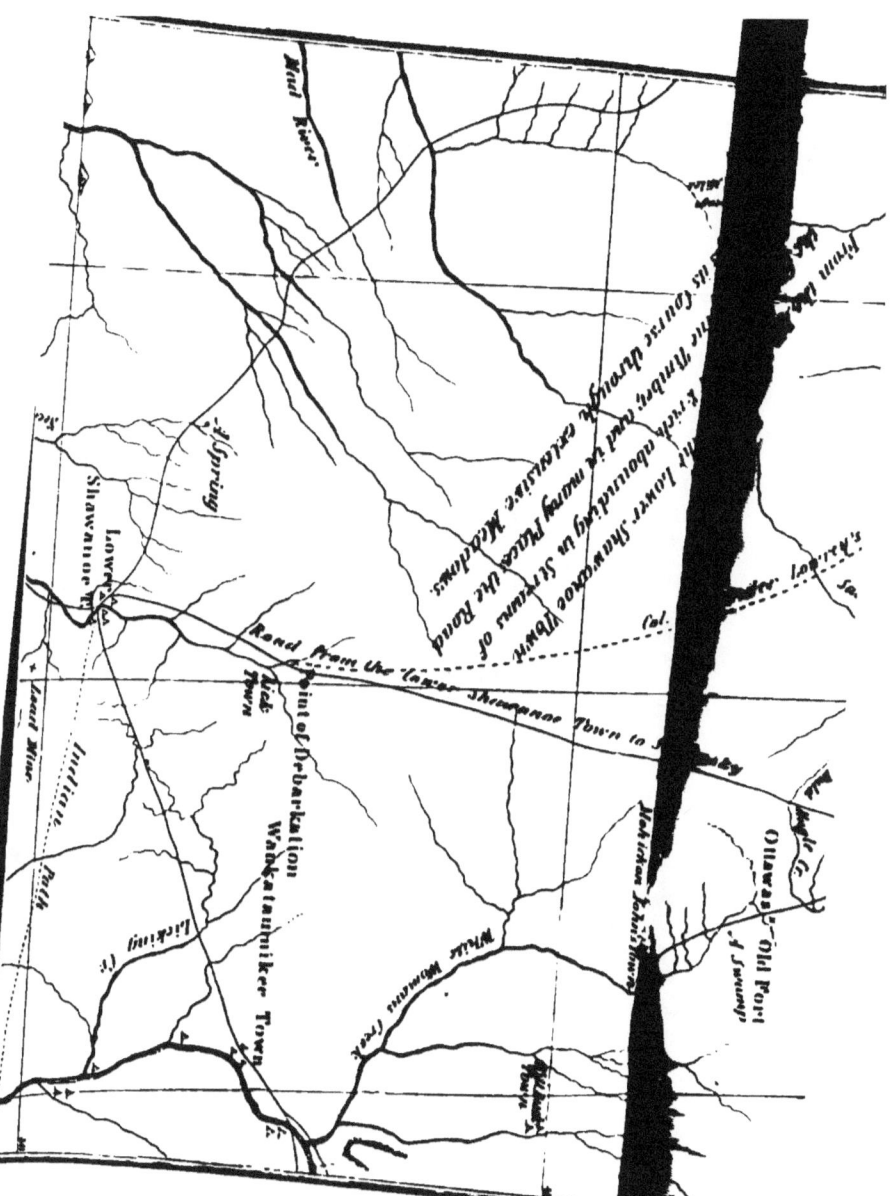

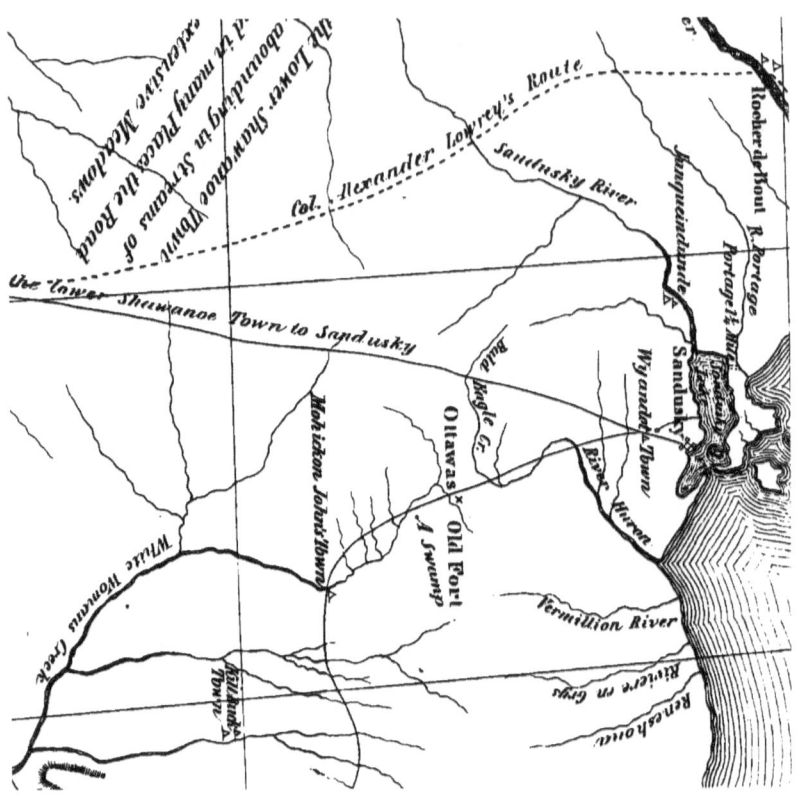

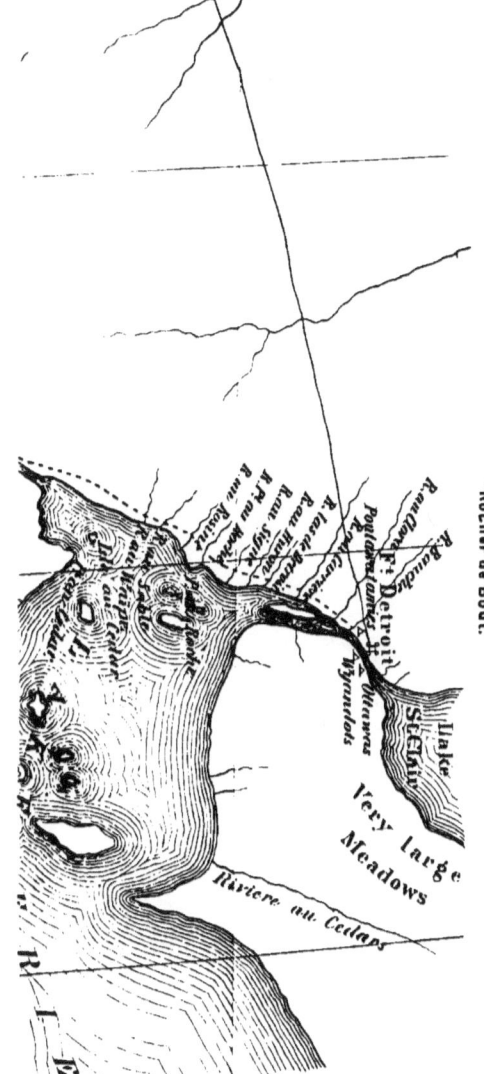

the Scioto; up that stream to the forks [now Columbus, Ohio]; and you may proceed above the forks, twenty miles.[1] Thence you shape your course for Rocher de Bout;[2] — a direct line from the salt lick town to that place will carry you clear of those streams I have before mentioned, as you will pass the heads of them and your route will be through a fine country, full of prairies (glades or savannas) and the woodlands are clear from underbrush.[3] The distance to Detroit is one hundred and forty or one hundred and fifty miles.

Boats large enough to carry an eighteen pounder may mount the Scioto at the aforesaid season (the spring). By this route you reduce your march more than one-half and escape the harassments of the savages; and the country, from its being so open, will not be so advantageous for these devils to act in. You may run down from Fort Pitt to Scioto in eight days; up the Scioto to the place of debarkation, in six days; and thence to Detroit, I suppose, in fifteen days, for he assures me

---

means to the service of his country. He was greatly beloved by his neighbors, and during his long life shared with his associate and friend, Colonel Galbraith, the confidence and leadership accorded to both in public, church, and local affairs.— Wm. H. Egle, in *Penn. Mag. of Hist. and Biog.*, Vol. IV, pp. 90-92.

It is evident from the wording of Mr. Gibson's letter, that Irvine had solicited him to make inquiries of Colonel Lowrey concerning the most practicable route from Pittsburgh to Detroit, for an army to travel; and, after making the inquiry, he (Gibson) gave the result of it to Irvine in the letter above.

[1] The point of debarkation cannot be determined with certainty for the reason that Col. Lowrey does not say which of the forks it was the custom to proceed up "twenty miles," whether the Scioto proper or the Olentangy.

[2] Rocher de Bout is not put down on any of the old maps. It was, no doubt, the Roche or Rocher de Bout — "Rock on End" — called, in English, "Standing Rock," located on the Maumee river, above the rapids at Waterville, some three or four miles above what is now Perrysburg and on the west side of the stream. In Howe's Hist. Coll. of Ohio, it is erroneously called "Rocher de Bœuf."

[3] It is quite impossible to trace, except approximately, the route taken from the point of debarkation to Rocher de Bout, from the description of it given by Colonel Lowrey. The only certainty about it is, that it was the shortest practicable route which kept clear of "the many small rivulets that disembogue into Sandusky river," which, "in the spring, were swelled to large, deep streams." The "glades or savannas" mentioned are the Sandusky plains (See, post p. 366, note 2).

the road may be made as fast as the troops can march. . . He (Mr. Lowrey) has gone frequently from the salt lick town to Detroit in eight days with pack horses.[1]

IV.— IRVINE TO COLONEL JOHN EVANS.[2]

FORT PITT, *March* 28, 1782.

Sir:—You will see by the enclosed resolutions of congress[3] the object of my command in this quarter, and I make no doubt you will easily conceive that from the jarring interests and other reasons, the advice and assistance of some of the principal people of this country will be necessary (indeed, indispensably so) for me.

I therefore wish to see you and such of your field officers as you may think proper to warn (at least one from every battalion in your county) at this post on Friday, the fifth day of April next. Punctually to the day will be necessary, as I have written to a number of gentlemen requesting their attendance at the same time. Whatever difference local situations may make in sentiments respecting territory, etc., a combination of forces to repel the enemy is clearly, I think, a duty we owe ourselves and country.[4]

V.— COLONEL RICHARD BUTLER[5] TO IRVINE.

CARLISLE, *March* 28, 1782.

Dear General:— I was yesterday honored with a letter from his excellency [General Washington], wherein he mentions his wish of the troops here being got in readiness as fast as

---

[1] This letter was directed to Irvine at Philadelphia.

[2] Lieutenant of Monongalia county, Virginia.

[3] Ante, p. 72, note 1.

[4] A similar letter was sent the same day to Col. David Shepherd, lieutenant of Ohio county, Virginia. The last clause, however, was not added to the letters of the same date sent to the lieutenants of Westmoreland and Washington counties, Pennsylvania. (Ante, p. 323.) It was thus the skillful and diplomatic writer poured oil upon the troubled waters of the boundary controversy.

[5] Richard Butler was made a lieutenant-colonel in the eighth Pennsylvania regiment, being promoted from major, March 12, 1777; he was afterward

possible to move, but not to march until his further orders.
He says he has ordered some clothing, etc., to be forwarded
and given the necessary orders to the quarter-master general
to provide camp equipage and carriage, etc., for the men on the
march; but, *if I divine right*, there is a hope of the enemy
evacuating Charlestown; if so, I shall hope an order [will be
given to march] *another way*. The French have taken Brimstone Hill by capitulation the most generous. The Dutch, it
is expected, will make peace with Britain. High debates [are
going on] in the British parliament for changing the mode of
the war. It is said Massachusetts has agreed to the duty on
imports; if so, then Delaware and Maryland, it is hoped, will
also; *and then* —

I waited on Mrs. Irvine to-day. She is very well, also the
children. I hope you and the other gentlemen have got up
safe and that you find matters better than you expected.[1] You
see, my dear general, I am determined to have you in debt in
the letter way. Please present my compliments to Colonel
Bayard[2] and assure him of my good wishes for him, and accept
the best wishes of your sincere friend.

VI.— Charles Campbell[3] to Irvine.

Sewickley,[4] *March* 28, 1782.

Sir:— I received instructions from Colonel Edward Cook to
make a draft in Colonel Pumroy's battalion and send them to

(June 9th) transferred to Morgan's rifle corps; he was, in 1781 and 1782, colonel of the fifth Pennsylvania. In 1783, he was at the head of the third regiment of that state. He was afterward agent of Indian affairs in the west;
and, in the expedition of St. Clair against the Indians, in 1791, was second in
command. He led the right wing of the army with the rank of major-general.
He was killed by the savages on the 4th of November, after receiving several
wounds, being tomahawked and scalped by the merciless foe. His brothers
were Lieutenant-Colonel William, Major Thomas, and Captain Edward.

[1] Butler has here reference to Irvine's return to Fort Pitt, this letter being
directed to him at that post, where he arrived, it will be remembered, the 25th
of March.

[2] From this it will be seen that Colonel Bayard had already returned to Fort
Pitt.

[3] Sub-lieutenant of Westmoreland county, Pennsylvania.

[4] Sewickley creek, a tributary of the Youghiogheny river, empties into the

Ligonier. But there are no arms nor ammunition to equip them, to go on their tour, nor yet are the officers in those parts willing to obey the orders that come from Colonel Cook as their county lieutenant. If your excellency sends me orders, they are much more willing to obey them, until some small disputes are settled. You will please let me know if you will supply the men with arms and the number that are to be called out. I would be glad to be informed if we are to be supplied with any men from below.[1]

VII.— Nathaniel Seidel[2] to Irvine.

Bethlehem [Pa.], *April* 11, 1782.

Esteemed Sir:— The bearer, Mr. Schebosh [Joseph Bull], having acquainted me and my brethren of the many marks of kindness and attention you were so condescending to show him on his being recaptured from the British and brought to your post last winter,[3] emboldens me in behalf of myself and the elders of the United Brethren's church, to recommend him to your further and particular notice. Any fresh kindness shown him will greatly add to that sense of gratitude we already have the satisfaction to feel, and any assistance in money will be punctually repaid.

We are exceedingly anxious by reports from sundry persons lately from Pittsburgh, importing that ninety-five Christian Indians, men, women and children, had been massacred[4] (by a

---

parent stream on the right about half way from the mouth of Jacob's creek to the confluence of the Youghiogheny with the Monongahela.

[1] That is, from over the mountains.

[2] Bishop of the Moravian church, or, as he calls it, "the United Brethren's church."

[3] Ante, p. 342, note 2.

[4] The reports about which the bishop was so anxious were those contained in Leinbach's "Relation" (ante, p. 237, note) and in three letters: one from Mr. John Etwine, dated Litiz, March 31, 1782, and two from Mr. George Niser, dated at York Town — the first on the 4th of April, 1782, the other the next day. In Etwine's letter was this information: "It is reported from Lancaster [Pa.], that 160 militia men from Ohio have destroyed two Delaware towns [and] have killed 95 Indians." In the first letter from Niser was this sentence: "I have seen a letter written by a woman at Pittsburgh, dated March 21, which contains these particulars: 'The militia have killed 99 of the Moravian

large number of volunteers[1] from the frontiers) in the towns on the Muskingum built by Indians in common with our church, but who were carried prisoners to Sandusky last fall, ere they had gathered their corn: this last circumstance adds much to our concern; fearing hunger had actually driven them back in search of food, and that they have met with so cruel a death.

It is further reported that a new expedition of the same kind, but composed of a larger number, was preparing to cut off the remainder at Sandusky.[2] Our anxiety on this head is very great; as well for the safety of our poor Indian congregation as also for our brethren, the missionaries. I therefore take the liberty of communicating my apprehension to your honor, hoping your authority will be extended to the utmost for their protection. Mr. Schebosh entertains some hopes of proceeding to his family at Sandusky.[3]

Indians, namely, 33 men and 66 women and children.'" The following is an extract from Niser's second letter: "The Moravian Indian congregation at Sandusky is butchered, as it is reported by the Scotch. They came and told them they must prepare directly for death. The Indians requested but an hour's time for this purpose, which was granted. They went to their meeting house to join in prayers to the Lord. After the hour had passed, they fell upon them and butchered all of them in cold blood, in the meeting house and then set fire to the house." (Compare, in this connection, Penn. Arch., vol. IX, p. 525.)

[1] This use of the word "volunteers" was wholly unwarranted, as Leinbach's "Relation" and the extracts from the letters of Etwine and Niser given in the preceding note conclusively show, without further reference. The men who went to the "Muskingum" are there spoken of as "militia," not as "volunteers," at all.

[2] The "further report" which the bishop here speaks of reached him in Leinbach's "Relation" and Etwine's letter. The former ends with these words: "Before these informants came away [that is, before Leinbach's two neighbors came from the Monongahela], it was agreed that 600 men should meet on the 18th of March, to go to Sandusky which is about 100 miles from Muskingum." In the letter of Etwine was this sentence: "There were 600 men ready to make another tour [after the return of the 160 'militia'] further up the country." (See Penn. Arch., vol. IX, p. 525.) From these reports, the bishop concludes that the object was to "cut off the remainder" of the Moravian Indians at Sandusky; but this conclusion had no other foundation than in his own imagination. (See p. 282 and note 3 thereto.)

[3] But these hopes were frustrated and he returned to Bethlehem, Pa. (See letter No. IX, following.)

VIII.—Lieutenant Samuel Bryson[1] to Irvine.

Fort McIntosh, *April* 29, 1782.

Sir:—I send you under guard, John Phillips and Thomas Steed, for behaving in a mutinous manner. I shall not, at this time, enter into a description of the manner in which they behaved, as the two men who guards them can give you particular information, they being the only ones who spiritedly took my part.

Phillips, who was sober, I cannot think myself justifiable in ever letting him out of the garrison with his life. But not having arms immediately in my power when I got rescued from him and observing a general sourness amongst the men — with his extraordinary conduct — induced me to suspect a premeditated design against me. Certain it is, from every thing I can learn, with the manner in which they embodied, that three-fourths of them were ready to join the mutineers; for which reason, I thought it most prudent for the safety of myself and the garrison to apply moderate measures first.[2]

There was a rascally boat's-crew lying under cover of the fort a night and part of a day, who found means to convey seven quarts of whisky to the men after roll-call yesterday morning; which, for some time, gave me an amazing trouble. Had it not been want of men I would have sent the crew to you, particularly from my being informed they were under guard at Pitt for the same crime. I had them searched; and to prevent any such trouble in future will suffer none to lay here longer than I examine them.

I wish to have two good men to replace the prisoners — and have nothing to fear in future; though the duty is much harder, it is done without a syllable of grumbling. I have experienced more insolence and grumbling for barely obliging them to do their duty consistent with the post since here, than I have met with in the army before.

There is not any appearance of an enemy yet. The plan of sending out patrols from the large plain which surrounds the

---
[1] Of the 2d Pennsylvania regiment.
[2] See p. 111 and note 2 thereto; also, p. 172.

fort might, I think, be fatal to the men; as the enemy, from an adjacent hill, can see every man who leaves the fort. Of course, they can concert a plan to ambuscade them under the cover of large trees bordering the plain. In place of that, I have four or five active woodsmen, whom I think of sending out with rifles, two of a night, and limit them to bounds of five, or six miles, on a hunting cruise and make their hours of coming in, the next day. They will have an equal chance with any scouting parties. If you disapprove of this plan, I shall hope to be informed by the bearer. I did not look upon your orders concerning the patrols as peremptory but discretionary.

IX.— IRVINE TO SEIDEL.

FORT PITT, *May* 8, 1782.

Sir:— I received your letter of the 11th April last, by Mr. Schebosh;[1] any attention paid him, when a prisoner, by me, was not meant to lay him, or any person for him, under the smallest obligation; it was dictated by humanity.[2]

As he can inform you verbally of the transaction at Muskingum, it will be unnecessary for me, at this time, to trouble you with an account of it.[3] He can also inform you of my intentions respecting future measures.

---

[1] See the bishop's letter to Irvine, ante, p. 358.

[2] An account of the capture of Joseph Bull (Schebosh) has already been given (see p. 342, note 2).

[3] By "the transaction at Muskingum" Irvine means the "Gnadenhuetten affair." It may here be stated, concerning this "transaction," that the reason why the militia were ordered out by Marshel at all was, because of Indian marauds and the belief that the towns upon the Tuscarawas were occupied by the marauders. Upon this point, contemporaneous evidence is positive (ante, p. 99, note 2; p. 239, note 4). The next question is, against *what* Indians were the militia sent? Here, too, contemporaneous evidence is unequivocal. The answer is, against "enemy Indians;" that is, hostile savages — marauding Indians, or those believed to be such (ante, p. 99, note 2; p. 237, note 1; p. 239, note 4, second paragraph; and p. 240, note 1). Marshel's ordering out the militia, therefore, "to go to Muskingum" was in accordance with legitimate warfare. Whatever acts were committed by them — whatever

I believe the missionaries are safe, and I can assure you it will always be pleasing to me to be able to render them service. I hope (and think it probable) they have removed farther than Sandusky; that being now a frontier, and one of the British and Indian barrier-towns, they cannot rationally expect to be safe at it.[1]

they did *after the valley of the Tuscarawas was reached*, he is not to be held accountable for. His intentions were patriotic, notwithstanding a "dark transaction" was the result.

[1] At the time that Bishop Seidel wrote the letter to which the above is an answer, he also wrote one of a like tenor to Col. Gibson. The answer of the latter was as follows:

"FORT PITT, *May* 9, 1782.

"*Sir:*— Your letter by Mr. Schebosh [Joseph Bull] of the 11th ultimo, came safe to hand. I am happy to find that the few small services I rendered to the gentlemen of your society in this quarter meet with the approbation of you and every other worthy character.

"Mr. Schebosh will be able to give you a particular account of the late horrid massacre perpetrated at the towns on Muskingum by a set of men, the most savage miscreants that ever degraded human nature. Had I have known of their intention before it was too late, I should have prevented it by informing the poor sufferers of it. I am in hopes in a few days to be able to send you a more particular account than any that has yet transpired, as I hope to obtain the deposition of a person who was an eye-witness of the whole transaction and disapproved of it. Should any accounts come to hand from Mr. [David] Zeisberger, or the other gentlemen of your society, you may depend on my transmitting it to you. Please present my compliments to Mr. William Henry Jr., &c.

"Believe me, with esteem, your most obed't humble servant,

"JNO. GIBSON,

"Rev. NATHANIEL SEIDEL. Col. 7th Va. Regiment."

The following extract is from Loskiel's "Hist. of the Mission of the United Brethren [Moravian]," P. III, p. 176: "Hearing that different companies of the believing Indians ["Moravians"] came occasionally from Sandusky to the settlements on the Muskingum [Tuscarawas branch] to fetch provisions, a party of murderers, about one hundred and fifty in number, assembled in the country near Whiling [Wheeling] and Buffaloe [Buffalo creek], determined first to surprise these Indians [the "Moravians"] and destroy the settlements and then march to Sandusky, where they might easily cut off the whole [Moravian] Indian congregation. As soon as Col. Gibson, at Pittsburgh, heard of this black design, he sent messengers to our Indians [the "Moravians"] on the Muskingum to give them timely notice of their danger: but they came too late." Upon what authority it is here affirmed that Gibson sent messengers to the Tuscarawas, is unknown. It could hardly have been upon the statements in his letter just given.

X.—Colonel William Crawford to Irvine.

Colonel Canon's,[1] *May* 20, 1782.

Sir:— At my arrival at this place,[2] I found a number of volunteers from Westmoreland county — about one hundred men. The Washington county people are to rendezvous at the Mingo Bottom [on the east side of the Ohio]. If common report can be true, there will be about three or four hundred men. I am afraid the smallest number. I should be happy to see you at the Mingo Bottom if it is convenient for you. I am much afraid guides will be wanting. None seem to be fixed on that I can find that will go. I can hear nothing of Thomas Nicholson[3] for scouting. To-morrow we shall be at the Mingo Bottom. About Wednesday we shall cross the Ohio and be able to begin our march on Thursday morning or Wednesday evening. I must beg your assistance in requesting Dr. Knight's coming as soon as possible. I can find him a horse from Colonel Canon's, if he can come that far. I shall write you from time to time as opportunity may offer.

XI.—Colonel Crawford to Irvine.

Mingo Bottom,[4] *May* 24, 1782.

Dear General:— Yours of the 20th was handed me by Major Rose, for which I am much obliged to you.

After much confusion in crossing the river [Ohio], having

---

[1] Now Canonsburgh, Washington county, Pennsylvania, then the home of John Canon. (See p. 284, note 2.)

[2] Crawford was on his way to meet the volunteers, who were to march against Sandusky.

[3] Thomas was a brother of Joseph Nicholson, who was famous as a scout, he having seen, perhaps, more service in that line, than any other person in the western country. He was with Washington in 1770, down the Ohio, to the Great Kanawha, proving himself upon that occasion, a useful guide. In Dunmore's war of 1774, he acted as pilot. He was also engaged in the same capacity in several expeditions, during the revolution, from Fort Pitt. After the war, he settled at Pittsburgh and died there.

[4] On the west side of the Ohio.

only four small canoes to ferry over men, horses and baggage,— we this day got over four hundred and sixty-eight men and to-morrow morning at eight o'clock we are to march; which I hope will be done. I shall endeavor to do all in my power for the good of my country; but, as those whom I command are volunteers and subject to alter their minds, I can only say I will do all I can for the best, and as far as I can. The whole at present seem determined to fight; and I am resolved they shall have an opportunity if I can [give them one] with a color of success. I shall take every precaution to prevent being surprised or getting into confusion.

Should it so happen that I can write to you before I return, I will.

I humbly thank you for favoring me with Major Rose, as he will be of great service to me.[1]

XII.—LIEUT. JOHN ROSE[2] TO IRVINE.

MINGO BOTTOM, *Friday, May* 24, 1782.

Sir:—The Mingo bottom is not a very long day's journey from Fort Pitt. Notwithstanding, I did not arrive here until the next day, late in the afternoon. I found everybody crossing, with the utmost expedition, the Ohio; and I myself pushed over immediately after my arrival. My fears that the present expedition would miscarry have been dispelled this very moment only. Colonels [David] Williamson and [William] Crawford did seem to have numerous and obstinate adherents. The latter carried the election this day but by five votes; and I cannot but give Colonel Williamson the utmost credit for his exhorting the whole to be unanimous after the election had been made known, and cheerfully submitted to be second in command. I think if it had been otherwise, Crawford would have pushed home and very likely we should have dis-

---

[1] This, it is believed, was the last letter ever written by the unfortunate colonel. The original is now in the possession of Lyman C. Draper, LL. D., of Madison, Wisconsin. The expedition started for Sandusky the next morning.

[2] Rose, it will be remembered, was aid-de-camp to Irvine. (See p. 117.)

Appendix M.

persed; which would have been likewise the case if Williamson had not behaved with so much prudence. One Colonel [Thomas] Gaddis is third in command; Colonel [John] McClelland, fourth; and Major [James] Brenton, fifth in command.

My presence caused, seemingly, uneasiness. It was surmised I had been sent to take command. An open declaration of mine, at a meeting of the officers, that I did not intend to take upon me any command of any kind whatsoever but to act as an aid-de-camp to the commanding officer, seemed to pacify everything, and all goes on charmingly. We expect to set out early to-morrow morning and are only detained by the want of some ammunition which has been sent for yesterday to McIntosh. We march, as you know, in four columns, etc. Our number is actually 480[1] men,— young, active, and seemingly spirited. I have the most sanguine hopes of our undertaking and am very sorry Colonel [James] Marshel [lieutenant of Washington county] does not march with us, who was within three or four votes of being third commander. I think him very popular, as much so as Colonel Williamson.

The report of an attack from the enemy upon the Rapids [Louisville, Kentucky] seems a mere invention. The men said to come from there have not been seen by anybody.

Major [William] Pollock has furnished me and Dr. Knight forty-five pounds of bacon. I cannot persuade him to take any pay for it, but a mere receipt. I do not understand upon what principles they furnish these articles.

I must beg the favor of you to receive my half-boots from Patrick Leonard and one pair of shoes, as I am already almost barefooted.[2]

---

[1] In Crawford's letter just given the number is stated at 463 that had then got over the river, but Rose's letter was, probably, written later in the day, when 12 more had succeeded in crossing.

[2] This letter gives much information concerning the organization of the expedition against Sandusky not obtainable from other sources. It was written at the Mingo bottom, on the west side of the Ohio, in what is now Jefferson county, Ohio, not far below Steubenville, as was the previous letter by Col. Crawford.

XIII.— COL. DAVID WILLIAMSON[1] TO IRVINE.

June 13, 1782.

Dear Sir:— I take the opportunity to make you acquainted with our retreat from the Sandusky plains,[2] June 6th. We were reduced to the necessity of making a forced march through their [the enemy's] lines in the night, much in disorder; but the main body marched round the Shawanese camp and was lucky enough to escape their fire. They marched the whole night, and the next morning were re-enforced by some companies which I cannot give a particular account of, as they were so irregular and so confused; but the number lost, I think, cannot be ascertained at this time. I must acknowledge my-

---

[1] He was colonel, it will be remembered, of the 3d battalion of Washington county militia, and second in command upon the Sandusky expedition. He was a son of John Williamson, and was born in 1752, near Carlisle, Pennsylvania. He came to the western country when a boy; he afterward returned home and persuaded his parents to emigrate beyond the Alleghanies. They settled upon Buffalo creek, in what was subsequently Washington county, about twelve miles from the Ohio. At that point, David had a "station" during the revolution, which, though often alarmed, was never attacked. From the commencement of Indian depredations, Williamson took an active part in the defense of the western border, having previously, during Dunmore's war, held a captain's commission. He was every where recognized as a true lover of his country — willing to make any sacrifice for its welfare. His activity in guarding the defenseless inhabitants of the frontier settlements was untiring. After the return of the Sandusky expedition, he was soon actively engaged in watching the exposed border — continuing his services until the restoration of peace. He was afterward popular with the people of his county, being first, county lieutenant and then elected, in 1787, to the office of sheriff. He was unsuccessful, however, in business, and died in poverty.

[2] That is, the retreat of the volunteers who, under Col. Wm. Crawford, had marched against Sandusky. The plains he speaks of, lie within the present counties of Crawford, Marion and Wyandot, Ohio, south and west of the Sandusky river, seldom reaching to its banks. This stream, however, may be said to bound them on the north in Crawford, and on the east in Wyandot county. In the former county, their eastern boundary is the Olentangy; in Wyandot, their western boundary is the Tymochtee. In general terms, we may bound the plains on the north by the Sandusky, on the east by the Olentangy, on the south by the Scioto, and on the west by the Tymochtee. Their extreme length, east and west, is something over forty miles; their greatest breadth, north and south, nearly twenty miles.

self ever obliged to Major Rose for his assistance both in the field of action and in the camp. His character, in our camp, is estimable, and his bravery cannot be outdone. Our country must be ever obliged to General Irvine for his favor done in the late expedition. Major Rose will give you a particular account of our retreat.[1] I hope when your honor takes into consideration the distress of the brave men in the present expedition, and the distress of our country in general, you will do us the favor to call the officers together, as our dependence is entirely upon you, and we are ready and willing to obey your commands when called upon. I have nothing more particular to write you.

P. S.—Colonel Crawford, our commandant, we can give no account of since the night of the retreat.[2]

XIV.— Lieut. Rose to Irvine.

Mingo Bottom, *June* 13th, 1782.

Sir:— Those volunteers who marched from here on the 24th of May last, under the command of Colonel Wm. Crawford, are this moment returned, and recrossing the Ohio with Colonel Williamson. I am very sorry to observe, they did not meet with that success which so spirited an enterprise and the heroic bravery of the greater part deserved.[3]

So small a body could only expect success by surprising the enemy. We therefore begun a rapid and secret march in the

---

[1] See next letter.

[2] Crawford, as previously mentioned, became separated from most of the volunteers; and, on the 7th of June, 1782, while endeavoring to make his way back, in the rear of his retreating forces, was captured by the savages, being four days after, tortured to death, in what is now Wyandot county. Upon the return march of the main force, the command devolved upon Williamson, who, after his arrival at the Mingo bottom, on the west side of the Ohio, sent the above letter to Irvine as his official report of the expedition,— but, to a great extent, as he indicates, leaving it to Lieut. Rose to give the details.

[3] This letter and the one immediately preceding are the American official reports of Crawford's campaign against Sandusky, both of which were written

straightest direction through the woods for the towns of Sandusky. Our horses soon tired under their heavy loads in those enormous hills and swamps, we had to cross. This obliged us to incline to the southward towards the Moravian towns, into a more level country, though more frequented by hunters and warriors. On crossing the Muskingum [Tuscara-

---

at the Mingo bottom on the west side of the Ohio. The following is the British and Indian official correspondence concerning the expedition:

[I.—JOHN TURNEY TO MAJOR A. S. DE PEYSTER, COMMANDING AT DETROIT.]

"CAMP UPPER SANDUSKY, *June* 7, 1782.

"*Sir:*—I am happy in having the pleasure of acquainting you with our success on the 4th and 5th instant. On the 4th, about 12 o'clock, the enemy appeared about two miles from this place. Captain [William] Caldwell, with the rangers and about two hundred Indians, marched out to fight them, and attacked them about 2 o'clock. The enemy immediately retreated to a copse of wood at a little distance, where they made a stand and had every advantage of us as to situation of ground people possibly could wish for; as there was but a small neck of woods that we could get possession of, which, when we once gained, the action became general and was dubious for some time till we obliged them to retreat about fifty yards, after which we were able to cover most of our men. The battle was very hot till night, which put a stop to firing. Both parties kept their ground all night.

"On the 5th at daybreak, we again commenced firing, which we kept up pretty briskly till we found the enemy did not wish to oppose us again. However, we kept firing at them whenever they dared show themselves. They made two attempts to sally, but were repulsed with loss. About 12 o'clock, we were joined by one hundred and forty Shawanese, and had got the enemy surrounded; but, through some mistake of the Indians, there was one pass left unguarded, through which they made their escape about 12 o'clock at night, though some of the Indians pursued them.

"They [the Indians] never alarmed our camp until daybreak. As soon as I heard of it [the retreat of the Americans], I pursued them with the rangers about two miles. The enemy were mostly on horseback. Some of the Indians who had horses followed and overtook them, killed a number, and it was owing to nothing but the country being very clear that any of them escaped.

"Captain Caldwell was wounded in both legs, the ball lodging in one. He left the field in the beginning of the action. Our loss is very inconsiderable. We had but one ranger killed and two wounded. Le Villier, the interpreter, and four Indians were killed and eight wounded. The loss of the enemy is one hundred killed and fifty wounded, as we are informed by the prisoners. The number of the killed we are certain of.

"Captain Caldwell started for Lower Sandusky on the evening of the 4th instant. I intend to march there likewise in a day or two, where I shall wait

was branch] on the 28th, we were unfortunate enough to be discovered by the enemy, which gave them sufficient time to prepare for our reception and alarm the adjacent Indian nations. Notwithstanding our small numbers, amounting in the whole to four hundred and eighty, we continued our march with great precaution and met the enemy the 4th of June at your orders unless something should turn up before I hear from you. They say [General George Rogers] Clark will be in the Shawanese country and that Sandusky is the most proper place for us to be at, till such time as we are certain the report is true.

"Too much cannot be said in praise of the officers and men and the Indians. No people could behave better. Captain [Matthew] Elliott and Lieutenant Clinch in particular signalized themselves. JOHN TURNEY,
"Major DE PEYSTER. Lieut. Corps of Rangers."

[II.—SAME TO SAME.]

"CAMP UPPER SANDUSKY, *June* 7, 1782.

"*Sir:*—I am desired by the Wyandots to return you thanks for the assistance you have sent them just in time of need, and they hope their Father will send them some provisions, ammunition and some clothing, as they say they are quite naked. They beg if possible a few more men; and the Half King a little rum to drink his majesty's health and the day on which he was born, as that was the day on which they defeated the enemy. They hope you will tell the Indians in general at Detroit to be ready to come to their assistance as soon as they send a runner, which may be in a few days as the enemy are coming into the Shawanese country. I am your most obedient, humble servant. JOHN TURNEY,
"Lieut. of the Rangers, commanding Upper Sandusky.
"Major DE PEYSTER."

[III.— SPEECH OF CAPTAIN SNAKE ON BEHALF OF THE MINGOES, SHAWANESE AND DELAWARES TO DE PEYSTER.]

"UPPER SANDUSKY, *June* 8 [7], 1782.

"*Father:*— What we asked of you this spring, it is needless to repeat, you granted to us. Your assistance came in good time. We have, with your people, defeated the enemy. There is another army coming against us from Kentucky. This we are certain of, not only from prisoners, but from our young men who are watching them.

"Father! We hope you will again grant our request and let the rangers remain at Lower Sandusky about ten days and then march for our villages. We hope, if possible, you will send some more of your people and stores, such as are necessary for warriors, with cannon and provision sufficient to maintain the Indians you may send to us. This you cannot do too soon, as we are determined if the enemy do not come into our country that we will go

the plains of Sandusky. Our advanced light horse fell in with them a short distance from their town, and at 4 P. M., the action was general, close and hot. Both parties contended obstinately for a piece of woods, which the enemy was forced to quit at sunset, with the loss of several scalps. We had five killed and nineteen wounded. The firing began early on the

into theirs; and we will give you all the assistance in our power to transport your provision and what other necessaries you may send for your people.

"We hope, Father! you will not fail but send us all assistance possible. [Three strings of black wampum.] CAPTAIN SNAKE.

"To Major DE PEYSTER, Commanding Detroit and dependencies."

[IV.— ALEX. McKEE OF THE BRITISH INDIAN DEPARTMENT TO DE PEYSTER.]

UPPER SANDUSKY, *June* 7, 1782.

"*Dear Sir:*— You have already an account of the repulse of five hundred of the enemy who advanced near to this place and were surrounded by near an equal number of Indians with the rangers; but, being too sure of taking the whole, and an unlucky maneuver of the Indians ordering the sentinels posted around them to fire, showed the enemy their weakest part through which they escaped under cover of a dark night. However, they were pursued and dispersed. But it is difficult to ascertain the numbers killed, as the Indians are still bringing in prisoners and scalps, and numbers are still after them whose intentions are to follow them to the Ohio. Many, by the prisoners' accounts, must perish in the woods, having left their clothes and baggage.

"The chiefs assembled here have also spoken to you their sentiments, which is to go against the enemy, provided they find the enemy is not coming soon against them from Kentucky; though it is generally believed they will; and that ten days or a fortnight will put us in certainty of their designs; in the mean time, that our forces be collected and wait at Sandusky until they send word what is further to be done. They likewise beg you to send them what further assistance you can, with a further supply of ammunition and stores suitable for warriors; as that on the way they think will not be sufficient and having already expended all they had. I shall go hence to Lower Sandusky where Captain Caldwell is and wounded, to see how matters can be settled there with the Indians, and thence proceed to the Shawanese towns. I am, with great respect, dear sir, your most obedient and very humble servant,

"Major A. S. DE PEYSTER, A. McKEE.

"Of the king's regiment, commanding Detroit, etc."

[V.— CAPTAIN WILLIAM CALDWELL, OF THE RANGERS, TO DE PEYSTER.]

"[LOWER] SANDUSKY, *June* 11, 1782.

"*Sir:*— No doubt but you must ere this have received Lieutenant Turney's letter from Upper Sandusky. At the time it was written, we were not able to ascertain properly the enemy's loss as the pursuers were not all returned. I

fifth. The enemy had received so severe a blow the preceding evening that he did not venture an attack, but contented himself to annoy us at a distance. We were so much encumbered with our wounded and sick, that the whole day was spent in their care and in preparing for a general attack the next night, which was thought dangerous with a part only. But our intentions were frustrated by the arrival of a large body of mounted rangers and two hundred Shawanese in the after-

now have the pleasure of transmitting to you as true an account as possible, which is, killed and wounded, two hundred and fifty. Amongst the prisoners [are] Colonel Crawford and some of the officers; amongst the killed is Major McClelland. Their officers I believe suffered much. Our loss is very inconsiderable: one ranger killed, myself and two wounded; Le Vellier killed; four Indians killed and eight wounded. The white men that are wounded are in a good way and I hope will be fit for service in a fortnight. The Delawares are still in pursuit, and I hope we will account for most of the six hundred. The lake Indians are very tardy. We had but forty-four of them in the action. I should be glad they would hasten, as I expect we will have occasion for them.

"I hope something will be done this summer. Clark, I believe, will soon be on his way for the Shawanese country; if so, we will have occasion for as many as possibly can be gathered. The Indian demands are great, and I have not a single thing to suffice them with. Provision is mostly their cry, which I hope you will send us a fresh supply of. Ammunition, tobacco, and such other things as are necessary for warriors, are requisite, if you please to send them.

"The Chief-with-one-Eye and Dewantale, with their bands, are going to Detroit; as it is their custom after striking a blow to return and see their families; but whatever you may tell them, they will do with pleasure. They behaved very well whilst with me. Sindewaltone, your friend, the little old chief, remains with me. I find him very useful, as he seems willing to do every thing in his power for the good of the service. He is of great service to me and a better soldier never went into the field.

"I received a ball through both my legs which obliged me to leave the field. If I had not been so unlucky I am induced to think, from the influence I have with the Indians, the enemy would not have left the place we surrounded them in. The young man who goes in with letters is a deserving young man and I hope you will reward him well. Please send us some pack ropes and stuff for bags as they will be very requisite. Capt. McKee sets out to-day for the Shawanese towns.   WM. CALDWELL,

"Major DE PEYSTER.   Captain Commanding at Sandusky.

"P. S.— I must beg leave to recommend Abraham Corn, whom I found very useful."

noon. As these succors rendered the enemy so vastly superior to us in numbers, and as they could collect all their forces in a circuit of about fifty miles, who kept pouring in hourly from all quarters to their relief, prudence dictated a retreat. This was effected in the night of the 5th and morning of the 6th instant.

The whole body was formed to take up their line of march,

[VI.— DE PEYSTER TO BRIG. GEN. H. W. POWELL, COMMANDING AT NIAGARA.]

"DETROIT, *June* 12, 1782.

"*Sir:*— I have the pleasure to inform you that the rangers and confederate Indians from this post, have been successful in opposing the enemy at Sandusky. I herewith enclose letters and Indian speeches to that purpose. You will see how they push me for more assistance, which it is not in my power to grant in the ruinous state the new fort is at present,— it having almost undergone an inundation. If this weather continues I fear it will level our works. The oldest people here do not remember such a rainy season. We are much at a loss for tools to carry on the works, and I shall want iron both for this place and Michillimackinac. If there is any on the communication, I hope you will be pleased to order it to be forwarded. A'T S. DE PEYSTER.

"Brig. Gen'l POWELL."

[VII.— DE PEYSTER TO THOMAS BROWN, SUPERINTENDENT OF INDIAN AFFAIRS.]

"DETROIT, *July* 18, 1782.

"*Sir:*— I am happy to inform you that the Indians from this quarter have gained a complete victory over six hundred of the enemy who had penetrated as far as Sandusky, with a view of destroying the Wyandots, men, women, and children, as they had done with ninety-six of the Christian Indians at Muskingum [Tuscarawas] a few weeks before.

"The affair of Sandusky happened on the 4th of June, when the enemy left two hundred and fifty in the field; and it is believed that few of the remainder escaped to Wheeling.

"Their major, [John] McClelland, and most of the officers were killed in the action. Colonel Crawford, who commanded, was taken in the pursuit and put to death by the Delawares, notwithstanding every means had been tried by an Indian officer [Matthew Elliott] present, to save his life. This the Delawares declare they did in retaliation for the affair of Muskingum [the 'Gnadenhuetten affair'].

"I am sorry that the imprudence of the enemy has been the means of reviving the old savage custom of putting their prisoners to death, which, with much pains and expense, we had weaned the Indians from, in this neighborhood. . . . A'T S. DE PEYSTER.

"THOS. BROWN, Sup't Indian Affairs."

and we had called in all our sentinels, when the enemy observing our intentions begun a hot fire. We secured all our wounded and retreated in four parties, of which that one suffered most, that retired along the common road between the encampments of the Shawanese and Delawares in our rear. In a body trained to the strictest discipline, some confusion would have arisen, upon such an occasion. Several were con-

[VIII.—Gen. Haldimand to Sir Guy Carlton.]

"Quebec, *July* 28, 1782.

" . . . It is necessary to acquaint your excellency, which I do with much concern, that a few days ago I had advice from Detroit that a party of rangers and Indians had fallen in with the enemy on the 4th and 5th ultimo as far advanced to destroy the Indian villages at Sandusky. The rebels were near six thousand strong and were severely dealt with, having two hundred and fifty killed and wounded. A most unfortunate circumstance which attended this recounter, though extremely bad in itself, will as usual be exaggerated. A Colonel Crawford (who commanded) and two captains were tortured by the Indians in retaliation for a wanton and barbarous massacre of about eighty Moravian Indians, lately committed at Muskingum by the Virginians, wherein it is said Mr. Crawford and some of that very party were perpetrators. I hope my letter will arrive time enough to prevent further mischief, though I am very fearful it will not stop here. This act of cruelty is to be more regretted, as it awakens in the Indians that barbarity to prisoners which the unwearied efforts of his majesty's ministers had totally extinguished. . .

"Frederick Haldimand."

[IX.—De Peyster to Gen. Fred'k Haldimand.]

"Detroit, *August* 18, 1782.

"I am just honored with your excellency's letter of the 11th of July, approving the conduct of the officers at the affair at Sandusky, and regretting the cruelty committed by some of the Indians upon Colonel Crawford, desiring me to assure them of your utter abhorrence of such proceedings. Believe me, sir, I have had my feelings upon this occasion; and foreseeing the retaliation the enemy would draw upon themselves from the Indians, I did every thing in my power to reconcile the Delawares to the horrid massacre their relations underwent at Muskingum, where ninety-three of those inoffensive people were put to death, by the people from American back settlements, in cool blood; and I believe I should have succeeded, had not the enemy so soon advanced with the intent, as they themselves declared, to exterminate the whole Wyandot tribe, not by words only, but even by exposing effigies, left hanging by the heels in every encampment.

"I had sent messengers throughout the Indian country, previous to the receipt of your excellency's letter, threatening to recall the troops, if they, the

sequently separated. But the main body was collected at day-break five miles from the place of action, on the ground where the town formerly stood. Here the command devolved upon Colonel Williamson, as Colonel Crawford was missing, whose loss we all regretted.

The enemy hung upon our rear through the plains. It was evidently their design to retard our march, until they could

---

Indians, did not desist from cruelty. I have frequently signified to the Indians how much you abhor cruelty, and I shall to-morrow dispatch a person I have great confidence in, to carry your instructions to the southern nations.

"We have been alarmed here with the accounts of a formidable body of the enemy, under the command of Gen. Hands, advancing this way, which occasioned my reinforcing Captain Caldwell, and sending Captain Grant to the Miamie with the armed vessels and gun-boats. Our scouts now report the enemy having retired. Captain Caldwell remains encamped on the banks of the Ohio, and Captain Grant arrived here yesterday. I have the honor to be, with great respect, sir, your excellency's most humble and most obedient servant,   A. S. DE PEYSTER.

"His Excellency General HALDIMAN, commander-in-chief, etc."

[X.— EXTRACT FROM A SPEECH DELIVERED TO BRIG. GEN. MCLEAN BY CHIEFS OF THE SIX NATIONS, 11 DEC., 1782.]

"We have hitherto, in general, refrained from retaliating their [the Americans'] cruelties, except in the instance of Colonel Crawford, the principal agent in the murder of the Moravians, and he was burned with justice and according to our custom."

The following extracts from American newspapers and a British periodical refer to Crawford's campaign:

I.

"It is reported, that a party of about 500 volunteers, who marched under the command of Colonel Crawford, from the neighborhood of Fort Pitt, against an Indian settlement called Sanduski, were attacked within nine miles of that place, and were obliged to retire. When the last accounts came from them they were at Muskingham, and it is said about thirty of the party are killed and wounded. Colonel Crawford is missing."— *Pennsylvania Packet*, July 4th, 1782.

II.

"Extract of a letter from Fort Pitt, 15 June, 1782:

'A party of volunteers, to the number of 400, under the command of Colonel William Crawford, formed a plan of surprising the upper town of Sandusky. We marched the 24th of May from the Mingo Bottom, on the Ohio river, with the utmost precaution and secrecy, through the woods, but were unfortunately discovered by some skulking Indians on crossing the Mus-

possess themselves of some advantageous ground in front, and so cut off our retreat, or oblige us to fight them to disadvantage. Though it was our business studiously to avoid engaging in the plains, on account of the enemy's superiority in light cavalry, they pressed our rear so hard, that we concluded upon a general and vigorous attack, whilst our light kingum [Tuscarawas] river. Notwithstanding our small number, we continued our march and met the enemy on the 4th of June in the plains of Sandusky a few miles from their town where they had sufficient time to collect their own forces and alarm the adjacent nations. A hot action ensued, which lasted from 4 o'clock P. M., until sunset. Both parties obstinately contended for an advantageous piece of ground, from which we drove the enemy with the loss of several scalps. We had 5 killed and 19 wounded in this action. The firing began at day-break on the 5th, and continued all day. Our party were so encumbered with their wounded that the whole day was spent in their care, in defending our guard, and in preparing for a vigorous attack the succeeding night. In the afternoon, a large body of mounted rangers and 200 Shawanese arrived to their relief. As this succor rendered the enemy so vastly superior to us and as all their forces lay in a circuit of 50 miles, who were hourly pouring in numbers, prudence dictated a retreat. This was effected on the morning of the 6th, with so much regularity that none of our wounded were left. The enemy pursued us twenty miles to the end of the plains and attempted to hinder us from entering the woods. This brought on a hot action for an hour, in which the enemy suffered so much, that they never afterwards attempted to molest us on our march. We had three killed and six wounded in this action. It is impossible for me to ascertain the loss of the enemy which was very considerable. Ours amounted in killed and missing to 30. Among the latter, Colonel Crawford.' "— *Pennsylvania Gazette*, July 17, 1782.

III.

"Extract of a letter dated Fort Pitt, July 6th, 1782:

'The expedition formed by Colonel Crawford with about 500 militia I suppose you have heard of, but now I have it in my power to give you the particulars as near as can well be collected. I think it was about the 6th of June, they arrived within two or three miles of Upper St. Dusky [Sandusky], an Indian town within 200 miles of Fort Pitt, near a northwest course, where the savages lay in ambuscade for them, and a warm action ensued, commencing about 3 in the afternoon, but in the utmost disorder; our people were obliged to retreat at dark. The Indians in company with some red-coats, mounted horses for speed and overhauled our people at a certain plain, 25 miles from the town, where they fought for a considerable time, but were again forced to make their best way home, the enemy hanging on their rear until they came to the Ohio. The details are so irregular it is not easy to ascertain the loss on our part, but I believe it is from 50 to 70 missing. Yesterday one Dr.

horse secured the entrance of the woods. In less than an hour the enemy gave way on all sides and never after attempted to molest us any more on our march. We had three killed and eight wounded in this action, besides several missing, who afterwards joined us again, before we crossed the Muskingum [Tuscarawas] on the 10th instant, between the two upper Moravian towns.

Knight who was taken with Col. Crawford arrived here after living for 21 days upon herbs in the woods. He says that five days after they were taken the Delaware Indians burnt the Col. with the most excruciating pain, first tied him to a long post with room to walk round it, then cut off his ears, after that blew squibs of powder on different parts of his body; then the squaws procured hickory brands and darted against such parts as they thought might most affect him; they then scalped him and slapped the scalp in the Dr.'s face,—told him that was his big captain; the Col. was still alive. This he thinks was an hour after the Col. was tied up, when he (the Dr.) was taken away. Just as he was leaving him the Col. leaned upon his knee and elbow for rest, when a squaw took a shovel of hot embers and threw upon his back to put him again in motion. The next day under the guard of one man the Dr. passed the same place and saw some of the Col.'s bones in the ashes. The Col. he says made little noise; he begged one Simon Girty, whom he formerly knew at Fort Pitt, to shoot him, but Girty said with a laugh he had no gun, that examples must take place. The Moravian towns were destroyed and inhabitants by our militia, and then told the Dr. there were Delaware towns which also must have an example, for which purpose he (the Dr.) must be sent there the next day. After one day's journey, with the one man guarding him, the morning following, the Indian loosed the pinions which bound the Dr. and fell to repairing the fire, when the Dr. picked up a stick and tho, weak, knocked him almost down and secured his gun, snapped her at the Indian, but could not get her off; however, the Indian ran and the Dr. made his escape. He says that the Delawares took nine besides himself and the Colonel; that the squaws and children as well as the men were employed in tomahawking them till the nine were killed. Such as fell into the hands of the Shawanese are well treated. The militia are greatly enraged and determined on having ample satisfaction.'"—*Pennsylvania Journal and Weekly Advertiser*, July 23, 1782.

IV.

"A gentleman from Fort Pitt informs, that another of Col. Crawford's party had escaped from the Indians by slipping from his guards whilst they were asleep. He says they tied Col. Harrison, who was taken in the same party, and was Col. Crawford's son-in-law, to a stake where they fired powder at him till he died; when they quartered him and left the quarters hanging on four poles. He adds that about 40 of the party had fallen into the hands of the savages."—*Same*, July 27, 1782.

The unremitting activity of Colonel Williamson surmounted every obstacle and difficulty, in getting the wounded along. Several of them are in a dangerous condition and want immediate assistance, of which they have been deprived since the loss of Dr. Knight.

V.

" Extract of a letter from Westmoreland county, Pa., 16 July, 1782:

'In a former letter I informed you of the unhappy fate of Col. Crawford, since which a man has made his escape from the Indians who says that fire was made for his torture, when a very heavy rain came on and obliged them to defer his execution. During the night he was left tied in the care of three Indians who fell asleep; that he got loose and escaped without waking the Indians and arrived here seven days after. He says the Indian from whom Dr. Knight escaped came to the town he was in, with his head much cut; that the Delawares applied to the Muncies for Col. Wm. Harrison (son-in-law to Crawford), who being given up was tortured in the most cruel manner, they having bound him to a stake, fired powder through every part of his skin for an hour, after which they cut him in quarters and hung them on stakes. This and other similar acts of barbarity the Indians said they did in revenge for the murders and robberies committed by our frontier inhabitants on their relations, the Moravians; and that in future they would spare none of our people.'"— *Pennsylvania Packet*, July 30, 1782.

VI.

"Richmond (Virginia), August 17th. . . After the barbarous massacre of Colonel Crawford, as mentioned in one of our late papers, the Delawares demanded his son-in-law, Colonel William Harrison, and his nephew [William] Crawford, of the Shawanese, by whom they had been taken; and they were accordingly given up. They both experienced the most horrid tortures until they were dead. Colonel Harrison was then quartered and stuck up on poles. One Slover was to have been put to death in the same manner; the fire had been once kindled for him, but a heavy shower of rain falling saved his life then, and before the next day he fortunately escaped."— *Same*, August 27, 1782.

VII.

"Ex'ract of a letter from a gentleman at Quebec, to his friend at Edinburgh, dated July 17, 1782. 'The resolutions of parliament to put an end to the American war, are, I am afraid, not transmitted to Canada, for the bloody butchery is still carrying on in the upper parts of this province. A Colonel Clark, commanding a large party of Americans in the Illinois country, has been for some years meditating an attempt upon Fort Detroit, but hitherto has always been defeated by the vigilance and activity of the Indians. This year Clark had assembled about 4,000 men, and by late letters we have heard, that he was on his march to Detroit. He had ordered a Major Crawford to

Since my arrival here, I find that different small parties who were separated from us either by the enemy or by fear, are arrived before us. Our loss will not exceed thirty men, at a moderate computation, in killed and missing. Colonel Crawford has not been heard of since the night of the 5th instant, and I fear is among the killed.

XV.—IRVINE TO COL. EVANS.

FORT PITT, *June* 18, 1782.

Sir:—I received your letter by Mr. Thomas in answer to mine of the 5th of April, and have ever since that time expected a direct application from you for a supply of ammunition, but your silence on that head leads me to think you had been provided at some other quarter; however, if you have not, and will take the trouble to send, I will furnish you with some; and, any assistance in my power to afford, you may depend on. I am informed by the secretary at war of Virginia that a company has been sent from Hampshire to your relief or assistance.

---

advance before his main body, with about 500 men, and they had actually reached St. Douskie, in the neighborhood of Detroit, when intelligence was brought to Major De Peyster, the commanding officer at the fort. He instantly collected all the Indians he could, and sent a Mr. Caldwell, a young American, with them, and a party of regulars, to surprise Major Crawford, before he was joined by Clark; he did so effectually, for he completely routed the party, and took about two hundred prisoners. The Indians, who were the chief actors in this scene, gave over the prisoners to their women, who instantly tomahawked every man of them with the most horrid circumstances of barbarity. It is unusual for the Indians to put their prisoners to death, but the Americans had this spring destroyed an Indian village, and put their women and children to the sword, for which inhuman act the Indian nations are resolved to take full revenge, as Crawford and his party wofully experienced."— *The Remembrancer* (Lond. 1782), Part II, pp. 255, 256.

XVI.— Captains Robert Beall and Thomas Moore[1] to Irvine.

Xings,[2] *June* 23, 1782.

Sir:— The unfortunate miscarriage of the late expedition [under Col. Crawford against Sandusky], the common interest of our country, and the loss of our friends, induce us to be thus forward in proposing another — the plan whereof we have herewith transmitted to you, the appearance it hath of being carried into execution, and our sincere wishes it may meet with your approbation. But if conceived impracticable, we rest assured some method will be by you adopted to lead us into the field where our actions shall more loudly proclaim the sentiments of our hearts than words can do here.

We do not wish to be understood as giving our own private sentiments, but those of the people generally in our quarter; for which purpose we are authorized to address you. And from accounts well authenticated, we assure you it is the wish of the people on this side the Monongahela river without a dissenting voice.

Mr. Benjamin Harrison will have the honor of delivering this, to whom we refer you for particulars if required, on whose information we wish you to depend, as it will be confined to strict truth.[3]

XVII.— Irvine to Captains Beall and Moore.

Fort Pitt, *June* 26, 1782.

Gentlemen:— I received your favor by Captain Harrison. Inclination as well as duty is a continual spur to me not only to acquiesce in, but to encourage every measure adopted for

---

[1] Robert Beall and Thomas Moore were captains in the Westmoreland militia.

[2] "Stewart's Crossings;" these "Xings" were nearly opposite the present town of Connellsville, Fayette county, Pennsylvania.

[3] On the 22d of the same month, these men also sent Irvine a proposition for "carrying" another expedition against Sandusky (see p. 123, note 2). Compare, in this connection, pp. 175, 303, 327, 329.

the public good. Your proposals on this occasion are so truly patriotic and spirited, that I should look on myself unpardonable were I to pass them unnoticed. As Captain Harrison is in full possession of my ideas on the subject, he can inform you better verbally than would perhaps be proper to commit fully to paper on some points. Your intention of putting yourself under my direction I have a most grateful sense of, and you may rest assured my constant endeavors shall be to merit the confidence and esteem of so worthy a body of men as those you represent.

XVIII.— COLONEL EVANS TO IRVINE.

MONONGALIA COUNTY, *June* 30, 1782.

Dear Sir:—It is his excellency, the governor's orders to me, that for the more effective protection of our western frontiers everything relative thereto should be submitted to your direction.[1]

I am therefore under the necessity of informing you by express of the dangerous situation of our frontiers in this state. The enemy are frequently in our settlements murdering, and we are situated in so scattering a manner that we are not able to assist one another in time of need. There are the Horse-Shoe, Tygart's Valley, West Fork, Dunkard Bottom and where I live, to defend; and, in the whole, we have not more than three hundred militia fit for duty. Those settlements are a very great distance apart, and no one settlement able to furnish men to the relief of the others. One article we are destitute of — that is provision; we have it not amongst us. The company from Hampshire I have stationed at Tygart's Valley, Horse-Shoe and West Fork. I have got a small supply of ammunition from government.

I pray you may adopt some mode of the men being furnished with provision, with orders to me for the number of men you may think proper to be kept in service. Provision is the greatest article and without your assistance I much fear our settlements will break. The defeat of Colonel Crawford

[1] The same orders from the governor of Virginia were sent to David Shepherd, the lieutenant of Ohio county (ante, p. 356, note 4).

occasions much dread. I fear what will be the event, without relief. I must make bold to apply to you for some paper to do the public writing on as I am quite without [any]. You will please to write your sentiments by the express so that I may be enabled [to know] in what manner to act.

XIX.— Michael Huffnagle to Irvine.

Hannastown, *July* 14, 1782.

Dear Sir:— At the request of Major Wilson, I am sorry to inform you that yesterday about two o'clock, this town was attacked by about one hundred Indians, and in a very little time the whole town except two houses was laid in ashes.[1] The people retired to the fort where they withstood the attack, which was very severe until after dark when they left us. The inhabitants here are in a very distressed situation, having lost all their property but what clothing they had on.

At the same time we were attacked here, another party attacked the settlement. What mischief they may have done we have not been able as yet to know; only that Mr. Hanna, here, had his wife and his daughter Jenny taken prisoners. Two were wounded — one out of the fort and one in. Lieutenant Brownlee and one of his children with one White's wife and two children were killed about two miles from town.

This far I wrote you this morning. The express has just returned and informs that when he came near Brush Run the Indians had attacked that place, and he was obliged to return. If you consider our situation, with only twenty of the inhabitants, seventeen guns and very little ammunition, to stand the attack in the manner we did, you will say that the people behaved bravely. I have lost what little property I had here, together with my papers. The records of the county, I shall, as soon as I can get horses, remove to Pittsburgh, as this place will in a few days be vacated. You will please to mention to Mr. Duncan to do all he can for the supplying of the garrison until I shall be able to get a horse, having lost my horse, saddle and bridle.

---

[1] Ante, pp. 250–253, 303; also, post, p. 383.

XX.—Irvine to Colonel Evans.

Fort Pitt, *July* 16, 1782.

Sir:—I did not receive your letter of the 30th of June until last night. How an express could be so long on the way is unaccountable to me. It is impossible for me to determine the number of men that would be necessary for the defense of the country you mention, not being acquainted with the situation, inroads of the enemy, nor any circumstances, except by slight information. But as government has already made arrangements for your defense on your representation, I do not wish to make any alteration, as long at least as those arrangements will answer the end. When they fail, I will doubtless give every assistance in my power. I am sorry, however, to inform you that I am straitened in all respects. As to provisions, if they are not in the country, it will be totally out of my power to give any assistance. Provisions for all parts of the army are now found by contract, at a certain sum for each ration; and a long regulation for the mode of issues, and directions ascertaining what will be vouchers for the contractors, are given, which would be too long for a letter. Upon the whole, unless you can find some person who will contract to furnish rations, I know not what is to be done. If any such person can be found in your quarter, who can give good security for his performance, I will enter into a contract. No money is to be advanced, but the contractor is to find the supplies and will be paid at a time agreed on. For this and other purposes, it would be best for you or some other intelligent person to come here, whom you may send, as the business cannot be transacted by letter. There is not an ounce of public salt now anywhere. The contractors find a proportion of salt with the rations.

P. S.—Inclosed is the present system for issuing provisions, which must be invariably adhered to, or the contractors cannot be paid.[1]

---

[1] These regulations are lengthy and are omitted, as possessing little interest.

XXI.— MICHAEL HUFFNAGLE TO IRVINE.

HANNASTOWN, *July* 17, 1782,— 4 o'clock, P. M.

Dear General:— I just this moment received yours by the soldier. I should have sent you an express on Saturday night, but could get no person to go, as the enemy did not entirely leave us until Sunday morning. A party of about sixty of our people went out last Monday and found where they were encamped within a mile of this place. And from the appearance of the camp they must have staid there all day Sunday. We have had parties out since and find their route to be towards the Kiskiminetas and that they have a large number of horses with them. They have likewise killed about one hundred head of cattle and horses and have only left about half a dozen horses for the inhabitants here.

Last Sunday morning, the enemy attacked at one Freeman's upon Loyalhanna, killed his son and took two daughters prisoners. From the best account I can collect, they have killed and taken twenty of the inhabitants hereabouts and burn and destroy as they go along. I take the liberty of mentioning if a strong party could follow that they might still be come up with them; having so much plunder and so many horses with them, I imagine they will go slow. As for the country rousing and following them, I am afraid we need not put any dependence on it; as several parties, some of thirty, others of fifty [men], would come in on Sunday and Monday last and stay about one hour, pity our situation, and push home again.

I am much afraid that the scouting parties stationed at the different posts have not done their duty. We discovered where the enemy had encamped and they must have been there for at least about ten days; as they had killed several horses and eat them about six miles from Brush run and right on the way towards Barr's fort. This morning about four miles from this place towards the Loyalhanna one of the men from this fort discovered four Indians whom he took to be spies.

I have mentioned to the inhabitants the subject of making

a stand here. They are willing to do everything in their power if assistance could be given them. It will take at least fifty men to keep a guard in the garrison and guard the people to get in their little crops, which ought to be done immediately; otherwise, they will be entirely lost. By a small party that returned last evening, I am informed from the different camps they saw, there must at least have been about two hundred of the enemy; and from the different accounts we have from all quarters, it seems that they had determined to make a general attack upon the frontiers.

Sheriff Jack has been kind enough to let me have a horse; to-morrow morning, I shall set out, and in a few days shall supply you with some whisky and cattle. I have just this moment been informed that Richard Wallace and one Anderson who were with Lochry, made their escape from Montreal and have arrived safe in this neighborhood. As soon as I shall be able to procure what intelligence they have, I shall inform you.

P. S.— The inhabitants of this place having lost what provisions they had, they made application to me to supply them with some. I had a quantity of flour and some meat. I took the liberty of supplying them and hope it will meet with your approbation; and when I shall see you [you can] give me particular directions for that purpose.

XXII.— IRVINE TO MRS. MARY WILLARD.

FORT PITT, *July* 21, 1782.

Madam:— The bearer informs me you have sent him to apply for the Indian to be delivered up to you who killed your family.[1] You know I offered to deliver him on your

---

[1] "In Pittsburgh (Pennsylvania), about the year 1782, one evening just in the twilight, there was found sitting in a porch, an Indian with a light pole in his hand. He spoke in broken English to the person of the house who first came out, and asked for milk. The person (a girl) ran in and returning with others of the family they came to see what it was that had something like the appearance of a human skeleton. He was to the last degree emaci-

other application, but through the advice of some of your friends, because you had some hope your daughter was not killed, you chose to have him remain with me to try to get her exchanged for him. In addition to your husband, you are

ated, with scarcely the semblance of flesh upon his bones. One of his limbs had been wounded; and it had been on one foot and by the help of the pole that he had made his way to this place. Being questioned, he appeared too weak to give an account of himself, but asked for milk, which was given him, and word sent to the commanding officer of the garrison at that place (General William Irvine), who sent a guard and had him taken to the garrison. After having had food and now being able to give some account of himself, he was questioned by the interpreter (Joseph Nicholson). He related that he had been on Beaver river trapping, and had a difference with a Mingo Indian who had shot him in the leg, because he had said he wished to come to the white people.

"Being told that this was not credible, but that he must tell the truth, and that in so doing he would fare the better, he gave the following account, to wit: that he was one of a party which had struck the settlement in the last moon, and attacked a fort, and killed some and took some prisoners.

"This appeared to be a fort known by the name of Waltour's fort by the account which he gave, which is at the distance of twenty-three miles from the town on the Pennsylvania road towards Philadelphia, and within eight miles of what is now Greensburg. He stated that it was there that he received his wound.

"The fact was that the old man Waltour, his daughter and two sons were at work in the field, having their guns at some distance, and which they seized, on the appearance of the Indians, and made towards the fort. This was, one of those stockades or block-houses to which a few families of the neighborhood collected in times of danger, and going to their fields in the day returned at night to this place of security.

"These persons in the field were pursued by the Indians and the young woman taken. The old man with his son kept up a fire as they retreated and had got to the distance of about an hundred and fifty yards from the fort when the old man fell. An Indian had got upon him and was about to take his scalp, when one in the fort directing his rifle, fired upon the Indian who made a horrid yell and made off, limping on one foot. This was in fact the very Indian, as it now appeared, that had come to the town. He confessed the fact, and said, that on the party with which he was, being pursued, he had hid himself in the bushes a few yards from the path, along which the people from the fort in pursuit of them came. After the mischief was done, a party of our people had pursued the Indians to the Alleghany river, tracing their course, and had found the body of the youmg woman whom they had taken prisoner but had tomahawked and left. The Indian, as we have said, continuing his story to the interpreter, gave us to understand that he lay three days without moving from the place where he first threw himself into the bushes,

now certain she is killed; you, therefore, wish to retaliate your vengeance on him, not considering there are numbers of people in the same situation as yourself.

Some of your near neighbors at Hannastown are killed and

until a pursuit might be over, lest he should be tracked; that after this he had got along on his hands and feet, until he found this pole in the marsh which he had used to assist him, and in the mean time had lived on berries and roots; that he had come to a post some distance, and thought of giving himself up, and lay all day on a hill above the place thinking whether he would or not, but seeing that they were all militia men and no regulars, he did not venture.

"The Indians well knew the distinction between regulars and militia, and from these last they expect no quarter.

"The post of which he spoke was about twelve miles from Pittsburgh on the Pennsylvania road at the crossings of what is called Turtle creek. It was now thirty-eight days since the affair of Waltour's fort, and during that time this miserable creature had subsisted on plants and roots and had made his way on one foot by the help of the pole. According to his account, he had first attempted a course to his own country by crossing the Alleghany river a considerable distance above the town, but strength failing to accomplish this, he had wished to gain the garrison where the regular troops were; having been at this place before the war; and, in fact, he was now known to some of the garrison by the name of Davy. I saw the Indian in the garrison after his confession, some days, and was struck with the endeavors of the creature to conciliate good-will by smiling and affecting placability and a friendly disposition.

"The question now was what to do with him. From the mode of war carried on by the savages, they are not entitled to the laws of nations. But are we not bound by the laws of nature, to spare those that are in our power; and does not our right to put to death cease, when an enemy ceases to have it in his power to injure us. This *diable boiteux*, or devil on two sticks, as they may be called — his leg and his pole — would not seem to be likely to come to war again.

"In the mean time the widow [Mrs. Mary Willard] of the man who had been killed at Waltour's fort and mother of the young woman who had been taken prisoner and found tomahawked, accompanied by a deputation of the people of the settlement, came to the garrison, and addressing themself to the commanding officer, demanded that the Indian should be delivered up that it might be done with him, as the widow and mother and relations of the deceased should think proper. After much deliberation, and the country being greatly dissatisfied that he was spared, and a great clamour prevailing through the settlement, it was thought advisable to let them take him, and he was accordingly delivered up to the militia of the party which came to demand him. He was put upon a horse and carried off with a view to take him to the spot where the first mischief had been done (Waltour's fort).

it is said some of them are prisoners. You ought, therefore, to consult the feelings of others as well as your own and do nothing rashly till you have the advice of the justices of the peace and principal inhabitants of the country. To these I

But, as they were carrying him along, his leg, the fracture of which by this time was almost healed, the surgeon of the garrison having attended to it, was broken again by a fall from the horse which had happened some way in the carrying him. The intention of the people was to summon a jury of the country and try him, at least for the sake of form, but, as they alleged, in order to ascertain whether he was the identical Indian that had been of the party of Waltour's fort; though it is not very probable he would have had an impartial trial, there having been a considerable prepossession against him.

The circumstance of being an Indian would have been sufficient evidence to condemn him. The idea was, in case of a verdict against him, which seemed morally certain, to execute him, according to the Indian manner, by torture and burning. For the fate of [Colonel William] Crawford and others, was at this time in the minds of the people, and they thought retaliation a principle of natural justice. But while the jury were collecting, some time must elapse, that night at least; for he was brought to the fort, or block-house in the evening. Accordingly, a strong guard was appointed to take care of him, while, in the mean time, one who had been deputed sheriff, went to summon a jury, and others to collect wood and materials for the burning, and to fix upon the place, which was to be the identical spot where he had received his wound, while about to scalp the man whom he had shot in the field, just as he was raising the scalp halloo, twisting his hand in the hair of the head, and brandishing his scalping-knife. It is to be presumed that the guard may be said to have been off their guard somewhat on account of the lameness of the prisoner, and the seeming impossibility that he could escape; but so it was, that while engaged in conversation on the burning that was to take place, or by some other means inattentive, he had climbed up at a remote corner of the block-house, where he was, and got to the joists, and thence upon the wall-plate of the block-house, and thence as was supposed got down on the outside between the roof and the wall-plate; for the block-house is so constructed that the roof overjuts the wall of the block-house, resting on the ends of the joists that protrude a foot or two beyond the wall, for the purpose of those within firing down upon the Indians, who may approach the house to set fire to it, or attempt the door. But so it was that, towards morning, the Indian was missed, and when the jury met, there was no Indian to be brought before them. Search had been made by the guard every where, and the jury joined in the search, and the militia went out in all directions, in order to track his course and regain the prisoner. But no discovery could be made, and the guard were much blamed for the want of vigilance; though some supposed that he had been let go on the principle of humanity that they might not be under the necessity of burning him.

The search had been abandoned, but three days, when a lad looking for

deliver him [the Indian], particularly. On his arrival with you, you will have the justices of the peace sent to and requested to attend on a certain day; on which day several militia officers and other inhabitants will likewise attend, when

his horses, saw an Indian with a pole or long stick, just getting on one of them by the help of a log or trunk of a fallen tree; he had made a bridle of bark as it appeared which was on the horse's head and with which and his stick guiding the horse he set off at a smart trot, in a direction towards the frontier of the settlement. The boy was afraid to discover himself, or reclaim his horse, but ran home and gave the alarm, on which a party in the course of the day was collected and set out in pursuit of the Indian. They tracked the horse until it was dark, and were then obliged to lie by; but in the morning taking it again, they tracked the horse as before, but found the course varied taking into branches of streams to prevent pursuit, and which greatly delayed them, requiring a considerable time tracing the stream and to find where the horse had taken the bank and come out; sometimes taking along hard ridges, though not directly in his course, where the tracks of the horse could not be seen; in this manner he had got on to the Alleghany river where they found the horse with the bark bridle, where he appeared to have been left but a short time before. The sweat was scarcely dry upon his sides; for the weather was warm and he appeared to have been ridden hard; the distance he had come was about ninety miles. It was presumed the Indian had swam the river, into the uninhabited (and what was then called the Indian) country, where it was unsafe for the small party that were in pursuit to follow.

"After the war, I took some pains to inform myself whether he had made his way good to the Indian towns, the nearest of which was Sandusky, at the distance of about two hundred miles; but it appeared that, after all his efforts, he had been unsuccessful, and had not reached home. He had been drowned in the river or famished in the woods, or his broken limb had occasioned his death."—H. H. Brackenridge.

The following account, written by Ephraim Douglass at Fort Pitt (see *Penn. Mag. of Hist. and Biog.*, vol. I., pp. 46–48), gives particulars, also, of the escape of the "pet Indian":

"PITTSBURGH, *July* 26, 1782.

"*My Dear General:* . . . Some three months ago, or thereabouts, a party of Indians made a stroke (as it is called in our country phrase) at a station [Waltour's] distinguished by the name of the owner of the place, Wolthower's (or, as near as I can come to a German name), when they killed an old man and his sons, and captivated [captured] one of his daughters.

"This massacre was committed so near the fort that the people from within fired upon the Indians so successfully as to wound several and prevent their scalping the dead. The girl was carried to within about six miles of this place, up the Alleghany river, where her bones were afterwards found with manifest marks on her skull of having been then knocked on the head and scalped. One

doubtless some form of trial will be gone into. I have enjoined the people who have charge of him not to suffer him to be hurt till this is done.[1] If after all due deliberation it is thought most expedient to spare his life for the present in furtherance of political purposes, and it will be inconvenient to secure him, he must be brought back here where he shall be kept safe for further investigation.

of the Indians who had been wounded in the leg, unable to make any considerable way and in this conditioned deserted by his companions, after subsisting himself upon the spontaneous productions of the woods for more than thirty successive days, crawled into this village in the most miserable plight conceivable. He was received by the military and carefully guarded till about five days ago, when, at the reiterated request of the relations of those unfortunate people whom he had been employed in murdering, he was delivered to four or five *country warriors* deputed to receive and conduct him to the place which had been the scene of his cruelties, distant about twenty-five miles. The wish, and perhaps the hope of getting some of our unfortunate captives restored to their friends for the release of this wretch, and the natural repugnance every man of spirit has to sacrificing uselessly the life of a fellow-creature whose hands are tied, to the resentment of an unthinking rabble, inclined the general to have his life spared, and to keep him still in close confinement. He was not delivered without some reluctance, and a peremptory forbiddance to put him to death without the concurrence of the magistrate and most respectable inhabitants of the district; they carried him, with every mark of exultation, away. Thus far, I give it you authentic; and this evening, one of the inhabitants returned to town, from Mr. Wolthower's neighborhood, who finishes the history of our pet Indian (so he was ludicrously called) in this manner: That a night or two ago, when his guards, as they ought to be, were in a profound sleep, our Indian stole a march upon them and has not since been seen or heard of.

"I may, perhaps, give you the sequel of this history another day; at present, I bid you good-night; my eyes refuse to light me any longer.

"PITTSBURGH, 4th of *August*, 1782.

"*Dear Sir:* To continue my narrative — our pet Indian is certainly gone; he was seen a day or two after the night of his escape very well mounted, and has not since been seen or heard of; the heroes, however, who had him in charge, or some of their friends or connection, ashamed of such egregious stupidity, and desirous of being thought barbarous murderers rather than negligent block-heads, have propagated several very different reports concerning his supposed execution, all of them believed to be as false as they are ridiculous. . . . EPHRAIM DOUGLASS.

"To Gen'l JAMES IRVINE."

[1] The following was the order issued by Irvine:

"You are hereby enjoined and required to take the Indian delivered into your charge by my order, and carry him safe into the settlement of Brush

XXIII.— EBENEZER ZANE[1] TO IRVINE.

WHEELING, *July* 22, 1782.

Sir:— I applied to Colonel Marshel for powder to furnish this garrison of that you have sent to Mingo Bottom. He tells me it is already issued to the militia, which lays us under the necessity of applying once more to you for thirty or forty pounds. Any powder you now furnish for the use of this garrison I will undertake to account for and replace if not burnt at the enemy.

Five militia are all the strength we have at present, except the inhabitants of the place. A few Indians have been viewing our garrison yesterday and have returned on their back track, in consequence of which we may shortly expect an attack. If any aid can be afforded, it will be very acceptable; if it cannot, we mean to support the place or perish in the attempt.

XXIV.— LIEUT.-COL. STEPHEN BAYARD TO COL. McCLEERY.

August 4, 1782.

Sir:— I have sent you by the bearer, William Hathaway, eight pounds powder and sixteen pounds lead for the particular use of Jackson's fort, which is all I could undertake to send in the general's [Irvine's] absence, who marches this morning with a party of regulars toward the Mingo Bottom.[2]

---

creek. You will afterward warn two justices of the peace, and request their attendance at such place as they shall think proper to appoint, with several other reputable inhabitants. Until this is done and their advice and direction had in the matter, you are, at your peril, not to hurt him nor suffer any person to do it. Given under my hand at Fort Pitt, July 21, 1782.

"To Joseph Studibaker, Francis Birely, Jacob Rudolph, Jacob Birely, Henry Willard, and Frederick Willard."

[1] Ebenezer Zane was born in Berkeley county, Virginia, October 7, 1747, and died in 1811. At an early day, he emigrated to the west and settled on the site of the present city of Wheeling, West Virginia.

[2] The following letter explains the reason for Irvine's march:

"PITTSBURGH, *August* 4, 1782.

"*My Dear General:*— . . . The Indians appear at length to have taken up the business of killing us in good earnest. Within this week, they made an attempt (happily a fruitless one) within a mile and a half of this place, upon a number of people — whites and slaves at work in the cornfield of a

Appendix M.

When he returns, you will no doubt be supplied with ammunition for the rangers.[1]

gentleman living in town [Pittsburgh]. They were pursued without success. Since this, they have been frequently seen in our neighborhood and have killed several within a few miles of us. The general [William Irvine] has had so many alarming accounts by expresses from Washington county of the numbers and probable designs of the savages at or toward Wheeling, that this morning he marched in person with so many of his regulars as he thought prudent to take from the defense of this post, in order to join a body of militia or volunteers assembled for the purpose. With these, he means to make a trial of the spirit of the Indians; and, from the complexion of the commander and forwardness of the troops, I think he will push them hard if they stay his arrival. The number of the enemy is estimated at about one hundred. The gentleman who first viewed them and made this computation was Major [Samuel] McCullogh [McColloch], a militia officer of invincible spirit and acknowledged enterprise. On his first discovery of them, they had not yet crossed the river. He returned to a neighboring fort, from whence he wrote letters to apprise the country, and at the same time communicated it [sic] to the county lieutenants. [See Marshel to Irvine, July 30, 1782, ante, p. 306.] Still desirous of keeping a strict watch upon their motions, he returned towards the river with his brother and some others accompanying him. In his way, he came upon the track of some of the en my who had crossed the river, and having penetrated some distance into the country were now on their return; in all probability, they had discovered McCullogh's party, for, having with their usual artfulness made a *double* upon, and way-laid their own track, they fired upon them undiscovered, and the unfortunate major lost his life, justly regretted by all who know his character. The rest of the little party fled, but not till the brother of the unfortunate had shot the Indian who attempted to scalp him. About the same time, two young men were fired upon in a canoe almost within sight of Wheeling (Milnes and Smith), the latter wounded in the flesh of his thigh, the other's thigh broken by one of the thirteen balls that entered his body and limbs; they were both alive when the accounts came away. . . .

"EPHRAIM DOUGLASS.

"To GEN. JAMES IRVINE."—[*Penn. Mag. of Hist. and Biog.*, Vol. 1, p. 43. For a biographical sketch of McColloch, see Doddridge's *Notes* (new ed.), p. 301]

[1] Col. William McCleery was one of the sub-lieutenants of Washington county(ante, p. 279, note 1). He wrote the following letter to Irvine which called out, in the general's absence, the letter of Col. Bayard above:

"TRAVELLER'S REST, WASHINGTON COUNTY, *August* 3, 1782.

"*Dear Sir:*— The bearer will call upon you for powder, lead and flints for the use of the ranging company allotted for the defense of our frontiers [two months] the time proposed for their continuance.

"Permit me to observe that a small magazine kept at this place for the purpose of furnishing those men men that may be called upon to repel the

XXV.— BRIG.-GEN. GEORGE ROGERS CLARK[1] TO IRVINE.

FORT NELSON,[2] *August* 10, 1782.

Sir:—By Major Walls, I learn that you intend to make a grand push against the enemy on the lakes this fall,[3] which enemy from time to time, should they penetrate into our settlements, would render essential service both to ourselves and country. I intended to have consulted you upon this matter at Catfish [ante, p. 303, note 1], but in the hurry and confusion of that day, it was neglected. However, should you think such a proceeding consistent, you will be good enough to augment the quantity allotted for the rangers, so as I may be enabled to furnish for the above purposes. At the same time, please to observe that men living in the woods, exposed to the weather (as these rangers must be), will need more ammunition than those stationed at a garrison. Also, be good enough to order us good rifle powder, as that sent me before was really bad. I should be glad if you would write me by the return of this express, the situation of matters relative to the late incursion of the enemy. Inclosed I have sent your newspapers, which I forgot to return to you at Catfish."

[1] George Rogers Clark was born in Albemarle county, Virginia, on the 19th of November, 1752. He was originally a land surveyor. He commanded a company in Dunmore's war of 1774. The year following, he went to Kentucky and took command of the armed settlers there. In the spring of 1778, Major Clark was entrusted with the command of an expedition against the Illinois country, then in possession of the British. The enterprise was undertaken under the auspices of Virginia, and was entirely successful. He was promoted to a colonelcy by the authorities of his native state, and while engaged in a pacification of the Indian tribes upon or near the Mississippi, he learned that Lieutenant Governor Henry Hamilton, of Detroit, had captured Vincennes, and that further blows were to be struck against American posts. Anticipating the enemy, Colonel Clark marched, on the 7th of February, 1779, with one hundred and seventy-five men, against Vincennes. He had to traverse a wilderness and the drowned lands of Illinois, suffering every privation from wet, cold and hunger. Vincennes surrendered. Hamilton was made prisoner and sent to Virginia. In August, 1780, Clark led a force against the Shawanese Indians, located upon the waters of the Mad river, in what is now the state of Ohio, defeating them with considerable loss. During Arnold's invasion, he took a temporary command under Baron Steuben. His next enterprise was directed against Detroit, the site of the present city of that name in the state of Michigan. He was now a brigadier general. This expedition proved a failure. (Ante, pp. 53, 76, etc.) In the fall of 1782, he made a successful campaign from Kentucky against the Indians (see, letters, p. 401), but upon a like service in 1786, was unsuccessful. He died near Louisville, Kentucky, February 13, 1818.

[2] At Louisville, Kentucky.

[3] Referring to General Irvine's contemplated expedition against Sandusky.

information occasions me to send this express to know of you the time you march and what is your object. If you will be so good as to favor me with such intelligence it may be much to the public interest, as it will be in our power to make a diversion much in favor of you if nothing intervenes to prevent us.[1]

XXVI.—Brig.-Gen. Edward Stevens[2] to Irvine.

Virginia, Culpeper Court House, *August* 25, 1782.

Sir:— In consequence of the information that the executive of this state has received respecting the apprehensions that Fort Pitt, in a little time, will be invested by an army of English and Indians, the governor has ordered a body of militia in the most convenient counties to hold themselves in readiness to march at the shortest notice (in case of necessity) to the relief of that place. And as I am appointed to the command of these men, I think it necessary that a correspondence should be opened between the commanding officer there and myself, as my movements altogether will be governed by the intelligence I may receive from that quarter.

---

[1] What Clark refers to here is, a contemplated march against the Shawanese upon the upper waters of the Great Miami river, in the western part of what is now the state of Ohio. This letter was received by Irvine, Sept. 2, 1782.

[2] Edward Stevens was born in Culpeper county, Virginia, in 1745, and died at his seat there, August 17, 1820. At the commencement of the revolution, he commanded with distinction a battalion of riflemen at the battle of Great Bridge, near Norfolk, Virginia. He was soon after made colonel of the 10th Virginia regiment, with which he joined Washington. At the battle of Brandywine, September 11, 1777, by his gallant exertions, he saved a part of the army from capture, checked the enemy, and secured the retreat. He also distinguished himself at Germantown; and, being made a brigadier general of Virginia militia, fought at Camden, also Guilford Court House, where his skilful dispositions were exceedingly serviceable to the army, and where, though severely wounded in the thigh, he brought off his troops in good order. General Greene bestowed on him marked commendation. At Yorktown, he performed important duties; and all through the war he possessed a large share of the respect and confidence of Washington. He was a member of the state senate from the adoption of the state constitution until 1790.

XXVII.— IRVINE TO BRIG.-GEN. STEVENS.

FORT PITT, *September* 3, 1782.

Sir:— I have received your favor of the 25th ult. About the middle of July, appearances were threatening.[1] Hanna's, a county town, was attacked and burned, and a number of the inhabitants killed and taken. At the same time, Wheeling was, in some degree, blockaded; a large body of Indians kept skulking about it for five or six days. In short, they appeared almost in every quarter, and the people of the county were alarmed beyond conception. Since the first of August, every thing has been perfectly quiet. As I am not apprised at present of the enemy's intentions against this place, except what Governor Harrison and your letters contain, I am at a loss to know whether congress or the secretary of war ground their fears on the alarming accounts received from here in July, or on intelligence from some other quarter. Should we be threatened with danger or the enemy make actual approaches, you shall have the earliest information in my power; your aid, in that case, will be much wanted and of course very acceptable.

I have been meditating for some time an excursion into the Indian country. If effected, my troops will be chiefly volunteer militia of the country, who propose, on this occasion, not only to equip and feed themselves, but also to provide provisions for such continental troops as I shall be able to take from this post. If we succeed, I hope it will nearly put an end to the Indian war in this quarter. I am made the more sanguine in this business by an express last night from General Clark,[2] in order to concert measures for a descent from his quarter at the same time.

---

[1] "Every new day produces events worse than the past, besides a thousand false and groundless reports attended with all the evil consequences to the defenseless and terrified inhabitants that the reality of them could produce; our settlements are almost every day contracted and every new frontier more timid than the last."— *Ephraim Douglass.*

[2] See Clark to Irvine, August 10, 1782, p. 392.

XXVIII.—Irvine to Captain Hugh Willy.[1]

Fort Pitt, *September* 8 [18?],[2] 1782.

Sir:—You will please to take John Freeman, a negro (a deserter from the enemy), in charge, and as his character is rather suspicious, you will not let him escape, at least till you get over the mountain.[3] He says his master lives in the state of New York; and, as it will be proper he should be sent to him, I mean to have inquiry made in the course of this winter, into the truth of his assertion. In the mean time, you may keep him and make him work for his maintenance until you receive further direction from me. But, in case of accident to me, so that you receive no instructions before the first of March next, you will, in that case, please to advertise him in the public papers, in order that his master (if he has any) may have a fair chance of reclaiming him.

P. S.— If the fellow should prove refractory or difficult to be dealt with, you had best send him to Carlisle jail, there to be advertised or dealt with according to law.[4]

---

[1] Willy was a captain of militia, doubtless from Cumberland county, sent over the mountains to Irvine. (See, post, Willy to Irvine, October 4, 1782.) Irvine's letter was probably directed to him at Hannastown.

[2] Irvine in copying this letter has made a mistake in the date; for, in his communication to Lincoln of September 12, 1782 (ante, p. 182), he says that the militia of York and Cumberland had not arrived. So, also, in his letter the day after, to Moore (p. 256), he says: "I could almost wish the militia may not come up." It probably was written the 18th of September.

[3] It is probable that this was the deserter mentioned by Marshel in his letter to Irvine of September 16, 1782 (ante, p. 315).

[4] "Pennsylvania provided for the gradual abolishment of slavery within her borders by the act of March 1, 1780, the immortal preamble to which is said to have been written by George Bryan, vice president of the supreme executive council, member of the legislature, and subsequently a judge of the supreme court. A section of the act provided for the registration on or before November 1, 1780, of all slaves; the registry to contain the name, occupation and residence of the owner, and the name, age and sex of the slave.

"Owing to the fact that the boundary controversy was still unsettled, and that the people of Westmoreland and Washington counties were still subject to and recognizing a divided jurisdiction, no attention was paid to the matter until, on April 13, 1782, a special act was passed upon the petition of the inhabitants of those counties, one provision of which extended the time of the

XXIX.— IRVINE TO GENERAL CLARK.

FORT PITT, *September* 9, 1782.

Sir:— I received your favor of the 10th of August, eight days ago. My reason for detaining your express so long was, if possible, to inform you positively what you might depend on from us;— as the passage may be precarious, I must refer you for full information to Messrs. Sullivan and Floyd. Being informed by Major Craig that you are scarce of three-pound shot, I have sent you fifty. And you will also receive the latest newspapers for your amusement.

XXX.— ROBERT MAGAW[1] TO IRVINE.

PHILADELPHIA, *September* 10, 1782.

Dear Sir:— Though I have but a few minutes to write, I could not miss the opportunity by Mr. Parkison to inform you briefly of our proceedings which I know will give you pleasure. The house on reading some memorials from your quarter and Northumberland stating the distressed state of the frontiers took the same under consideration and appointed me, with General Potter[2] deputed by council, to wait on his excellency, General Washington. We found him at Verplank's Point, at which place he had arrived the day before with the army from West Point. They are composed of the Jersey, New York, Rhode Island, Connecticut, and Massachusetts

---

registration of slaves to January 1, 1783. I have before me the original of the registry of slaves of Washington county,— a venerable looking document. It is headed, 'Washington County: List of Negroes Registered Pursuant to the Late Act of Assembly for Redress of Certain Grievances in the Counties of Westmoreland and Washington.'"— Boyd Crumrine, in *The Washington* (Pa.) *Observer,* August 11, 1881.

[1] Magaw, of Carlisle, was member of the Pennsylvania assembly from Cumberland county. He was commissioned major, June 25, 1775; promoted to colonel of the fifth Pennsylvania regiment, January 3, 1776; taken prisoner November 16, following; was exchanged October 25th, 1780. He died at Carlisle, January 7, 1790.

[2] James Potter was vice president of the supreme executive council of Pennsylvania, having been elected to that office November 14, 1781.

lines. I dare say no troops were ever in better clothing or in higher discipline. His excellency readily agreed to spare the recruits of this state and Hazen's regiment now at Lancaster, in concert with volunteers and militia, to form two expeditions into the Indian country; the one to consist of twelve hundred men under your command against the Delaware and Wyandot towns; the other under Colonel Richard Butler or General Hazen against some of the Genesee towns on Susquehanna waters.

I begin to fear as many regular troops will not be sent you as I could wish. It is talked by the minister at war to send you Hazen's regiment, consisting of about three hundred men. They are the best disciplined troops, but those of Pennsylvania would I think be more agreeable to you and more numerous; but the internal strength and ardor of your country is much counted on. However, this matter will not be finally settled before Monday. His excellency, General Washington, has given no direction in the matter, but informed us that the two New Hampshire regiments were at Saratoga and German Flats; and, in case he was not obliged to call them to his assistance, they should be employed to call the attention of the enemy as much as possible to that quarter.

There is no money in the treasury and none with the army; and we have appropriated last winter all our resources to the requisitions of congress; and have not a shilling now in our power but five thousand pounds we have borrowed of the bank for the sole purpose of the extra expenses of those expeditions, for which the financier will give us credit, though he can give us no assistance in money, being from hand to mouth in supplying provisions, taxes come in so slowly.

Excuse this hasty scrawl and expect to hear from me more fully in a few days.

XXXI.— EBENEZER ZANE TO IRVINE.

WHEELING, *September* 17, 1782.

Sir:— On the evening of the 11th instant, a body of the enemy appeared in sight of our garrison. They immediately formed their lines round the garrison, paraded British colors, and demanded the fort to be surrendered, which was refused. About twelve o'clock at night, they rushed hard on the pickets in order to storm, but were repulsed. They made two other attempts to storm before day, but to no purpose.

About 8 o'clock next morning, there came a negro from them to us and informed us that their force consisted of a British captain and forty regular soldiers and two hundred and sixty Indians. The enemy kept a continual fire the whole day. About ten o'clock at night, they made a fourth attempt to storm to no better purpose than the former. The enemy continued around the garrison until the morning of the 13th instant, when they disappeared. Our loss is none. Daniel Sullivan, who arrived here in the first of the action, is wounded in the foot.

I believe they have driven the greatest part of our stock away, and might, I think, be soon overtaken.

XXXII.— IRVINE TO GENERAL CLARK.

FORT PITT, *October* 3, 1782.

Sir:— Since I dispatched Mr. Floyd, sundry obstacles have intervened to prevent my moving at the time proposed. I have therefore thought proper to send this express as well to inform you of the causes of my detention that you may know what to depend on, as of my present expectations and views. If he cannot arrive at the Falls [Louisville] in time, I flatter myself he will meet you and perhaps at such a place as it may be no great inconvenience for you to halt a few days, in case that step should appear expedient on his account of my intentions. I cannot be more explicit for reasons I mentioned in my former letter, and must refer you to the bearer or his companions— Mr. Tate and James Amberson. You may credit what they inform you for me. I have promised them you will give them provision while they remain and assist them to return if necessary.

I presume much will depend on keeping good time;— I mean that one should not be long before the other.[1]

XXXIII.— Captain Willy to Irvine.

Hannastown, *October* 4, 1782.

Sir:— I had the honor to receive your letter of the 21st ult., and acknowledge your goodness in supplying us with the ammunition which I wrote for. The kettles were not brought, which I believe must have been the neglect of the express. We have not been able to make any provision for an expedition, as the men have no money with them, and indeed if they had it would be a hard matter to procure leather for moccasins. The men are also exceedingly ill prepared with clothing for cold weather, which must soon be expected.

Our county lieutenant[2] informed me that our business would be scouting on the frontier, which was the means of our coming out in the most light order that the season would admit of. We have been reasonably well supplied with provisions since a few days after our arrival here; and I keep out a scout of between twenty and thirty men on the frontier. I labor under some difficulties which I would take it as a singular favor if the general would indulge me with his opinion of. There was a packhorseman sent with us to carry our little baggage to this post and my orders were to discharge him when I arrived here; but when I found the difficulty of getting flour and that grain could be got ground by carrying about forty miles and no horses could be employed here, I ventured to detain him awhile; and from your verbal orders to me I have kept him yet. The contractors refuse paying him for any time but when he is actually carrying for them, and the man cannot afford to stay here on expense without being made sure of some compensation.

---

[1] That is, that Clark's expedition against the Shawanese should strike that tribe at the same time that Irvine should reach the Wyandots, upon the Sandusky.

[2] The writer probably means the lieutenant of Cumberland county, Pennsylvania.

There is also a certain John Vance of the York county militia who was drafted at the same time with those who came up lately. He joined me at our rendezvous, marched with me, and has done his duty very well, and I am at a loss to know whether I should return him to his captain, as he may refuse perhaps to return him on his pay roll, because he was not all his time under his command.

I enclose you a return of a lieutenant and a few men who came up since as will appear. I have nothing of importance to communicate. Our scouts have made no discoveries; and they are of opinion the coasts are pretty clear of the enemy.

XXXIV.— IRVINE TO GENERAL CLARK.

FORT PITT, *November* 7, 1782.

Sir:—I appointed [a day][1] for the general rendezvous of the militia at Fort McIntosh, and should have been able to have taken up my line of march on the 20th following. The day previous to this, a report of a cessation of arms spread, seemingly deserving credit, as I received intelligence that the march of the continental troops from below was countermanded. This news gained universal belief with the country and I fear would have mutilated my plan if the report had proved premature. But, at the time I proposed to march, I received letters from the continental secretary at war countermanding the expedition, as General Washington had been assured by the British general that all the savages were called in from the frontiers, and were not to commit any farther depredations upon the inhabitants.

I was exceedingly uneasy when I considered it was then impossible to communicate to you the intelligence before you marched. A report of the defeat of a large number of the inhabitants in Kentucky[2] was circulating at the same time and persuaded me almost that it would oblige you to drop your

---

[1] The day mentioned is illegible.
[2] The defeat here referred to was suffered at the battle of the Blue Licks, in the month of August previous.

design. Yet, in case this should either be false, or not incapacitate you from proceeding against the Shawanese, I determined to draw the attention of the Wyandots by sending them information that I was prepared to attack Sandusky with a numerous force,—the only stratagem left me to make use of in your favor.

XXXV.—GENERAL CLARK TO IRVINE.

MIAMI, *November* 13, 1782.

Sir:—I fell in with your late express [1] on the 2d inst. at the mouth of the Licking creek.[2] I was happy to find that our design was likely to be well-timed. We marched on the 3d. The 10th, surprised the principal Shawanese town, Chillicothe;[3] but not so completely as wished for, as most of the inhabitants had time to escape. We got a few scalps and prisoners. I immediately dispatched strong parties to the neighboring towns. In a short time, laid all of them in ashes, with all their riches. The British trading post[4] at the carrying-place, shared the same fate.[5] I can not find, from the prisoners, that

---

[1] Referring to the one which left Fort Pitt, October 3d.
[2] Opposite the site of the present city of Cincinnati, Ohio.
[3] Now Piqua, Miami county, Ohio.
[4] Known, at that time, as Loramie's store, at or near the present Loramies, Shelby county, Ohio.
[5] The official report of Clark of his invasion of the Shawanese country was as follows:

"LINCOLN [COUNTY, Ky.], *Nov.* 27th, 1782.

"*Sir:*—I embrace the earliest opportunity by Capt. Morrison, of acquainting you with our return from the Indian country. We left the Ohio on the 4th inst. with one thousand and fifty men, and surprised the principal Shawnee [Shawanese] town [now Piqua, Miami county, Ohio] on the evening of the 10th inst. Immediately detaching strong parties to different quarters, in a few hours two-thirds of the town was laid in ashes and everything they [the Shawanese] were possessed of destroyed, except such articles as might be useful to the troops; the enemy had no time to secrete any part of their property which was in the town. The British trading post [Loramie's store] at the head of the Miami, and carrying-place [portage] to the waters of the lake [Erie], shared the same fate, at the hands of a party of one hundred and fifty horse commanded by Col. Ben Logan. The property destroyed was of great amount,

they had any idea of your second design; and I hope you will completely surprise the Sanduskians. I beg leave to refer you to Mr. Tate and his companions for further particulars, for reasons well known to you.

XXXVI.— CHRISTOPHER HAYS[1] TO IRVINE.

NEAR CROSS CREEK, *November* 19, 1782.

Dear Sir:— We have proceeded this length in running the north line of Pennsylvania[2] and have enjoyed a peaceable pro-

and the quantity of provisions burned surpassed all idea we had of the Indian stores.

"The loss of the enemy was ten *scalps*, seven prisoners, and two whites retaken; ours was one killed and one wounded. After lying part of four days in their towns, and finding all attempts to bring the enemy to a general action fruitless, we retired, as the season was far advanced and the weather threatening. I could not learn from the prisoners that they had the least idea of Gen. Irwin's [Irvine's] penetrating into their country; should he have given them another stroke at Sandusky, it will have more than doubled the advantage already gained. We might probably have got many more scalps and prisoners, could we have known in time whether we were discovered or not. We took for granted we were not, until getting within three miles, some circumstances happened which caused me to think otherwise. Col. John Floyd was then ordered to advance with three hundred men to bring on an action or attack the town, while Major Walls with a party of horse had previously been detached by a different route, as a party of observation. Although Col. Floyd's motions were so quick as to get to the town but a few minutes later than those who discovered his approach, the inhabitants had sufficient notice to effect their escape to the woods, by the alarm cry which was given on the first discovery. This was heard at a very great distance, and repeated by all that heard it. Consequently our parties only fell in with the rear of the enemy.

"I must beg leave to recommend to your excellency the militia of Kentucky, whose behavior on the occasion does them *honor*, and particularly their desire to save prisoners. Subscribed,   G. R. CLARK.

"[To Gov. BENJ. HARRISON, of Virginia.]"

[1] Hays was employed by the state of Pennsylvania to assist in running the temporary boundary line between that state and Virginia from the end of Mason & Dixon's line to the Ohio river. He was a prominent citizen of Westmoreland — a member of the supreme executive council of the state, and judge of his county, he having been commissioned July 24th, of that year.

[2] That is, the boundary line on the west side of Pennsylvania, south of the Ohio river. Hays speaks of it as a "north line," because a meridian line

gress hitherto, and expect to strike the Ohio river about Thursday next between Fort McIntosh and Baredon's Bottom.

Sir, I am reduced to the necessity of troubling your honor to send me by the bearer one keg of whisky, two pounds powder, and four pounds lead, and your compliance will much oblige [me].[1]

P. S.— I will replace the whisky with all convenient speed. Please to bring it in your own boat if you come to meet us.[2]

---

was being run from the southwest corner of the state to the Ohio river; the twenty-three miles to that corner from the point east where it had been previously stopped, having been completed. This was the finishing of the temporary boundary line which Alexander McClean endeavored to commence the running of on the previous 10th of June, but was stopped by a number of horsemen — "Virginians, as they called themselves "— but which was afterward resumed. (See pp. 248, 268, 294–296, 326, 327.)

The question of the boundary line between Pennsylvania and Virginia was settled by commissioners of those states at Baltimore, in August, 1779; but, as we have seen, the line remained unrun. This fact, as already frequently indicated, was the cause of a great deal of trouble in the western department. As an expedient to "quiet the minds of the people and compel militia service," until a permanent line could be run based upon astronomical observations, the governor of Pennsylvania addressed the executive of Virginia May 14, 1781: "For the sake of settling the minds of the people and preventing disputes among the borderers, [we suggest] to have a temporary line run by common surveyors from the termination of Mason and Dixon's line to the Ohio; or, if that should not be agreeable, to extend it twenty-three miles from the end of Mason and Dixon's line, that being the extent of five degrees according to common computation. In this case, we only propose to mark the trees, avoiding as much as possible unnecessary expense. We hope this last proposition, in which we have no other intentions than to quiet the minds of the people and compel militia service, will be acceptable to your excellency, as the best and indeed the only expedient which can now be adopted."

The first attempt to run this temporary line and its results have already been spoken of on previous pages. The next attempt (and the successful one) was commenced November 4, 1782, by McClean and Neville, and carried forward as indicated in Hays' letter. Of course, Virginia had no interest in the western boundary of Pennsylvania *north* of the Ohio.

[1] It will be noticed that whisky is the article *first mentioned;* more to be desired than powder and lead, notwithstanding the Indians were still hostile!

[2] The following from McClean to the governor of Pennsylvania, dated March 13, 1783, refers to the finishing up of the temporary line:

"Sir:— Enclosed is an account of expenses, in addition to the bill I laid before you. I take the liberty to inform you that I was under the necessity of

XXXVII.— HENRY TAYLOR[1] TO IRVINE.

WASHINGTON COUNTY, *November* 20, 1872.

Sir:—There is a certain Crail, a soldier now belonging to the troops at Pittsburgh, who was attached some time ago for forgery. At the time he was before the court, the grand jury was discharged, therefore no bill of indictment was prepared. The state attorney and the court thought it most prudent to order him to the service as it was the safest place to secure him and the public requiring his service, no jail being yet in

---

defraying or assuming the expense herein set forth, to prevent the business being entirely frustrated; as the militia expected from this state could not be drawn out in time to answer the purpose; and the Virginia troops being on the spot, we concluded to proceed with the guard we were then possessed of; and as Colonel Hays could not possibly overtake us, I kept the troops from Virginia until their provisions were expended and then discharged all that I could spare, giving them an order to draw provisions at Beeson's Town [now Uniontown, Fayette county, Penn.] for their return home."

For the history of "Mason and Dixon's Line," with accounts of running the permanent line west of Dunkard and north to the Ohio river, see "A Memoir," etc., by James Dunlop, in "Mem. of the Hist. Soc. of Penn.," Vol. I (1826); Craig's "Olden Time," Vol. I (1846); U. S. Senate (Ex.) Doc., No. 21, 30 Cong. (1848); Col. J. D. Graham's Report, Penn. Senate Jour., Vol. II (1850); "Hist. of Mason and Dixon's Line," by J., H. B. Latrobe (1855); "Mason and Dixon's Line," by James Veech (1857). Consult, also, in this connection, the Penn. Archives and Col. Records and the Calendar of Virginia State Papers.

[1] President judge of Washington county. He was from Cecil county, Maryland, from which place he emigrated in 1771, to a place near what is now Washington, in Washington county. Before the organization of that county, Taylor was an adherent of the Virginia side of the boundary controversy. He was a major of militia and a justice of the courts of Yohogania county, under the authority of that province. He subsequently filled several important civil and military positions in Washington county. He died October 8, 1801, aged sixty-three years. (See "The Washington County Centennial,"— Address by Boyd Crumrine, p. 42.)

"I have before me a duplicate of the [land] warrant to Henry Taylor, the first justice who presided in the courts of Washington county [Pa.], . . . which warrant was signed by John Penn, and is dated February 1, 1771, for 150 acres on the Middle Fork of Chartiers creek, and on the path leading from Catfish Camp [now Washington, county-seat of Washington county] to Pittsburgh."— Boyd Crumrine, in *The Washington* (Pa.) *Observer*, Aug. 11th, 1881.

the county to secure him and it was not known at the time when we should have an opportunity of having him tried.

There is a court of oyer and terminer and general jail delivery to be held for this county the 25th instant at Catfish Camp [Washington, the present county-seat of the county]. The judges have required me to give you the above information, not doubting your ready compliance in delivering him up for trial. In compliance on my part of the request I send this with an officer, who will deliver it, and has an order for receiving him if you will please to order him in his custody.[1]

I have not heard all the testimony that will be against Crail, but from the information I have got I am of opinion there will be no danger of losing a soldier. . . ,.

XXXVIII.—CHRISTOPHER HAYS AND EDWARD COOK TO IRVINE.

WASHINGTON COUNTY, *December* 25, 1782.

Sir:— Mr. Crail[2] we return to you again, as no evidence appeared against him. There is a certain William Hanks convicted of a rape upon a child and under sentence of death. There is no place in this county to secure him in until his death warrant arrives. It is therefore requested that the general will do the county the favor of securing him. The sheriff will throw in such supplies as may be necessary for his support.[3]

---

[1] The request made to Irvine was complied with. (See next letter.)
[2] See letter from Taylor to Irvine next preceding.
[3] This letter was signed by both Hays and Cook, who, though judges of Westmoreland, were also members, at that time, of the Washington county court, under a special commission, as the following shows:

"IN COUNCIL, PHILADELPHIA, *July* 25th, 1782.

"*Ordered,* that a special commission of oyer and terminer and general jail delivery, directed to the Honorable Christopher Hays and Dorsey Pentecost, Esquires, and Edward Cook, Esquire, be now issued to the counties of Westmoreland and Washington, for the trial of divers persons now confined in the jails of the said counties charged with high crimes and misdemeanors."

XXXIX.— IRVINE TO MAJOR ISAAC CRAIG.[1]

CARLISLE, *April* 1, 1783.

Dear Major:— As Mr. Rose[2] will carry you all the particulars of peace, etc., the present is only to congratulate you on

---

[1] Isaac Craig was born at Ballykeel Artifinny, County Down, Ireland, of Presbyterian parents, about the year 1742, emigrating to America at the close of the year 1765 or beginning of 1766, and settled in Philadelphia, working as a journeyman house carpenter, which trade he had previously learned, becoming finally a master builder and laboring with success until the breaking out of the revolution. In November, 1775, he received an appointment as the oldest lieutenant of marines in the navy, and, in that capacity, served ten months, being promoted, after some active service, to a captaincy of marines. Having joined the army with his company as infantry, he was present at the crossing of the Delaware, the capture of the Hessians at Trenton, and at the battle of Princeton. On the 3d of March, 1777, he was appointed a captain of artillery in the regiment of Pennsylvania troops under the command of Colonel Thomas Procter, in which regiment he continued to serve until it was disbanded at the close of the war. He was engaged with his company in the battles of Brandywine and Germantown.

Early in the spring of 1778, Captain Craig was ordered to Carlisle to learn practically the art of the military laboratory. Here he remained until August, 1778. On the 29th of March, 1779, he was ordered to the command of the fort at Billingsport on the Delaware, below Philadelphia, being relieved May 2d following. He was ordered with his regiment to Easton, May 20, 1779, and marched with Sullivan in his expedition against the Six Nations, returning to Easton October 18, following. In January, 1780, he was with the army at Morristown, New Jersey. On the 20th of April, he was ordered to Fort Pitt with artillery and military stores, reaching that post on the 25th of June. He continued in command of the artillery there until the 29th of July, 1781, when he left with his detachment for the Falls (Louisville) in aid of Clark, as before narrated; getting back to Fort Pitt on the 26th of November.

On the 12th of March, 1782, Captain Craig was promoted to be major, his commission bearing date March 13, 1782, to rank from October 7, 1781. His duties at Fort Pitt and the confidence reposed in him by General Irvine have already been indicated in previous pages. Major Craig continued at that post until the close of the war, when he became a citizen of Pittsburgh.

In February, 1785, Major Craig married Amelia Neville, the only daughter of Colonel John Neville. In February, 1791, he was made deputy quartermaster and military store-keeper at Pittsburgh. He soon after superintended the construction, at the same place, of Fort Fayette; also of smaller works at La Bœuf, Presq' Isle and Wheeling. He died May 14, 1826.

[2] This letter was taken by Lieutenant John Rose, Irvine's aid, to Major Craig, at Fort Pitt.

the glorious end to the war. It has been with hard work and much assiduity, in Mr. Rose, that subsistence and pay have been obtained for the post. But after all, you will find the post has been, on the whole, better supplied than any other part of the army. Not a rag has the main army got this winter. A late commotion of the officers at headquarters has occasioned some attention from congress.

It is said the army will be settled with before they are disbanded. I will wait here some time and watch every motion. Everybody must remain in *statu quo* for some time. A peace establishment is talked of. What do you think of that? Do let me know your inclination soon.

XL.— EPHRAIM BLAINE[1] TO IRVINE.

PHILADELPHIA, *April* 2, 1783.

Dear Sir:— I expected being at Carlisle the first of this month, but my public accounts will prevent my getting away before the 15th. I should wish to see you before your de-

---

[1] Ephraim Blaine, the son of James Blaine, an early Scotch-Irish settler on the Conodoguinet, was born near Carlisle, Cumberland county, Pennsylvania, on the 26th of May, 1741. His father being a man of means, the son received a classical education, under the care of the Rev. Dr. Allison. The breaking out, however, of the French and Indian war, brought Ephraim away from his books to the duties of a soldier on the frontiers. During the Bouquet expedition of 1764, he was commissary-sergeant of the second provincial regiment. At the outset of the war for independence, he assisted in raising a battalion of associators, and as an officer of these "minute men" of the revolution he continued until his appointment as county lieutenant of Cumberland county, April 5, 1777, a position, however, he resigned in August following, when he entered the commissary department of the continental line. He was commissioned commissary general of purchases, February 19, 1778, a position he held over three years, including one of the most trying periods of the war — the cantonment at Valley Forge. On the 7th of July, 1780, he accepted the position of issuing commissary for his county; Owing to his personal sacrifices during the war, Col. Blaine's estate became impaired, although his fortune remained ample. He was a warm personal friend of Gen. Washington, and it was at his house the first president remained during his week's stay at Carlisle when on the so-called "Whisky Insurrection" of 1794. Col. Blaine died at his seat near Carlisle, February 16, 1804, in the sixty-third year of his age. He was twice married: first, to Rebecca Gal-

parture to Fort Pitt, and hope the 18th will answer that purpose. If I can get my cash accounts settled with the public, I shall certainly go to Pittsburgh in July, in order to settle some disputes which I have about lands in that neighborhood. Mr. Wilson has settled his accounts of two months' issues, and Mr. Morris gave him part payment in his own notes, which he refused taking until he assured him he had written you to lift them. You will greatly oblige me by doing it, as Mr. Wilson will be necessitated for money and would not have taken them upon any other principle.[1]

XLI.— LIEUT.-COL. STEPHEN BAYARD[2] TO IRVINE.[3]

FORT PITT, *April* 5, 1783.

Dear General:— About ten days ago I received an express from Waltour's giving me an account of the Indians killing

---

braith; secondly, to Mrs. Duncan, whose husband had fallen in a duel. There were two sons, both by his first wife — James and Robert. James Blaine went abroad in 1791 as a merchant, and became an attache to the American legation in Paris, but returned as bearer of dispatches connected with Jay's treaty. At that period, he was considered the most accomplished gentleman in Philadelphia. He died in Washington county, Pennsylvania, whither he had removed after his father's death. His son Ephraim was the father of James G. Blaine, who was born in Washington county, removed to Maine, and was lately the distinguished senator from that state. Ephraim Blaine's other son, Robert, married Anna S. Metzgar and left issue.

[1] Directed to Irvine at Carlisle.

[2] In command at Fort Pitt during General Irvine's absence. (Ante, p. 141, note.) Stephen Bayard was born in Maryland, in 1748. He belonged to a Huguenot family from Languedoc. He was brought up by his uncle, John Bayard, of Philadelphia. He settled after the revolution in Pittsburgh, where he was in partnership with Isaac Craig. After retiring from business, he made his home on his lands on the Monongahela, fourteen miles above Pittsburgh. There he laid out a town which he named Elizabeth, after his wife. He built there the first vessel launched upon the waters of the Monongahela. He died at Pittsburgh, December 13, 1815. He was captain in the third Pennsylvania regiment, ranking from January 5, 1776; promoted major of the eighth, March 12, 1777; appointed lieutenant-colonel September 23, same year; transferred to the sixth, January, 1781; to the first, January 1, 1783.

[3] This letter was directed to Irvine at Carlisle, the general reaching there, it will be remembered, on the 4th of March previous.

James Davis [and] his son, and taking two prisoners about half a mile from that fort. The 31st of March, Mr. Zane [1] writes by express that one man was found killed and scalped and another taken prisoner at Wheat's Narrows on Wheeling creek. An express came to me last night from Col. Shepherd [2] giving an account of six persons being killed, six wounded and five made prisoners within seven miles of Catfish.[3] This moment I was informed by a man from the widow Myres' that one Thomas Lyon who lived about four miles from her house was yesterday killed and scalped. The certainty of Indians being about, killing and taking prisoners, is now beyond doubt, and has induced me to send this express. I should have done it before, but could not altogether rely on the accounts given me. I dare say the account will to you be unexpected, as it really was to me, and seems so to the country people, who can scarcely believe it yet, having heard so much of a peace and Indians being called in.

Your representation of the matter will no doubt have great weight and probably be of infinite service to this unhappy country.

I have given them every assurance of assistance consistent with the safety of this post, should they stand fast and act spiritedly.

P. S.— The officers here that are to retire are very anxious to know whether they will be retired. The sub-lieutenant of Washington county has written (by the express) to the president [of the supreme executive council of Pennsylvania], representing the situation of the county.[4]

---

[1] Ebenezer Zane, of Wheeling.

[2] Colonel David Shepherd, lieutenant of Ohio county, Virginia.

[3] Now Washington, county-seat of Washington county, Pennsylvania.

[4] J. Dickinson was president of Pennsylvania, elected November 7, 1782. (Ante, p. 260, note.) The letter referred to as written him by the sub-lieutenant of Washington county, was as follows:

"WASHINGTON COUNTY, *April* 5, 1783.

"*Sir:*— The expectation of peace gave the inhabitants of the western frontiers hopes of being eased of the calamities of war, at least for some time; but it is our great mortification the savages have begun anew their depredations. They took one Mrs. Walker prisoner on the 27th ult., on Buffalo

XLII.—MAJOR CRAIG TO IRVINE.

FORT PITT, *April* 5, 1783.

Dear General:— Notwithstanding General Carleton's assurance of the savages being restrained and the Indian partisans being called in, we have almost every day accounts of families being murdered or carried off. The frontier inhabitants of

creek, but she happily made her escape. This woman says that two parties of Indians are gone against the inhabitants. Two days after there were two men taken prisoners at Wheeling;—the day following, a man was wounded on Short creek. The 1st of April they took the Wison Boice and family consisting of eight persons, and a man was killed the day following, near Washington county court house. Same time two Indian rafts were seen on the Ohio, between Wheeling and Grave creek. In short, the inhabitants are in the utmost consternation, especially on the frontiers; and, unless timely relieved, their case must be truly deplorable.

"The commandant of Fort Pitt (Col. Bayard) has generously supplied us with ammunition, and is ready to give us every assistance in his power. We are with great respect, sir, your most obed't and humble servants,

"WM. PARKER, } Sub. L'ts W. C."
"JAMES ALLISON,

The following letter from the Washington county member of the supreme executive council of Pennsylvania to the governor of the state gives particulars of these inroads and of their subsidence:

"WASHINGTON COUNTY, *May* 4, 1783.

"*Sir:*— I have no doubt but that Gen. Irvine has informed your excellency and council of the early inroads of the savages this spring, and with what uncommon inhumanity they marked their horrid murders, as also the great success they met with owing to the unexpectedness of the stroke. I think in one week they killed and captured seventeen persons, two of whom (a woman and a boy) have since made their escape. The people were so entirely easy under the expectation of a general peace, that those butchers of mankind met with no kind of obstruction in their progress; for it is said, and I believe with truth, that they continued about the frontiers of this county for several days without a single scout pursuing them. However, they have at length left the country of their own accord; and I have the pleasure of informing your excellency that I have not heard of any disturbance from them for several weeks past. . . . Your excellency's most ob't humble serv't,

"DORSEY PENTECOST."

The following is from the *Pennsylvania Packet* of June 19, 1783 (No. 1056):

"Extract of a letter from a gentleman at George's creek, on Monongahela, to his brother, an officer in the Pennsylvania line, dated May 7, 1783:

"'The Indians have been worse this spring than any other time since the commencement of the war; killing, captivating and burning upon all quar-

Washington and Ohio counties are moving into the interior settlements. The inhabitants of Westmoreland, it is said, will follow their example, and we have reason to believe that the post of Wheeling is or will' shortly be evacuated.

It appears there are several parties of the enemy, or detachments of some large party, as they are ranging the country in several places at the same time. Colonel Bayard's letter[1] will further inform you. Applications and petitions for ammunition and assistance have come in from all quarters.

Prospects of peace on this side the mountains seem to vanish. The British either have very little influence over their savage allies or they are acting a most deceitful part. I hope, however, that the assurances we have of the pacific disposition of England will give congress an opportunity of sending a sufficient force to extirpate or at least properly chastise these marauding rascals.[2] Should an expedition be determined on in which artillery is to be employed, I hope it will be remembered that there is not a three-pounder fit to be carried into the field at this place, and that at least two of that calibre will be wanted, according to my opinion. I hope I shall have the pleasure of battering the Wyandot blockhouses in the course of the ensuing summer and perhaps of taking possession of Detroit.[3]

---

ters of our frontiers, and the only support that we have is a faint hope that his excellency, General Washington, will send us relief. My dear brother, if you have any influence in this case, I pray that you would exert it to the utmost.'

"It is astonishing how men in power can bear of our poor frontiers, suffering under the barbarous hands of cruel savages, and take no measure to bring to justice a race of mankind who glory in killing women and children.

"Have we lost all feelings in Philadelphia? Or can we be so void of the principles of justice as to suppose that a people, who are not protected by us, owe allegiance to us."

[1] See previous letter, same date as the above.

[2] "The inhabitants of the frontiers seem more discouraged than they have been, having flattered themselves with the most sanguine hopes of peace, which hopes they now think are frustrated."—*John Cummins to Pres't Dickinson, from Hannastown, March 29*, 1783.

[3] Directed to Irvine at Carlisle.

XLIII.—Lieut.-Col. Bayard to Irvine.[1]

Fort Pitt, *April* 15, 1783.

Dear General:— I thank you for your kind favor by Major Rose. Since my last by express, the Indians have done no more mischief; but signs have been discovered and the country people are yet prodigiously scared and say they will make another stroke soon; as they swear they will be revenged on the frontiers [that is, the frontier people will be revenged], be it peace or be it war.

The retired officers seem greatly distressed and dissatisfied at receiving no cash by Mr. Rose; as they are in debt, have no money nor credit, and have a great way to go home. Their case is really hard and they are to be pitied, but you will say that is cold comfort.

I have not made up my mind fully on the questions you were good enough to put to me; but incline as soon as peace is established to lay aside the tomahawk and scalping-knife and retire to a private life. However, on this and every other interesting subject, I shall always pay a great deference to your advice.

The soldiers have said, as soon as peace was concluded, they would immediately go home, as they then considered themselves free men. I have not heard them say so, nor spoke to them on the subject; but I dare say I shall be able to keep them together till further orders. Duncan is not yet arrived; I hope to have the pleasure of a line from you by him.

[P. S.]—I hear the Virginians are making improvements over the Ohio from Beaver creek to the Muskingum. Dr. Rogers sends his respectful compliments to you.

XLIV.— Lieut.-Col. Bayard to Irvine.[2]

Fort Pitt, *April* 28, 1783.

Dear General:— Mr. Duncan handed me your favor of the 9th instant, for which I thank you. I make it a point to give

---
[1] Directed to Carlisle.
[2] Directed to Irvine at Carlisle.

you a few lines by every opportunity, though they contain very little novelty, and are only a repetition of the same dull scene, which can give no entertainment, yet may be satisfactory.

I sent last week a scout to Wheeling of 19 men to be out eight days; that time is elapsed and they are not yet returned. Probably they may have met with Indians which has detained them; if so, I shall know in a day or two. Immediately on its return I propose sending another to Fort Crawford *via* widow Myres', which will give confidence and keep people at home. The people of Westmoreland have been at me for ammunition but I chose rather to send a scout than give it them.

Mr. Rose will inform you of the troops refusing to receive their pay in the way directed; they will have no objections, I am informed, to receive a full month's pay at once though they grumble a good deal at that, and have said (not in my hearing) that if they were not settled with soon, they would lay down their arms; but these may be words, of course. I hope soon to have the pleasure of seeing you, when all these affairs will be settled to everybody's satisfaction.

McIntosh I hope is safe; not an Indian nor sign been seen for a long time.

P. S.— Please inform Mr. Bryson what Mr. Rose says with respect to his pay. The party from Wheeling has just come in; no Indians nor signs seen.

XLV.— EPHRAIM DOUGLASS[1] TO IRVINE.

FORT PITT, *June* 4, 1783.

Sir:— Presuming on your inclination equally with the request of the honorable the secretary at war, to afford me every

---

[1] Douglass was an officer of the revolution, of the eighth Pennsylvania regiment and afterward an aid to General Lincoln. Upon the erection of Fayette county, Penn., in 1783, he was appointed prothonotary and clerk of the courts, offices which (with others, civil and military) he held until 1808. He died in 1833.

assistance,[1] I beg leave to trouble you with a request for two horses, one riding saddle, three blankets, one hundred weight of flour, forty pounds of dried bacon ham and one quart of salt, in addition to the one horse and such articles as I have already received out of the public stores.

XLVI.—Ephraim Douglass to Irvine.

FORT PITT, *June* 7, 1783.

Dear Sir:— The delay of yesterday will probably deny me the pleasure of seeing you, as I flattered myself I should at Fort McIntosh, where I proposed to have taken my leave of you, and to have submitted to your better judgment the propriety of informing [General George Rogers] Clark of a messenger being sent to the Indians with offers of peace; and whether, in your opinion, it might not possibly be a means of restraining the people of that country from attempting anything against the Indians till it shall be known how the proposals of congress will be received.

If your opinion coincides with my wishes on this head, I would beg you take the trouble to write him on the subject, from a conviction that your name will give a sanction to whatever you may think to suggest to him.

XLVII.—Ephraim Douglass to Irvine.

DETROIT, *July* 6, 1783.

Dear Sir:— For the purpose of writing to the honorable, the secretary at war, as well as to give you the information

---

[1] For the request of the secretary at war to Irvine of which Douglass speaks, see p. 188. Douglass, when he wrote the above letter, was *en route* to the Indian country "charged with a message to the Indian nations," because of their hostilities continued upon the border, as mentioned in the letters of Colonel Bayard and Major Craig, just given. (Ante. p. 188, note 2.)

[2] Before Douglass' arrival at Detroit, he sent in an open letter by an Indian to Mr. Elliott, which letter was taken to De Peyster, the commandant, who immediately dispatched Elliott into the Indian country to meet him and conduct him in. De Peyster, at the same time, wrote Douglass, requesting him not to enter into any negotiations with the Indians before his arrival.

of my safe arrival at this place, I have caused Mr. Elliott to return by the nearest way to your post; and am happy in communicating to you that, though I have not been able to answer entirely the expectations of the public, I have found the Indians highly disposed, from the pains which had been taken with them before my arrival, to cease from further hostilities against the inhabitants of the United States, provided that, on their part, they [the latter] show the same disposition to avoid the offer of every cause of just complaint, and particularly to confine themselves to that side of the [Ohio] river, which neither prudence nor the laws of the country forbid their entrance.

I expect to depart to-morrow for Niagara, where I am encouraged to hope such instructions will shortly arrive as that the officer [Gen. Allan McLean] commanding the district will find duty and inclination conspire to promote and effectuate the business of my mission. At present, the want of official information induces Colonel De Peyster, the gentleman commanding here, to think it incompatible with his duty, as it is repugnant to his opinion, to suffer the message of the United States to be delivered before he is possessed of such authenticated accounts of the treaty as will justify his concurrence with me.[1] Exclusive of the reasons I have already mentioned, I have yet another which I am very earnest to make known to you: The possibility that curiosity — the desire of visiting their relations or the confidence of an hospitable reception — might lead some of the Indians to Fort Pitt, while our reception in their country was still unknown,—and that some injury might, in consequence, be offered to them by an unthinking populace,— all bid me wish to advertise you of their friendly disposition, from the opinion that you will see the justice and necessity of affording them protection and

---

[1] But Douglass was disappointed. Upon his arrival at Niagara he was not suffered "to assemble the chiefs [of the various Indian tribes of the west] and to make known to them the message" he was charged with by the United States; his mission was, therefore, a failure in one sense, but it tended to lessen the inroads of the savages upon the frontiers and was, as a consequence, productive of much good, thanks to the kind offices of the humane De Peyster.

suitable assistance. In this case, I am well assured that whatever humanity and good policy could suggest, you would order to be done, if our *fate* was *not* so intimately connected with theirs.[1] Let me beg that you will excuse the liberty of offering to trouble you with the enclosed.

XLVIII.— Lieut.-Col. A. S. De Peyster[2] to Irvine.

Detroit, *July* 10, 1783.

Sir:— By this favorable opportunity of Mr. Elliott, I have permitted Mr. Little to return to Fort Pitt, on his

---

[1] The following extract from a letter afterward written by the commandant at Detroit, Colonel A. S. De Peyster, to his superior officer, Brigadier General Allan MacLean, commanding at Niagara, explains, as he understood it, one of the causes operating to protract hostilities between the borderers and the savages:

"Runners are just come in from the Indian country with accounts that the Kentucky people had attacked and carried off a number of horses belonging to the Indian hunters who were hunting on their own grounds at a considerable distance on this side of the Ohio. The Indians, not willing to lose their property, pursued the Virginians, attacked them, and killed two men, and had one of their own number mortally wounded, who is since dead. I have made every possible inquiry, and can assure you the Kentuckians were the aggressors. I mention the particulars that they may be fairly related, to prevent any misfortune that might ensue from misapprehensions of these lawless people, the Indians being heartily disposed to peace and friendship with the people on the frontiers of the United States."

[2] Arent Schuyler de Peyster was born in New York city, on the twenty-seventh of June, 1736. His father, Pierre Guillaume, was the seventh son of Abraham de Peyster. His mother was Catharine Schuyler, sister of Peter Schuyler, famous in the history of our country. Arent Schuyler was their second son. He entered the eighth, or king's regiment of foot, British army, on the tenth of June, 1755. Having served in various parts of North America, he, finally, as captain, took command of the post of Mackinaw, in 1774. While there, the revolution was inaugurated, which, in the end, as we have already shown, secured to the British interest all the western Indians. In the management of the wild tribes within his jurisdiction, De Peyster displayed extraordinary discretion. After the capture early in 1779, of Lieutenant-Governor Henry Hamilton by George Rogers Clark, De Peyster, now holding the rank of major, was assigned to the command of Detroit. At this time, all the Ohio and Lake Indians were firm allies of the British, the Delawares alone excepted; and the principal part of that tribe soon joined their fortunes with the neighboring nations.

private affairs. Mr. Douglass, before he left this for Niagara, informed me that he had written to you fully upon the sub-

Brought into closer relation with hostile operations along the border, the command at Detroit was a very difficult and perplexing one to the urbane, humane, and chivalric De Peyster. His policy, so different from that of his predecessor, is well disclosed in one of his speeches to the Delawares in 1781, while securing the alienation of that nation from the Americans: "Bring me," said he, "some Virginian prisoner,—I am pleased when I see what you call *live meat*, because I can speak to it and get information; *scalps* serve to show that you have seen the enemy, but they are of no use to me, I cannot speak with them." That he made all haste to send succor from Detroit to his allies upon the Sandusky upon the approach of Crawford and his army, is nothing to his discredit. As an officer in the British army, he could do no less. His words to his superior, upon learning the fate of that unfortunate commander, are highly creditable to him: "I have sent messengers throughout the Indian country, threatening to recall the troops if they — the Indians — do not desist from such cruelty." As an officer, although, at times, quite arbitrary, De Peyster won considerable distinction at Detroit. In some respects, however, his acts were open to criticism, especially in securing for himself a large grant of land from the Indians, but which was not confirmed to him. Concessions without authority of law of public property to private individuals and unnecessary bias to certain parties engaged in the fur-trade, have been charged against him,—possibly with some exaggerations. On the whole, his administration of affairs at that post must be considered as characterized by fairness as well as firmness.

After the conclusion of hostilities with the revolted colonies, De Peyster continued in the service, remaining at Detroit until 1784; having risen to be lieutenant-colonel during that conflict; he afterward went to England where he received his commission as colonel. He was located at different stations, commanding, at one time, the garrison at Plymouth; subsequently retiring to Dumfries, Scotland, his wife's native town. At the period of the French revolution, he embodied and trained the first regiment of Dumfries volunteers, of which corps the poet, Burns, was a member. One of the sparkling effusions of the latter is addressed to De Peyster, commencing,—

> My honor'd Colonel, deep I feel
> Your int'rest in the Poet's weal;
> Ah! how sma' heart hae I to spee!
> The steep Parnassus,
> Surrounded thus by bolus pill,
> And potion glasses."

De Peyster was not only "a warrior, true and bold," but a writer of no insignificant power and pretensions. Besides many fugitive poetical efforts, he left behind him a volume of "Miscellanies," wherein he recorded some of his services in the northwest from 1774 to 1779, which contains also consider-

ject of his voyage. I have given a pass to a lad taken after the peace concluded, to return to his friends.¹

The annexed advertisement² will give you a description of certain slaves, deserters from this neighborhood after the peace concluded betwixt Great Britain and the United States of America; the owners having requested of me to transmit it to you, in hopes you will give orders for their being apprehended.

Mr. Elliott will deliver you a letter from me to General Lincoln in answer to his letter to me of the 3d of May.³

XLIX.—Major William Croghan⁴ to Irvine.

Fort Pitt, *July* 28, 1783.

Sir:—When at Winchester barracks about two months ago, Captain John Stith had just returned from Philadelphia with one month's pay for the troops at that post, the whole of

---

able information in regard to incidents transpiring in that region during the period indicated. He died in Dumfries, in November, 1822. His remains were interred in St. Michael's church-yard, in presence of a greater crowd than had ever entered or surrounded the walls of the same place since the funeral of Robert Burns. At the time of his death, he was probably the oldest officer in his majesty's service. He was buried with military honors.

¹ John Burkhart. He was taken by a war-party of savages headed by Simon Girty, in May previous, five miles from Pittsburgh, at the mouth of Nine Mile Run. Guns were firing in Fort Pitt at the very time of the boy's capture, on account of the reception of the news of peace. This fact was made known to Girty by the lad; and still he was taken to Detroit, but was, of course, returned to his friends by De Peyster, at the first opportunity. Burkhart was well treated by Girty, as, indeed, were other persons in his power after De Peyster assumed command at Detroit.

² This advertisement has not been found, which is a matter of regret, as the citizens of Detroit would, doubtless, be interested in reading a description of certain negro slaves held by residents of their city only five years before the passage of the Ordinance of 1787.

³ A search for copies of these letters has proved fruitless.

⁴ William Croghan was a native of Ireland. He entered the American army in 1776, as captain of infantry in the Virginia line. He fought at Brandywine, Germantown and Monmouth, but was made prisoner of war May 12, 1780, at Charleston, under General Lincoln and released on parol. He was present at the siege of Yorktown and the capture of Cornwallis, but

which he paid both officers and soldiers (then present) at one payment;—my being particular in mentioning their being paid the month's pay at once, is on account of the orders I was informed were sent to Fort Pitt when the month's pay was sent there, which said the soldiers should receive no more than half a dollar per week of the month's pay until the whole was paid.[1]

could only participate in the stirring scenes by his presence, as he was not exchanged at that date, but had been previous to the writing of this letter to Irvine. At the close of the war, he was the senior major of the Virginia line. He moved to Kentucky in 1784, where he married a sister of George Rogers Clark. He died at Locust Grove, Jefferson county, that state, in September, 1822, in the seventieth year of his age.

[1] The following correspondence explains why the above letter was addressed to General Irvine:

"WINCHESTER BARRACKS, *July* 13, 1783.

"*Dear Sir:*—I am directed by the honorable Major General Lincoln to send an officer to Fort Pitt to discharge the men belonging to the Virginia line enlisted for the war and to give them three months' pay. I have, therefore, to request you will undertake this business as quick as possible. Colonel Wood will furnish you with twenty-five hundred dollars Morris's notes, and a number of printed furloughs or discharges. You will permit the men discharged to carry their arms and accouterments with them. I am, sir, your most obedient humble servant. P. MUHLENBERG, B. G'l.

" P. S.— The officers only who were arranged last January receive pay. If any others are on duty they must transmit their accounts to General Lincoln.

"Major CROGHAN."

"FORT PITT, *July* 23, 1783.

"*Sir:*—The above is an extract of my orders from General Muhlenberg for discharging and paying the Virginia line at Fort Pitt. I have the honor to be your most humble and obedient servant,

"W. CROGHAN, Major Virginia Line.

"General IRVINE."

Immediately afterward, Irvine issued the following: "Orders. Fort Pitt, July 24, 1783. In consequence of orders from the honorable the secretary at war, Major [William] Croghan will begin to-morrow to furlough (which will serve as discharges as soon as the definitive treaty of peace is concluded) the troops of the Virginia line at this post, and will pay them in notes for the months of February, March, and April last. Lieutenant Rose will pay them in specie for the month of January, at the same time.

"The general has reason to expect directions in a few days for discharging the Pennsylvanians on similar principles. The men will be allowed to take their arms with them. As Captain [Uriah] Springer's company will be first settled with, none of them are to be detailed for duty to-morrow.

"General Irvine has not a doubt but the notes will be equal to specie at

L.—Major Croghan to Irvine.

WARM SPRINGS, *August* 30, 1783.

Dear General:— Having received letters from Pointy [Point of] Fork and meeting with people here with whom I had business, added to the agreeable company here (which amounts to near six hundred), among whom are Generals Gates, Gist, Morgan and Williams, I have delayed longer than I intended.

I have enquired when the Maryland company are to march to Fort Pitt, and am informed they are in Fredericktown, Maryland, and that about a week ago an express was sent to the war office to receive orders for and respecting their march.

General Morgan received a letter from Colonel Lamb to the same purport of that you got from him. He is apprehensive he will have to pay his part of the bill.

The officers of the Virginia line are to have a meeting at Fredericksburg the beginning of October, respecting the society now forming by the officers of the different states, when they will choose their officers for it,[1] and consult on other matters for our general benefit.

LI.—Irvine to Lieutenant Colonel De Peyster.

FORT PITT, *August*, 1783.

Sir:— I have been honored with your letter of the 10th of July by Mr. Elliot, and have transmitted the enclosed letter to General Lincoln.

Report says the definitive treaty has arrived at New York;

---

the time they become due; he therefore earnestly advises the men not to part with them at an undervalue. The several states will certainly make good their engagements with the troops;—their now adopting ways and means to pay the interest on certificates is a proof of their inclination to do justice.

"The general flatters himself this advice will have weight with the men as they must be convinced he can have no self-interested motives in view, and that he has never on any occasion shown a disposition to deceive them by promising what he had not clearly a right to expect done for them."

[1] Reference is here made to the Society of the Cincinnati.

the enclosed newspapers, which I send for your amusement, contain all I can say of it, as I have not any official communication on that subject; the probability, however, is in favor of its being true. No fugitive negroes have come into this country for upwards of nine months past that I have heard of. I will cause the advertisement to be made public, and if all or any of the described negroes can be found during my command here, their owners may expect that they will be sent to Detroit the first proper opportunity.[1]

LII.— IRVINE TO CAPTAIN JOSEPH MARBURY.[2]

FORT PITT, Oct. 1, 1783.

Sir:— By official information respecting your appointment and orders for taking command of this post I am persuaded you must arrive in a few days.[3] The troops have been already

---

[1] When General Irvine returned home he proposed immediately to free the few slaves he held under the laws of Pennsylvania, as he remarked it was inconsistent for a man who had been so long contending for liberty to hold men in bondage. My grandmother told me, on her consent the negroes were all called in, and when he told them they were free, they were overjoyed, and his body servant Tom said: "Master, am I free to do as I please?" "Yes," was the reply, "as free as I am, and what do you want to do now?" So Tom (whom he had purchased from a self-righteous man of Boston — a Mr. R———) said he would like to go back and see the old folks. He was fitted out with clothing and money and was off to Boston. Several years elapsed; one day the general was passing by the kitchen door, when he noticed a miserable, ragged negro seated inside. He went in, asked him who he was, and what he was doing there. The fellow jumped up and said: "Oh, Master, don't you know old Tom? he has come back to live and die here; he's found that thing you call liberty is all sham;" and he did live and die there. In the case of the Detroit people, General Irvine was actuated by a regard to the rights of others as then recognized; but, when it became a question where his *own* property was concerned, he did not hesitate to let the instinct of humanity be paramount.— Communicated by Dr. Wm. A. Irvine.

[2] In 1780, Captain Marbury of the Maryland line acted as quartermaster to the Maryland division of the army.

[3] That is, by a letter received from General Lincoln or rather from his assistant, W. Jackson (ante, p. 195). Irvine, however, as appears by the following letter to his wife, had previously a clue as to who his successor was to be:

"FORT PITT, *September* 8, 1783.

"*My Dear Love:*—Since Mr. Rose left this, letters have arrived here addressed to a Captain Marbury, by General Lincoln, which convinces me he

detained so much longer than any others that they are impatient, though perfect tranquility is reigning. For these reasons, and because of the urgent necessity for my attending immediately to private concerns, I have left Captain John Finley in command, with a small detachment only, till your arrival, having furloughed the rest.[1]

thinks I have left the place. Marbury, however, is not yet come. He is the officer to take command. Some accident must have happened him or his party. Matters will, I hope, be adjusted soon, at furtherest when Mr. Rose returns. If Captain Marbury should come in a few days, it is probable I may set out immediately and not wait for Mr. Rose's return, but of this I am not certain. You may inform Mr. Rose of this part of this letter; and also if I do set out, I shall take the Glade road.

"I swapped Callender's pony yesterday for another — a real beauty and I am told it runs fast, but this may be against it for his safety; however, I believe it is good humored. It is a great runaway and hard to catch; its name — Mingo. I have let Colonel Gibson have it for his little daughter to ride to Carlisle, who promises to deliver it as soon as she gets there. This serves him and saves me the trouble and expense of taking it down.

"WM. IRVINE."

[1] "Orders. Fort Pitt, September 28, 1783. Lieutenant John Mahon is appointed agent to settle the accounts of the troops of the garrison with the auditor at Philadelphia and to distribute the certificates to the individuals; each man will, previous to receiving his furlough, inform Mr. Mahon where he means to reside next winter, in order to know where will be most convenient to advertise them to assemble, for a final adjustment of their accounts. The officers present will give him all necessary assistance, and before they depart render him accounts of clothing issued to the men. He is also to call on Lieutenant Reed for a settlement for the time he acted as paymaster, and all others concerned."

"Orders. Fort Pitt, September 30, 1783. Captain John Finley will remain in command at this post with the detachment already formed for that purpose until the arrival of the new garrison. Lieutenant [John] Mahon will also remain. All other officers have leave of absence as soon as they furnish Mr. Mahon with necessary vouchers and accounts to enable him to proceed to a liquidation of the accounts of the troops, agreeably to his appointment."

The following was dated Fort Pitt, Oct. 1, 1783: "By a resolution of congress dated July 4, 1783, the paymaster general is authorized and empowered to settle, and appoint persons finally to adjust, all accounts whatsoever between the United States and the officers and soldiers of the army. Being requested by him to appoint an agent who should examine and receive the vouchers of such persons whose accounts are connected with this settlement of the different detachments constituting this garrison, you are hereby authorized by virtue of the powers vested in John Pierce, Esq., paymaster general,

This gentleman has charge of all the stores and will deliver them with returns to you. He is well informed of all matters necessary for you to know relative to the post and has my orders also to communicate some private ideas by way of advice, which I hope will be taken as intended (friendship for a brother officer).

Inclosed you have a copy of an extract from a letter of the secretary at war addressed to me dated the 15th inst.[1]

LIII.—Captain Marbury to Irvine.[2]

Pittsburgh, *October* 28, 1783.

Sir:— On my arrival at this post I received your letter of the 1st instant. I am exceedingly obliged to you for your friendly advice through Captain Finley[3] and will strictly adhere to it. I shall always be ready to give Mr. Mahon[4] all the aid and assistance in my power.[5]

---

by the honorable the continental congress to call to account such regimental paymasters whether they be actually in service or discontinued, and demand such papers as you may judge requisite for your sufficient information, of persons possessed of them.

"For your transactions on this occasion, provided they be agreeable to the existing resolves of congress, this shall be your warrant.

"Wm. Irvine, B. Gen'l.

"Lieutenant John Mahon, 2d Penn'a Regt."

[1] Irvine should have written "15th ult." See Jackson to Irvine, September 15, 1783, p. 195.

[2] This letter was directed to Irvine at Carlisle.

[3] Captain John Finley. See previous letter.

[4] Lieut. John Mahon (ante, p. 422, note 1).

[5] "We have long been puzzled," wrote Neville B. Craig in January, 1847 ("The Olden Time," Vol. II, p. 48), "to know why the street which runs right by our dwelling to the Alleghany river, was called Marbury street [now, 1882, Third street]. We have often made inquiries of old residents, but never until within a short time got any information. Judge Wilkins, a few days ago, informed us that an application had been made to him to prepare the papers to procure from government some arrears of pay or pension due to an old soldier. Upon examining the necessary documents, he discovered that the soldier had belonged to the company of a Captain Marbury, and that he was discharged from the service at Fort Pitt, in June, 1784."

INDEX.

Albert, G. Dallas, 176, 177.
"Alleghany," how to spell, 136.
Allison, Col. James, 410.
Amberson, Wm., 152.
Arbuckle, Capt. Matthew, 14.
Ashcraft, Sergeant John, 324.
Audebert, Philip, 148.
Augusta county, Va., 4.
Bailey, Francis, 128, 129.
Bayard, Lieut.-Col. Stephen, 41, 54, 68, 74, 75, 108, 142, 148, 159, 187, 320, 340, 350, 357, 390, 408, 410, 411, 412, 414.
Beall, Capt. Robt., 37, 124, 328, 379.
Beard, Col. Geo., 330.
Beckett, Capt. Joseph, 324.
Biggs, Capt. Benj., 120, 352.
Biggs, Capt. John, 299, 343.
Blaine, Alex., 211.
Blaine, Ephraim, 209, 210, 220, 221, 407.
Blaine, James G., 408.
Block houses: Carnahan's, 323, 324; Rice's, 313; Rook's, 161.
Blue Jacket, a Shawanese chief, 332, 333.
Blue Licks, battle of, 333.
Board of War, letters to, from Gen. Irvine, 157-165.
Boggs, Capt. John, 312.
Boggs, James, 264.
Boundary troubles, 4, 34, 36, 64, 80.
Brackenridge, H. H., 126, 128, 129, 304, 384.
Braddock's road, 1, 177.
Brady, Capt. Samuel, 41, 74, 88, 112, 134, 159, 319, 336, 350.
Brant (Thayendanegea), Capt. Joseph, 55, 110, 230.
Brenton, James, 122, 365.

Brodhead, Col. Daniel, 22, 23, 34, 35, 36, 37, 38, 39, 40, 41, 42, 43, 48, 49, 51, 52, 53, 54, 56, 58, 62, 74, 75, 76, 83, 97, 103, 110, 170, 193, 194, 304, 340.
Brown, Thomas, 372.
Bryson, Lieut. Samuel, 111, 146, 360, 413.
Bull, Joseph, 236, 341, 342, 362.
Burkhart, John, 418.
Butler, Capt. Edward, 357.
Butler, Col. Richard, 96, 97, 98, 168, 178, 199, 356, 397.
Butler, Lieut.-Col. Wm., 97.
Butler, Maj. Thomas, 357.
Butler's Rangers, 305.
Caldwell, Capt. Wm., 122, 127, 305, 332, 333, 368, 370, 371, 378.
Callender, Anne (Mrs. Wm. Irvine), 65, 340-348, 357.
Callender, Mrs. Robert, 340, 350.
Callender, Robert, 65.
Campbell, Capt. Thomas, 46.
Campbell, Col. Charles, 104, 324, 331, 357.
Campbell, Lieut.-Col. Richard, 27, 38.
Canada, conquest of, 1.
Canon, John, 204, 205, 206, 241, 234.
Carleton, Gen. Sir Guy, 124, 128, 135, 337, 410.
Carmichael, Maj. James, 105, 285.
Carmichael, John, 285.
Carnahan, Col. John, 210, 257, 258, 260.
Carpenter, John, 100, 101, 102, 197, 240, 243.
Catfish (Catfish Camp), 280, 303, 306, 308, 314, 316, 330, 392, 405.
Chief-with-one-Eye, 371.

Index.

Clark, Geo. Rogers, 14, 15, 53 *et seq.*, 76, 77, 83, 139, 154, 155, 229, 230, 231, 259, 271, 273, 275, 332, 333, 368, 371, 377, 378, 392, 393, 394, 396, 398, 400, 401, 414.
Clark, Capt. John, 31, 74, 88, 108, 159, 194, 351, 352.
Clark, Ensign John, killed, 37.
Conolly, Dr. John, 71, 172.
Cook, Col. Edward, 104, 248, 253, 282, 295, 296, 310, 317, 320, 321, 323, 324-327, 329, 331, 334, 335, 336, 338, 339, 345, 405.
Cook, Paden, 330.
Cornstalk, a Shawanese chief, 14.
Coshocton Campaign, 53, 305.
Coverly, Col. Wm., 291.
Cracraft, Maj. Charles, 230.
Craig, Maj. Isaac, 48, 55, 56, 76, 77, 88, 108, 113, 130, 137, 138, 139, 140, 174, 231, 343, 350, 351, 396, 406, 408, 410, 414.
Craig, Neville B., 78, 139, 423.
Craig, Thomas, 97.
Crockett, Col. Joseph, 55.
Crawford, Col. Wm., 75, 107, 114-117, 118, 119, 122, 123, 125, 127, 128, 131 *et seq.*, 174, 244, 246, 247, 249, 250, 274, 278, 289, 291, 292, 293, 294, 305, 332, 363, 364, 366, 367, 370, 374, 375, 376, 378, 387.
Crawford, Hanna, 131.
Croghan, Col. Geo., 170.
Croghan, Maj. Wm., 292, 345, 418, 419, 420.
Crooks, Col. Thomas, 105, 297, 302, 308, 316, 320.
Crumrine, Boyd, 396, 404.
Cummins, John, 411.
Davies, Col. Wm., 272-276, 292.
Davis, Col. Benjamin, 295, 325, 327, 330.
De Peyster, Lieut.-Col. A. S., 7, 51, 60, 77, 82, 124, 135, 230, 368, 369, 370, 371, 372, 373, 374, 378, 414, 415, 416, 417, 420.

Detroit, an expedition against, 21 *et seq.*; deferred, 23; Clark's expedition against and its failure, 53 *et seq.*; why the post should be demolished, 79, 83; supposed plan against, 125.
Dewantale, an Indian, 371.
Dickinson, Pres't John, 188; letters to, from Gen. Irvine, 260, 261; letters to Irvine, 262-265; elected Pres't of Sup. Ex. Council of Pa., 260, 409.
District of West Augusta, 24, 272.
Dixon, Jeremiah, 248.
Dod, Thaddeus, 307.
Dougherty, Benard, 348.
Douglass, Ephraim, 57, 188, 252, 388, 391, 394, 413, 414, 415, 417.
Draper, LL.D., Lyman C., 364.
Duncan, David, 81, 152, 154, 159, 161, 165, 202, 208, 217, 239, 252, 254, 317, 348, 352, 381, 412.
Dunlavy, Francis, 10, 27, 28.
Dunmore, Lord, 115, 170.
Dunmore's War, 115, 278, 341, 349, 363.
Edgar, James, 105, 284.
Eels, John, 107, 108, 120.
Egle, Dr. Wm. H., 177, 284, 235, 353-355.
Elliott, Andrew, 69.
Elliott, Capt. Matthew, 17, 58, 60, 127, 305, 332, 341, 369.
Emes, Capt., 223.
Emerson, John, 198.
Enoch, Col. Henry, 308.
Evans, Col. John, 24, 266, 272, 275, 356, 378, 380, 382.
Fincastle county, Va., 4.
Finley, Capt. J. L., 159, 353.
Finley, Capt. John, 159, 353, 422, 423.
Finley, Maj. Samuel, 85.
Fisher, Myndert, 72, 82.
Forbes Road, 3, 176, 177.
"Foreman's defeat," 18.
Foreman, Charles, 329, 330.

Index. 427

Forts: Armstrong, 13, 41; Andrew Donnelly's, 19; Crawford, 39; "Dunmore," 80, 115; Duquesne, 8, 71, 171; Fincastle, 8, 278; Hand, 24, 39; Henry, 10, 13, 35, 270, 278, 397; Jackson's, 298; Laurens, 28, 32, 36, 37, 38; Le Bœuf, 110, 111; Ligonier, 41, 176, 254; McIntosh, 26, 35, 78. 79; Miller, 251; Nelson, 144, 231; Pitt, 2, 71, 78, 80; Presq' Isle, 111; Schlosser, 143; Randolph, 10, 13, 35, 40; Richard Wells', 297; Venango, 110, 111; Wallace, 29.

Fowler, Alexander, 62, 152, 159, 166.
Freman, John, 315, 395.
Gaddis, Col. Thomas, 122, 365.
Gardner, Joseph, 94.
Gibson, Col. John, 22, 28, 31, 42, 56, 57, 67, 71, 73, 74, 85, 89, 95, 103, 108, 117, 131, 153, 165, 241, 267, 282, 285, 322, 337, 340, 344, 349, 351, 353, 362.
Gibson, George, letter to Irvine, 353.
Girty, George, 55.
Girty, James, 25, 55.
Girty, Simon, 17, 31, 47, 55, 126, 127, 293, 332, 342, 376, 418.
Girty, Thomas, 291.
Gist, Christopher, 78.
Glenn, David, 59.
"Gnadenhuetten affair," the, 67, 99, 127, 236-239, 240, 241, 242, 282, 288, 289, 361, 372, 373, 374, 377.
Gordon, James, 120, 253.
Grant, a British captain, 374.
Greene, Gen. Nathaniel, 178, 185.
Haldimand, Gen. Fred'k, 124, 135, 230, 373.
Half King, a Wyandot chief, 18, 61.
Hamilton, Lieut.-Gov. Henry, 7, 9, 77, 392.
Hanks, Wm., 405.
Hannastown, 4, 161, 177, 250, 251, 252, 253, 254, 270, 303, 336, 350, 381, 383, 386, 394.
Hanna, Robert, 176.

Hand, Brig.-Gen. Edward, 10, 11, 20, 22, 71, 116.
Hardin, Lieut. John, 43, 152.
Hardin, Maj. John, 274.
Harmar, Lieut.-Col. Josiah, 197, 198, 199.
Harrison, Col. Benj., 327, 328, 329, 330, 331, 379, 380.
Harrison, Col. Wm., 107, 127, 294, 376, 377.
Harrison, Gov. Benj., 76, 266, 268, 269, 270, 401.
Hart, Barney, 225.
Hay, Lieut. John, 231, 343.
Hays, Christopher, 94, 161, 255, 322, 327, 329, 330, 338, 402, 404, 405.
Hazen, Brig.-Gen. Moses, regiment of, 133, 134, 181, 183, 258, 397.
Heckewelder, John, 51.
Hilligas, Michael, 148, 212, 213.
Hinds, John, 72.
Hogdon, Samuel, 222-224.
Hoge, John, 322.
Howell, Jacob S., 225, 228.
Huffnagle, Michael, 81, 161, 165, 167, 201, 204, 208, 240, 250, 253, 254, 263, 281, 383.
Hughes, Capt. John, 226, 287, 283, 310, 311, 330, 343.
Humpton, Col. Richard, 96, 97, 235.
Hunter, Robert, an Oneida chief, 169.
Hutchins, Thomas, 78.
"Indiana," Indian land grant, 295.
Indian Moses, 88.
Indians: Chippewas, 333; Delawares, 9, 10, 13, 14, 16, 25, 42, 43, 51, 52, 58, 90, 100, 113, 122, 124, 135, 179, 333, 349, 369, 374, 377; "Lake," 122; Mingoes, 5, 13, 14, 18, 45, 48, 122, 124, 333, 341, 369; Monseys, 16, 58, 113, 124, 333; "Moravians," 27, 59, 60, 61, 67, 90, 91, 99, 101, 106, 236, 237, 238, 241-243, 245, 250, 282, 288, 289, 293, 294, 305, 342, 343, 344; Ottawas, 2, 91, 113, 333; "Pluggy's-town," 9, 11; Shaw-

428   Index.

anese, 5, 7, 10, 13, 14, 25, 45, 58, 91, 113, 124, 259, 292, 332, 333, 341, 342, 349, 360, 374; Six Nations, 42, 172; Senecas, 42, 349; Wyandots, 13, 18, 45, 48, 58, 113, 122, 124, 135, 333.
Indian treaty, 25.
Irvine, Mrs. Wm., 65, 340–348, 357.
Irvine, Callender, 341, 346, 348, 422.
Irvine, Brig.-Gen. Wm., 64, 65–70; correspondence of, 71–152, 153–423.
Irvine, Dr. Wm. A., 341, 421.
Irwin, John, 200, 219, 259.
Jack, Capt. Matthew, 46, 235, 384.
Jackson, W., 195.
Johnson, Lieut. Richard, 330.
Johnson, Guy, 63.
Johnson, Sir John, 110, 143.
Jones, Lieut., 236.
Killbuck, a Delaware, 10.
Killbuck, Jr., John, 25, 81, 106.
Knight, Dr. John, 117, 122, 123, 125, 126, 128, 129, 249, 363, 365, 376, 377.
Knox, Brig.-Gen. Henry, 96.
Laurel Hill, 90.
Lee, H., 262, 263.
Leet, Daniel, 122.
Leeth (Leith), John, 7, 304.
Leinbach, Fred'k, 237, 233.
LeVillier, Francis, 305, 368.
Lewis, Andrew, 25.
Lincoln, Maj.-Gen. Benj., 81, 157, 166–193, 212, 353, 419.
Loyd, Capt. James, 351.
Lochry, Col. Archibald, 24, 55, 56, 77, 154, 229, 230, 233.
Logan, Col. Benj., 401.
Logan, the Mingo Chief, 5, 283, 344.
Lowrey, Col. Alex., 92, 264, 353, 354.
Lyon, John, 119.

Magaw, Col. Robert, 255, 256.
Mahon, Lieut. John, 422, 423.
Malott, Catharine, 47.
Marbury, Capt. Joseph, 189, 192, 195, 199, 421, 422, 423.

Marshel, Col. James, 50, 67, 81, 84 85, 106, 239, 240, 245, 246, 248, 277–320, 331, 338, 361, 365, 390.
Marshall, Col. John, 302, 308, 311, 316.
Martin, Capt. Hugh, 331.
Maryland corps, 39, 40, 48, 164.
Masonic Fraternity in the West, 172.
Mason and Dixon's Line, 82, 248, 249, 402, 403, 404.
Mason, Charles, 248.
McClean, Alex., 248, 249, 268, 294, 295, 326, 327, 328, 329, 330, 337, 403.
McClelland, Maj. John, 122, 123, 365, 371.
McCleery, Col. Wm., 279, 391.
McClure, John, 262, 263.
McColloch, Ebenezer, 312.
McColloch, Maj. Samuel, 52, 306, 391.
McDonald, Maj. Angus, 115, 278.
McGruder, Capt. Hez., 329, 330.
McIntosh, Brig.-Gen. Lachlan, 20, 26, 27, 28, 33, 116.
McKean, Thomas, 153.
McKee, Alex., 16, 17, 29, 126, 230, 332, 333, 342, 370.
McKee, Capt. Wm., 18.
"McKee's Rocks," 78.
McLean, Gen. Allan, 415, 416.
Meason, Isaac, 234, 235.
Miles, Samuel, 163, 217–221.
Miller, Gavin, 236.
"Mohawk Pluggy," 9.
Montour, Andrew, 163.
Montour, Madame, 169.
Montour, John, 52, 168, 169.
Moore, Capt. Thomas, 124, 325, 328, 379.
Moorhead, Capt. Samuel, 11, 13, 39, 46.
Moore, Pres't Wm., 233–258.
Morgan, Col. Geo., 9, 10, 17.
Morris, Robert, 81, 84, 95, 109, 145, 161, 166, 189, 195, 200–213, 221, 222, 258, 325, 326, 327, 408.
Moylan, John, 178, 225–227.

Muhlenberg, Brig.-Gen. P., 419.
Neill, Wm., 346.
Nelson, Thomas, 76.
Neville, Amelia, 406.
Neville, Capt. John, 8, 9, 71, 406.
Neville, Joseph, 249.
"New state scheme," 64, 196-199.
Nicholson, Joseph, 152, 363.
Nicholson, Thomas, 122, 363.
Ohio County, Va., 24.
Ormsby, John, 152, 294, 295, 296, 297, 347.
"Pan-handle," 272, 297.
Parker, Col. Wm., 279, 297, 319, 410.
Parkison, Capt. Thomas, 203, 204, 205, 206, 208, 209, 287, 296, 308, 396.
Peachy, Col. Wm., 116.
Pentecost, Dorsey, 94, 232, 235, 241, 242, 284, 292, 322, 405, 410.
"Pet Indian," 384-390.
Phillips, Col. Theoph., 330.
Phillips, John, 111, 112, 172, 360.
Pittsburgh, beginning of, 3; early growth, 4.
Pierce, John, 146, 147, 211, 214-216 353.
Pluggy, the Mohawk, 9.
Pluggy's-town Indians, 9, 11.
Plumer, George, 354.
Poe, Adam, 61, 277.
Poe, Andrew, 61, 277.
Point Pleasant, battle of, 5.
Pollock, Maj. Wm., 302, 303, 309, 365.
Polke, Maj. Edmond, 590, 300.
Porter, Sergeant, 338.
Postlethwait, Mr., 223.
Potter, Gen. James, 255, 336, 396.
Procter, Col. Thomas, 406.
Proctor, John, 234, 235.
Pumroy, Col. John, 324, 325, 330.
Quebec bill, 136.
Rawlings, Col. Moses, corps of, 39, 40, 48, 164.
Redick, David, 265.
Reed, Pres't, 230.

Redstone-old-fort, 15.
Reno, Wm., 129.
Ritchie, Col. Matthew, 279, 306.
Rogers, David, 44, 45.
Rocher (Roche) de Bout, 93, 355.
Rose, Lieut. John, 117, 121, 122, 125, 138, 145, 147, 148, 151, 185, 186, 187, 195, 212, 213, 215, 247, 258, 290, 292, 319, 335, 346, 348, 350, 364, 367, 406, 407, 412, 419, 422.
Ross, Alex., 332.
Sample, Samuel, 31, 86, 152, 154, 159, 219.
Sandusky Plains, 355, 366.
Sandusky, expeditions against, proposed, 11, 57, 74; are abandoned, 11, 61, 74; a third proposed and given up, 282, 359; Crawford's expedition against, see Crawford, Col. Wm.; a fifth expedition, projected, 123 *et seq.*; laid aside, 134 *et seq.*
Sappington, John, 344.
Schebosh, Rev., 237, 341, 362.
Scott, Maj., 105.
Scott, Thomas, 100, 322.
Seidel, Rev. Nathaniel, 238, 289, 343, 361.
Seitz, Andrew Adam, 217, 218.
Seneca Indians, Brodhead's expedition against, 42.
Shepherd, Col. David, 24, 52, 105, 193, 266, 302, 318, 356, 380, 409.
Sinn, Andrew, 330.
Slover, John, 122, 123, 127, 128, 129, 304, 334, 377.
Small, John, 350.
Smallman, Thomas, 170.
Smith, Devereux, 152.
Smith, Col. James, 30.
Snake, Capt., a Shawanese chief, 369, 370.
Springer, Capt. Uriah, 106, 107, 108, 139, 351, 419.
Springer, Zadock, 330.
"Squaw Campaign," the, 15, 16.
St. Clair, Arthur, 66, 97.

Steed, Thomas, 111, 112, 119, 172, 360.
Stevens, Gen. Edward, 269, 393, 394.
Stewart, Walter, 97.
Stokely, Capt. Nehemiah, 46, 330.
Stokely, Thomas, 230.
Sullivan, Daniel, 396, 398.
Sullivan, Maj.-Gen. John, 42, 110.
Surplus, Robert, 17.
Swearingen, Capt. Andrew, 308.
Tannehill, John, 146, 214, 215, 351, 352, 353.
Taylor, Henry, 404.
Thayendanegea (Capt. Joseph Brant), 55, 110, 230.
Thompson, A., 230.
"Triangle," the, 69.
Turney, Lieut. John, 368, 369.
Vallandigham, Lieut.-Col. Geo., 104, 279, 288, 289, 308.
Vernon, Maj. Fred'k, 33, 38, 75.
Virginia, boundaries of, 7.
Wallace, Geo., 219.
Wallace, Robert, 99, 101, 240, 318.
Walls, Maj., 392, 402.
Walter, Wm., 322.
Ward, Maj. Edward, 71, 170, 171, 360.
Warring, Thomas, 330.
Washington County, Pa., 50.
Washington, Gen. George, 10, 20, 34, 62, 64; correspondence of, 71–152.

Wayne, Brig.-Gen. Anthony, 97.
Weiss, L., 238.
West Augusta, District of, 24, 272.
"West Augusta Regiment," 11, 75.
Western Department, extent of, 75.
Western Border War, 7 *et seq.*; 13 *et seq.*; 35 *et seq.*
Westmoreland County, 4.
White Eyes, a Delaware, 25.
White, Maj. John, 289.
Willard, Mrs. Mary, 384.
Williamson, Col. David, 67, 99, 100, 101, 104, 121, 122, 125, 236, 237, 240, 244, 245, 282, 286, 288, 297, 305, 303, 311, 316, 318, 319, 320, 364, 365, 366, 367, 374, 377.
"Williamson's Expedition," 99, 236, 244, 288.
Wilson, Capt., a Delaware, 52, 103.
Willy, Capt. Hugh, 395, 399.
Wilson, Lieut.-Col. Samuel, 275, 330.
Winganund, a Delaware, 51.
Woods, James, Journal of, 10.
Wuibert, Lieut.-Col., 108, 112, 113, 130, 170.
Yohogania County, Va., 24.
Yorktown, siege of, 71, 73.
Zane, Ebenezer, 390, 397, 409.
Zane, Jonathan, 122.
Zeisberger, Rev. David, 58, 59, 63.
Zingly, Capt., 223.

www.ingramcontent.com/pod-product-compliance
Lightning Source LLC
Chambersburg PA
CBHW020525300426
44111CB00008B/541